DATA PROTECTION

Data Protection

A Practical Guide to UK and EU Law

Fifth Edition

Edited by
PETER CAREY

OXFORD
UNIVERSITY PRESS

OXFORD

UNIVERSITY PRESS

Great Clarendon Street, Oxford, OX2 6DP,
United Kingdom

Oxford University Press is a department of the University of Oxford.
It furthers the University's objective of excellence in research, scholarship,
and education by publishing worldwide. Oxford is a registered trade mark of
Oxford University Press in the UK and in certain other countries

© Peter Carey 2018

The moral rights of the author have been asserted

Fourth Edition published in 2015
Fifth Edition published in 2018

Impression: 1

Published in the United States of America by Oxford University Press
198 Madison Avenue, New York, NY 10016, United States of America

British Library Cataloguing in Publication Data
Data available

Library of Congress Control Number: 2017960259

ISBN 978–0–19–881541–9

Printed and bound by
CPI Group (UK) Ltd, Croydon, CR0 4YY

Foreword

It's a great honour to be introducing the new edition of Peter Carey's practical guide to data protection.

This is a pivotal time for data protection and privacy. The laws we regulate are converging globally, consumer trust is ever more central to both business and the public sector, and a rapidly expanding digital economy is asking more questions of us all.

UK citizens are better informed about their information rights than ever before.

But alongside that increased awareness of the law, a lot of people feel they've lost control of their own data—and that impacts their trust in organizations.

For me, the end game in the data protection field is always about increasing public trust and confidence in how their personal data are used.

And the way our personal information is handled has never been more important.

Which of us doesn't consider ourselves a citizen of the digital world today? Whether it's the digital services we see every day on our phones and tablets, or the digital infrastructure that underpins everything from banking to manufacturing.

Technology is moving so fast. And consumer trust needs to follow it. That's why a new law was needed. And that's what we're getting with the Data Protection Bill, which will include the provisions of the General Data Protection Regulation within its broader scope.

The GDPR builds on the previous legislation; it provides more protections for consumers, and more privacy considerations for organizations. But this is a step-change. It's evolution, not revolution.

There are specific new obligations for organizations, for example around reporting data breaches and transferring data across borders. But the real change for organizations is understanding the new rights for consumers.

They'll have the right to request that personal data be deleted or removed if there's no compelling reason for an organization to carry on processing it, and they'll enjoy new rights around data portability and how they give consent.

It's vital that organizations are prepared to comply; but they can also prosper in the new regulatory landscape.

If your organization can demonstrate that good data protection is a cornerstone of your business policy and practices, you'll see a real business benefit.

An upfront investment in privacy fundamentals offers a payoff down the line, not just in better legal compliance, but a competitive edge. Whether that means attracting more customers or more efficiently meeting pressing public policy needs, I believe there is a real opportunity for organizations to present themselves on the basis of how they understand and respect the privacy of individuals.

I hope this new edition helps you be transparent, be accountable, and give people back control of their data.

Elizabeth Denham
Information Commissioner

Contents—Summary

Table of Cases   xv
Table of UK Legislation   xvii
Table of UK Secondary Legislation   xxiii
Table of European and International Legislation   xxv
Contributing Authors' Biographies   xxvii
List of Abbreviations   xxxi
Introduction   xxxiii

1. Territorial Scope and Terminology   1

2. Data Protection Principles   32

3. Fair, Lawful, and Transparent Processing   42

4. Special Categories of Data   66

5. Data Security and Breach Notifications   88

6. International Data Transfers   105

7. The Rights of Individuals   122

8. Enforcement and the Role of the Regulator   155

9. Outsourcing Personal Data Processing   175

10. Electronic Communications   184

11. Data Protection Impact Assessments   205

12. Accountability and the Role of the Data Protection Officer   223

13. Creating a Data Protection Compliance Programme   240

Appendix 1: Regulation (EU) 2016/679 of the European Parliament
    and of the Council   251
Appendix 2: Addresses and Websites   351
Index   355

Contents

Table of Cases   xv
Table of UK Legislation   xvii
Table of UK Secondary Legislation   xxiii
Table of European and International Legislation   xxv
Contributing Authors' Biographies   xxvii
List of Abbreviations   xxxi
Introduction   xxxiii

1. **Territorial Scope and Terminology**   1
   Damien Welfare and Peter Carey

   Introduction and Historical Perspective   2
   Territorial Scope   5
   Introduction to Terminology   7
   Personal Data   8
   Processing   15
   Filing System   16
   Controller   18
   Processor   19
   Special Categories of Personal Data   20
   European Economic Area   21
   Main Establishment   21
   Data Subject   22
   Pseudonymization   23
   Profiling   23
   Personal Data Breach   24
   The Data Subject's Consent   24
   Child   24
   Genetic Data   25
   Biometric Data   25
   Recipient   25
   Data Protection by Design   26
   Data Protection by Default   26
   Codes of Conduct   26
   Joint Controllers   27
   European Data Protection Board   27
   Delegated Acts   28
   Certification   28
   One Stop Shop   29
   Directive on Security of Network and Information Systems   30
   Directive on Personal Data Processed for Criminal Law Enforcement   31

2. **Data Protection Principles**   32
   Peter Carey

   Introduction   32
   Lawfulness, Fairness, and Transparency   33
   Purpose Limitation   34
   Data Minimization   35
   Data Accuracy   37
   Storage Limitation   38
   Integrity, Confidentiality, and Security   39
   Exemptions   40
   Accountability   40
   Data Protection by Design and by Default   41
   Processors   41

3. **Fair, Lawful, and Transparent Processing**   42
   Estelle Dehon and Peter Carey

   Introduction   42
   Obtaining Data—Duty Not to Mislead   43
   Obtaining Data in a Transparent Manner—Information to Be Supplied
       to the Data Subject   44
   Other Unfair Processing   50
   The Lawfulness Conditions   50
   Other Unlawful Processing   59
   Cases of Significance   61
   Summary   65

4. **Special Categories of Data**   66
   Nicola Fulford and Peter Carey

   Introduction   66
   The Conditions for Processing   69
   Personal Data Relating to Criminal Convictions and Offences   81
   Advice on Processing Special Category Personal Data   83

5. **Data Security and Breach Notifications**   88
   Ann Bevitt and Peter Carey

   Introduction   88
   Obligations of the Controller and Processor   91
   Privacy by Design and Privacy by Default   95
   Pseudonymization   96
   Privacy Enhancing Technologies   97
   ISO 27001   97
   Security and Outsourcing   98
   Security and Exports   98
   Security Breaches   98
   Notifying Security Breaches   100
   Advice on Breach Notification   104

6. **International Data Transfers** 105
   Eduardo Ustaran

   Introduction 105
   Examples of International Transfers 107
   Scope of Data Transfers 108
   Adequate Level of Protection 108
   Transfers to the United States—Privacy Shield 110
   Providing Adequacy Safeguards 114
   The Contractual Route 115
   Codes of Conduct and Certification Mechanisms 116
   Binding Corporate Rules 117
   The Derogations 119
   Non-repetitive Transfers 121
   Advice for Organizations 121

7. **The Rights of Individuals** 122
   Heledd Lloyd-Jones and Peter Carey

   Introduction 122
   Responding to Individuals 123
   Exemptions 125
   The Right of Access 126
   Data Portability 137
   Rectification 139
   Rights to Object 140
   The Right to Object to Direct Marketing 140
   Right to Erasure 143
   Right to Restriction of Processing 147
   Automated Decision-taking 149
   Compensation 151
   Right to a Judicial Remedy 153
   Complaints to the Commissioner 154

8. **Enforcement and the Role of the Regulator** 155
   Alison Deighton and Peter Carey

   Introduction 155
   Supervisory Authority Enforcement Role 156
   Other Remedies 162
   Consistency Mechanism 162
   Cross-border Processing and Appointing a Lead
       Authority 163
   UK Enforcement Action 166
   UK Enforcement Procedures 166
   Information Notice 167
   Assessment Notice 169
   Enforcement Notice 170
   Monetary Penalty Notices 171

Appeals   173
Powers of Entry and Inspection   173

9. **Outsourcing Personal Data Processing**   175
   Suzanne Rodway and Peter Carey

   Introduction   175
   The Nature of a Processor   177
   Obligations on Processors   178
   Choice of Processor   179
   Ongoing Assurance   179
   The Written Contract   180
   Pre-GDPR Arrangements   181
   Sub-processors   181
   Processor Versus Controller   182
   Cloud Services   183
   Foreign Processors   183

10. **Electronic Communications**   184
    Peter Given and Peter Carey

    Introduction and Historical Background   184
    Definitions   186
    Email Marketing   189
    Text Message Marketing   194
    Telephone Marketing   195
    Fax Marketing   196
    Location Data   197
    Cookies and Similar Devices   198
    Limitations on Processing of Traffic Data   200
    Calling and Connected Line Identification   200
    Telephone Directories   202
    Non-itemized Bills   202
    Termination of Unwanted Call Forwarding   202
    Security   202
    Breach Notification   203
    Enforcement   203

11. **Data Protection Impact Assessments**   205
    Olivia Whitcroft

    Introduction   205
    What Is a DPIA?   206
    When to Carry Out a DPIA   207
    Identifying Whether a DPIA Is Required   210
    Who Should Carry Out a DPIA   211
    How to Conduct a DPIA   212
    Reporting and Publication of the DPIA   221

12. **Accountability and the Role of the Data Protection Officer**   223
Jenai Nissim

  Introduction   223
  The Accountability Requirement   224
  The Role of the DPO   226
  When Is a DPO Mandatory?   226
  Accessibility   231
  Expertise and Skill of the DPO   233
  Involvement of the DPO   234
  Necessary Resources   235
  Independence   236
  Security of Tenure   236
  Conflict of Interest   237
  Data Protection Impact Assessments   238
  Record Keeping   238
  Policies and Procedures   239

13. **Creating a Data Protection Compliance Programme**   240
Jenai Nissim

  Introduction   240
  Stage 1—Assessing Data Processing Activities   241
  Stage 2—Creating Data Protection Policies   242
  Stage 3—Data Protection Training and Raising Awareness   244
  Stage 4—Implementing Controls to Reduce and Monitor Risk   246
  Stage 5—Monitoring Compliance   248
  Stage 6—Reporting   249
  Stage 7—Annual Review Process   249

*Appendix 1: Regulation (EU) 2016/679 of the European Parliament
  and of the Council*   251
Appendix 2: Addresses and Websites   351
Index   355

Table of Cases

AB v Ministry of Justice [2014] EWHC 1847 (QB) 152–153
Baronetcy of Pringle of Stichill [2016] UKPC 16 68
Brown (Andrea) v Commissioner of Police for the Metropolis and Chief Constable of
    Greater Manchester Police (2016) Claim No. 3YM09078 & A53YP250
    (CC, Central London) 153
Campbell v Mirror Group Newspapers [2004] UKHL 22; [2002] EWHC 299;
    [2002] All ER (D) 448 (Mar) 15, 57, 63, 64, 68
Chief Constable of Humberside Police and Others v Information Commissioner
    [2009] EWCA Civ 1079. 51
Coco v A N Clarke (Engineeers) Ltd [1968] FSR 415 59–60
College van burgemeester en wethouders van Rotterdam v Rijkeboer [2009] C-553/07. 128
Common Services Agency v Scottish Information Commissioner [2008] UKHL 47 12
Dawson Damer and Others v Taylor Wessing LLP [2017] EWCA Civ 74 . . . . .128, 129
Deer (Dr Cécile) v The University of Oxford [2017] EWCA Civ 121 . . . . 129, 130, 136
Dunn v Durham County Council [2012] EWCA Civ 1654 128
Durant v Financial Services Authority [2003] EWCA Civ 1746 . . . . 11–13, 16, 17–18, 128
Edem v IC & Financial Services Authority [2014] EWCA Civ 92 12–13
Elliott v Lloyds TSB Bank plc and Another [2012] EW Misc 7 128
Esch and Others v European Central Bank (2004) T-320/02. 74
Ezsias v Welsh Ministers [2007] All ER (D) 65 129
Google Inc. v Vidal Hall and Others [2014] EWHC 13 (QB). 152
Google Spain SL & Google Inc. v Mario Costeja Gonzalez [2014] C-131/12 . . . . 7, 15–16, 146–147
Gurieva and Another v Community Safety Development (UK) Ltd [2016]
    EWHC 643 (QB). 124, 128
Halliday v Creation Finance Ltd [2013] EWCA Civ 33. 152
Huber v Germany [2009] CMLR 49 50
Iesni v Westrip Holdings [2011] 1 BCLC 498. 128
Ittihadieh v 5-11 Cheyne Gardens RTM Company Ltd [2017] EWCA Civ 121 . . . . .13, 129
Johnson v Medical Defence Union [2004] EWHC 347. 130
Johnson v Medical Defence Union [2007] EWCA Civ 262. . . . . .50, 64, 128
Kololo v Commissioner of Police for the Metropolis [2015] EWHC 600 (QB) 128
Law Society and Others v Kordowski [2011] EWHC 3185 (QB) 50, 64–65
Lin v Commissioner of Police for the Metropolis [2015] EWHC 2484 (QB). 128
Lindqvist, Bodil v Kammaraklagaren (C-101/01) [2004] 1 CMLR 20 (ECJ). 63–64, 68, 108
Netherlands Immigration Minister v M & S (17 July 2014) C-141/12 & C-372/12 13
R (Kelway) v The Upper Tribunal (Administrative Appeals Chamber) and Northumbria
    Police and R (Kelway) v Independent Police Complaints Commission [2013]
    EWHC 2575 12
R (on the application of B) v Stafford Combined Court [2006] EWHC 1645 75
R v Secretary of State for the Home Department, ex p Lord [2003] EWHC 2073
    (Admin). 131, 135–136
Robertson (Brian Reid Beetson) v Wakefield Metropolitan Council, Secretary of State
    for the Home Department [2001] EWHC 915 (Admin). 61, 62
Smith v Lloyds TSB plc [2005] EWHC 246 . . . . 14, 17, 130
Southern Pacific Personal Loads Ltd [2013] EWHC 2485 (Ch) 128
Stone v South East Coast SHA (formerly Kent and Medway SHA) [2006] EWHC 1668. 77

TLT and Others v Secretary of State for the Home Department [2016] EWHC 2217 (QB)......153
V & EDPS v European Parliament (2011/C 282/92) 72
Valsts policijas Rīgas reģiona pārvaldes Kārtības policijas pārvalde v Rīgas pašvaldības SIA
    'Rīgas satiksme' (Case C-13/16) [2017] ECLI:EU:C:2017:43........................58
YS v Minister voor Immigratie [2014] C-141/12 and C-372/12 128

Table of UK Legislation

Please note that page numbers in **bold** refer to actual text (in Appendix 1). Please refer to Index for references to Working Parties, e.g. Article 29 Working Party.

EUROPEAN UNION PRIMARY LEGISLATION

Charter of Fundamental Rights of the
European Union (Nice Charter) 268
Art 8. 4
Art 8(1) 251
Art 47. 282
Council of Europe Convention (1981) 275
Lisbon Treaty 2009. 4

Treaty on European Union
Title V 3
Chapter 2. 291
Title VI 3

Treaty on the Functioning of the
European Union (TFEU)
Art 5. 289
Art 16. 251
Art 16(1) 251
Art 16(2) 253
Art 17. 289
Art 101. 285
Art 102. 285
Art 179(1) .80, 288
Art 263. .283, 284
Art 267. 283
Art 290. 289
Art 338(2) 288

EUROPEAN UNION SECONDARY LEGISLATION

Decisions

Commission Decision 2000/518/
EC on adequate protection of
personal data (Switzerland) 110
Commission Decision 2002/2/EC on
adequate protection of personal
data (Canada). 110

Commission Decision 2003/490/EC
on adequate protection of
personal data (Argentina) 110
Commission Decision 2003/821/EC
on adequate protection of
personal data (Guernsey) 110
Commission Decision 2004/411/EC
on adequate protection of
personal data (Isle of Man) 110
Commission Decision 2008/393/EC
on adequate protection of
personal data (Jersey) 110
Commission Decision 2010/147/EU
on adequate protection of
personal data (Faroe Islands) 110
Commission Decision 2010/625/EU
on the adequate protection of
personal data (Andorra) 110
Commission Decision 2011/61/EU
on the adequate protection of
personal data (Israel). 110
Commission Decision 2012/484/EU
on the adequate protection of
personal data (Uruguay) 110
Commission Decision 2013/65/EU
on the adequate protection of
personal data (Uruguay) 110

Directives

Directive 93/13/EEC (Unfair Terms
in Consumer Contracts) 260
Directive 95/46/EC (Data Protection
Directive) . . . . xxxi, 3, 4, 7, 10, 15,
20, 38, 40, 61, 72, 74, 109,
111, 146, 180, 181, 190,
251, 252, 253, 282, 290
Chapter I (Arts 1–4)
Art 2(a) 8
Art 2(c). 16
Art 2(d) 18
Chapter II (Arts 5–21)
Art 14. 62

Chapter IV (Arts 25–26)
  Art 25(6) 275, 321, 322, 349
  Art 26(2) 323
  Art 26(4) 275, 323
Chapter VI (Arts 28–30)
  Art 29. 349
Directive 97/66/EC
  (Telecommunications
  Sector Directive). 195
Directive 2000/31/EC (E-Commerce
  Directive). . . . . Arts 12–15, 255, 291
Directive 2002/58/EC (E-Privacy
  Directive). 185, 186, 191,
  193–194, 198, 199, 203, 290, 305, 349
  Art 9. 197
  Art 13. 189–190
  Art 13(2) 192
  Recital 41. 192
Directive 2003/98/EC (on re-use of
  public sector information) 286
Directive 2009/136/EC (E-Privacy)
  (Amendment) Directive 185
Directive 2011/24/EU (Cross-Border
  Healthcare). 258
Directive 2015/1535 (Technical
  Standards and Regulations Directive)
  Art 1(1) .54, 294
Directive 2016/680 (Law Enforcement
  Directive). 20, 83, 224, 254
  Chapter II (Arts 5–11) 31
  Art 6. 31
Directive 2016/1148 (Network and
  Information Security Directive) 30

Recommendations

Commission Recommendation
  2003/361/EC on the
  definition of micro, small
  and medium-sized enterprises
Annex, Art 2. 253

Regulations

Regulation (EU) 45/2001 (on
  European data protection
  supervision) 254
  Art 28(2) 290
  Art 98. 291
Regulation (EC) 1049/2001 (on
  public access) 342
Regulation (EU) 765/2008 (on
  accreditation and market
  surveillance). 29, 319
Regulation (EC) 1338/2008 (on
  public health and safety statistics) . . 263

Regulation (EC) 223/2009 on
  transmission of data subject to
  statistical confidentiality) 288
Regulation (EU) No 182/2011 (on
  control of Commission's exercise
  of implementing powers) 275,
                                              289, 348
  Art 5. 349
  Art 8. 349
Regulation (EU) 1215/2012 (on
  jurisdiction and enforcement of
  judgments). 284
Regulation (EU) 536/2014 (on clinical
  trials on medicinal products). 288
Regulation (EU) 2016/679 (General
  Data Protection Regulation
  (GDPR). 2, 14, 37, 38,
      59, 92, 107, 155, 158, 173, 174,
      175–176, 181, 186, 189, 192, 203,
      204, 220–221, 223, 240, 245, **251–350**
Recitals
  Recital 15. 16
  Recital 24. . . . . .6, 229
  Recital 26. . . . . .22, 23
  Recital 27. 16
  Recital 33. 81
  Recital 34. 25
  Recital 38. 54
  Recital 42. 70
  Recital 43. 70
  Recital 45. 57
  Recital 47. . . . . .57, 58
  Recital 49. 93
  Recital 51. . . . . .68, 69
  Recital 63. 128
  Recital 66. 146
  Recital 68. 137
  Recital 72. 149
  Recital 78. 95
  Recital 81. . . . . .98, 99
  Recital 83. . . . . .88, 89
  Recital 84. 213
  Recital 85. . . . . .100, 101
  Recital 86. . . . . .100, 101
  Recital 87. . . . . .100, 101
  Recital 88. . . . . .100, 101
  Recital 90. 215
  Recital 91. . . . . .208, 228
  Recital 97. . . . . .227–228, 233, 236
  Recital 101. 106
  Recital 112. 56
  Recital 146. 152
  Recital 155. 72

Recital 157 80
Recital 158 80
Recital 159 80
Recital 160 80
Recital 162 80
Chapter I (Arts 1–4) **290–294**
Art 1 . . . . **290**
Art 1(1) 8
Art 2 290–291
Art 2(2)(a) 4
Art 2(2)(b) 4
Art 2(2)(c) 4
Art 2(2)(d) 4
Art 3 . . . . .6, **291**, 316, 318
Art 3(1) 18
Art 3(2) 159, 307
Art 4 . . . . .67, 130, **291–294**
Art 4(1) 8, 9, 13, 22
Art 4(2) 15
Art 4(4) 23
Art 4(6) 16
Art 4(7) 18
Art 4(8) 19, 177
Art 4(9) 25
Art 4(11) 24, 52
Art 4(12) 24, 98
Art 4(13) 25
Art 4(14) 25
Art 4(16) 21
Art 4(17) 22
Art 4(23) 163
Art 4(26) 106
Chapter II (Arts 5–11) **294–298**, 346
Art 5 . . . . 32, 33, 39, 71, 82,
   85, 125, **294**, 306, 345
Art 5(1)(a) 42
Art 5(1)(c) 217
Art 5(1)(d) 139
Art 5(1)(f) 246
Art 5(2) 40, 224
Art 5(e) 143
Art 6 . . . . 33, 34, 43, 50, 65,
   69, 70, 71, 74, 75, 81, 85,
   144, 164, **294–295**, 345
Art 6(1) 50, 51, 298, 300,
   301, 303, 304, 313, 328
Art 6(1)(a) . . . 24, 51, 53, 54, 70, 74, 81
Art 6(1)(a)–(f) 42
Art 6(1)(b) 55, 75
Art 6(1)(c) 55–56, 72, 75
Art 6(1)(d) 56
Art 6(1)(e) 56–57, 75, 78, 79, 81
Art 6(1)(f) 57, 74, 81
Art 6(d) 73

Art 7 . . . . .31, 225, **296**, 345
Art 7(1) 24, 70
Art 7(3) 24, 70
Art 8 . . . . .43, 54, **296**, 345
Art 8(1) 24, 54–55, 303
Art 8(2) 25
Art 9 . . . . 33–34, 43, 65, 76, 82, 85,
   217, 219, 227, **296–298**, 315, 345
Art 9(1) 10, 20, 25, 66, 207,
   305, 308, 310, 313
Art 9(2) . . . 20, 25, 42, 66, 69, 144, 300,
   301, 303, 304, 305
Art 9(2)(a) 24, 53, 70
Art 9(2)(b) 71, 83
Art 9(2)(f) 74
Art 9(2)(h) 86
Art 9(3) 78, 303
Art 10 . . . . . . 20, 43, 81, 207, 227, **298**,
   308, 310, 313, 315
Art 11 . . . . **298**, 345
Art 11(2) 125, 298
Chapter III (Arts 12–23) . . . 153, **298–306**,
   309, 346
Art 12 . . . . 43, 44, 45, 122,
   123–124, 126, 138, 139, 142,
   143, 147, 148, 177, **298–299**
Art 12(1) 125
Art 12(3) 127–128
Art 12(4) 124
Art 12(5) 128
Art 12(7) 44, 340
Art 12(8) 348
Arts 12–22 . . . . .306, 345
Art 13 . . . . 27, 43, 46–47,
   132, 150, 177, 216, 298,
   299–300, 307, 323, 325
Art 13(2)(f) 23
Art 14 . . . . 27, 43, 47–48, 132, 177,
   298, 299, **300–302**, 307, 323, 325
Art 14(2)(g) 23
Art 15 . . . . 126–127, 130, 135,
   150, 298, 299, **302**, 347
Art 15(2) 133
Art 15(3) 127
Art 16 . . . . 139, 298, 299, **302**,
   304, 331, 347
Art 17 . . . . 143, 145, 146, 147,
   298, 299, **303**, 304, 331
Art 17(1) 304
Art 17(1)(c) 147
Art 17(2) 146, 331, 339
Art 17(3) 146
Art 18 . . . . 147, 148, 298,
   299, **303–304**, 331, 347

Art 19. . . . . 139–140, 145–146,
148, 298, 299, **304**
Art 20. . . . . .137, 298, 299, **304**
Art 20(4) 139
Art 21. . . . . 23, 140, 225,
298, 299, **304–305**, 347
Art 21(1) 142, 143, 144, 146,
147, 148, 303, 304
Art 21(2) 144, 303
Art 21(6) 142
Art 21(6) 143
Art 22. . . .23, 149, 150, 298, 299, **305**, 323
Art 22(1) 126, 300
Art 22(2) 339
Art 22(3) 150
Art 22(4) 126, 300
Art 23. . . . . **305–306**
Art 23(1) 295
Art 23(1)(i). 134–135
Chapter IV (Arts 24–43) . . .40, **306–320**, 346
Art 24. . . . . . . .225, 242, **306–307**, 316
Art 25. . . . . 41, 95–96, 172, 205,
225, **307**, 316, 344
Art 25(1) 26, 225
Art 25(2) 26, 225
Arts 25–39 345
Art 26. . . . . .27, 152, 172, **307**
Art 26(1) 182–183
Art 27. . . . . .22, 172, **307–308**
Art 27(3)(a) 147
Art 28 . . .98, 99, 152, 172, 225, **308–309**
Art 28(1) 19, 99, 178
Art 28(3) 19, 85, 99, 180
Art 28(4) 99
Art 28(8) 329, 331, 335
Art 28(9) 180
Art 28(10) 85
Art 28(h) 179
Art 29. . . . . 172, **310**
Art 30. . . . . 71, 85, 172, 224,
225, 238, **310**, 325
Art 30(1) 211, 238
Art 30(2) 238
Art 30(5) 85
Art 31. . . . . .157, 172, **311**
Art 32. . . . . 40, 88, 89, 91, 99, 172,
217, 308, 309, **311**, 316, 344
Art 32(1) 310
Art 32(4) 94
Art 33. . . . . 24, 99, 100, 101–102,
103, 172, 225, 309, **311–312**
Art 33(1) 339
Art 33(2) 339
Art 33(3) 100, 312

Art 34. . . . . 24, 99, 100, 102, 172,
298, 299, 306, 309, **312**
Art 34(1) 339
Art 34(2) 100, 103
Art 34(3) 103
Art 35. . . . . 86, 99, 172, 225,
238, 309, **312–314**, 316
Art 35(1) 206, 207, 218
Art 35(2) 234, 238
Art 35(3) 207, 208, 209
Art 35(4) 210, 329, 335
Art 35(5) 210
Art 35(7) 206
Art 35(7)(a) 212
Art 35(8) 214
Art 35(9) 206
Art 35(10) 210
Art 35(11) 207, 221
Art 36. . . . . 99, 172, 206, 220,
238, 309, **314**, 316, 331
Art 36(2) 329
Art 36(5) 331
Art 37. . . . . 86, 172, 225, 226,
229, **314–315**, 323–324
Art 37(1) 227, 228
Art 37(1)(b) 227
Art 37(1)(c) 227
Art 37(5) 233
Art 38. . . . . .172, 226, **315**
Art 38(1) 234
Art 38(2) 235
Art 38(3) 236
Art 38(6) 237
Art 39. . . . . . . .172, 226, 238, **315–316**
Art 40. . . . . 26, 27, 89, 99, 311,
313, **316–317**, 322, 339, 344
Art 40(1) 329
Art 40(5) 329, 331
Art 40(7) 335
Art 40(9) 340
Art 41. . . . . .27, **317–318**, 330
Art 41(1) 317
Art 41(3) 335
Art 41(4) 345
Art 42. . . . . 28, 89, 96, 99, 225,
307, 309, 311, **318–319**,
322, 331, 339, 344, 345
Art 42(1) 96, 320, 329
Art 42(2) 96
Art 42(5) 319, 320, 329, 331
Art 42(7) 157, 330, 339
Art 43. . . . . 28, 309, 318,
319–320, 330, 331, 339, 345
Art 43(3) 335, 339

Art 43(6) 339
Art 43(8) 339, 348
Chapter V (Arts 44–50) 98, 105–106,
            183, **320–326**, 349
Art 40. . . . . .114, 307, 309
Art 42. 114
Art 44. . . . . 106, **320**
Arts 44–49 345
Art 45. . . . . **321–322**, 325
Art 45(1) 108
Art 45(3) 322, 324
Art 46. . . . . . . 127, 300, 301, **322–323**,
                        324, 325
Art 46(2) 316–317, 318, 329,
                        331, 335
Art 46(3) 330, 331, 335
Art 47. . . . . 114, 300, 301, 322,
         323–324, 330, 331, 335, 339
Art 48. **324**
Art 49. . . . . **324–325**
Art 49(1) 300, 301, 310, 339
Art 50. . . . . 166, **326**
Chapter VI (Arts 51–59). **326–332**,
                        346, 348
Art 51. . . . . **326**
Art 52. . . . . **326–327**
Art 53. . . . . **327**
Art 54. . . . . **327–328**
Art 54(2) 339
Art 55. . . . . . . 101–102, 311, 317, 318,
         319, 320, 328, **328**, 335, 342
Art 55(1) 334
Art 56. . . . . 164, 317, 318, 319,
                320, **328–329**, 342
Art 56(1) 334
Art 56(4) 334
Art 57. . . . . .156, 317, **329–330**
Art 57(1)(f) 154
Art 58. . . . . .157, 317, **330–331**
Art 58(1) 339, 345, 347
Art 58(2) . . . 319, 330, 332, 339, 344, 345
Art 58(3) 318, 339
Art 59. . . . . **331–332**
Chapter VII (Arts 60–76) 331,
                        346, 349
Art 6. 78
Art 60. . . . . .165, 328, **332–333**, 337
Art 60(3) 328
Art 60(4) 336
Art 60(7) 337
Art 60(8) 337
Art 60(9) 337
Art 61. . . . . . . .329, 332, **333–334**, 335
Art 62. . . . . .329, 332, **334–335**

Art 63 . . . 309, 313, 317, 318, 319, 320,
        323, 326, 332, **335**, 337, 341
Art 64. . . . .**335–336**, 337, 338
Art 64(1) 336, 340
Art 64(2) 340
Art 64(3) 337
Art 65 . . . . 163, **336–337**, 338, 340, 341
Art 65(1) 336
Art 65(2) 337
Art 66. . . . . .165, 333, **337**, 340
Art 66(1) 334
Art 66(2) 334, 335
Art 67. . . . . **338**
Art 68. . . . . .27, 313, **338**
Art 69. . . . . **338**
Art 70. . . . . **338–340**
Art 70(1) 338, 340
Art 70(2) 338
Art 71. . . . . 338, **340**
Art 72. . . . . **340**
Art 73. . . . . **341**
Art 74. . . . . **341**
Art 75. . . . . **341**
Art 76. . . . . 340, **341–342**
Chapter VIII (Arts 77–84) 318, 320,
                        342–346
Art 77. . . . 154, 166, 316, 342, **342**, 343
Art 78. . . . . .342, **342**, 343
Art 79. . . . . .316, 323, **342–343**
Art 79(2) 344
Art 80. . . . . 329, **343**
Art 80(1) 154
Art 81. . . . . **343**
Art 82. . . . . . . .104, 151, 309, **343–344**
Art 82(2) 85, 176
Art 83. . . . . . . 159, 160, 309, 331, 339,
                        344–345
Art 84. . . . . 309, **345–346**
Chapter IX (Arts 85–91). 295, 345,
                        346–348
Art 85. 346
Art 86. 346
Art 87. 346
Art 88. . . . . **346–347**
Art 89. . . . . .79, 80, 347
Art 89(1) . . . 49, 79, 294, 301, 303, 305
Art 90. . . . . **347–348**
Art 91. . . . . **348**
Chapter X (Arts 92–93) **348–349**
Art 92. . . . . .28, 29, 320, **348**
Art 93. . . . . 340, **348–349**
Art 93(2) 309, 317, 320,
                321, 322, 324, 334, 338
Art 93(3) 322

Chapter XI (Arts 94–99). 349–350
    Art 94. 349
    Art 95. 349
    Art 96. 349
    Art 97. 349–350
    Art 98. 350
    Art 99. 350
E-Privacy Regulation
    (Proposed) . . . . xxxi, 54,
        141, 185, 186, 187, 188, 189,
        191, 192, 193, 194, 195–196,
        198, 199, 200, 203, 204

Art 15. 202
Art 16. . . . . .191–192, 194
Art 16(6) 194
Art 23. 186

INTERNATIONAL

European Convention on Human Rights
    and Fundamental
    Freedoms 1950. . . . . .4, 78, 268
Art 8. . . . . .61, 62
First Protocol, Art 3 . . . . .61, 62

Table of UK Secondary Legislation

Electronic Commerce (EC Directive)
Regulations 2002 (SI 2002/2013). . . . 187
Privacy and Electronic Communications
(EC Directive) Regulations 2003
(SI 2003/2426) (PECR) 54, 156, 173,
174, 185, 186, 193, 199, 203–204
Reg 6 198
Reg 7(2) 200
Reg 7(3) 200
Reg 14 197–198
Reg 15 201–202
Reg 16 198
Reg 16A 198, 200
Reg 19 195
Reg 20 195

Reg 21 195
Reg 22 . . . . .190, 191
Reg 22(3)(a) 192–193
Reg 23 . . . . .191, 194
Reg 26 196
Privacy and Electronic Communications
(EC Directive) (Amendment)
Regulations 2011 (SI 2011/1208). . . 156, 185
Representation of the People (England
and Wales) Regulations 2001
(SI 2001/3111). 62
Representation of the People Regulations
1986 (SI 1986/1081) 62
Reg 54 61

Table of European and
International Legislation

Communications Act 2003. 189
Companies Act 1985, s 735(1) 188
Companies Act 2006 188
Computer Misuse Act 1990 61
Data Protection Act (DPA) 1984 . . . . .2, 3
Data Protection Act (DPA) 1998 . . . . xxix, xxx,
       xxxi, 3–4, 7, 10, 42, 63, 66–67, 73,
       74, 77, 78, 80, 87, 129, 131, 175, 180
  s 1(1) 8
  s 2 68
  s 10 65
  s 11 . . . . .61, 62
  s 11(3) 191
  s 13(2) 152
  s 70(2) 37
  Sch 1, Prt II 43
  Sch 3(3) 72
Data Protection Bill 2017 (new Data
    Protection Act) . . . . .xxx, xxxi, 6, 7,
           22, 143, 145, 168, 240
  Prt 1
    cl 2(2). 9, 13
    cl 2(4). 15
    cl 2(7). 16
  Prt 2 (Chapters 1–3). 5, 81, 82
    cl 5 18
    cl 5(2). 18
    cl 8 24
    cl 8(6). 24
    cl 9 20
    cl 10 . . . . .20, 81
    cl 16 29
  Prt 3 (Chapters 1–6) 5, 19, 31, 69, 83
    Ch 2 82
  Prt 4 (Chapters 1–6) 5, 82
    Ch 6 . . . . Sch 11, 69
  Prt 5 5
  Prt 6 . . . . .5, 156, 166

Prt 7 5
cl 186 6
s 18 80
s 28 227
s 33(8) 82
s 34(3) 83
s 39 83
s 67 . . . . .225, 226–227
s 69(2) 225, 239
s 160(2) 85
s 183 78
s 184 67
Sch 1 69
  Prt 1 . . . . .71, 81
  Prt 2 . . . . .75, 81
  Prt 2(6). 77
  Prt 2(11). 77
  Prt 2(14). 77
  Prt 3 81
  Prt 4 . . . . .71, 85
Schs 2–4. . . . . .125, 131
Sch 5 29
Sch 6 6
Sch 7 224
Sch 8 . . . . .82, 83
  Prt 3 73
Sch 9 . . . . .Prt 4, 73
Sch 10 . . . . .73, 80, 83
Equality Act 2010. 71–72
Freedom of Information Act 2000 . . . .133, 222
  Sch 1 59
Freedom of Information (Scotland)
    Act 2002 59
Human Rights Act 1998. 61
Investigatory Powers Act 2016 . . . . .69, 77
Police and Justice Act 2006 61
Representation of the People Act 1983 61
Serious Crime Act 2007 61

Contributing Authors' Biographies

Ann Bevitt is a Partner at Cooley LLP. Ann assists clients with privacy and data security compliance and risk management and advises on issues such as effecting data transfers, drafting privacy policies, rolling out new technologies in the workplace, contractual arrangements with third party service providers, corporate acquisitions and investments, electronic marketing, monitoring employees, whistleblowing hotlines, dealing with e-discovery, undertaking internal investigations (domestic and cross-border), responding to subject access requests, and notifying breaches. Ann works with a wide range of clients, from governments and multinationals to small, medium, and large corporations, from a broad spectrum of industry sectors including technology, venture capital and private equity, insurance, hotel and leisure, music, banking and financial services, recruitment and employment, biotechnology, and pharmaceuticals. Ann has rights of audience in all civil courts, and significant experience as an advocate. She was called to the Bar in 1992 and practised as a barrister before qualifying as a solicitor in 2000. Ann is recommended and described as a 'key figure' for data protection work in the 2016 edition of The Legal 500 UK.

abevitt@cooley.com

Peter Carey is a solicitor and internationally recognized expert on data protection. He advises national and international clients on data protection compliance matters. Peter was a Consultant with London law firm Charles Russell Speechlys for 17 years before moving abroad and setting up his own consultancy. Before joining the firm, Peter was a Senior Lecturer at the University of Law for six years, and was Visiting fellow at the London School of Economics until 2014. Peter travels the world providing bespoke training courses on all aspects of data protection compliance, and he is a contributor of articles to *Privacy & Data Protection* journal. Peter is a Member of the Examination Board on the Practitioner Certificate in Data Protection Programme.

peter.carey@dataprotectionlaw.com

Estelle Dehon is a public law barrister practising at Cornerstone Barristers. She works across a wide range of areas, including information law and environmental law. She and is a member of the European Commission's Multistakeholder Expert Group on the GDPR, which assists the Commission in dealing with potential challenges in implementing the GDPR across Europe. Estelle's information law practice entails providing advice and advocacy in matters concerning data protection and the GDPR, freedom of information, and environmental information. She has experience of appearing before the First-Tier Tribunal and of pursuing and resisting damages claims in the High Court alleging breaches of the Data Protection Act. Estelle is a Member of the Examination Board for the Practitioner Certificate in Data Protection.

estelled@cornerstonebarristers.com

Alison Deighton is head of TLT's Data Protection & Privacy team. She advises a wide range of businesses and public sector clients on all aspects of information law. She regularly conducts data protection compliance reviews and advises on privacy strategies and freedom of information issues. Alison also has extensive experience dealing with subject access requests, ICO investigations, and breach management issues. Alison frequently advises on State Aid matters, advising both public bodies and private companies on State Aid compliance issues.

alison.deighton@TLTsolicitors.com

Nicola Fulford is a Partner and head of the Data Protection and Privacy department at Kemp Little. She specializes in privacy and data protection, advising on the full range of related issues including international data transfers; responding to data security breaches and inquiries from data protection authorities; privacy policies; notices and consents; online profiling, cookies, and marketing; subject access; interception; surveillance and monitoring; compliance strategies and projects; and dealing with sensitive data such as health data and personal data of children. Nicola advises clients on the use of personal information across a range of sectors, including technology, social media, financial services, health care, retail, and travel. She also has extensive experience of outsourcing and complex technology transactions, acting for both customers and providers.

Nicola.Fulford@kemplittle.com

Peter Given is a Legal Director at Womble Bond Dickinson, specializing in data protection and privacy law. He advises clients on a wide range of data protection matters in a variety of contexts, including in relation to general data protection compliance (including GDPR preparedness and remediation), data processing and outsourcing arrangements, direct marketing, subject access requests, data breaches and cross-border transfers of data. Peter has previously undertaken secondments to a global US-based financial institution and a major European pharmaceutical organization. In both secondments Peter supported the internal legal teams on a variety of matters and projects, including those relating to data protection and privacy. He also spent time as a Judicial Assistant to Lord Justice Jackson, assisting him with his review of the costs of civil litigation in England and Wales. Peter regularly contributes articles to *Privacy & Data Protection* journal.

Peter.Given@wbd-uk.com

Heledd Lloyd-Jones is an Associate at Bird & Bird in the Privacy and Data Protection Group. Heledd has particular expertise in the management of complex information requests, having acted for clients both in the courts and in the Information Tribunal in connection with disputed requests. She also provides non-contentious advice on general data protection compliance, data security breach management, international data transfers, and contractual matters. She has a special interest in data protection challenges arising in the fields of health care provision, health regulation, and life sciences.

Heledd.lloyd-jones@twobirds.com

Jenai Nissim is Legal Director at TLT Solicitors. She has extensive experience advising UK and US businesses on European privacy requirements, negotiating multinational data transfer agreements, handling breach notifications and investigations, and undertaking data protection audits. Jenai holds the Practitioner Certificate in Data Protection.

Jenai.Nissim@TLTsolicitors.com

Suzanne Rodway is Group Head of Privacy for the Royal Bank of Scotland Group, with responsibility for oversight of the organization's compliance with data privacy, bank secrecy, and freedom of information laws, worldwide. Suzanne trained with global law firm Linklaters, where after completing a number of years in the Technology, Media & Telecoms practice, she moved to an in-house role to advise the firm on its own privacy and information risk management issues. With the experience gained in this role Suzanne then undertook a secondment to Barclays as their interim head of data protection. She joined Barclays permanently in December 2006 as their Privacy Director within the Legal & Compliance team. Most recently Suzanne was the Chief Privacy Officer at NBCUniversal. She represents Privacy on the Executive Committee of the Women's Security Society, which aims to encourage the advancement of women working in today's security world through the exchange of information and creation of collaborative relationships. Suzanne is a Member of the Examination Board for the Practitioner Certificate in Data Protection.

Suzanne.Rodway@rbs.com

Eduardo Ustaran is a Partner at Hogan Lovells and an internationally recognized expert in privacy and data protection. He advises international clients, including leading FTSE 100 companies, on the adoption of global data protection compliance strategies. Eduardo wrote the data exports chapter of the Law Society's *Data Protection Handbook* and is co-author of the book *E-Privacy and Online Data Protection*. He is a regular contributor of articles to *Privacy & Data Protection* journal.

eduardo.ustaran@hoganlovells.com

Damien Welfare, Barrister, came to the Bar in 2001 after a career in local government. He specializes in data protection, freedom of information, and the Environmental Information Regulations. He appears in the Information Tribunal, advises on all aspects of information law, and speaks and writes regularly on information law matters. Damien is a Member of the Examination Board for the Practitioner Certificate in Data Protection.

damienw@cornerstonebarristers.com

Olivia Whitcroft led the data protection practice at PricewaterhouseCoopers Legal LLP for several years before setting up her own specialist firm. Olivia specializes in all aspects of data protection compliance, including conducting compliance audits and reviews, drafting data protection policies, contracts and frameworks, and advising on compliance and good practice. Olivia has worked on projects across a wide range of industries including financial services, media, technology, retail, education, and the public sector. She has advised both large multinationals and small UK companies alike, each benefiting from her experience of understanding and addressing the different needs of businesses of different sizes, and at different stages in their evolution. Olivia is a Member of the Examination Board for the Practitioner Certificate in Data Protection.

olivia.whitcroft@obep.uk

List of Abbreviations

BCR	Binding Corporate Rules
CJEU	Court of Justice of the European Union
CLI	Calling Line Identification
CSIRT	Computer Security Incident Response Team
DPA	Data Protection Act 1998
DPIA	data protection impact assessment
DPO	Data Protection Officer
EDPB	European Data Protection Board
EEA	European Economic Area
EFTA	European Free Trade Area
EU	European Union
FSA	Financial Services Authority
GDPR	General Data Protection Regulation
GMC	General Medical Council
ICC	International Chamber of Commerce
ICO	Information Commissioner's Office
IoT	Internet of things
MMS	multimedia messaging services
PECR	Privacy and Electronic Communications (EC Directive) Regulations 2003
PETs	privacy enhancing technologies
UKAS	United Kingdom Accreditation Service

Introduction

Considerable excitement and trepidation has surrounded the advent of the European Union's new Regulation on the protection of natural persons with regard to the processing of personal data and on the free movement of such data (the 'General Data Protection Regulation' or 'GDPR').

So much so, that one could be forgiven for thinking that the GDPR beholds the dawn of a new era in data protection law. However, the reality is that the Regulation mostly represents an updating measure which tweaks the pre-GDPR legal requirements that organizations were already required to undertake when processing personal data.

The real revolution was the beginning of data protection law itself, back in the 1970s. Since then, the content of the law has not altered to any Earth-shattering extent. The majority of the obligations on organizations that previously existed under Directive 95/46/EC (the former EU data protection law that was abolished by the GDPR, and upon which the UK's Data Protection Act 1998 was based) remain substantially the same under the new law. Examples include the obligation to ensure that only a minimum quantity of data are used for any particular purpose (data minimization), the obligation to process only such information on people as is relevant to the purpose/s of the processing (purpose limitation), the obligation to supply a copy of their personal data to anyone making a request (data subject access), the obligation to apply appropriate security provisions to personal data processing, and the obligation to destroy or delete data held after they have become obsolete.

Some of the 'new' obligations, such as the requirement to conduct data protection impact assessments ('DPIAs'), are only new in terms of the obligation to carry them out. They are not new in terms of their concept. For example, many organizations had been conducting DPIAs (previously known as 'privacy impact assessments') for many years prior to the GDPR's inception. Similarly, the virtues of creating products and services with personal data protections in mind from the beginning of the creation process (privacy by design) have been extolled to management by many a Data Protection Officer for years prior to it being mandated by the GDPR.

But for organizations to sit back and breathe a collective sigh of relief would be mistaken for two reasons. The first is that, whilst much of the previously applicable law is reproduced in the GDPR, several new obligations present a significant challenge in both time and money—in particular, the requirements to publish certain documentation, to appoint a Data Protection Officer, and to notify breaches to both national regulators and potentially affected individuals.

The second is that many organizations are somewhat unprepared for the new law—not because they haven't taken steps to comply with the GDPR (although they may not have done), but because they didn't properly implement the *pre*-GDPR data protection legal requirements. They therefore have some catching up to do.

One possible explanation for the explosion of interest in, and awareness of, data protection legal requirements under the GDPR is the significant increase in levels of penalties that can be imposed. In particular, monetary penalties (fines, in effect) of up to 20 million euros or 4 per cent of global annual turnover are available to the national data protection regulators. Another is the global awareness that has been sparked by the apparent extra-territorial applicability of the GDPR—the law attempts to regulate organizations based outside of the EU which supply products or services to EU citizens, even where such organizations have no EU presence or establishment.

Yet a third might be that the EU chose a Regulation rather than a Directive to create the new law. To understand why this is significant, it is useful to understand the differences between a Directive and a Regulation. A Directive, which is the most common method of EU law formation, is a somewhat cumbersome legal instrument that requires implementation in each individual Member State—it sets out the goals to be achieved, and then requires Member States to implement appropriate measures in their own territories. As an example, the Data Protection Directive was implemented in the UK by the Data Protection Act 1998. France also created a Data Protection Act. As did Ireland. And as did all the remaining members of the EU. The problem with this method of law creation, especially when dealing with compliance issues across national boundaries within the EU, is that it produces twenty-eight somewhat different national laws. Even though the decisions of the Court of Justice of the European Union (which are binding in all Member States) are designed to harmonize the legal landscape across the entire region, the reality is that differences remain.

A Regulation, on the other hand, is a legal instrument that has immediate binding effect in all Member States, without any further action being required by those States. Although Regulations can (and the GDPR does) include provisions that allow Member States to create additional rules, such as exceptions to certain requirements, the main cut and thrust of the provisions of the legal instrument is identical across the EU. This is intended to provide greater certainty for organizations that operate in multiple jurisdictions. And it should mean that their compliance operations will be simpler to implement and maintain. It also means that Member States' parliaments have no opportunity to 'water down' the law's requirements (as they do with a Directive) except to the extent specifically permitted under the terms of the Regulation.

In terms of guidance on what the law means, a Regulation (just like a Directive) contains both Recitals and Articles. The Articles are the important operative bits, whereas Recitals are statements that are produced by the legislators which explain the rationale behind the law. The latter are often used as 'persuasive' guides to interpretation, but they are not legally binding. In this book, we refer to Recitals where it helps to explain the intention behind the content of the Articles.

But the fact that the new law has been created by a Regulation does not mean that national parliaments have no role. At the time of going to print, several Member States had introduced national legislation which provides clarification on the GDPR's applicability, including (where permitted by the GDPR) defining the scope of exceptions to some of the GDPR's provisions. The UK's own draft legislation, the Data Protection Bill 2017, is somewhat unusual in this regard since it additionally attempts to deal with the UK's legal position as regards data protection matters after

Brexit. Although the Bill had not had the opportunity to become an Act at the time of going to print, we refer to the provisions of the Bill where relevant throughout the text. Readers should check the final wording of the Act before relying on the book's view or interpretation of the Bill's provisions.

Although Chapter 1, on terminology, sets out the definitions of words and phrases that arise in data protection law, it might be helpful here to set out a few guidelines on the common abbreviations in the text.

- When referring to the UK Data Protection Act 1998, we use, for the sake of variety, 'the 1998 Act' and 'the DPA'.
- 'Directive 95/46/EC on the protection of individuals with regard to the processing of personal data and on the free movement of such data' is referred to throughout the book as 'the Directive' or 'the Data Protection Directive'.
- The General Data Protection Regulation is referred to as 'the Regulation' and 'the GDPR'.
- The UK's Data Protection Bill 2017 is referred to as 'the Bill'.
- The European Commission's proposal for a new Regulation on the processing of personal data in the electronic communications sector is referred to as the 'E-Privacy Regulation'.
- We have used 'data subject' and 'individual' interchangeably.
- We also use both 'national law' and 'Member State law' interchangeably.

As regards the appendices to the book, these have been reduced in quantity since the last edition. The full text of the Data Protection Act 1998 has been removed (since it is abolished by the Bill), as have the statutory instruments made under the 1998 Act. For other important documents that are referred to in the book, we have created a web page which lists them and provides links to their full text online (see <http://www.dpdocuments.com>). The new Data Protection Act will be added to the online list of documents at the point that it receives Royal Assent.

In producing this new edition, we faced a timing issue. Should we wait for the UK to leave the European Union so that the UK's legal position vis à vis the remaining Members of the EU would become clearer prior to publication, or would it suffice to have the final wording of the GDPR at the time of writing? We chose the latter, mostly because the Regulation has direct effect in the UK from 25 May 2018, which is at least several months prior to the earliest date that Brexit can take effect.

In any event, organizations across Europe need to take measures to adapt their data processing operations in order to meet the GDPR's requirements. As far as the UK is concerned, this cannot wait for Brexit, as the new law (including the Commissioner's revised powers) is effective from May 2018. We hope this new edition, even though it may be considered premature by some, will assist in this regard.

Peter Carey

November 2017

1

Territorial Scope and Terminology

Damien Welfare and Peter Carey

Introduction and Historical Perspective	2
Territorial Scope	5
Introduction to Terminology	7
Personal Data	8
Processing	15
Filing System	16
Controller	18
Processor	19
Special Categories of Personal Data	20
European Economic Area	21
Main Establishment	21
Data Subject	22
Pseudonymization	23
Profiling	23
Personal Data Breach	24
The Data Subject's Consent	24
Child	24
Genetic Data	25
Biometric Data	25
Recipient	25
Data Protection by Design	26
Data Protection by Default	26
Codes of Conduct	26
Joint Controllers	27
European Data Protection Board	27
Delegated Acts	28
Certification	28
One Stop Shop	29
Directive on Security of Network and Information Systems	30
Directive on Personal Data Processed for Criminal Law Enforcement	31

Introduction and Historical Perspective

Data protection law gives people rights in their personal information, and it restricts the ways in which organizations can use people's personal information.

The perceived need for data protection legislation arose out of the growing use of computers in the 1970s and the threat to personal privacy that rapid manipulation of data potentially posed. In the UK the existing law at that time (which consisted of not much more than a possible action in breach of confidence) was insufficient to deal with concerns about the amount of information relating to individuals that was held by organizations in electronic form.

Thus the UK created one of the world's first comprehensive legislative measures on the protection of people's personal information. The Data Protection Act 1984 introduced in the UK a new regime for holding and processing 'information recorded in a form in which it can be processed by equipment operating automatically in response to instructions given for that purpose'. For the first time, data users—those organizations that held data—were obliged to register with a supervisory authority: then known as the Office of the Data Protection Registrar. The 1984 Act introduced criminal offences for failing to comply with its provisions and a system of compensation for individuals who suffered damage by non-compliance.

The regime under the 1984 Act was underpinned by certain fundamental principles, which formed a code for the proper processing of personal data. The principles, with two notable exceptions, were not dissimilar to those now contained in the General Data Protection Regulation, and were as follows:

1. The information to be contained in personal data shall be obtained, and personal data shall be processed, fairly and lawfully.
2. Personal data shall be held only for one or more specified and lawful purposes.
3. Personal data held for any purpose or purposes shall not be used or disclosed in any manner incompatible with that purpose or those purposes.
4. Personal data held for any purpose or purposes shall be adequate, relevant and not excessive in relation to that purpose or those purposes.
5. Personal data shall be accurate and, where necessary, kept up-to-date.
6. Personal data held for any purpose or purposes shall not be kept for longer than is necessary for that purpose or those purposes.
7. An individual shall be entitled—
   (a) at reasonable intervals and without undue delay or expense—
      (i) to be informed by any data user whether he holds personal data of which that individual is the subject; and
      (ii) to access to any such data held by a data user; and
   (b) where appropriate, to have such data corrected or erased.
8. Appropriate security measures shall be taken against unauthorised access to, or alteration, disclosure, or destruction of, personal data and against accidental loss or destruction of personal data.

The European Directive 95/46/EC on the protection of individuals with regard to the processing of personal data and on the free movement of such data (referred to in this book as 'the Data Protection Directive' or 'the Directive') was adopted as a legislative measure in October 1995. The Directive was a general framework legislative provision, which had, as its principal aims:

(a) the protection of an individual's privacy in relation to the processing of personal data; and

(b) the harmonization of data protection laws of the Member States.

It set out the conditions under which the processing of personal data was lawful, the rights of data subjects, and the standards of data quality. In this way, the Directive sought to establish an equivalent level of protection for personal data in all Member States so as to facilitate the transfer of personal data across national boundaries within the European Union. The Directive applied to personal data processed wholly or partly by automatic means, and to manual data held in filing systems structured by reference to individuals, but did not apply to activities that fell outside the scope of EU law. It excluded areas within Titles V and VI of the Treaty on European Union, public safety, defence, state security (including the economic well-being of the state when the processing relates to state security matters), and the activities of the state in areas of criminal law. It also specifically excluded domestic or household activities. The principles of personal data processing established by the Directive were largely similar to those contained in the UK's 1984 Act, with the addition of a restriction on transferring personal data outside the European Economic Area ('EEA') and a restriction on the processing of certain categories of personal data (such as health-related information).

Each Member State of the European Union implemented the Directive by national legislation. The Data Protection Act 1998 (referred to in this book as 'the 1998 Act' or 'the DPA') implemented the Directive in the UK, and came into force on 1 March 2000. It provided a new definition of 'processing' (which included virtually anything that could be done with data) and incorporated the following features which represented significant changes to the 1984 Act regime:

(a) *Manual processing*—The 1998 Act applied to certain paper-based records in addition to electronically (automatically) processed personal data.

(b) *Legitimacy of processing*—New conditions for processing were introduced as a minimum threshold requirement before processing could be lawfully undertaken.

(c) *Sensitive data*—A new category of personal data was created. Sensitive personal data could not be processed unless one of a set of pre-conditions was satisfied.

(d) *Data exports*—Transfers of personal data to countries outside the European Economic Area were banned unless certain conditions were satisfied.

(e) *Data security*—The security requirements were extended and new requirements regarding data processors were established.

(f) *Individual rights*—Significantly more and stronger rights for individuals existed under the 1998 Act, including the right to compensation for damage or distress caused by unlawful processing.

In December 2000, all three bodies of the European Union that have legislative functions—the European Commission, the European Parliament, and the Council—agreed in Nice (hence the 'Nice Charter') the Charter of Fundamental Rights of the European Union. The Charter represented the first occasion when the EU institutions had agreed on a set of individuals' rights, separate and distinct from (although related to, in terms of content) the Council of Europe's Convention for the Protection of Human Rights and Fundamental Freedoms ('ECHR'). The Charter sought to give more effective legal force to existing rights by enshrining them as a 'fundamental' aspect of the EU.

Article 8 of the Nice Charter, with the title of 'Protection of Personal Data', provides as follows:

1. Everyone has the right to the protection of personal data concerning him or her.
2. Such data must be processed fairly for specified purposes and on the basis of the consent of the person concerned or some other legitimate basis laid down by law. Everyone has the right of access to data which has been collected concerning him or her, and the right to have it rectified.
3. Compliance with these rules shall be subject to control by an independent authority.

In 2009, the Lisbon Treaty granted legally binding force to the Nice Charter, consolidating the existence in EU law of the fundamental right to the protection of personal data.

The General Data Protection Regulation ('GDPR'), which is the main subject of this book, takes data protection requirements to the next level of complexity. The Regulation has direct effect throughout the European Union from 25 May 2018. As such it replaces Directive 95/46/EC on the protection of individuals with regard to the processing of personal data and on the free movement of such data ('the Data Protection Directive').

As far as the UK and Brexit are concerned, the GDPR will be incorporated into UK law by virtue of the EU (Withdrawal) Bill (or 'Great Repeal Bill'), if enacted, from the date of the UK's departure from the European Union.

The Regulation does not apply in the course of an activity which falls outside the scope of EU competence (Article 2(2)(a)); nor to the processing of personal data for law enforcement, or national security data processing (Article 2(2)(d)). The Regulation also does not apply to processing by member states for border checks, asylum or immigration activities (Article 2(2))(b)); nor to the processing of personal data by a natural person (i.e. a living individual) in the course of a 'purely personal or household activity' (Article 2(2)(c)).

Under the GDPR, Member States are permitted to create national exemptions from some of its requirements, and additional provisions as regards others. The UK had begun the process of supplementing the GDPR at the time of writing by introducing the Data Protection Bill 2017. The Bill acknowledges that most personal data processing operations in the UK are subject to the GDPR, and goes on in Part 2 to apply the same rules as those contained in the GDPR to areas of UK activity that would otherwise not be covered by the Regulation, because they fall outside EU competence (which the Bill calls the 'applied GDPR regime')—with the exception of law enforcement and processing by the intelligence services. The Bill and the GDPR (effectively in combination, for the remainder of the UK's membership of the EU from 25 May 2018) are intended by the UK government to apply 'substantively the same standards to the majority of data processing in the UK'. Part 3 of the Bill makes provision for law enforcement data processing (implementing EU Directive 2016/680, which obliged member states to implement a parallel data protection regime for law enforcement by the same date as the GDPR). Part 4 provides for data processing by the intelligence services.

The Bill applies the relevant Articles of the GDPR to processing outside the scope of EU law as set out in Schedule 6 of the Bill (the 'applied GDPR regime'). The Bill simultaneously modifies certain Articles of the GDPR in their application in a context where EU law does not apply.

The Bill also deals with the powers of the Information Commissioner (Part 5) and enforcement (Part 6, and offences in Part 7).

The distinction between personal data inside and outside the scope of EU law will disappear when the UK leaves the EU, and the government intends that GDPR standards of processing will continue to apply to the areas of processing within Part 2 of the Bill (i.e. the areas that have been outside EU law while the UK has been a member). At the time of writing, the government therefore intends, when the GDPR is brought within the UK's domestic law, to make provision to enable a 'single domestic legal basis' to apply the GDPR's data processing standards.

In other words, it appears that a further single UK measure is intended to unify the regimes in the GDPR and the Data Protection Bill (excluding national security data processing, and possibly leaving law enforcement data processing to be covered, as before, by Part 3 of the Data Protection Bill).

This chapter refers to the combination of the GDPR and the Data Protection Bill, and their possible replacement in the future by a single provision, as the 'UK replacement'. The chapter reflects the Data Protection Bill as first introduced into the House of Lords and assumes that equivalent provisions would be enacted in a single provision, if one were introduced.

The remaining chapters of this book will use 'GDPR' to apply both to the GDPR itself, and the combined regime which is intended to replace it in the UK.

Territorial Scope

Territorial scope refers to the applicability of the legislation on a geographical basis.

Data protection law has historically applied primarily to organizations located in the European Union—for example, where a UK company holds and uses information on its employees it is obliged to comply with data protection legal requirements. Organizations located in the EU have also, however, had to observe European requirements in relation to transfers of personal data to jurisdictions which do not have broadly equivalent data protection regimes, often through bilateral arrangements such as model contractual clauses, or the 'Safe Harbor' or 'Privacy Shield' agreements (approved by the European Commission) with major companies in the United States, to secure data protection standards.

However, the GDPR seeks somewhat wider applicability. Article 3 of the Regulation states, in effect, that the law applies to any activity that has data protection consequences for individuals in the European Union (including in this context, this countries of the European Economic Area, or EEA). It does this by applying to:

- the processing of personal data by a controller or a processor which has an establishment in the EU, where the processing is within the context of the activities of the organization which is so established, regardless of whether the processing itself takes place in the EU or not; or
- the processing of personal data of data subjects who are in the EU by a controller or processor which is not established in the EU, where the processing activities are related to:
  - the offering of goods or services to data subjects in the EU, irrespective of whether a payment by the data subject is required; or
  - the monitoring of their behaviour, so far as that behaviour takes place within the EU.

The Data Protection Bill modifies this in respect of processing that was outside the scope of EU law before Brexit. By complex provisions in Clause 186, and Schedule 6, paragraph 8 (involving substituting Article 3 of the GDPR with a modified version of Clause 186), controllers established outside the UK and offering services to individuals in the UK or monitoring their behaviour, or processors working for controllers established outside the UK, who are undertaking such processing, are excluded from these rules.

Although there is no definition of 'monitoring the behaviour' in the GDPR, Recital 24 implies that this occurs where individuals are tracked on the internet with data processing techniques that consist of applying a 'profile' to an individual in order to make decisions concerning the individual or for analysing or predicting an individual's personal preferences, behaviours, and attitudes. Behavioural advertising could therefore be covered by this description. Non-EU organizations, particularly those which sell into several EU Member States, may be subject to the law of every Member State in which they operate.

The Regulation (and its UK replacement) also applies, like the previous Directive, to processing by a controller which is not established in the EU (or the UK), but in a place where the law of the Member State applies by virtue of public international law. An example is an EU Member State's embassy in a Far Eastern country—the data protection laws applying to the embassy's activities are those of the Member State by virtue of treaties applying to embassies, rather than the local law of the state in which the embassy is sited.

In general terms, the data protection law of the Regulation applies within the UK and the Member States of the European Union, plus Norway, Liechtenstein, and Iceland (the latter being the remaining three European Free Trade Area ('EFTA') members which are also members of the EEA).

In terms of the UK, and on the basis of the above, UK data protection law after Brexit will apply to all organizations in the UK, but not to non-UK organizations that offer goods or services to data subjects in the UK, or which monitor the behaviour of persons in the UK.

The Regulation (and its UK replacement) refers to the concept of 'establishment'. This term has a complex definition which depends to some extent on the type of organization concerned. Essentially we can say that an organization is established in the UK if it carries out activity in the country. Thus, where an organization is located in the UK, it is fairly obvious that the data protection law of the UK will apply. However, the Regulation (and hence its UK replacement) states that the data processing needs only to be undertaken in the context of the activities of that establishment. This concept is wider than merely requiring the data processing to be undertaken by the organization that is established in the Member State. It includes processing undertaken by a legal entity that is not itself established in a Member State where the processing is undertaken in the context of the activities of an organization which is so established. Such was the case under the former Directive in *Google Spain SL & Google Inc. v Mario Costeja Gonzalez* [2014] C-131/12, where the well-known search engine operated by Google Inc., a US corporation, was held to be processing personal data in Spain due to the presence and activities of its subsidiary there.

The Regulation thus covers both processing undertaken in the EU/EEA (and the UK) by a subsidiary within the Union and the offering of goods or services to individuals in the Union by a controller or processor outside that territorial scope, or a controller or processor which is monitoring behaviour within the EU from outside. These approaches may overlap in some situations. The limitation proposed by the Data Protection Bill in respect of processing not subject to EU law during the period of the UK's membership, however, is referred to above.

At a practical level, it is difficult to see how non-compliance by organizations outside the EU/EEA (or, after Brexit, the UK) would be enforced.

Introduction to Terminology

In order to understand the application of data protection law, it is necessary to become familiar with certain terms that are used repeatedly throughout the legislation. This chapter sets out the definitions of key terms from the Regulation (and, where relevant, compares them with the equivalent definitions in the 1998 Act or the Data Protection Directive).

It is useful to bear in mind that the purpose of the 1998 Act was to give effect, in the UK, to the Data Protection Directive. However, the definitions in the 1998 Act (and in the implementing legislation of other Member States) did not always exactly match their counterparts in the Directive. This sometimes led to understandable confusion amongst organizations as to how to implement data protection measures properly, most particularly where operations were undertaken at the fringes of the definitions. This problem is reduced with the Regulation since it largely harmonizes the law across all Member States. Most queries over definitions in the UK replacement should not, at least initially, arise from different wording between the EU and UK provisions, unless they relate to differences over the definitions of exceptions. There may, however, be divergences of substance in the future over such expectations, or if the UK law is amended in ways that distinguish it from the Regulation.

Rather than being set out in alphabetical order, the terms below appear in a sequence that seems, to the authors, to be more conducive to an understanding of their meaning and application.

Personal Data

The legal restrictions contained in the Regulation apply only to 'the processing of personal data' (Article 1(1)). Thus, an accurate determination of what amounts to 'personal data' is crucial to any data protection compliance regime. In the UK, the term was previously defined somewhat differently as between the Directive and the Act (see Box 1.1 below).

Box 1.1 Comparison of the Definition of 'Personal Data'

Article 2(a) Data Protection Directive

Any information relating to an identified or identifiable natural person (data subject); an identifiable person is one who can be identified, directly or indirectly, in particular by reference to an identification number or to one or more factors specific to his physical, physiological, mental, economic, cultural or social identity.

Section 1(1) Data Protection Act

Data which relate to a living individual who can be identified—

(a) from those data, or

(b) from those data and other information which is in the possession of, or is likely to come into the possession of, the data controller, and includes any expression of opinion about the individual and any indication of the intentions of the data controller or any other person in respect of the individual.

Article 4(1) GDPR

Personal data means any information relating to an identified or identifiable natural person. An identifiable natural person is one who can be identified, directly or indirectly, in particular by reference to an identifier such as a name, an identification number, location data, an online identifier or to one or more factors specific to the physical, physiological, genetic, mental, economic, cultural or social identity of that natural person.

Personal data means, under the GDPR, any information relating to an identified or identifiable natural person ('data subject'). An identifiable natural person is 'one who can be identified, directly or indirectly, in particular by reference to an identifier such as a name, an identification number, location data, an online identifier or to one or more factors specific to the physical, physiological, genetic, mental, economic, cultural or social identity of that natural person' (Article 4(1)). The GDPR moves the UK definition into line with that applying in the rest of the EU. It is also much closer to the definition in the outgoing Directive than has been the definition in the DPA.

The previous complication in relation to identification, caused by there having been a different definition under the DPA from the Directive, is removed under the Regulation (see below). Under the Regulation, if a natural person (rephrased by Clause 2(2) of the Bill to a 'living individual') can be identified, or is identifiable (potentially by anyone else), and the information relates to that natural person, it constitutes personal data about him or her. The person does not have to be identified, or to be identifiable, from the particular information under consideration, since it is sufficient if the identification (or potential identification) is made 'indirectly' (i.e. from other information). Nor, again in contrast to the DPA, does such information need to be possessed by, or be likely to come into the possession of, the 'controller' (formerly, the data controller).

Identification (based on the Information Commissioner's guidance under the DPA) amounts to distinguishing a person from a group, and 'identifiable' may be interpreted as meaning that a natural person (or living individual) is capable of such identification.

As outlined above, the definition in the GDPR sets out a non-exhaustive list of factors by which a person may be identified or identifiable (it follows, therefore, that another means of identification or identifiability would be as valid). The list gives as examples of potential identifiers:

- a person's name;
- an identification number (e.g. a patient number, national insurance number, or the reference number of their complaint);
- location data (e.g. a GPS location reference from a person's mobile telephone); or
- an online identifier (e.g. an individual's identity as used on social media, an email address including one not incorporating their name, or a reference number used to make a profile of their internet use).

Of these, most were in place in the Directive, and only a person's name, location data, and an online identifier are new as between the Directive and the GDPR. The use of these terms is new, however, in the UK legislation.

The list extends to 'factors' relating to more personal aspects of a natural person's identity, such as:

- physical factors (e.g. a photograph showing their appearance, or a reference to a health condition affecting them);
- genetic factors (e.g. a record of their DNA profile);

- mental aspects (e.g. a record of their mental health, or their intellectual abilities);
- economic aspects (e.g. a record of their income, wealth, or employment);
- cultural aspects (e.g. their ethnicity, or a culture in which they originated); or
- social identity (e.g. a socio-economic class to which they are deemed to belong).

Of these, only genetic data (and biometric data, referred to in Article 9.1) are new as between the Directive and the GDPR. As above, however, the use of these terms is new in the legislation in the UK.

The Information Commissioner's guidance in the UK (under the DPA) has been that a broad approach should be taken to the scope of information 'relating' to a natural person, reflecting the application of the Directive generally in the EU, and there is no reason to doubt that this will continue to be the case under the GDPR or its UK replacement. It extends, therefore, to the following:

- Information that is obviously about an individual that can be linked to them in a way that discloses something about them (e.g. a salary figure linked to a postholder).
- Information that is processed to inform or influence actions or decisions affecting an individual (e.g. information about a house's consumption of energy, used to generate a bill to the occupier for payment; or, information used to consider or determine the outcome of a complaint by a person).
- Information that has some biographical significance in relation to a person (e.g. a record of their activities on a certain day) which focuses or concentrates on them, rather than on some other person, object, transaction, or event. (Information on the other hand which only refers to that person in passing, but is actually about someone else, or concerns some other object, transaction, or event, will not be included.)
- Information about an object or thing, where it contains information about an individual which has an impact on that person (e.g. a test of machinery which reveals differences in the productivity of two workers, leading the company to make changes to their working pattern or training).

Under the DPA and Directive, some courts in the UK took a narrower approach to the scope of personal data than the Information Commissioner had done (see below). Where relevant to the new definition, these cases may still need to be taken into account as persuasive under the Regulation, and its UK replacement, though this may prove to be limited given that the wording of the Regulation clearly points to a wider interpretation (as did the wording of the Directive).

As shown above, the definition in the Regulation is similar to that in the Directive. The DPA, however, was more restrictive in that 'other information' alongside the data in question, from a combination of both of which a data subject could be identified, had to be in the hands (or be likely to come into the possession) of the data controller, rather than other persons. In practice, this limited who could identify data subjects to the data controller, rather than the wider community. There was also no reference to 'identifiability'. On the other hand, the DPA specified that personal data included expressions of opinion about a data subject and any indication of the intentions of the data controller or another person towards the data subject. These two aspects should continue to be borne in mind as likely to indicate that information is personal data.

From a practical perspective, in most cases it will be obvious whether information that is being used by an organization amounts to an individual's personal data. For example, in the case of a customer of a bank, the bank will hold and electronically process the customer's information in the form of her name, address, date of birth, account number, debit or credit card details, payments into and out of her account, and certain other information (such as her credit rating, or suitability for a loan)—this is clearly personal data. Similarly, in relation to information held by an employer on its employees, it will usually be obvious that personal data are being held about, and used in relation to, staff members.

However, there are circumstances where it can be less clear whether an organization is processing personal data; or, where, if it is undertaking such processing, what information amounts to personal data. In those cases it will be crucial to make an appropriate determination on that issue, as the obligations under data protection law apply only to the processing of personal data. Equally, without an adequate awareness of the potential breadth of personal data, there is a risk that activities may be undertaken in relation to the information which do not comply with the legal requirements.

Past interpretations by the courts

The Court of Appeal in England and Wales often took a narrower view than the Commissioner of the scope of personal data, although the cases it decided (as well as the decisions of other courts) were not consistent. However, even under the GDPR, they may remain relevant and persuasive.

In *Durant v Financial Services Authority* [2003] EWCA Civ 1746, the Court of Appeal looked at the issue of information 'relating' to an individual. Mr Durant was in dispute with Barclays Bank over the recovery of a mortgage loan made by Barclays Bank to Mr Durant's company. In the course of his dispute with the bank he made a complaint to the Financial Services Authority ('FSA') (a predecessor of the Financial Conduct Authority) and then subsequently made a subject access request to the FSA. Mr Durant felt the FSA's response was inadequate and so took action to obtain the disclosure from the FSA of information not provided in response to his subject access request, including the disclosure of information from the FSA's manual (paper-based) files.

In the course of his judgment, Lord Justice Auld made the following observation about personal data which subsequently proved to be highly controversial:

. . . not all information retrieved from a computer search against an individual's name or unique identifier is personal data within the Act. Mere mention of the data subject in a document held by a data controller does not necessarily amount to his personal data. Whether it does so in any particular instance depends on where it falls in a continuum of relevance or proximity to the data subject, as distinct, say, from transactions or matters which he may have been involved in to a greater or lesser degree. It seems to me that there are two notions which may be of assistance. The first is whether the information is biographical in any significant sense, that is going beyond the recording of the putative data subject's involvement in a matter or an event which has no personal connotations, a life event in respect of which his privacy cannot be said to be compromised. The second is one of focus. The information should have the putative data subject as its focus rather than some other person with whom he may have been involved or some transaction or event in which he may have figured or had an interest, for example, as in this case, an investigation into some other person's or body's conduct that he may have instigated. In short it is information that affects his privacy, whether in his personal or family life, business or professional capacity.

By requiring there to be either a 'biographical' or a 'focus' element to any particular data in question, the judge was taken to be seeking to narrow the application of the definition of personal data compared to that in the Directive. The European Commission subsequently expressed its dissatisfaction with the case and took steps to commence legal proceedings (which were later dropped) against the UK for failing to implement the Data Protection Directive adequately.

Following the controversy produced by the *Durant* case (and other concerns regarding the apparent ambiguity of the definition of personal data in the Directive), the Article 29 Working Party (a grouping of equivalents of the Information Commissioner in member states, and the forerunner of the European Data Protection Board) produced an Opinion document in June 2007 (WP 136) in an attempt to clarify the definition of personal data. In that document, the Working Party reiterated the breadth of the definition, effectively denying the validity of the more controversial (and arguably narrowing) interpretation of the *Durant* judgment. The Working Party stated that in general terms information could be considered to relate to an individual where it was about that individual. Later in 2007, the Information Commissioner's Office ('ICO') produced its own guidance on the definition of data protection, in a document (revised in December 2012) entitled 'Determining what is personal data' (this guidance remains current at the date of writing but will need to be revised for GDPR purposes).

A wider approach to the definition of personal data was supported by several other UK cases. In *Common Services Agency v Scottish Information Commissioner* [2008] UKHL 47, the House of Lords (as the Supreme Court was then known) referred to *Durant* in a manner that could be interpreted as limiting *Durant's* applicability to the narrow circumstances disclosed by that case's particular facts. In the High Court decision of *R (Kelway) v The Upper Tribunal (Administrative Appeals Chamber) and Northumbria Police* and *R (Kelway) v Independent Police Complaints Commission* [2013] EWHC 2575, the judge said that although *Durant* should be considered as one of the tests for personal data, other factors should also be looked at, and these are the Article 29 Working Party and ICO guidance documents referred to earlier, as well as (of course) the legislative wording of both the DPA and the Directive.

In the case of *Edem v IC & Financial Services Authority* [2014] EWCA Civ 92, the Court of Appeal was asked to consider whether data that records a person's name was automatically personal data (because it identified and related to a particular individual) or whether, in order to be personal data, it had to be processed in a context which provided additional information about the individual. The court took the former approach, namely that a name, of itself, was indeed personal data (unless the name was so common that without further information, such as its use in the context of a person's work, a person would remain unidentifiable from its disclosure). The court cited a passage from the ICO's guidance document, which it may be helpful to reproduce here:

It is important to remember that it is not always necessary to consider 'biographical significance' to determine whether data is personal data. In many cases data may be personal data simply because its content is such that it is 'obviously about' an individual. Alternatively, data may be personal data because it is clearly 'linked to' an individual because it is about his activities and is processed for the purpose of determining or influencing the way in which that person is treated. You need to consider 'biographical significance' only where information is not 'obviously about' an individual or clearly 'linked to' him.

In the case of *Netherlands Immigration Minister v M & S* (17 July 2014) C-141/12 & C-372/12, the European Court of Justice held that whilst the information contained in an application for a residence permit, and the data contained in the legal analysis that related to the permit, amounted to the personal data of the applicant, the legal analysis itself was not personal data.

The position left after the *Edem* case was complicated, however, at least in England and Wales, by another decision of the Court of Appeal which reverted, at least in part, to the approach in *Durant*. In *Ittihadieh v 5-11 Cheyne Gardens RTM Company Ltd* [2017] EWCA Civ 121, the requester made a subject access request to the property management company for his home, whose directors were also his neighbours. He stated that he was concerned about their use of his personal data, indicating a likelihood of various claims against them and the company. The court again (following *Durant*) accepted that the mere fact that a person's name was mentioned in a document did not, without more, mean that it contained the individual's personal data. It also observed, however, that data revealing a person's whereabouts may amount to their personal data.

This left a somewhat confused position before the introduction of the Regulation in 2018. Nevertheless, in the context of the GDPR, it is strongly suggested that the breadth of its wording should be taken as a clear indication that a wide interpretation should be placed on the scope of personal data. (On the specific issue of a name as personal data, as noted above, the GDPR provides for this in Article 4(1).)

A further and separate consideration is that in order to be personal data, the information must relate to a 'natural person'. There are two points to be made here which, whilst obvious, are nevertheless worth mentioning. The first is that, in order to relate to a natural person, the data must relate to a living individual—once a person has died, her rights under the legislation (and the obligations of the controller in respect of her personal data) cease. (The Data Protection Bill converts the definition to refer to a 'living individual' in the UK context, in Clause 2(2). Having said that, it should be borne in mind that information relating to a deceased person may constitute the personal data of a living individual—an example is the value of a deceased person's estate where there is just one beneficiary.

The second is that the definition applies only to individuals. A database containing information relating to limited companies is therefore not caught (see, for example, *Smith v Lloyds TSB plc* [2005] EWHC 246 where it was held, under the DPA, that information concerning a loan made to Mr Smith's company did not amount to information about Mr Smith). However, where such a database includes the names of officers or employees within a company (e.g. contact names), it will fall within the definition of personal data because a living individual can be identified by his name and place of work. The Regulation makes no distinction between information processed on people in their work or professional capacity on the one hand, and in their personal capacity on the other.

The final part of the definition in the Act referred to information which indicated an opinion of, or an intention towards, an individual (see Box 1.1 above). Examples in the context of information processed by a personnel or human resources department of an organization would have included a manager's statement of intentions concerning an employee's promotion or demotion, or a manager's opinion that an employee is unsuitable for a particular role.

It should be noted that personal data can relate to more than one person. For example, the location of a person at any particular time may also constitute the personal data of other known individuals in the same location. Joint property ownership can amount to the personal data of two persons. The content of an email sent by a tenant living in an apartment block complaining about his neighbour may contain information relating to both the complainer and the person about whom the complaint was made. A page of text recording a discussion between two individuals, perhaps including a detailed exchange of views or a disagreement, may be the personal data of both.

Whilst the definition of personal data is complicated at its fringes, it should be remembered that the concept is defined widely. Once the threshold of identification has been reached, virtually anything that may relate to an individual can fall within

---

Box 1.2 Examples of Information About Individuals Capable of Amounting to 'Personal Data'

Name	Shoe size	Last time/place credit card used
Address	DNA sample	Geographical location
Date of birth	Blood group	Medical history
NI number	Credit card number	Sexual preference
Passport number	Favourite restaurant	Destination of air travel

the definition, provided it also relates to the individual in a broad sense. A non-exhaustive list of examples of personal data is shown in Box 1.2.

Processing

The Regulation defines processing as:

any operation or set of operations which is performed on personal data or on sets of personal data, whether or not by automated means, such as: collection, recording, organization, structuring, storage, adaptation or alteration, retrieval, consultation, use, disclosure by transmission, dissemination or otherwise making available, alignment or combination, restriction, erasure or destruction (Article 4(2)).

Clause 2(4) of the Bill applies a similar definition.

By comparison with the previous Directive, the term 'structuring' is added, and 'restriction' is substituted for 'blocking'.

This definition of processing is very wide and includes almost anything that can be done with data. Significantly, the definition extends to the mere storage of information on a computer hard drive, server, CD-Rom, or any portable memory device including a USB stick. It also includes the activities known as data matching, data sharing, data mining, and data warehousing. The recording of CCTV images of people's faces or other identifying characteristics also constitutes processing.

Essentially almost everything that can be done with data by an organization in the lifecycle of the data, including the initial obtaining and the eventual destruction, as well as storage in between, or any use of the information, amounts to processing, and is therefore caught within the data protection legal regime.

The breadth of the term 'processing' under the Directive and the DPA was considered in *Campbell v Mirror Group Newspapers* [2002] EWHC 299, when it was held to include everything that was done with Naomi Campbell's information by the *Mirror* up to and including the publication in hard copy. An extract from the Court of Appeal judgment is as follows:

the definition of processing is so wide that it embraces the relatively ephemeral operations that will normally be carried out by way of the day-to-day tasks, involving the use of electronic equipment such as the laptop and the modern printing press, in translating information into the printed newspaper.

In its judgment in the 2014 Google case (also decided under the Directive), the Court of Justice of the European Union confirmed that a search engine collects (and therefore processes) personal data by its usual activities, namely 'searching automatically, constantly and systematically for information published on the internet'. According to the judgment, other processing operations conducted by search engines include retrieving, recording, organizing, storing, disclosing, and making available.

Filing System

As well as being applicable to electronically processed personal data, data protection law applies to information contained in certain manual (paper-based) records. Such paper-based records must usually form part of a 'filing system' (previously known as a 'relevant filing system' under the DPA) in order to be caught within the legislative regime. The definition from the Regulation, which is identical to that in Article 2(c) of the former Directive, appears in Box 1.3.

In the context of the DPA, there was some argument over precisely what was included within the definition of a 'relevant filing system'. This arose partly because of the narrow definition placed on such systems by the *Durant* case. It seems that the key characteristics of a relevant filing system remain the structuring by reference to individuals and/or the ready accessibility of specific information. Recital 15 of the Regulation, in referring to manual files, states: 'Files or sets of files, as well as their cover pages, which are not structured according to specific criteria should not fall within the scope of this Regulation'. (Recital 27 of the Directive contained very similar wording.)

In her 'Overview of the GDPR', the Commissioner says that the GDPR 'applies to both automated personal data and to manual filing systems where personal data are accessible according to specific criteria. This is wider than the DPA's definition and could include chronologically ordered sets of manual records containing personal data.' It is fair to conclude, therefore, that the scope of manual filing systems under the Regulation should be treated more broadly than previously.

Clause 2(7) of the Bill refers to a filing system as a structured set of personal data held by automated means or manually, thus similarly extending the definition of a filing system to include an electronic one.

Under the Commissioner's guidance in relation to 'relevant filing systems' (under the DPA) an example of such a system was a set of manual personnel files held in the workplace, where each alphabetically filed record related to a specific employee and contained clearly indexed information concerning that employee. On the other hand, a single ring binder containing an individual's personal data might not have been a structured file, and therefore would not necessarily have formed part of a relevant filing system, if it did not have information sub-divided

---

Box 1.3 Definition of 'Filing System'

Article 4(6) GDPR
any structured set of personal data which are accessible according to specific criteria, whether centralised, de-centralised or dispersed on a functional or geographical basis.

by category within it, particularly if there was a substantial quantity of it. In the *Smith* case the court held that an unstructured bundle of papers kept in boxes did not amount to a relevant filing system.

By way of background, in his judgment in the *Durant* case, Lord Justice Auld considered four different manual files held by the FSA:

1. Major Financial Groups Division systems file—Two volumes relating to Barclays Bank's own systems, controls, and money laundering procedures. The file, which was arranged in date order, contained a few documents concerning Mr Durant's complaint about the bank.

2. Complaints file—Documents relating to Mr Durant's complaint about the bank were stored under a divider marked 'Mr Durant', in date order.

3. Bank Investigations Group file—A file held by the bank investigations group relating to matters concerning the bank. A section of the file contained documents relating to Mr Durant. The file sections were organized by reference to cases or issues but not necessarily by reference to an individual save the name of Mr Durant on the sub-file itself.

4. Company Secretariat papers—A set of papers held by the company secretary relating to a complaint by Mr Durant concerning the FSA's dealings with him. The file was not organized chronologically or by any other criteria.

The court took the view that the structure of the four files did not satisfy the definition of a relevant filing system and that the documents did not have to be, and should not be, disclosed. In adopting a narrow interpretation of 'relevant filing system', Lord Justice Auld stated that a manual filing system must be 'on a par' with a computerized system in order to be caught by the definition. He said that Parliament's intention was to apply the DPA to manual records only if they were of sufficient sophistication to provide the same or similar ready accessibility as a computerized filing system. In particular, the judge stated that a 'relevant filing system' for the purposes of the DPA was limited to a system:

1. in which the files forming part of it were structured or referenced in such a way as clearly to indicate at the outset of the search whether specific information capable of amounting to personal data of an individual requesting it was held within the system and, if so, in which file or files it was held; and

2. which had, as part of its own structure or referencing mechanism, a sufficiently sophisticated and detailed means of readily indicating whether and where in an individual file or files, specific criteria or information about the applicant could readily be located.

It remains to be seen to what extent *Durant* is regarded in the future as correctly reflecting the law as to filing systems under the Regulation; although since the wording in the Directive is almost identical, it would seem likely to be regarded as at least persuasive, notwithstanding its somewhat restrictive approach. The Commissioner's guidance on relevant filing systems, interpreting *Durant*, may also remain relevant during at least the early period of the operation of the definition, for the same reason.

Controller

A 'controller' (formerly a 'data controller' under the DPA, although not under the Directive) is the entity that is responsible for complying with data protection law. Article 4(7) of the Regulation defines a controller as meaning:

the natural or legal person, public authority, agency or other body which, alone or jointly with others, determines the purposes and means of the processing of personal data.

Article 2(d) of the Directive defined the controller in almost identical terms. Where the purposes and means of such processing are determined by EU or Member State (or UK) law, that law may also determine who is the controller. Clause 5 of the Data Protection Bill amends the definition slightly in the UK context over minor differences relating to the Crown and to Parliament. Where personal data is processed only for the purposes of a statutory requirement, the Bill proposes that the UK will treat the person who has the duty to process the data as the controller (Clause 5(2)).

In general, all sole traders, self-employed professionals, partnerships, and companies will be controllers—this includes all online or 'bricks and mortar' businesses such as banks, insurance companies, law firms, supermarkets, betting shops, opticians, dentists, medical practices, Internet search engines, pharmaceuticals companies, telecommunications businesses (including internet service providers ('ISPs')), and construction firms. Additionally, unincorporated associations will be controllers, as well as schools, local authorities, police forces, fire services, hospitals, government departments, and quangos.

The use of the word 'jointly' in the definition makes it clear that there can be more than one controller in relation to any given piece of personal data, or personal data processing operation.

The Regulation, by virtue of Article 3(1), applies to controllers regardless of whether the processing takes place in the Union or not (see 'Territorial Scope' above). The different position in relation to processing that has not been subject to EU law during the period of the UK's membership is referred to above (also under 'Territorial Scope'). Notwithstanding the limitation, the UK measure will claim to apply to many EU controllers doing business in the UK, and the Regulation will claim to continue to apply to UK controllers with an establishment in the EU, or offering goods or services to EU data subjects, or monitoring their behaviour within the EU.

A controller should be distinguished from a 'Data Protection Officer' ('DPO') (whether or not that person is formally appointed as a 'statutory' DPO under the Regulation—see Chapter 12). The DPO, in an informal sense, is an individual person within an organization who has responsibility for data protection compliance within that organization. Under the Regulation, it is compulsory for many organizations to appoint a DPO with statutory functions. However, where not required to do so, many medium-sized and large data controllers will choose to appoint one or more DPOs informally to carry out data protection functions and to ensure the compliance of the organization with data protection legal requirements. Generally speaking, a DPO will not be liable for the data protection breaches of the controller.

A controller must also be distinguished from a 'processor'—the latter is an entity that processes personal data on behalf of a controller (see below and Chapter 9). The Regulation imposes formal responsibilities on the processor (formerly, the 'data processor') for the first time—but controllers remain legally responsible for some of the processing operations carried out by the processor.

Processor

A 'processor' is defined in the Regulation (Article 4(8)) using the same wording as in the Directive, namely:

a natural or legal person, public authority, agency or any other body which processes personal data on behalf of the controller.

Clause 30(3) defines a processor (in similar terms to the DPA) as 'any person who processes personal data on behalf of the controller (other than a person who is an employee of the controller)'.

Controllers often use third party companies to process their data due to the time and cost savings involved. As long as the third party merely acts on the instructions of the controller and does not itself determine the purposes or means of the processing of the data, it will be a processor. The distinction is, in some circumstances, less critical than under the Directive, due to the creation of obligations on the processor. However, it is still important to understand the respective roles since the responsibilities of processors differ from, and are still less onerous than, those of the controller. Further, the controller continues to have important responsibilities where it enters into arrangements with processors.

Outsourcing arrangements (see Chapter 9), whereby the controller passes certain tasks to a processor, are of course very common—most controllers in the EU engage in this type of activity in one form or another. Examples include the farming out to third party suppliers of the following activities of a business: payroll administration, debt collection, website hosting, telephone call centres, paper waste handling and destruction, and private investigation.

As well as holding statutory responsibilities under the Regulation, processors should expect to be required, by their controllers, to enter into a written contract or agreement which obliges them to give guarantees as to data protection compliance, including security provisions, and to process personal data only on the instructions of the relevant controller (Article 28(1) and (3)).

For further detail on processors and their relationship with controllers, see Chapter 9.

Special Categories of Personal Data

The Data Protection Directive and the DPA created a category of data called 'sensitive personal data'. This has been replaced by 'special categories' of personal data, under the Regulation.

As a general principle, a controller is not permitted to process these special categories of personal data (Article 9(1)). However, processing is permitted if it falls into one or more of a number of exceptions (or 'conditions') in Article 9(2). While the exceptions are set out in the Regulation, Member States (and the UK after Brexit) may create their own additional conditions (including limitations) that permit or apply to the processing of certain of the special categories of personal data.

'Special categories of personal data' is defined in Article 9(1) of the Regulation to mean personal data consisting of information as to:

(a) the racial or ethnic origin of the data subject;

(b) his political opinions;

(c) her religious or philosophical beliefs;

(d) whether he is a member of a trade union;

(e) genetic data (for the purpose of identifying a unique person);

(f) biometric data (for the purpose of identifying a unique person);

(g) data concerning her health; or

(h) data concerning a natural person's sex life or sexual orientation.

Information about the commission or alleged commission of an offence, or any proceedings concerning offences or alleged offences, their disposal legally, or any sentence in relation to them, has been removed from the definition of special categories of data, and (so far as relevant to processing under the GDPR) is dealt with in a separate Article of the GDPR (Article 10—see Chapter 4). (The main provision in relation to processing by law enforcement agencies and the criminal justice system will be Part 3 of the Data Protection Bill, implementing the Law Enforcement Directive (EU) 2016/680.)

Special category personal data, including the conditions for processing such information, are considered in more detail in Chapter 3. Clauses 9 and 10 of the Data Protection Bill make detailed provision relating to processing of special category data in the UK.

Box 1.4 EEA Countries

Austria	Greece	Norway
Belgium	Hungary	Poland
Bulgaria	Iceland	Portugal
Croatia	Ireland	Romania
Cyprus	Italy	Slovakia
Czech Republic	Latvia	Slovenia
Denmark	Liechtenstein	Spain
Estonia	Lithuania	Sweden
Finland	Luxembourg	UK
France	Malta	
Germany	Netherlands	

European Economic Area

The EEA consists of the Member States of the European Union, plus Iceland, Liechtenstein, and Norway. The complete list of the countries, at the date of writing, is shown in Box 1.4.

Main Establishment

For organizations with more than one establishment in the EU, the GDPR introduces the concept of a 'main establishment' (Article 4(16)). The location of the main establishment determines which national data protection regulator ('supervisory authority') will deal with the organization.

The main establishment of a controller in the EU is its administrative centre, unless its decisions on the purposes and means of processing are taken in another establishment within the EU which has the power to have its decisions implemented (in which case, that establishment will be the main one). The main establishment of a processor in the EU is its administrative centre, or if it has none within the EU, the place within the EU where the main processing activities (in the context of the activities of an establishment) take place.

If a controller or processor is based outside the EU, it will have to appoint a representative (subject to certain exceptions) in one of the EU Member States where the data subjects (to whom goods or services are offered, or whose behaviour is monitored) are located to act on behalf of the controller or processor, and to deal with the supervisory authorities and with those data subjects. This will apply to many UK companies after Brexit.

A 'representative' is defined as a natural or legal person, established in the EU, who is designated by a controller or processor in writing, and who represents the controller or processor with regard to their respective obligations under the Regulation (Article 4(17)).

The exceptions are where the processing is only occasional, does not include the processing of special categories of data on a large scale, and is unlikely to result in a risk to the rights and freedoms (e.g. the privacy) of individuals (Article 27). A public authority or body is also exempt from the requirement.

After Brexit, where a controller or processor is based outside the UK, but offers goods or services to data subjects in the UK (or monitors their behaviour), the controller or processor is likely to have to appoint a representative in the UK (as well as another in the EU) except where the same exceptions as above apply. The representative is likely to need to be established within the UK. The limitation proposed by the Data Protection Bill, in respect of processing that was outside EU law during the period of the UK's membership, has been noted above (under 'Territorial Scope').

Data Subject

A data subject is, in a general sense, the person about whom any given personal data record information, or to whom the data relate.

The definition of data subject in the GDPR, which forms part of the definition of 'personal data' in Article 4(1) rather than being afforded its own defining subparagraph, refers to a person who is either 'identified or identifiable'.

The concept of 'identifiability' broadens the previous definition of data subject to include individuals whose identity is not known at the time the data are collected but who may be identified in the future—for example, where a controller undertakes additional research or investigation, or adds additional data.

Recital 26 states that, in order 'to determine whether a natural person is identifiable, account should be taken of all the means reasonably likely to be used, such as singling out, either by the controller or by another person to identify the natural person directly or indirectly. To ascertain whether means are reasonably likely to be used to identify the natural person, account should be taken of all objective factors, such as the costs of and the amount of time required for identification, taking into consideration the available technology at the time of the processing and technological developments'. The Recitals indicate the background and purpose of the legislation. The reference to identifying a person 'indirectly' means identifying them from other information.

Location data and online identifiers are included in the list of factors which may lead to an individual being 'identified or identifiable'. This broader definition will pose particular challenges in a 'big data' context.

Helpfully, as noted above, the definition of 'data subject' clarifies that the restriction in the DPA—that where identification relied on combining the information in issue with other information, the latter had to be in the possession of the data controller (or likely to come into its possession)—no longer applies. This means, for example, that the data protection implications of publishing statistics which may make individuals identifiable within a community—perhaps because the statistics concern small numbers of people, and other information about those concerned is known within that community—will have to be borne more clearly in mind.

Pseudonymization

Pseudonymization means the processing of personal data so that the data can no longer be attributed to a specific data subject without the use of additional information, provided such additional information is kept separately and is subject to technical and organizational measures to ensure that the person is not identified or made identifiable.

In effect, the data subject is given a different identity for the purposes of the processing, and the controller or processor has a separate 'key' to unlock the identity, which it keeps secure.

Unlike anonymized data, however, personal data which has been pseudonymized remains personal data (Recital 26).

See Chapter 5 for further information on pseudonymization.

Profiling

Article 4(4) defines 'profiling' to mean:

any form of automated processing of personal data consisting of the use of personal data to evaluate certain personal aspects relating to a natural person, in particular to analyse or predict aspects concerning that natural person's performance at work, economic situation, health, personal preferences, interests, reliability, behaviour, location or movements.

This definition is linked to a right to object to profiling in certain circumstances (Articles 21 and 22), to be informed about the existence of profiling, and of measures based on profiling, and to be provided with meaningful information about the logic involved, as well as the significance and the envisaged consequences of profiling for the data subject (Articles 13(2)(f) and 14(2)(g)). The main instances of the use of profiling are likely to arise from the use of cookies on a website to analyze observed preferences in the browsing carried out by an individual.

For an insight into the practical risks associated with profiling, see Bevitt A and Dietschy L, 'The Risks with Data Profiling', *Privacy & Data Protection*, Volume 17, Issue 2 (<http://www.pdpjournal.com>).

Personal Data Breach

'Personal data breach', by virtue of Article 4(12), refers to a:

breach of security leading to the accidental or unlawful destruction, loss, alteration, unauthor-ised disclosure of, or access to, personal data transmitted, stored or otherwise processed.

The definition is used in Article 33 of the GDPR, which obliges a controller to report personal data breaches to the supervisory authority unless it is unlikely to result in a risk to the rights and freedoms of natural persons (a very high threshold before there is no duty to report). It is also used in Article 34, which requires personal data breaches to be reported to data subjects where the breach is 'likely to result in a high risk to the rights and freedoms of natural persons'.

Chapter 5 contains more detail of the data breach notification requirements.

The Data Subject's Consent

Article 4(11) defines the data subject's consent as 'any freely given, specific, informed and unambiguous indication' of his or her wishes by which the data subject, either 'by a statement or by a clear affirmative action, signifies agreement' to personal data relating to them being processed.

Consent remains a legal basis for processing personal data (Article 6(1)(a); and Article 9(2)(a) in relation to 'explicit consent'), but the circumstances in which con-sent will be valid have been narrowed.

Where a controller is relying on consent to justify processing, Article 7(1) requires the controller to be able to demonstrate the consent. Where it is given in the form of a written declaration which also concerns other matters, the request for consent must be presented in a manner 'clearly distinguishable' from other matters, in 'an intelligible and easily accessible form, using clear and plain language'. The data sub-ject must have the right to withdraw his or her consent at any time, and it must be as easy to withdraw consent as to give it (Article 7(3)).

Child

Under Article 8(1), the processing of personal data in the context of providing infor-mation society services to a person below the age of sixteen is lawful only with the consent of the child's parent or custodian.

It should be noted, however, that the restriction applies only where those services are provided on the basis of an individual's consent. The law of the Member State (or UK law after Brexit) may provide for a lower age, down to thirteen years. Clause 8 of the Data Protection Bill proposes that the age in the UK should be 13 years. Clause 8(6) excludes preventive or counselling services from 'information society services'.

The introduction of the requirement to obtain parental consent for personal data relating to a person under sixteen (or the lower age, if specified in a given country) raises several practical difficulties. In particular, although the principle is straightforward, it is not clear how and at what point parental consent can, and should, be obtained; although Article 8(2) places a responsibility on the controller to make reasonable efforts to verify the adult's consent, 'taking into consideration available technology'.

For a consideration of the GDPR's specific application to the personal data of children, see Fenelon J, 'Children and Parental Consent', *Privacy & Data Protection*, Volume 17, Issue 8 (<http://www.pdpjournal.com>).

Genetic Data

Genetic data are defined in Article 4(13) as any data which relate to 'inherited or acquired genetic characteristics of a natural person (i.e. 'living individual') which give unique information about the physiology or the health' of that person, and which result from, for example, an analysis of a biological sample from that natural person. Recital 34 gives, as examples, chromosomal, deoxyribonucleic acid (DNA), or ribonucleic acid (RNA) analysis, or the analysis of another element enabling equivalent information to be obtained. Under Article 9(1), genetic data are included as a 'special category of personal data' and therefore afforded additional protection.

A controller wishing to process genetic data (or any other special category of personal data) must meet one of the further exceptions (or conditions) prescribed in Article 9(2) for processing such data.

Biometric Data

Biometric data means personal data resulting from technical processing 'relating to the physical, physiological or behavioural characteristics of a natural person' which allow or confirm a unique identification of that person (Article 4(14)). These types of data include facial images, or dactyloscopic data (i.e. fingerprints).

Recipient

Article 4(9) defines a recipient as meaning a natural or legal person, public authority, agency, or other body, to which personal data are disclosed, whether or not by a third party.

Public authorities that receive personal data as part of an inquiry conducted under EU or UK law are not regarded as recipients of those data (although their processing of the data must be undertaken in compliance with the relevant data protection rules).

Data Protection by Design

The principle of data protection by design requires the controller, both when determining the means of processing and at the time of the processing itself, to implement in an effective manner 'appropriate technical and organisational measures, such as pseudonymisation', which are designed to ensure compliance with data protection Principles such as data minimization.

In other words, principles such as processing the least quantity of personal data consistent with the data protection purpose, the use of secure identities (by pseudonymization), and data compliance in general should be built into the design of processing operations from the outset. The necessary safeguards to protect privacy and the rights of data subjects should also be integrated into the processing (Article 25.1).

Data Protection by Default

Data protection by default means that the controller is required to implement appropriate technical and organizational measures to ensure that, by default, only personal data which are 'necessary for each specific purpose of the processing are processed'. This takes the design process a stage further.

The obligation applies to the amount of personal data collected, the extent of processing, the period of storage, and the accessibility of the data. The measures are to ensure that by default personal data are not made accessible to an 'indefinite number of natural persons' without the intervention of the individual (meaning, presumably, some action demonstrating his or her consent) (Article 25(2)).

Codes of Conduct

Article 40 makes provision for Member States, supervisory authorities, the European Data Protection Board, and the European Commission to encourage the drawing-up of codes of conduct intended to assist in applying the Regulation.

Bodies representative of categories of controllers and processors may prepare codes to apply the legislation, especially in relation to areas such as: fair and transparent processing; the legitimate interests of controllers; information provided to children, and their protection; data protection by design and default; security and notification of breaches to supervisory authorities and data subjects; and the resolution of disputes. Accredited bodies are to be allowed under codes to carry out mandatory monitoring.

Codes (and amendments or revisions to them) are subject to the approval of supervisory authorities. Codes covering processing in several Member States are to be submitted by the supervisory authority, before giving approval, to the European Data Protection Board for an opinion as to whether the proposed safeguards are adequate. If approved, the European Commission may, by an implementing act, decide that the code will have general validity within the EU.

Codes of conduct approved by the supervisory authorities, and given general validity by the European Commission, may also be adhered to by controllers and processors outside the territorial application of the Regulation in order to give safeguards in transfers to third countries.

The Board is required to collect approved codes (and amendments to them), and to make them publicly available.

Article 41 provides for the monitoring of approved codes. An accredited body with an appropriate level of expertise may monitor compliance with a code. It must demonstrate to the supervisory authority its independence and expertise and that it has established procedures to assess the eligibility of controllers and processors to apply the code.

It will similarly have to show that it has procedures in place to handle complaints of infringements, and that it has no conflicts of interest.

A supervisory authority's first draft of its criteria for the accreditation of such a body must be submitted to the European Data Protection Board. A code-making body's accreditation may be revoked by the supervisory authority. The system of codes of conduct in Articles 40 and 41 does not apply to public authorities or other public bodies.

In the UK, there will need after Brexit to be a parallel system of code-making, both in general and in relation to third country transfers (including EU countries).

Joint Controllers

Under Article 26, where two or more controllers jointly determine the purposes and means of processing, they are 'joint controllers'.

Where this situation arises, the joint controllers are required to determine their respective responsibilities in a transparent manner, particularly regarding the exercise by individuals of their rights, and the controllers' duties to provide information to individuals (Articles 13–14; formerly called Fair Processing Notices or Privacy Notices, under the DPA).

This should be done by an arrangement between the controllers, including possibly a single contact point for data subjects, unless EU or Member State (or UK) law determines otherwise. The 'essence' of these arrangements must be made available to data subjects (although it is unclear at what point). The individual may, irrespective of any such arrangement, exercise his or her rights against each data controller.

European Data Protection Board

Article 68 establishes the European Data Protection Board ('EDPB') as an EU body with legal personality.

The Board is composed of the head of the relevant supervisory authority in each EU Member State (or their representative). The European Commission has a right to participate, but does not have a vote. The UK's Information Commissioner is part of the EDPB until Brexit (remaining the supervisory authority in the UK afterwards).

The Board has a similar membership to the former Article 29 Working Party, which advised on the interpretation of data protection law in the EU, but has an expanded role and an independent secretariat. Its new functions include resolving disagreements between supervisory authorities, ensuring a consistent application of the Regulation, giving advice and guidance, and approving EU-wide codes and certification. The Board is tasked with producing an annual report on data protection in the EU (or, where relevant, third countries and international organizations).

Delegated Acts

Article 92 gives the European Commission power to adopt 'delegated acts' in relation to certain types of information, subject to conditions. These relate either to standardized icons that may be used in data processing notices, or to mechanisms for certification under Article 43 (see below).

The acts are subject to revocation by the European Parliament or the Council of Ministers, but otherwise come into force within three months if there is no objection by either body (or sooner if they give notice of no objection within that time). The timescale may be extended to six months if either body gives notice that a further three months is required.

Certification

Under Article 42, Member States, supervisory authorities, the EDPB, and the European Commission are required to encourage the establishment of data protection certification mechanisms, and of data protection seals and marks, to demonstrate compliance by controllers and processors with the Regulation. Seals and marks may also be gained by controllers outside the territorial scope of the Regulation in relation to international data transfers to third countries.

Certification is voluntary and the process is required to be transparent. It does not reduce the level of compliance nor replace the need for it. Certificates are issued by certification bodies under Article 43, or by the supervisory authority, on the basis of criteria approved by the latter, or by the European Data Protection Board (which may lead to common European certification, at least in some areas). Controllers or processors seeking certification are required to provide all the information and access to their processing necessary to the application procedure.

A certificate lasts for a maximum of three years, and is renewable if the conditions continue to be met. It may be withdrawn by the certificating body, or by the supervisory authority, if the conditions are not met. The European Board is tasked with collating all certification mechanisms and seals across the EU into a public register.

Certificating bodies with appropriate data protection expertise may issue and review certificates, after informing the supervising authority (so that it can withdraw them, or order the certificating body to do so). Certificating bodies are to be accredited by either or both of the supervisory authority or the national accreditation organization under EU accreditation rules (Regulation 765/2008; in the UK, this is the United Kingdom Accreditation Service ('UKAS')).

To earn accreditation, a body must demonstrate its independence and expertise, and give an undertaking to respect the criteria approved by the supervisory authority or EDPB. It must be able to demonstrate the established procedures for issuing, reviewing, and withdrawing certificates, and for handling complaints about infringements. Accreditation is for a maximum of five years, which is renewable.

The criteria for certificates are to be published by the supervisory authority in an easily accessible form, and collated into a public register by the Board. Accreditation arrangements must be revoked when the conditions are no longer met, or if actions infringe the Regulation.

Under Article 92, the Commission may adopt delegated acts to specify the requirements to be taken into account for certification mechanisms. The Commission may also adopt (in accordance with the EU's 'examination procedure') implementing acts setting down technical standards for certification mechanisms, and for data protection seals and marks, and mechanisms to promote and recognize them.

Clause 16 and Schedule 5 of the Data Protection Bill set out the proposed arrangements for accreditation in the UK, involving the Commissioner and UKAS.

One Stop Shop

The concept of One Stop Shop was first proposed in an attempt to deal with the situation that arises when an organization, for example because it works across multiple Member States, is subject to the oversight of more than one national data protection regulator. The GDPR attempts to resolve this difficulty by designating a 'lead authority' as the relevant regulator for any particular controller or processor. The lead authority is the one for the country in which the organization's main establishment is located.

For an excellent and detailed consideration of the operation of One Stop Shop, including the meaning of 'main establishment' and the challenges that can arise in identifying a lead authority, see Treacy B, 'Preparing for One Stop Shop', *Privacy & Data Protection*, Volume 17, Issue 4 (<http://www.pdpjournal.com>).

Directive on Security of Network and Information Systems

The Directive (Directive 2016/1148) represents the first EU-wide rules on cyber-security. The objective is to achieve a high common level of security within the EU by three means:

(a) improving capabilities in relation to cyber-security at national level;

(b) increasing cooperation at EU level; and

(c) placing obligations concerning the management of risk, and reporting of incidents, onto operators of essential services and digital service providers.

In relation to the first of these means (a), each Member State is required to adopt a national strategy on security, defining strategic objectives and appropriate measures of policy and regulation. It is required to designate a national-level authority to monitor the application of the strategy, and also to designate a Computer Security Incident Response Team ('CSIRT') to (amongst other activities) monitor incidents at national level, provide early warning, respond to incidents, and participate in a wider network.

To assist the second means (b), a cooperation group of Member States is to facilitate strategic cooperation and exchange of information, and provide a network of national CSIRTs.

As regards the third means (c), operators of essential services are private businesses or public entities with an important role for society or the economy. Identified operators will have to take appropriate security measures, including preventing risks, ensuring the security of their systems, and handling incidents to minimize their impact. Serious incidents should be notified to the national authority.

The operators concerned are to be identified by the Member States on the basis of criteria such as their importance to critical societal or economic activities, or the effects of a security incident on that service, such as in the case of the energy, transport, banking, financial, health, water, and digital information sectors. Digital service providers (those providing online market places, cloud computing services, or search engines) are also covered unless they are small enterprises.

The Directive came into force in August 2016, with a period of twenty-one months for implementation into national law, and a further six months to identify the entities affected. Thus EU Member States are obliged to have transposed the Directive into national law by May 2018 and identified operators of essential services by November 2018, with a review of progress by the Commission in May 2019.

As well as being part of the initial implementation, the UK will doubtless develop its own cooperative arrangements with the European system along similar lines after Brexit.

Directive on Personal Data Processed for Criminal Law Enforcement

Directive 2016/680 applies to processing for policing and judicial activities concerning criminal matters, both nationally and across borders.

It includes processing by law enforcement agencies for prevention, investigation, detection, or prosecution of criminal offences, or the execution of criminal penalties, or for public security. It does not apply to processing by EU institutional bodies, or to activities outside the scope of EU law.

The Directive covers a number of areas of similar ground to the GDPR, in relation to lawful principles of processing; collection for specific and not excessive purposes; and access and other rights for individuals. Controllers have similar obligations in relation to the designation of a DPO and assessing the potential impact of processing likely to result in high risk. The supervisory authorities can be the same, and there are rules on mandatory mutual assistance. The activities of the EDPB include this Directive. Data subjects are entitled to compensation for processing contrary to the rules.

Transfers to a third country of personal data covered by the Directive may only occur if required for law enforcement processes, and if the European Commission has adopted an adequacy decision in respect of that country, or (as under the GDPR) under appropriate safeguards or in specific circumstances.

On the other hand, under Article 6 of the Directive controllers are required to distinguish the personal data of different categories of data subjects—for example those with regard to whom there are serious grounds to suspect that they have committed, or are about to commit, a criminal offence; persons convicted of a criminal offence; victims of crime; or other parties to a criminal offence, such as witnesses. Article 7 introduces a distinction, to be made so far as possible, between personal data based on facts and personal data based on personal assessments. Overall, the Directive appears to give greater control than under the GDPR to Member States.

The Directive came into legal effect on 5 May 2016, setting a deadline for its translation into national law of 6 May 2018. Part 3 of the Data Protection Bill transposes the Directive into UK law. It should be noted that arrangements under the Directive in relation to transfers to third countries will need to be applied to the UK by other EU countries (and probably vice versa) after the country leaves the Union.

2

Data Protection Principles

Peter Carey

Introduction	32
Lawfulness, Fairness, and Transparency	33
Purpose Limitation	34
Data Minimization	35
Data Accuracy	37
Storage Limitation	38
Integrity, Confidentiality, and Security	39
Exemptions	40
Accountability	40
Data Protection by Design and by Default	41
Processors	41

Introduction

Data protection law requires compliance with a number of rules, which are set out in Article 5 of the GDPR (see Box 2.1). This chapter provides an introduction to each of the rules, known as 'Principles', several of which are discussed in more detail in the following chapters.

The key thing to understand about the Principles is that, unless a relevant exemption applies, *all* of the Principles should be observed in relation to *all* aspects of personal data processing. In other words, complying with some, or even most, of the Principles is never sufficient. For example, an organization will breach data protection law where it:

- stores inaccurate data on a person, even where the information was obtained after a transparency notice had been properly made available;

- keeps data on a person longer than is necessary for the purpose for which those data were acquired, even where the organization's records meet excellent security standards; or

- collects too much data for the stated purpose, even where it has the consent of the relevant individual to the collection.

Box 2.1 The Data Protection Principles

(GDPR, Article 5)

(1) Personal data shall be processed lawfully, fairly and in a transparent manner in relation to the data subject ('lawfulness, fairness and transparency')

(2) Personal data shall be collected only for specified, explicit and legitimate purposes, and not further processed in a manner that is incompatible with those purposes ('purpose limitation')

(3) Personal data shall be adequate, relevant and limited to what is necessary in relation to the purposes for which they are processed ('data minimization')

(4) Personal data processed shall be accurate and, where necessary, kept up to date ('accuracy')

(5) Personal data shall be kept in a form which permits identification of data subjects for no longer than is necessary for the purposes for which the personal data are processed ('storage limitation')

(6) Personal data shall be processed in a manner that ensures appropriate security of the personal data, including protection against unauthorised or unlawful processing and against accidental loss, destruction or damage, using appropriate technical or organisational measures ('integrity and confidentiality')

The importance of the Principles is underlined by the extent of the powers of national data protection regulators in relation to their breach, including powers of investigation and powers relating to issuing significant fines (see Chapter 8). Further, an individual may bring an action against a controller where he or she suffers damage as a result of a breach by the controller of one or more of the Principles.

Lawfulness, Fairness, and Transparency

Due to the wide definition of processing (see Chapter 1), the First Principle has a particularly extensive application to all usages of personal data. The First Principle can be divided into three obligations:

(1) to process personal data lawfully;

(2) to process such data fairly;

(3) to process personal data transparently.

As far as 'lawful' processing is concerned, all personal data processing (unless a relevant exemption applies) will be unlawful unless one of the conditions in Article 6 of the GDPR is met. The set of conditions in Article 6 can therefore be seen as a 'threshold' or minimum standard for the processing of personal data. The Article 6 conditions are discussed in detail in Chapter 3.

Article 9 requires that where the personal data being processed fall within certain special categories or types (e.g., data relating to health, religious beliefs, ethnic origin, political opinions, or membership of a trade union), processing will not be lawful unless one of a further set of conditions is met. It should be noted that the requirement for an Article 9 condition is *in addition* to the requirement for an Article 6 condition where an organization is processing special category personal data (see Chapter 4).

Compliance with Article 6 (and, where relevant, Article 9) is not sufficient to comply with the First Principle in its entirety, because such processing must also be 'fair'. Furthermore, the processing must be transparent. This means that the data subject must be provided with certain information at the point of data collection. The fairness and transparency requirements are discussed in Chapter 3.

Purpose Limitation

The purpose limitation Principle requires that data shall be collected only for specified, explicit, and legitimate purposes, and not processed in any manner that is incompatible with those purposes.

This Principle has two limbs. The first limb imposes an obligation on the controller to make known ('specify') the purposes for which the data are required. Further, such notice must be explicit and the purposes of the processing must be legitimate. The requirement to make available certain information to data subjects is discussed in detail in Chapter 3.

The second limb requires that personal data must not be processed in a manner incompatible with the purpose(s) for which they were obtained. Since a different purpose would not necessarily be an incompatible purpose, this Principle does not itself necessarily proscribe processing for a purpose other than those that have been specified. In determining whether the manner of processing is compatible with the specified purpose(s), one of the factors that the 1998 Act obliged controllers to bear in mind was the purpose or purposes for which the personal data were intended to be processed by any third party to whom the data were to be disclosed. Controllers could therefore consider requiring organizations (other than their processors) to which they disclose personal data to use those data only within the remit of the purposes for which the controller obtained the information.

In April 2013, an Opinion of the Article 29 Working Party (WP 203—see <http:/www.dpdocuments.com>) set out extensive guidance for controllers on the substantially similar principle in the Directive. The Opinion stated that all relevant circumstances must be taken into account when making an assessment of whether further processing is compatible with the original purpose. In particular, the following key factors should be considered:

- the relationship between the purposes for which the personal data have been collected and the purposes of further processing;
- the context in which the personal data have been collected and the reasonable expectations of the data subjects as to their further use;

- the nature of the personal data and the impact of the further processing on the data subjects;
- the safeguards adopted by the controller to ensure fair processing and to prevent any undue impact on the data subjects.

For further comment on the Working Party's Opinion, see Treacy B and Bapat A, 'Purpose Limitation—Clarity at Last', *Privacy & Data Protection*, Volume 13, Issue 6 (<http://www.pdpjournal.com>).

The GDPR makes reference to certain types of processing that will not be regarded as being incompatible for the purposes of this Principle. These purposes are: archiving in the public interest, scientific or historical research purposes, and statistical purposes.

Example of the purpose limitation Principle
XYZ Water plc, a UK water utility company, maintains a database of its customers. David, who moves into XYZ's area of operation is added to the database at the point he registers with XYZ for water services. The data protection notice provided to David states that personal data will be collected and used for all purposes associated with the provision of water and water-related products and services. Several months later, XYZ sells David's details to Mainstream Mobiles (MM) so that MM can send David marketing materials on its mobile telephone services. By providing David's personal data to MM, XYZ is in breach of the Second Principle.

Data Minimization

In order to comply with the data minimization Principle, organizations are required to ensure that their processing of personal data is adequate, relevant, and limited to what is necessary in relation to the purposes for which they are processed.

This Principle essentially obliges controllers to obtain and use only those pieces of information that are necessary for the controller's purpose(s) for processing such information. In practice, organizations are more likely to breach the 'relevant' and 'limited to what is necessary' aspects of this Principle than they are the 'adequacy' aspect, since organizations tend to collect too much information on people rather than too little.

Just like in the GDPR, the data minimization principle in the previous Directive required personal data processing to be 'adequate' and 'relevant'. But instead of requiring the processing to be 'limited' to what is necessary, it outlawed 'excessive' processing. The difference between these two concepts is the subject of some debate, but it seems likely that the former is somewhat narrower than the latter. Organizations will need to review their processing operations to ensure that their processing is limited to what's needed, rather than not being excessive.

Determining whether an organization is in compliance with the data minimization principle consists of two key steps. The first step is to ascertain the relevant purpose or purposes for processing. For example, the purpose of collecting information in an 'application for employment' form is to make a decision about whether the job applicant is suitable to be short-listed or interviewed for the position. The purposes of collecting information from a customer who is purchasing an item online may be to take payment, to deliver the item, and to send future marketing communications. Once the purposes have become clear (remember to document the purposes in a suitable statement), then the second step is to consider whether each proposed processing activity is actually needed in order to achieve the purpose(s). Organizations will breach the principle where they collect or use any personal data that are not needed for the specified purpose(s).

To achieve compliance with the Principle, controllers should initially review all aspects of data collection—such as employment application forms, customer details forms, call centre forms, and website and app registration forms—to ensure that information requested from individuals is adequate, relevant, and limited to what's needed for the purpose(s). The time of collection is an important one, because organizations cannot process what they don't have—limit the data collected, and you limit the circumstances where the data minimization principle can be subsequently breached.

However, the Principle does not *only* apply to data collection—it applies to all types of data processing. It is quite possible that data initially collected lawfully under the Principle can subsequently be processed unlawfully. The next step will therefore be to ensure that all processing (e.g. standard data usage operations within the organization) meets the requirements of the Principle.

Another example of where the Principle might be breached in circumstances other than where data are being collected is where the controller is making a determination as to which members of staff should have access to personal data. In making this determination, regard should be had to whether particular staff members need such access in order to carry out their functions. It would, for example, be 'more than necessary' for the entirety of an employee's personnel record (including information on qualifications, past employment, and sickness) to be made available to all staff members within the organization.

Example of the data minimization Principle

XYZ Recruiting Ltd requires job applicants to state their driving licence number on its standard client details form. James, who wishes to apply for a job that does not involve driving, fills in the form including details of his driving licence. In processing details of James' driving licence, XYZ Recruiting Ltd will breach the data minimization Principle.

It should be noted that it is not possible for an individual to consent to processing more of his or her personal data than is needed for the purpose(s). Thus it will be no defence for a controller to say that the data subject voluntarily submitted information in response to a 'non-compulsory' question (often marked by the use of, or absence of, an asterisk) in an online or offline application form.

In summary, this Principle requires 'data minimization'—only those personal data that are necessary to achieve the purpose(s) of processing should be collected, stored, and used by controllers. The holding of any additional personal data on individuals is unlawful.

Data Accuracy

The data accuracy Principle is relatively self-explanatory, and is substantially similar to the equivalent provision in the previous Directive. It provides that 'personal data must be accurate and, where necessary, kept up to date'.

Although the requirement to keep information up to date applies only where 'necessary', there is no such qualification to the requirement of accuracy. Thus the requirement to ensure that personal data are accurate is an absolute one. There is no definition of 'accurate' in the GDPR, but Section 70(2) of the 1998 Act gave a helpful definition of 'inaccurate':

For the purposes of this Act data are inaccurate if they are incorrect or misleading as to any matter of fact.

The presence of the word 'fact' in that provision would seem to indicate that an expression of opinion could not breach the data accuracy Principle, no matter how unreasonable or ridiculous the opinion.

It should be remembered that the obligation to ensure that personal data processed by the controller are accurate and up to date is an obligation on the controller, and cannot be delegated. Thus a statement given at the commencement of processing by controllers to data subjects, to the effect that data subjects must inform the controller of any subsequent change to the data, is unlikely to be enough, on its own, to satisfy the Principle. On the other hand, it would be unreasonable to interpret the Principle as requiring controllers to investigate data subjects' circumstances intrusively to check for data accuracy. In some cases, compliance with the Principle can be achieved by providing a method for data subjects to check and amend data held by the controller—this may be done, for example, by the provision of an annual statement to customers, setting out the information held (or providing a method for checking data, such as secure online access to customer details on a website) and requesting updates, as relevant.

In November 2012, Prudential was served by the Information Commissioner's Office with a monetary penalty of £50,000 when one customer received tens of thousands of pounds into his retirement fund in error—the money should have been paid into the retirement fund of a different customer, who had the same first name, last name, and date of birth. The two accounts had been mistakenly merged some years earlier and, despite being alerted to the error by one of the customers, the controller had failed to adequately investigate the issue.

Where the controller finds that it is in fact processing inaccurate data, the GDPR requires that every reasonable step must be taken to ensure that such inaccurate data, having regard to the purposes for which they are processed, are erased or rectified without delay. This provision goes beyond that which was required under the previous legislation, and requires organizations to manage their data assets more proactively.

The steps that are necessary to keep personal data up to date will depend on the type of data being processed and the purpose for its processing. Data kept in a record of a board meeting, for example, will not need to be updated where they consist of an accurate record of that meeting. Data kept, on the other hand, for determining a person's creditworthiness from time to time are likely to require regular updating amendments.

The obligations on controllers under the Principle dovetail with the right of individuals to have their personal data rectified or erased—see Chapter 7.

Storage Limitation

The storage limitation Principle provides that personal data shall not be kept for longer than is necessary for the purposes of processing. The basic objective of this Principle is that organizations do not retain obsolete data, and its wording is substantially similar to that contained in the previous Directive.

One difference between the old law and the GDPR is that pseudonymization (see Chapter 1) is now permitted as a method of complying with this Principle.

In general terms, the storage limitation Principle requires the deletion, destruction, anonymization, or pseudonymization of personal data that are no longer needed for their purpose(s). There are no interpretative provisions in the GDPR that relate to this Principle per se, and there are no set periods of time to which controllers must adhere. Thus controllers will usually be required to make their own determinations as to an appropriate retention period having regard to the purposes for which data were collected, and the information conveyed in the notice made available to data subjects.

Since this Principle concerns data storage and access, those responsible for data protection within an organization may consider it appropriate to gain at least rudimentary knowledge and skills in the field of records management. In any event, data retention is a necessary part of the overall records management strategy of an organization.

As a first step to complying with the Principle, controllers should undertake an analysis of all personal data processed, as well as the purpose(s) of such processing. Then it will be necessary to consider, in relation to each aspect of personal data processing, for how long those data will need to be kept for the relevant purpose(s). A useful methodology for compliance (and to demonstrate, or be accountable for, such compliance) is to draw up a 'data retention policy' or 'retention schedule' that sets out the relevant periods of time for which data in relevant categories may be held.

Where controllers are under a legal obligation (e.g., as a result of national law) to retain data on individuals for a certain specified period, the relevant data retention periods should be no shorter than that specified period. Similarly, personal data should be kept for at least the length of time equivalent to any relevant statutory limitation period for the purposes of litigation—thus accident-at-work records should be kept for at least three years following the date of the incident (the statutory limitation period in the UK for bringing personal injury claims is three years) and interview records (where the person has not been given the job) should be kept for at least three months (the period of time within which a person can bring a claim for discrimination in the UK). Specific industry sector rules or codes should also be considered, although it must be borne in mind that the legal requirement in data protection law to delete personal data that are no longer needed by the controller will override any conflicting non-statutory retention preferences.

A significant factor in determining a retention period for each type of personal data held is the purpose(s) for which the information was collected. This may necessitate a lengthy retention period (e.g., the home address of an employee will need to be retained for at least the duration of the person's employment), or a very short period (a document that is used solely to check a person's identity—for example, when an organization needs to confirm a person is indeed who they say they are before carrying out a particular function—must be destroyed as soon as the identity has been ascertained).

In some cases, there will be more than one purpose for holding information. In this situation, it is appropriate and acceptable to retain the information until all of the purposes have been satisfied. In the example of the identity check, where the document required is a copy of a driving licence, and the person is engaged as a driver, then retaining the personal data contained in the licence may be required for the duration of the person's employment.

The storage limitation Principle will not allow information to be held indefinitely or speculatively. The latter refers to the situation where a controller contends that it 'might need' the information in the future for some currently unascertained purpose. Further, guidance from the Information Commissioner states that personal data should not be kept 'just in case' it is needed if there is only a 'small possibility' that it will be used.

In the circumstances where a person has indicated that he or she no longer wishes to receive marketing materials, the controller should retain enough information ('suppression data') on the person to allow compliance with the request.

Upon the expiry of any retention period, the relevant personal data should be deleted, or destroyed. Anonymization, and in some cases pseudonymization, will be acceptable, although care should be taken to ensure that the data are successfully anonymized (see Graham N and Crowley S, 'Anonymisation and Pseudo-anonymisation of Personal Data', *Privacy & Data Protection*, Volume 10, Issue 2—<http://www.pdpjournal.com>). Since deletion, destruction, anonymization, and pseudonymization are all aspects of 'processing', those activities must comply with data protection legal requirements. Of particular relevance is the need for security in personal data processing (see Chapter 5).

Integrity, Confidentiality, and Security

The 'integrity and confidentiality' Principle requires that personal data be processed in a manner that ensures appropriate security of the personal data, including protection against unauthorized or unlawful processing and against accidental loss, destruction, or damage, using appropriate technical and organizational measures. Although the basic legislative provision is contained in Article 5 of the GDPR, this should be read in conjunction with Article 32, which provides further provisions on data security requirements.

This Principle is substantially similar to that contained in the previous Directive. However, the consequences of a 'personal data breach' (see Chapter 1) are considerably more significant and require greater work on the part of the controller (and processor) than in the previous legislation. In particular, in the case of serious breaches, organizations are required to inform both the relevant national regulator and all persons potentially affected. See Chapter 5 for a detailed discussion on the GDPR's requirements in relation to 'breach notifications'.

The aim of the legislative provisions on data security is to ensure that appropriate care is taken of personal data, and that the attention of controllers and processors is focussed on this objective (with significant adverse consequences if they do not).

Where the controller proposes to engage a processor to carry out data processing operations on its behalf, it must ensure that the processor provides sufficient guarantees to implement appropriate technical and organizational measures so that the processing meets the requirements of the Regulation. For further detail on the obligations that arise in the relationship between controllers and processors, see Chapter 9.

Exemptions

There are a number of exemptions from the application of the data protection Principles to particular types of processing. Some exemptions relate to certain individual Principles and some to only certain aspects of one or more of the Principles.

The exemptions are discussed where relevant throughout this book.

Accountability

Article 5(2) of the GDPR expressly provides that controllers (note, not processors) are responsible for, and must be able to demonstrate compliance with, the six Principles contained in that Article (see Box 2.1). This requirement, known as 'accountability', is a new one to data protection law, introduced by the GDPR.

In addition, Chapter IV of the GDPR imposes duties of responsibility and accountability on controllers. For example, controllers must adopt policies and implement appropriate measures to ensure and demonstrate that the processing of personal data complies with the GDPR. The measures to be implemented (which are discussed in detail in Chapters 12 and 13) are the criteria against which the accountability of the controller will be assessed. Controllers are required to maintain necessary documentation of all processing operations, implement appropriate security measures, perform Data Protection Impact Assessments (see Chapter 11), comply with requirements for prior notification or approval from the relevant supervisory authority, and designate a Data Protection Officer ('DPO') (see Chapter 12), if required.

Data Protection by Design and by Default

Article 25 of the GDPR requires controllers to implement appropriate technical and organizational measures:

- which are *designed* to implement the data protection Principles; and
- for ensuring that, by *default*, only the minimum quantity of personal data are processed for each purpose.

These requirements were defined in Chapter 1, and are discussed where relevant in several chapters in this book.

Processors

Processors' responsibilities have been significantly expanded when compared with the previous Directive.

The GDPR requires controllers to 'choose a processor providing sufficient guarantees of security'. It also imposes an obligation on both parties to enter into a contract governing the obligations of the parties. Both parties also have direct obligations for implementing appropriate technical and organizational measures.

Processors must document the processing operations for which they are responsible, and must (as well as the controller) cooperate with supervisory authorities, including by providing information and granting access to the processor's premises and processing equipment.

Processors may be ordered by the supervisory authority to comply with data subjects' requests to exercise their rights, even though the primary responsibility for such compliance rests with the controller.

The security obligations and the requirements concerning the appointment of a qualified Data Protection Officer apply directly to processors.

Most significantly, the supervisory authority's powers extend to processors, including the ability to impose monetary penalties. These provisions significantly affect the risk profile for processors, and will likely require amendments to existing services agreements.

The relationship between controllers and processors is considered in detail in Chapter 9.

3

Fair, Lawful, and Transparent Processing

Estelle Dehon and Peter Carey

Introduction	42
Obtaining Data—Duty Not to Mislead	43
Obtaining Data in a Transparent Manner—Information to Be Supplied to the Data Subject	44
Other Unfair Processing	50
The Lawfulness Conditions	50
Other Unlawful Processing	59
Cases of Significance	61
Summary	65

Introduction

The First Data Protection Principle, contained in Article 5(1)(a) of the GDPR, is broad in its application. It requires that all personal data processing be fair, lawful, and carried out in a transparent manner.

Processing will only be lawful if at least one of the conditions in Article 6(1) (a)–(f) apply, and controllers must be able to ascertain and pinpoint the relevant condition(s) before they commence the processing. Where special category personal data are processed, one of a further set of conditions in Article 9(2) must also be met.

In the 1998 Act, the 'fairness' obligation was particularly linked to the requirement to be transparent—that is, to be clear and open with individuals about how their information is used. Under the GDPR, transparency is brought out as an express requirement of the First Principle. However, the separate requirement to process personal data 'fairly' remains. This 'fairness' obligation means that the First Principle will usually be breached where personal data are obtained in a way that is misleading to the data subject, where the processing of the data is outside the data subject's reasonable expectations, or where it is in breach of other laws or legal obligations.

This chapter considers the practical implications for controllers of these requirements, which derive from Articles 6–10 and 12–14 of the GDPR.

Obtaining Data—Duty Not to Mislead

Obtaining or collecting personal data will be the first occurrence of personal data processing by any controller. The obtaining takes place when personal data are recorded or otherwise processed either electronically or in a relevant paper-based filing system (see the definitions of 'personal data' and 'filing system' in Chapter 1).

The 'fairness' element of the First Principle requires that the method by which controllers obtain information from any person must not deceive or mislead that person as to the intended purpose for processing the data. This was previously an explicit obligation in the UK, contained in Schedule 1, Part II of the 1998 Act. Under the GDPR, it is an implicit requirement, given that the First Principle imposes a separate requirement of fairness.

Personal data may be obtained unfairly even if the individual who is deceived or misled is not the data subject. For example, I might obtain data from you that relate to your brother; if you are misled as to my purpose for obtaining the data then the data may have been obtained unfairly even though your brother was neither deceived nor misled.

In *Innovations (Mail Order) Ltd v Data Protection Registrar* (DA92 31/49/1), a case which was decided under the 1984 Act but which remains of interest as an example of unfair obtaining of information, a mail-order company obtained business in two principal ways: by receiving orders from its catalogues and by receiving orders in response to its advertisements in the media. Customers coming via the media advertisements route were informed of the possibility of their details being used for other purposes only after their details had been obtained. The company engaged in the practice known as 'list rental' (trading in lists of customers' names and addresses) and many of the customer details obtained by both methods of data capture were used for this purpose. It was the Registrar's contention that all customers had to be informed of all intended uses for their personal details at the time the order was made—that is, at the time the customers supplied their details to the company. The company argued that the practical constraints this would cause for its general media advertising made such a practice unacceptable. The Data Protection Tribunal (as the Information Rights Tribunal was then known) found that the absence of a warning in the general media advertising might lead to an assumption on the part of individual members of the public that their details would not be traded. This meant that some members of the public would be misled and therefore that the obtaining of the information was indeed unfair.

Obtaining Data in a Transparent Manner— Information to Be Supplied to the Data Subject

A key aspect of the principle of 'transparency', set out in Article 12 of the GDPR, is that controllers must take 'appropriate measures' to provide the data subject with concise, intelligible information about the processing of personal data, in clear and plain language and in an easily accessible form. This means that any notice or communication must be unambiguous and genuinely informative, and must not mislead in any way. It must also be easy to understand, so legalistic or technical language should be avoided. By implication, it should be in the local language of the Member State where the controller is interacting with the data subject.

The need for clarity and precision is especially strong where any information is addressed to a child. Particular care must be taken with the language, so it is plain and easy for a child to grasp.

Article 12(7) allows for information to be provided in combination with standardized icons, in order to give a 'meaningful overview' of the information in an easily visible, intelligible, and clearly legible manner. This suggests that icons by themselves will not be sufficient, but will be an acceptable first layer of privacy information.

The extent and timing of the requirement to provide information depends on whether the personal data are collected directly from the data subject or from a third party—both of which are dealt with in more detail below.

The requirement for transparency also obliges the controller to inform data subjects about their rights (i.e. access, rectification, erasure, restriction, objection, portability, and the right not to be subject to automated decision-making—see Chapter 7). Article 12 imposes a number of procedural requirements in this regard, all of which contribute to transparency:

- the controller must facilitate the exercise of the data subject's rights;
- the controller must respond within specified time limits to requests exercising those rights; and
- the controller must give reasons for any refusal of the rights and inform the data subject of the possibility of lodging an appeal or taking further action.

The commonest method of compliance with the requirement of transparency is by making available a notice, which may be known as a 'fair processing notice', 'privacy notice' or (online) 'privacy policy', or 'data protection notice', that sets out the required information.

The method for providing the fair processing or privacy notice is shown in Box 3.1.

The requirement in Article 12 is that controllers take 'appropriate measures' to make the fair processing information 'easily available'. This means that it should be clear to the individual how to obtain or view the information, and there should be no charge for the provision of such information.

Box 3.1 Method of Providing Information to the Data Subject

(a) The information must be provided in writing or by other means, including electronic means where appropriate.

(b) The information may be provided orally, where requested by the data subject and provided the data subject has been able to prove his/her identity.

(c) The information may be provided through a website, particularly where there are a number of controllers or processors and a technologically complex process which may make it difficult for data subjects to know whether and by whom their personal data are being collected, and for what purpose—for example, in the case of online advertising (see Recital 58).

(d) Where personal data are collected off-line (e.g. when a form is filled in face-to-face with the consumer), information provided online is not a substitute for direct notice, which must be provided to the data subject when the data are collected.

The notice must not be concealed in terms and conditions or buried in a long document. If it is to be included with other matters in a single document, then it should be at the beginning and appropriately highlighted to ensure that the individual sees the notice.

Where the notice is provided electronically, it should feature prominently on the appropriate webpage, before the user provides any personal information. In relation to apps, the privacy information should ideally be provided before the user downloads the app, which could be done via an app store or via a link to a privacy policy. Where the information is provided after an app is downloaded and installed, it must be done before the app processes the relevant personal data.

Importantly, Article 12 does not require the consent of the individual to the terms of the notice. In fact, the relevant individual may never actually see the fair processing notice—that is of no consequence to the fulfilment of the fair collection requirement, provided that the controller took 'appropriate measures' to ensure the information contained in the notice was 'easily available'.

In some circumstances it will be impractical to provide the full extent of the fair processing information in one location. In such circumstances, a 'multi-layered' fair processing or privacy notice could be appropriate. Such an approach usually consists of an initial brief statement at the point of data collection and a more detailed statement in separate documentation. An example of where such an approach might be useful is a commercial website, where the initial statement would appear on the data collection page: 'Your information will be used to process your order and to let you know about our other products and special offers. To see more detailed information as to how we use your information, click here.' There should additionally be a link to a privacy policy, which contains the more detailed statement.

The multi-layered approach was approved by the Information Commissioner's Office ('ICO') in its Code of Practice on Privacy Notices, Transparency and Control (see <http://www.dpdocuments.com>), which states that a layered notice usually consists

---

Box 3.2 Information Required in Cases of Collection of Data from the Data Subject

---

Article 13 GDPR

The controller shall provide the data subject with all of the following information 'at the time when personal data are obtained':

(a) the identity and contact details of the controller and, where applicable, of the controller's representative;

(b) the contact details of the Data Protection Officer, where applicable (see Chapter 12 for the requirement to appoint a Data Protection Officer);

(c) the purposes of the processing for which the data are intended;

(d) the legal basis for the processing (i.e. the lawfulness condition on which the controller is relying), including the legitimate interests pursued by the controller, as applicable;

(e) the recipients or categories of recipients of the data, if any;

(f) where applicable, the fact that the controller intends to transfer the personal data to a third country or international organization, including the existence or absence of an adequacy decision or reference to the appropriate or suitable safeguards and the means by which to obtain a copy of them.

---

of a short notice plus a longer notice. The short notice must contain basic information, such as the identity of the organization, the way in which the information will be used, and any particular risks arising from that use. The short notice then contains a link to a second, longer notice which provides much more detailed information. The longer notice can, in turn, contain links to further material, explaining relatively specialist issues such as the circumstances in which information may be disclosed to the police.

The precise operation of the fair processing (privacy notice) provisions depends upon whether the personal data are to be obtained directly from the data subject herself or whether personal data on the data subject are to be obtained from some other person or organization.

Data obtained from the data subject

Article 13 (see Box 3.2) sets out the information which the controller must provide to the data subject at the time when the personal data are obtained. All of the information in Box 3.2 must be provided.

In addition, Article 13 identifies that the controller may need to provide the following further information where it is necessary to ensure fair and transparent processing:

- the period for which the data will be stored, or if that is not possible, the criteria used to determine the period;

- the existence of rights to request access, rectification, erasure, or restriction of the processing, or to object to the processing, and the right to data portability;

- where processing is based on consent, the right to withdraw that consent at any time;
- the right to lodge a complaint with the national data protection regulator, and contact details;
- whether the provision of the data is a statutory or contractual requirement, and the possible consequences of failure to provide the data; and
- the existence of any automated decision-making, including any profiling, based on the data, as well as 'meaningful information' about the logic involved and the significance and the envisaged consequences of such processing for the data subject.

Example 1

A website provides tailor-made news items which it sends by email to its registered members. To become a member, an individual must provide her name, address, email address, and the type of news items in which she is interested. Here the website must make easily available the details in Box 3.2. *The information could appear on the same website page as is used for data capture (sometimes referred to as a 'user registration page') or it could be briefly referred to there and set out more fully in an appropriate online privacy policy.*

Data obtained from a third party

Where data have not been obtained from the data subject, but from a third party, the controller must provide the data subject with the information set out in Box 3.3. Data may be obtained from someone other than the data subject where, for example, such data comprise a list of information transferred from one controller to another (e.g. list rental) or where the data are supplied by a friend or relative of the data subject to the controller (e.g. member-get-member schemes).

The information in Box 3.3 must be provided within 'a reasonable period' after obtaining the data, but at the latest within one month, having regard to the specific circumstances in which the personal data are provided. There is no definition of 'reasonable period' in the GDPR. This is likely to depend on the type of processing in question, the effect on the data subject, and the ease of providing such information.

If the personal data are to be used for communication with the data subject, then the information must be provided at the latest at the time of the first communication with the data subject. If disclosure to another recipient is envisaged, then the information must be provided at the latest when the personal data are first disclosed.

In addition, Article 14 identifies that the controller may need to provide the following further information where it is necessary to ensure fair and transparent processing:

- the period for which the data will be stored, or if that is not possible, the criteria used to determine the period;
- where the processing is based on legitimate interests pursued by the controller or a third party, what those interests are;

Box 3.3 Information Where the Data Have Not Been Obtained from the Data Subject

---

Article 14 GDPR

The controller shall provide the data subject with the following information:

(a) the identity and contact details of the controller and of his representative, if any;

(b) the contact details of the Data Protection Officer, where applicable;

(c) the purposes of the processing for which the data are intended;

(d) the legal basis for the processing (i.e. the lawfulness condition on which the controller is relying);

(e) the categories of personal data concerned;

(f) the recipients or categories of recipients of the data, if any; and

(g) where applicable, the fact that the controller intends to transfer the personal data to a third country or international organization, including the existence or absence of an adequacy decision or reference to the appropriate or suitable safeguards and the means by which to obtain a copy of them.

- the existence of rights to request access, rectification, erasure, or restriction of the processing, or to object to the processing, and the right to data portability;
- where processing is based on consent, the right to withdraw that consent at any time,
- the right to lodge a complaint with a supervisory authority;
- from which source the personal data originate and, if applicable, whether the data came from publicly accessible sources; and
- the existence of any automated decision-making, including any profiling, based on the data, as well as 'meaningful information' about the logic involved and the significance and the envisaged consequences of such processing for the data subject.

Example 2

A market researcher telephones Susie and asks her for information about her shopping habits. Susie tells the researcher which supermarket she uses and gives a list of some basic products that she and her husband, Mark, commonly purchase. Here Mark must be informed, as soon as practicable after the telephone conversation takes place, of the identity of the researcher or the researcher's employer, the purpose of requiring the information that Susie has given, and the remaining fairness information. Where the market researcher is acting as agent for another, Mark must be informed of those matters within a reasonable period of time.

There is an exception to the rule that, where the controller obtained personal data from someone other than the data subject, the controller must notify the data subject of the fair collection information. The exception applies where:

(a) the data subject already has the specified information (e.g. where the notice has been provided by a third party or a processor);

(b) the provision of the information would be impossible (e.g. where an internet search engine collects personal data from a vast number of websites);

(c) the provision of the information would involve a 'disproportionate effort', particularly where the data are being collected for scientific, historical, or research purposes in accordance with Article 89(1);

(d) the objectives of the processing would be impossible or seriously impaired were the notice requirements to be complied with.

As regards paragraphs (b), (c), and (d), the controller must take appropriate measures to protect the data subject's rights and freedoms and legitimate interests, including making the fair processing information publicly available.

Disproportionate effort

Where the controller obtains data on an individual from a third party, the fair processing information need not be made easily available by the controller where the effort required to do so is 'disproportionate'. There is no definition of 'disproportionate' in the GDPR, nor is there a precise description of what the disproportionate effort must relate to.

For this condition to operate, the effort involved in making the information easily available to the data subject must be disproportionate to the prejudice or disadvantage caused to the relevant individual(s) by the lack of any such information being supplied. Thus, where the effort needed to supply information is considerable, such effort may be disproportionate unless it is outweighed by severe consequences for the data subject, for example because it involves significant or otherwise important processing (e.g. of special category personal data).

The test thus appears to involve a balancing exercise and relevant factors will be the time and expense required for the controller to provide the relevant information, and the prejudicial effect on the data subject due to the absence of such information.

Therefore, the 'disproportionate effort' exemption might apply where the controller has obtained a massive database of personal data from a single source, so as to obviate the need to contact every data subject immediately.

Legal or confidentiality obligation

The fair collection provisions also do not apply (where data are obtained from someone other than the data subject) where the obtaining or disclosure of the personal data by the controller is necessary to comply with a legal obligation expressly laid down by Union or Member State law. Examples include statutory duties upon certain organizations to compile lists of individuals who belong to certain groups or professional bodies.

The fair processing information is also not required to be provided where the personal data must remain confidential subject to an obligation of professional secrecy regulated by Union or Member State law, including a statutory obligation of secrecy.

Other Unfair Processing

Whilst the specific types of unfair processing envisaged by the legislation are covered above—namely, obtaining data in circumstances where the data subject is misled and failing to make easily available a privacy notice—any other type of 'unfair' processing will potentially be open to review under data protection law.

This includes unfairness in any type of processing, not just at the obtaining stage. An allegation of unfair processing arose in the case of *Johnson v Medical Defence Union* [2007] EWCA Civ 262, which is considered further later in this chapter. In *Law Society and Others v Kordowski* [2011] EWHC 3185 (QB), the court held that the publication of libellous material about solicitors on the 'Solicitors from Hell' website amounted to unfair processing.

The Lawfulness Conditions

In order for processing of personal data to be lawful under data protection law, one of a set of conditions must be met for each and every aspect of such processing. Article 6 sets out six such conditions (see Box 3.4) and provides that processing is only lawful if and to the extent that at least one of those conditions applies to that processing.

Thus, for processing to be lawful, at least one of the six conditions in Article 6(1) must be met unless the controller is able to benefit from a relevant and applicable exemption. None of the conditions is any 'better', in a legal sense, than any of the others; they are all equal in terms of providing a lawful basis for the personal data processing in question. However, when more than one condition is potentially available, the effect and breadth of each of the conditions should be considered when controllers are making a decision as to which to prioritize.

For each of the conditions except the first (consent), the processing in question must be 'necessary' for the relevant reason. The term 'necessary' has a special meaning drawn from EU law, as has been explained in a number of CJEU and UK cases that are very likely to remain relevant to understanding the GDPR. 'Necessity' is a well-established part of 'proportionality', which means that the controller must adopt the least restrictive means for achieving the aim of the lawfulness condition, see *Huber v Germany* [2009] CMLR 49, which dealt with processing information on an official register. This interpretation, which has been adopted by national regulators and courts, has a bearing on whether a particular lawfulness condition is available to a controller in any particular circumstance, and means that processing which is just 'useful' or 'convenient', rather than 'necessary', will not fulfil the requirement.

Box 3.4 The Lawfulness Conditions

Article 6(1) GDPR

1. The data subject has given his consent to the processing of his or her data for one or more specified purposes.

2. The processing is necessary:

   (a) for the performance of a contract to which the data subject is a party, or

   (b) in order to take steps at the request of the data subject with a view to entering into a contract.

3. The processing is necessary for compliance with any legal obligation to which the controller is subject.

4. The processing is necessary in order to protect the vital interests of the data subject or another natural person.

5. The processing is necessary for the performance of a task carried out in the public interest or in the exercise of official authority vested in the controller.

6. The processing is necessary for the purposes of legitimate interests pursued by the controller or by the third party or parties, except where such interests are overridden by the interests or fundamental freedoms of the data subject which require the protection of personal data, in particular where the data subject is a child.

The legitimate interests condition does not apply to processing carried out by public authorities in the performance of their tasks.

In *Chief Constable of Humberside Police and Others v Information Commissioner* [2009] EWCA Civ 1079, the UK Court of Appeal looked at the word 'necessary' in relation to processing under the sixth ground (legitimate interests) and held that there should be a pressing social need justifying the processing, which must be proportionate as to means and fairly balanced as to ends. In its guidance, the ICO interprets 'necessary' somewhat restrictively, by suggesting that processing will be unnecessary (and hence will not benefit from the relevant condition) if a controller could arrive at the result to be achieved by the processing in some other less intrusive way.

The six conditions are briefly summarized in Box 3.5 and their practical application is considered in the following pages.

Consent

Article 6(1)(a) provides that personal data processing will be lawful for the purposes of the First Data Protection Principle where:

the data subject has given consent to the processing of his or her personal data for one or more specific purposes.

Contrary to some of the mythology which has grown around the GDPR, there is no requirement for a controller to seek an individual's consent to processing their

---

Box 3.5 The Processing Conditions (in brief)

---

1. Consent of the data subject
2. Contractual necessity
3. Legal obligation of the controller
4. Vital interests of an individual
5. Performance of a task in the public interest or in the exercise of official authority
6. Legitimate interests of the controller or a third party

---

personal data. In fact, where a controller would rely on a different lawful processing condition to continue processing the individual's data even if consent were withdrawn, then seeking purported consent may be misleading and should be avoided.

'Consent' is defined in Article 4(11) as:

any freely given, specific, informed and unambiguous indication of the data subject's wishes by which he or she, by a statement or by a clear affirmative action, signifies agreement to the processing of personal data relating to him or her.

Three things are clear from this definition: consent cannot be implied from silence, as it requires knowledge and active agreement; consent cannot be imposed upon another or implied where there is a significant power imbalance; and it is unlikely that consent will be achieved by the use of impenetrable or over-complicated notices or clauses.

Example 3—'Freely given' consent in a commercial transaction
An online fashion store requires customers to consent to their details being shared with other retailers before permitting them to create an account and buy products. The store is making consent a condition of sale, but it is clearly not necessary for that purpose, and so is not freely given. The store must allow customers the option to refuse but still be able to buy clothing through the site in order for consent to be valid.

Example 4—Consent 'freely given' to a public authority
A local housing authority needs to collect information about an individual's circumstances, including their health, in order to assess whether they are in priority need and should be provided with accommodation. It is inappropriate for the local authority to ask for the individual's consent for this, particularly as a condition of carrying out the assessment. The individual is likely to be in a vulnerable position and has no real choice but to provide the information. The local housing authority would require and would process the information even if the individual did not consent. Even if the processing is necessary to provide the accommodation, it is not freely given.

It would be different if the local authority asked local residents to participate in a trial of a new recycling scheme, allowing people to sign up and provide certain personal information if they wished, which would be used by the authority to decide whether the recycling scheme was viable. Those residents who agreed to participate in the scheme would freely be giving their consent to the local authority processing the personal data they provided for the stated purpose.

The requirement for signification by 'clear affirmative action' means that failure by the data subject to take action, such as un-ticking a pre-ticked box, cannot be used as a basis for implying consent. Similarly, the sending of a circular or other communication to an individual which states that consent will be *assumed* 'unless we hear from you to the contrary' (an opt-out opportunity) would be ineffective in obtaining consent where there is no response whatsoever from the data subject.

The requirement for consent to be 'specific' and 'informed' means that, before they give consent, individuals must be informed of the purposes for the processing, the processing activities, and the ability to withdraw their consent. Note that the ICO's GDPR Consent Guidance recognizes that it may not be possible to specify purposes in advance where controllers are carrying out processing for scientific research purposes. In that circumstance, it is possible to obtain consent by specifying the general areas of research, and where possible giving individuals granular options to consent only to certain areas of research or parts of the research project.

The ICO has indicated in her GDPR Consent Guidance that there are seven important elements of 'consent' in the GDPR:

- it must be 'unbundled'—it must be separate from other terms and conditions and should not be a precondition of signing up to a service unless it is necessary for that service;

- there must be 'active opt-in'—neither pre-ticked opt-in boxes nor opt-out boxes are valid. Either un-ticked opt-in boxes or similar opt-in methods must be used to obtain consent;

- consent must be 'granular'—options to consent to different types of processing should be given whenever appropriate;

- those relying on consent must be 'named'—not just the controller, but also any third parties who will be relying on consent;

- consent must be 'documented'—the controller must keep records to demonstrate what the individual has consented to, including what they were told and when and how they consented;

- consent must be 'easy to withdraw'—data subjects must be told that they can withdraw their consent at any time and how to do this. The method must be as easy as it was to give the consent;

- there must not be an 'imbalance in the relationship'—consent will not be 'freely given' where there is an imbalance in the relationship between the controller and the individual, such as might occur where the controller is a public authority or an employer.

'Consent', as required by Article 6(1)(a), should be contrasted with 'explicit consent' as required for the processing of special category personal data in Article 9(2)(a) (see Chapter 4). The ICO has indicated in her GDPR Consent Guidance that explicit consent must be expressly confirmed in words, rather than by any other positive action. One implication of this is that implied consent will not be acceptable.

Individuals will not be taken to have consented to processing of which they were not informed or could not reasonably have expected to occur. Thus, a controller that gathers personal data for one purpose will be acting without the consent of the data subject if such data are processed for another non-obvious purpose (in addition to such processing breaching the First Principle where none of the other lawfulness conditions applies, it is also likely to breach the Second Principle—see Chapter 2).

Example 5
A charity collects donors' personal information, including their physical addresses and their banking details, and properly obtains the individuals' consent to this in order to make donations. Some of the donors also consent to receive further marketing messages from the charity. The charity enters the information of those donors into a computer program that uses algorithms and online information to categorize them into 'wealth sectors' so that the charity can target them with specific marketing that is more likely to yield further donations. The donors would not expect their address and banking information to be used in this way and could not be taken to have consented to that processing.

The obtaining of consent for the purposes of electronic marketing (this includes email, text messages, and multimedia messaging service ('MMS')) is also subject to the provisions of the Privacy and Electronic Communications (EC Directive) Regulations 2003, shortly to be replaced by the E-Privacy Regulation—for further detail, see Chapter 10.

Where the individual has no genuine choice in the processing of their personal data, seeking purported consent may be misleading. Impermissible purported consent occurs where the controller would continue to process the individual's personal data on a different lawful basis if consent were refused or withdrawn, where consent is a precondition for services, or where the controller is in a position of power over the subject.

Consent of children

The GDPR is particularly concerned to protect children. Recital 38 makes it clear that children merit such special protection because they may be less aware of the risks, consequences, and safeguards surrounding personal data. Consent of a child obtained under Article 6(1)(a) will need to meet the same standard as applies to adults, and the controller must be satisfied that the child is capable of 'freely' giving consent.

Greater protections are required under Article 8 where the controller is offering 'information society services' direct to a child. These are defined by reference to Article 1(1) of Directive 2015/1535 as 'any service normally provided for remuneration, at a distance, by electronic means and at the individual request of a recipient of the service'. The reference to 'for remuneration' is not limited to payment for the service by the user—it can also encompass services that are free to the user but are remunerative to the service provider because of advertising. 'Information society services' therefore include social media sites and apps, as well as online retail and auction sites.

Where an information society service is offered direct to children, article 8(1) prohibits reliance on consent from a child under sixteen years of age without the authority of the holder of parental responsibility. Those providing such services direct to children will therefore need to develop methods of verifying age and obtaining the requisite consent from those with parental authority over the child. Member States are given flexibility to reduce the minimum age to 13, and the United Kingdom has chosen to this route, so all references to '16 years' in the GDPR are to be read as references to '13 years'. This reflects lobbying from both children's and parents' groups, which consider it is important to recognize the individual autonomy of children aged 14–16 years.

Contractual necessity

Article 6(1)(b) provides that personal data processing will be legitimate for the purposes of the First Data Protection Principle where:

[. . . the] processing is necessary—

(a) for the performance of a contract to which the data subject is a party, or
(b) for the taking of steps at the request of the data subject prior to entering into a contract.

Where the controller has entered into contractual relations with an individual, it is easy to envisage types of processing that will be necessary for contractual performance. Examples include passing a purchaser's details to the issuer of her credit card for payment purposes, sending an individual's name and address to a courier for the delivery of items bought by the individual, and using an employee's bank account details to pay his salary. In contrast, the future sending of direct marketing materials to a customer will not usually be a contractual necessity under the original purchase agreement.

It should be noted that this lawfulness condition refers to a contract to which the data subject is a party. It is thus not necessary for the controller to be a party to the contract on which it is relying for its processing to be lawful, but the contract must include the data subject.

The meaning of the word 'necessary' has been discussed above. Processing by a controller will not be necessary for contractual performance where the contract could reasonably be performed in some other way without the need for such processing.

It is unclear to what the 'steps at the request of the data subject' element of the contractual necessity ground relates. Some have suggested that it is intended to legitimize credit checks carried out by the controller on the data subject, but this seems unlikely due to the presence of the words 'at the request of the data subject'. Further, it is difficult to imagine a type of processing that would be legitimized under this element of the condition which would not also benefit from consent.

Legal obligation

Article 6(1)(c) of the GDPR provides that personal data processing will be legitimate for the purposes of the First Data Protection Principle where:

processing is necessary for compliance with a legal obligation to which the controller is subject.

Processing in furtherance of any statutory or other legal obligations imposed on the controller will be lawful where the processing is necessary to comply with that obligation. The obligation could be imposed by statute, statutory instrument, or regulation, but must amount to an 'obligation' and not simply a 'power' or a 'discretion'.

This condition would be fulfilled, for example, where a statute required an organization to make public a list of its members. The processing involved in making this public disclosure would be lawful because of the legal obligation placed on the controller. Similarly, this condition allows the transfer by an employer of employee records to the tax authority, where such transfer is necessary to comply with statutory taxation obligations. Complying with money laundering checks is a further example of processing that is necessary to satisfy a legal obligation.

The furnishing of certain information to the police (or other law enforcement or investigative bodies) where such information is necessary for the investigation of a criminal offence may also be legitimate under this condition, but controllers should take care to satisfy themselves that they are under a *legal obligation to supply* such information (which, it should be noted, is a different concept to that of the police having lawful authority to investigate an offence).

Vital interests

Article 6(1)(d) provides that personal data processing will be legitimate for the purposes of the First Data Protection Principle where:

processing is necessary in order to protect the vital interests of the data subject or of another natural person.

The word 'vital' is key to this condition and is likely to be construed narrowly. Recital 112 includes 'physical integrity or life' as examples of 'vital interests'. An emergency medical situation would therefore be covered. It is possible that 'vital interests', in addition to serious medical or health issues, could extend to circumstances involving serious and substantial damage to an individual's property—this has certainly been the case in some Member States, such as Ireland, prior to the GDPR coming into force (the wording in the previous legislation was virtually identical to that in the GDPR).

Example 6
Jo travels to France for a skiing holiday. She is caught in an avalanche while skiing off-piste and requires emergency hospital treatment. The French hospital requires Jo's medical records to be transferred from the UK, but Jo is unable to consent to such transfer, as she is unconscious. In this case, the processing by Jo's UK doctor (sending the records to France) is lawful for Article 6 purposes by virtue of the fact that it is necessary to Jo's vital physical well-being.

Public functions

Article 6(1)(e) provides that processing will be lawful where it is:

necessary for the performance of a task carried out in the public interest or in the exercise of official authority vested in the controller.

The 'exercise of official authority' will likely be based on whether there is a law determining the purpose of the processing and requiring or enabling the processing to take place by the controller. Recital 45 makes it clear that the GDPR does not require a specific law for each individual processing. A law as a basis for several processing operations based on a legal obligation to which the controller is subject or where processing is necessary for the performance of a task carried out in the public interest or in the exercise of an official authority may be sufficient.

Recital 45 also makes it clear that it is for each Member State to determine whether the controller performing a task carried out in the public interest or in the exercise of official authority should be a public authority or another natural or legal person governed by public law, or, where it is in the public interest to do so, including for health purposes such as public health and social protection and the management of health care services, by private law, such as a professional association. The definition of 'public authority' is considered further below. Although there is no definition of 'public interest' in the GDPR (as was the case with the Directive and the 1998 Act), there is a wealth of case law in the UK that deals with this point—see, for example, *Campbell v Mirror Group Newspapers* later in this chapter.

The 'public functions' condition is likely to be the basis on which public authorities carry out the bulk of their processing of personal data.

Legitimate interests

Article 6(1)(f) provides that personal data processing will be lawful for the purposes of the First Data Protection Principle where:

processing is necessary for the purposes of the legitimate interests pursued by the controller or by a third party except where such interests are overridden by the interests or fundamental rights and freedoms of the data subject which require protection of personal data, in particular where the data subject is a child.

The 'legitimate interests' condition is somewhat ambiguous and controversial. The starting point here is the existence of a legitimate interest of the controller. There is no definition of 'legitimate' in the GDPR, so the ordinary meaning of the word should be used. Recital 47 states that a legitimate interest could exist, for example, where the data subject is a client or in the service of a controller, and also acknowledges that the processing of personal data for direct marketing purposes may be regarded as carried out for a legitimate interest. This makes clear that business purposes, such as customer care or marketing, and staff purposes, such as wellbeing, can be legitimate interests. However, reliance on business purposes would justify more limited types of processing that a stronger interest, such as staff wellbeing.

The processing must be necessary for that legitimate interest. Finally, the legitimate interests must not be overridden by the interests or fundamental rights and freedoms of the data subject—a proportionality assessment is thus brought into play in which the legitimate interests of the controller or third party are to be weighed against the rights, freedoms, and legitimate interests of the relevant individual whose data are being processed, in order to assess if the latter override the former.

It is clear that the legitimate interests of third parties can justify reliance on the condition, including for the purposes of disclosure to such parties. However, in order to assess whether the condition applies before making the transfer of personal data to a third party, the controller will need to ascertain the third party's proposed purposes for processing so as to determine whether they are 'legitimate'.

As previously mentioned, some guidance on the meaning of a 'legitimate interest' is provided in Recital 47, which states:

[A] legitimate interest could exist for example where there is a relevant and appropriate relationship between the data subject and the controller in situations such as where the data subject is a client or in the service of the controller. At any rate the existence of a legitimate interest would need careful assessment including whether a data subject can reasonably expect at the time and in the context of the collection of the personal data that processing for that purpose may take place ... The processing of personal data strictly necessary for the purposes of preventing fraud also constitutes a legitimate interest of the data controller concerned. The processing of personal data for direct marketing purposes may be regarded as carried out for a legitimate interest.

The Court of Justice of the European Union ('CJEU') has considered the legitimate interests processing condition, although its judgment was not particularly illuminating. In the case of *Valsts policijas Rīgas reģiona pārvaldes Kārtības policijas pārvalde v Rīgas pašvaldības SIA 'Rīgas satiksme'* (Case C-13/16), the CJEU held that 'there is no doubt that the interest of a third party in obtaining the personal information of a person who damaged their property in order to sue that person for damages can be qualified as a legitimate interest'. In relation to 'balancing the opposing rights and interests at issue', the CJEU noted that this depended 'on the specific circumstances of the particular case'. It did suggest two relevant factors: 'the possibility of accessing the data at issue in public sources' and the age of the data subject in question.

In light of the intended supremacy of human rights legislation over other legal provisions it seems clear that where the interests of the controller and those of the data subject are perceived to be equal, national regulators and the courts will determine the interests of the data subject to be the most important. Even in the absence of the Human Rights Convention it should be remembered that data protection legislation is aimed principally at protecting the privacy of the individual.

In April 2014, the Article 29 Working Party published an Opinion (WP 217—see <http://www.dpdocuments.com>) on the legitimate interests ground for processing personal data within the European Union, based on the Directive. It is likely that much of the practical advice in this opinion remains relevant under the GDPR. Interestingly, the Opinion states that controllers should neither treat the ground as a 'last resort' for processing, nor should they 'automatically select' the ground on the basis that its use is less constraining than the other grounds. The Working Party proposes three factors that should be considered (amongst others that may be relevant in the circumstances of the proposed processing) in implementing the balancing test:

- the nature and source of the legitimate interest and whether the data processing is necessary for the exercise of a fundamental right, is otherwise in the public interest, or benefits from recognition in the community concerned;
- the impact on the data subject and their reasonable expectations about what will happen to their data, as well as the nature of the data and how they are processed;
- additional safeguards which could limit undue impact on the data subject, such as data minimization, privacy-enhancing technologies, increased transparency, general and unconditional right to opt out, and data portability.

The legitimate interests condition is not available to public authorities where they are processing personal data 'in the performance of their tasks'. This suggests that where the public authority is not performing an official function or 'task' (e.g. if it is acting as employer or as a commercial contracting party), it may be able to rely on the legitimate interests condition.

There is no definition of 'public authority' in the GDPR, but the government has indicated that it will adopt the same definition as in the Freedom of Information legislation. Accordingly, any body listed in Schedule 1 of the Freedom of Information Act 2000 or of the Freedom of Information (Scotland) Act 2002, or any authority or body designated by the Secretary of State in regulations, is a 'public authority'. These include central government departments and local authorities, the Houses of Parliament, the devolved administrations, the police, the armed forces, and maintained schools, NHS commissioning boards and clinical commissioning groups, various arts councils, the BBC and Channel 4 (in respect of any information held other than for the purposes of journalism, art, or literature), and a variety of regulatory bodies.

Other Unlawful Processing

The First Data Protection Principle requires that personal data must be processed 'lawfully'. This means that breach of a non-data protection legal provision in UK law (or, as relevant, any other Member State), which involves the processing of personal data, will amount to a breach of the First Principle.

Confidential information

The main restriction in the UK on processing data, outside the provisions of data protection legislation, is the law of confidentiality. Confidence will be breached (and thus an action for breach of confidence will lie) where, as Megarry J stated in *Coco v A N Clarke (Engineers) Ltd* [1968] FSR 415:

(a) the information has the necessary quality of confidence;

(b) the information has been imparted in circumstances importing an obligation of confidence; and

(c) there is an unauthorized use of the information to the detriment of the original communicator of the information.

Information will have the necessary quality of confidence when it is of a confidential character. The courts apply an objective test in determining whether information has a confidential character: would the reasonable man, in the position of the defendant, realize that the information in his possession is confidential? Information will not have the necessary quality of confidence if it is in the public domain.

The information will be imparted in circumstances imposing an obligation of confidence where there is a relationship between the parties that would lead the reasonable man to conclude that the information should be kept secret. Thus, a clearly audible exchange between A and B in a crowded market place will not lead to an obligation of confidence no matter how confidential the information. Others present in the market place who hear the conversation will not be under an obligation of confidence either, as there is no existing relationship between them and the speaker. There are, however, several types of relationship that the courts have held to be sufficient for this purpose—for example, the relationship which exists between an employee and employer, between two commercial concerns undertaking a business negotiation with each other, and between one family member and another.

A further type of relationship that may give rise to an obligation of confidence, and one that is of particular significance to the media, is that of a journalist and the person who provides him with information. The obligation will most commonly arise when the journalist is aware that the information is being provided covertly and the person providing the information is the original source of it. It is less clear whether an obligation of confidence arises if the information is sent to the journalist anonymously or where it is provided overtly by a person who has received the information from another.

Not every use of the information by the recipient will be sufficient to found an action for breach of confidence; it must be an unauthorized use. This rarely presents much difficulty for claimants in practice and in many cases the unauthorized use will involve some form of data processing. Once it has been established that the information was of a confidential character and was imparted in circumstances imposing confidentiality then it will rarely be difficult to show that the dissemination of that information is an unauthorized use.

Other legal provisions

Aside from the law of confidence, information will be processed unlawfully in the UK (and therefore in breach of the First Data Protection Principle) where it is processed in one of the following ways:

(a) in breach of contract;

(b) by a body acting outside of its allotted powers (*ultra vires*);

(c) in breach of copyright;

(d) in contravention of the provisions of the Computer Misuse Act 1990 as amended by the Police and Justice Act 2006 and the Serious Crime Act 2007; or

(e) in breach of the Human Rights Act 1998, particularly Article 8.

Cases of Significance

The following cases offer some examples of the ways in which the First Data Protection Principle was understood and applied under the Directive and the 1998 Act. It is unclear whether any of these cases will be binding under the GDPR. It is likely that cases on provisions which have not materially changed will still be persuasive.

Robertson

In *Brian Reid Beetson Robertson v Wakefield Metropolitan Council, Secretary of State for the Home Department* [2001] EWHC 915 (Admin), the refusal by an electoral registration officer to allow an elector to have his name removed from an electoral register before that register was sold to a commercial concern for marketing purposes was held to be:

(a) a breach of his right to respect for his private and family life under Article 8 of the European Convention on Human Rights;

(b) a breach of his right to have processing for direct marketing stopped under Section 11 of the Data Protection Act; and

(c) an invalid interference with his right to vote in free elections under Article 3 of the First Protocol to the European Convention on Human Rights.

In the Queen's Bench Division of the High Court, Mr Justice Maurice Kay granted an application, by Brian Robertson, for judicial review of the refusal of the electoral registration officer for the first defendant, Wakefield Metropolitan District Council, to accede to his request that his name and address should not be supplied to commercial organizations. The grounds for the application were twofold: (1) the refusal was unlawful in that UK domestic law did not comply with the Data Protection Directive, and, (2) it was both a breach of his right to privacy under Article 8 of the European Convention on Human Rights and his right to vote in free elections under Article 3 of the First Protocol thereto.

The judge said that, by virtue of the Representation of the People Act 1983 and the Representation of the People Regulations 1986 (SI 1986/1081), electoral registration officers were charged with the duty of preparing and publishing a register of Parliamentary and local government electors for their area annually and were required, under Regulation 54 to supply a copy to any person upon payment of the prescribed fee.

Although it was a criminal offence not to return the application form duly completed, the claimant had written to the electoral registration officer in Wakefield stating that he did not intend to complete the form for inclusion on the register because he opposed the practice of selling copies of the register to commercial companies. In response, the registration officer stated that the compilation of the register was separate to the uses to be made of it, and that he intended to include the claimant's name and address.

The claimant applied for judicial review on the ground that he was unlawfully being required to tolerate the dissemination of the register to commercial interests who utilized it for marketing purposes and that his enfranchisement could not lawfully be made conditional upon acceptance of that practice. Article 14 of the Data Protection Directive (and Section 11 of the 1998 Act) provides that an individual could object to the processing of personal data relating to him that the controller anticipated being processed for the purposes of direct marketing (see Chapter 9).

Since no provision had been made in the Representation of the People (England and Wales) Regulations 2001 (SI 2001/3111) for registers to be edited pursuant to requests for exclusion, domestic law failed to comply with Article 14 of the Data Protection Directive and electoral registration officers were wrongly administering the registers without regard to that Directive and Section 11 of the 1998 Act. In principle, an elector could enforce his right to object and it was incumbent on the courts to construe the 1986 Regulations and the 2001 Regulations in a manner that complied with the Data Protection Directive and was consistent with the 1998 Act.

The claimant's concern was the sale of his personal details by the authority to commercial organizations in the knowledge that they would be used for direct marketing purposes. In that the sale of the register affected electors as marketing targets and the interference with their private lives, exacerbated by technological advances, was both foreseeable and foreseen, Article 8 of the European Convention on Human Rights was relevant.

As, in his Lordship's judgment, the practice of selling the register to commercial concerns without affording individual electors a right of objection was a disproportionate way in which to give effect to the legitimate objective of retaining a commercially available register, it followed that the claimant's right to privacy under Article 8 was breached.

Furthermore, if and to the extent that the 1986 Regulations and 2001 Regulations made the right to vote conditional upon acquiescence in that practice, with no individual right of objection, they operated in a manner which contravened Article 3 of the First Protocol to the European Convention on Human Rights on the same reasoning of justification and proportionality that had applied to the Article 8 challenge.

The *Robertson* case altered the practice of the collection of personal details by local authorities for compilation of the electoral roll. There are now two registers: one for use by direct marketing companies, and one that cannot be used for marketing purposes. Individuals can now choose which register they would like to have their details entered on at the time they provide those details.

Campbell

In *Campbell v MGN Limited* [2004] UKHL 22, the model Naomi Campbell brought an action (which was founded in the law of confidence but included data protection pleadings) against *The Mirror* newspaper regarding its publication of the fact that she had, and was receiving treatment for, a drug addiction. The article was accompanied by a photograph of her on the street leaving a therapy session. The faces of those she was with had been pixellated but she was clearly recognizable. The article included details about the fact that she was receiving treatment at Narcotics Anonymous ('NA'), the nature of that treatment, and how often she attended.

At first instance, the court held that both the fact of the addiction and the additional details of her attendance at NA sessions were capable of protection under the law of confidence. On appeal, the newspaper successfully argued that the fact that she was a public figure and a role model made a difference to the status of the information. Ms Campbell had previously denied having a drug addiction and, therefore, had conceded at the outset that the newspaper was entitled to expose her misconduct and subsequent hypocritical concealment by stating that she had a drug addiction and that she was receiving treatment. What she had objected to was the publication of details of where and how she was receiving treatment and the photograph of her at the specific NA centre she attended.

The Court of Appeal decision ([2003] EMLR 2) held that where a public figure made false statements about his or her private life, the press was allowed to 'set the record straight' and the peripheral details, such as where and how she was receiving treatment, were part of the detail required to give the overall story credibility. Ms Campbell had courted publicity during her career, and the press was entitled to publish information about her untruthful statements. In relation to the data protection claim, the Court of Appeal had to consider the question of whether the publication of hard copy newspapers amounted to 'processing' under the 1998 Act. It held that 'where the controller is responsible for the publication of hard copies that reproduce data that has previously been processed by means of equipment operating automatically, the publication forms part of the processing and falls within the scope of the Act'.

The approach of the Court of Appeal was narrowly overturned (three to two) in the House of Lords. Finding for Ms Campbell, the Lords decided that the disclosure of the additional information conveyed in the story about where and when she attended for treatment and the photograph of her leaving NA was a breach of confidence. The House of Lords judgment did not deal with the data protection claim.

Lindqvist

The CJEU case of *Lindqvist* (Case C-101/01 [2004]) involved a web page which had been created by Mrs Lindqvist with personal information about some of her fellow parishioners. The information included sensitive personal data which related to a parishioner's leg injury. The page was composed by Mrs Lindqvist on her home computer and placed on the internet. She was prosecuted for processing personal data by automatic means. The national court in Sweden referred to the CJEU the following question:

Does it constitute 'the processing of personal data wholly or partly by automatic means' to list on a self-made internet home page a number of persons with comments and statements about their jobs and hobbies etc?

The CJEU held that the listing of the parishioners did constitute the processing of their personal data, and that the process had been 'performed, at least in part, automatically' because of the loading of the page on to the server. Although the selection of the data had been purely manual, there was no suggestion that the processing taken as a whole was not automatic.

Johnson

In the case of *Johnson v Medical Defence Union* [2007] EWCA Civ 262, Mr Johnson was a consultant orthopaedic surgeon who had, for several years, paid an annual fee to the Medical Defence Union ('MDU'), an organization which provided him with professional indemnity cover and other services. In 2002 the MDU wrote to Mr Johnson saying that it would not be renewing his membership at the expiry of its current period. Although the MDU initially furnished no reason for the decision, it later transpired that the MDU used a points-based allocation system to determine its risk of exposure to potential claims against its members. Mr Johnson asserted, *inter alia*, that the points-based allocation system constituted unfair processing of his personal data due to the fact that it was based on a scoring method which counted the number of allegations made against members rather than whether such allegations had any merit.

One difficulty for Mr Johnson was that, although much of the risk allocation system (including storage of personal data) used computers, the actual decision regarding termination of membership was taken by a human being. The trial judge held, following *Campbell*, that the human decision was part of a whole series of operations that was caught in its entirety by the definition of personal data processing. But a majority of the judges in the Court of Appeal distinguished *Campbell*, holding that the decision to not renew Mr Johnson's membership was not automatically processed (nor formed part of a relevant filing system) and so was not caught by data protection law.

Notwithstanding that Mr Johnson lost his case against the MDU on the basis that there was no relevant personal data processing, the Court of Appeal went on to consider the hypothetical question of whether, had the processing been caught by the 1998 Act, such processing would have been unfair. The conclusion that the MDU's policy (which was to count incidents of complaint rather than consider their merit) 'was not clearly unjustified' (per Buxton LJ at para 63) seems to have been based more in a desire for freedom of action for the business world than on more general concepts of fairness.

Kordowski

The case of *Law Society and Others v Kordowski* [2011] EWCH 3185 (QB) concerned a claim for an injunction to restrain the publisher of the 'Solicitors from Hell' website from continuing to publish the names of solicitors or law firms on that site or any similar site. The claimants based their action in libel, harassment, and data protection.

The site itself purported to be a service to the general public by providing an opportunity for disgruntled, aggrieved, or dissatisfied persons to 'name and shame' a lawyer or firm. The claimants objected to the site on the basis that it provided a forum for the publication of malicious and defamatory allegations against solicitors. A financial charge was made by the publisher of the site for any posting to the site, and lawyers were invited to make payments to have their details removed from the site.

As far as the data protection claim was concerned, the judge found that the site breached several aspects of data protection law, including the requirement for personal data to be processed fairly and lawfully. In respect of the latter, the unlawfulness of the processing was made out by virtue of the fact that it was both libellous and harassing. The judge granted an order under Section 10 of the Act for cessation of the publication.

Summary

In order to comply with the requirements of the First Data Protection Principle, controllers must:

1. obtain personal data from data subjects in a manner that does not deceive or mislead data subjects as to the purposes for the data;

2. ensure that, when data are collected, a 'fair processing' notice is easily available that sets out information on the identity of the controller, the purposes for processing, and any other information to enable the processing to be fair, such as the right to obtain subject access;

3. ensure that personal data are processed with fairness and in compliance with all applicable legal provisions;

4. ensure that all personal data processing meets one of the lawfulness conditions contained in Article 6 of the GDPR; and

5. ensure that the processing of special category personal data is made lawful by one of the conditions listed in Article 9 of the GDPR.

4

Special Categories of Data

Nicola Fulford and Peter Carey

Introduction	66
The Conditions for Processing	69
Personal Data Relating to Criminal Convictions and Offences	81
Advice on Processing Special Category Personal Data	83

Introduction

A special category of personal data is afforded stronger protection under the GDPR and the Bill than ordinary personal data. Similar restrictions on processing 'sensitive personal data' under the 1998 Act existed previously in the UK.

Article 9(1) of the Regulation provides a list of special categories of personal data and Article 9(2) sets out the conditions on which such data may be legally processed. The Bill supplements the rules on legitimate processing of special categories of personal data.

The types of personal data that form the special categories are listed in Box 4.1.

The list is similar to the types of data defined as 'sensitive personal data' under the Directive and the 1998 Act, with the notable addition of genetic and biometric data

---

Box 4.1 Special Category Personal Data

(a) Data revealing racial or ethnic origin

(b) Data revealing political opinions

(c) Data revealing religious or philosophical beliefs

(d) Data revealing trade union membership

(e) Genetic data

(f) Biometric data for purpose of uniquely identifying a natural person

(g) Data concerning health

(h) Data concerning sex life or sexual orientation

---

as well as data concerning a person's sexual orientation. As technology advances, the potential for capturing and using data to identify individuals (e.g. genetic and bio-metric data) increases and the Regulation and the Bill seek to keep pace in order to protect the privacy of individuals. The definitions of genetic and biometric data were drafted deliberately widely to include 'acquired genetic characteristics' and 'behav-ioural characteristics'.

Personal data relating to criminal convictions and offences (referred to in this chapter as 'criminal data'), which were previously within the definition of sensitive personal data under the 1998 Act and the Directive, are still afforded special protec-tion but are no longer within the 'special categories' of personal data as defined. See the discussion below on the protection of criminal data. 'Data concerning health' is broadly defined (in Article 4 of the Regulation and Section 184 of the Bill) and includes data relating to physical and mental health and personal data relating to the provision of health care services. Consumer groups question whether enough has been done to protect individuals against the risks from the growth of eHealth (health services delivered by electronic or digital means) and mHealth (health services delivered by mobile communication systems). The health care system has a poor track record for data breaches. In March 2017, the Information Commissioner's Office ('ICO') launched new resources aimed at improving records management in the health sector following audits which revealed numerous instances of data being sent to incorrect recipients and paperwork being lost or stolen. Many consumers remain unaware of the ways in which private companies use health data they gather, for example, from wearable technology and associated smartphone apps for the recording of data concerning diet and exercise.

Examples of special category personal data include:

- an airline's booking record showing that a particular passenger requires kosher food;
- the membership database of a political party;
- a school application form showing information about a pupil's religious beliefs;
- an employer's record of amounts deducted from employees' salaries relating to trade union membership fees;
- images captured by the facial recognition cameras at airport border control ePassport gates;
- fingerprint ('dactyloscopic') data recorded by school canteen payment and classroom registration systems;
- results of a genetic test to determine a patient's predisposition to various health conditions;
- DNA samples collected from a crime scene and analysed to determine the iden-tity of the perpetrator (which may qualify as special category personal data and criminal data);
- hotel booking data disclosing that wheelchair access is required for a particular guest;

- data from a wearable device about the number of steps walked, heart rate, sleep patterns, and the calories burned;
- publication of details of therapy received by Naomi Campbell at Narcotics Anonymous including photos with captions which betrayed her drug addiction (*Campbell v MGN [2002] All ER (D) 448 (Mar)*); and
- minutes of a meeting discussing alleged discrimination against an employee who has undergone gender reassignment surgery.

In the case of *Lindqvist ((2003) C-101/01)*, the Court of Justice of the European Union ('CJEU') held that the posting on a web page of details regarding an individual's leg injury did amount to the processing of sensitive personal data (the forerunner of special category personal data) and did violate the Directive's prohibition on 'processing data concerning health'. The case involved a church worker who had set up a website where she published a parish magazine that included information about other parish workers, including the fact that one worker had an injured leg and was working part-time as a result, without that worker's consent.

In the more recent case of *Baronetcy of Pringle of Stichill ([2016] UKPC 16)* DNA evidence was produced to help determine the identity of the rightful Baronet of Pringle of Stichill, and the Privy Council acknowledged that 'DNA was sensitive personal data as defined in section 2 of the 1998 Act as it contained information as to the data subject's racial or ethnic origin and possibly also his health or condition.'

There will always be grey areas and scope for debate about whether particular data are within one of the special categories of personal data. Could someone's place of birth—for example 'England'—be ethnic origin information? Arguably the ethnic mix in England today is so varied that 'England' alone does not reveal one's ethnic origin.

Personal data may need to be seen in context to determine whether they are actually special category personal data or not. For example, where an individual registers with a website which provides information on churches and other religious buildings and then undertakes a search for her local Baptist church, could the controller be processing special category personal data, being information on a 'religious belief'? The ICO has indicated that a pragmatic approach will be taken, suggesting that the purpose of the processing will be considered. Thus the question as to whether the racial or ethnic origin of a data subject could be gleaned from the processing of a surname or family name (e.g. Jones, Patel, McGregor, Abdullah) could be answered by considering whether the processing was for special category personal data reasons (e.g. to send marketing information on kilts to the McGregors) or merely to store a list of names (e.g. a general customer details database).

Where the language used in the Articles of the GDPR is ambiguous and the Bill does not give further clarity, the Recitals of the Regulation can be useful for assisting with interpretation. For example, the definition of biometric data refers to facial images but Recital 51 states that photographs will only qualify as biometric data and be deemed special category personal data 'when processed through a specific technical means allowing the unique identification or authentication of a natural person'. In other words, an ePassport scanner processes biometric data but copying a company's marketing brochure containing photos of its directors is not processing biometric data.

The Conditions for Processing

The Regulation contains ten conditions for the lawful processing of special category personal data. They are set out in Article 9(2), summarized in Box 4.2, and discussed below.

All personal data processing requires compliance with an Article 6 condition (see Chapter 3) and, therefore, the need for one of the special category conditions is an *additional* requirement for special category personal data processing (this is confirmed in Recital 51).

In the UK, the Bill provides supplementary conditions for the lawful processing of special category personal data, which are set out in Schedule 1. Separate conditions exist to govern processing by 'competent authorities' including the police and other law enforcement bodies (Part 3—Law Enforcement Processing) and MI5, MI6, and GCHQ (Part 4—Intelligence Services Processing). Law enforcement processing is covered below. This chapter does not deal in detail with intelligence services processing but it is worth noting that there are a number of exemptions available to the intelligence services (see Part 4, Chapter 6 and Schedule 11), the major exemption being the safeguarding of national security, which is anyway outside of the remit of EU law and therefore the GDPR. With counter-terrorism high on the government's agenda it will be interesting to see how the security services and the police exercise their covert surveillance powers under the Investigatory Powers Act 2016 and how an appropriate balance can be struck between privacy and public safety.

Box 4.2 Conditions for Processing Special Category Personal Data

(a) Explicit consent of the data subject

(b) Compliance with employment, social security, and social protection law obligations

(c) Vital interests of the data subject

(d) Processing by a not-for-profit body

(e) Personal data manifestly made public by the data subject

(f) Establishing, exercising, or defending legal claims or whenever courts are acting in their judicial capacity

(g) Substantial public interest

(h) Provision of medical or social care or treatment

(i) Public interest in the area of public health

(j) Archiving in the public interest, scientific or historical research, or statistical purposes

The data subject has given his or her explicit consent to the processing of the special personal data

The rules on obtaining consent from data subjects are somewhat stricter under the Regulation than they were under the preceding legislation. Consent is defined as any 'freely given, specific, informed and unambiguous indication of the data subject's wishes by which he or she, by a statement or by a clear affirmative action, signifies agreement to the processing of personal data relating to him or her'.

The Regulation places greater emphasis on, and clarity around, what organizations must do to ensure that consent is 'freely given'. Blanket consent for a range of nameless controllers, processors, and third parties will not be specific or granular enough to be valid (according to Recitals 42 and 43). It also must be easy for individuals to withdraw consent at any time and there must not be any penalty for withdrawing it (according to Article 7(3) and Recital 42). Detailed records of the consent obtained, by whom, for whom, for what processes and when, must be kept as evidence and must be refreshed where necessary (e.g. where the purpose of processing has changed or a child has become an adult) along with the details of any withdrawal of consent (according to Article 7(1)).

There is no definition of 'explicit consent'. According to the ICO's latest draft guidance at the time of writing, the key difference between consent and explicit consent is 'likely to be that explicit consent must be affirmed in a clear statement (whether oral or written)'. Implied consent, which is consent inferred from someone's action, is of course insufficient.

A signature box or a tick box (never pre-ticked) on a form is an acceptable means of obtaining explicit consent as long as the accompanying statement of consent is sufficiently specific and written in clear active language, for example 'I consent to X collecting and keeping a record of my medical conditions in order to provide me with appropriate assistance if required (e.g. in the event of an injury/incident)'. The controller must specify the type of special category personal data to be processed, give granular options to consent separately to different types of processing wherever appropriate, and not seek combined consent for multiple processing activities.

There is a presumption that consent is not 'freely given' if there is an imbalance of power between the individual and the controller. Public authorities and employers should, therefore, use an alternative condition for processing special category personal data where possible.

Explicit consent will be unavailable where an individual is prohibited by law from giving their explicit consent (Article 9(2)(a)). For example, in the UK an individual cannot give consent if they have certain mental disorders.

Where an individual gives explicit consent, such consent will also operate to legitimize the processing for Article 6 purposes (Article 6(1)(a) relates to obtaining the 'consent' of the data subject for the processing of ordinary personal data).

The processing is necessary for carrying out obligations and exercising specific rights of the controller or of the data subject under employment, social security, or social protection law, or a collective agreement

Special categories of personal data may be processed where necessary for the performance of obligations or the exercise of rights of the controller or the individual under:

- employment law;
- social security law; or
- law relating to social protection.

In the UK, the Bill provides supplementary guidance for controllers wishing to rely on this condition for processing. To use this exception the controller must have an appropriate policy document in place (Schedule 1, Part 1 of the Bill) (referred to in this chapter as a 'processing policy'). The processing policy requirement is new and is the UK's way of 'providing for the appropriate safeguards for the fundamental rights and interests of the data subject', as prescribed by Article 9(2)(b). The processing policy must:

- explain the controller's procedures for securing compliance with the principles in Article 5 in relation to the condition replied upon;
- explain the controller's policies for retention and erasure of personal data in relation to the condition replied upon;
- be reviewed and updated (if appropriate) from time to time;
- be made available to the ICO on request without charge; and
- be maintained from the time processing begins until six months after processing ceases.

The controller (or their representative) is also required to maintain a record (under Article 30 of the Regulation) (referred to in this chapter as a 'processing record') of:

- which condition is relied upon;
- how the processing satisfies Article 6; and
- whether the personal data are retained in accordance with the processing policy and if not why not.

This requirement is set out in Schedule 1, Part 4 of the Bill.

Examples of processing of special category personal data being necessary in order to comply with employment law include mandatory statutory disclosures of highly confidential employee data and processing necessary to meet health and safety requirements. For example, an employer would need certain details about an employee's disability in order to properly adapt their workstation.

The Equality Act seeks to protect employees against race and/or sexual orientation discrimination (two characteristics that fall within the special categories of personal data). This legislation requires employers to prevent unlawful discrimination.

As such, an employer would be able to collect and use special category personal data if, for example, there was evidence that an employee was using the employer's email system to engage in racial harassment, and there was no reasonable alternative to monitoring the employee's email to ensure the employer met its obligations.

One question is whether 'necessary' under employment law includes rights and obligations in an employment contract that allows for the processing of special category personal data. It is suggested that it does not.

Processing necessary for compliance with social security and social protection law did not exist under the 1998 Act or the Directive. These activities involve significant special category personal data processing so this will be a helpful addition for those delivering social services especially where the beneficiaries of those services are unable to give consent to the processing of their data, either physically or due to an imbalance of power.

The Regulation also permits processing of special categories of personal data where it is necessary under a collective agreement pursuant to Member State law where the law or collective agreement provides for appropriate safeguards for the fundamental rights and interests of the data subject. The reference to collective agreements is new to the Regulation but is not covered by the Bill. Recital 155 makes it clear that collective agreements may provide for specific rules on the processing of employees' personal data in the employment context. Policies relating to data protection obligations will often form part of workforce agreements that an employer is required to adhere to.

As for all conditions which require processing to be 'necessary', this condition will not be available where the purpose can be achieved by other reasonable means. The case of *V & EDPS v European Parliament (2011/C 282/92)* is an example of the courts finding that processing was unnecessary and that the purpose could have been achieved by less obtrusive means.

Processing that complies with this special category condition will usually also satisfy the condition in Article 6(1)(c) for the processing of ordinary personal data—that is, that the processing is necessary to comply with a legal obligation on the controller.

The processing is necessary to protect the vital interests of the data subject or another person

This condition allows for the processing of special category personal data where such processing is necessary to protect the 'vital interests' of the data subject or another person, but the data subject is 'physically or legally' incapable of giving his or her consent. The wording of this condition is identical to its predecessor in the Directive, so there is nothing new in this condition at EU level. However, the 1998 Act (in Schedule 3(3)) contained slightly different wording, reflecting a slightly different interpretation in the UK.

The ICO's Guide to Data Protection (which was produced under the preceding law) stated that the 'vital interests' condition in the 1998 Act applied only in cases of 'life or death', such as where an individual's medical history is disclosed to a hospital's A&E

department where the individual is being treated after a serious road accident. Other jurisdictions, for example Ireland, were more generous with their interpretations of vital interests, extending the definition to physical injury as well as damage to property.

This condition will be useful in an emergency situation where an individual cannot give consent (e.g., where he or she is unconscious), is a minor or otherwise legally incapacitated, or cannot be found.

Where an individual has a communicable disease and 'another person' is in danger of infection the individual may be capable of giving consent but may choose not to consent to the processing of their special category personal data. In these circumstances, in order to protect the vital interests of 'another person', the 1998 Act provided controllers with the ability to process the data where 'consent by or on behalf of the data subject has been unreasonably withheld'. There is no equivalent right in the Regulation. In the Bill, there is no vital interests condition for the processing of special category personal data except for processing by the 'intelligence services' and 'competent authorities'. The UK has chosen to remove the requirement for consent of the data subject, and the need to prove that the data subject has withheld consent for whatever reason, for ordinary processing by the 'intelligence services' (under Part 4 of the Bill in Schedule 9) and for sensitive processing for 'law enforcement purposes' (under Part 3 of the Bill in Schedule 8) where it is necessary to protect the vital interests of the data subject or another individual. For sensitive processing by the 'intelligence services' (in Schedule 10 of the Bill) the test is the same as that under the 1998 Act.

There may be some overlap between the 'vital interests' condition and the conditions for the provision of health or social care and public health (see below). It could be argued that 'vital interests' covers matters other than purely life-and-death health issues, such as cases involving significant damage to property. The condition for the provision of health care requires the processing to be carried out by a health professional. The vital interests condition is not limited in this way—it extends to processing by any person.

This condition is essentially a slightly stricter version of the vital interests condition in Article 6(d), which will be satisfied if the special categories personal data test is met.

The processing is carried out in the course of the legitimate activities of a not-for-profit body

In order to take advantage of this condition, the foundation, association, or other not-for-profit body must exist for political, philosophical, religious, or trade union purposes and the processing must:

- be carried out in the course of its legitimate activities with appropriate safeguards;
- relate only to members or former members of the body or to persons who have regular contact with it in connection with its purposes; and
- not involve disclosure of the personal data outside that body without the consent of the data subjects.

This condition is broadly the same as in the Directive and the 1998 Act, with the addition of 'former members'.

If the processing requires the disclosure of the data to third parties, the body will still require the explicit consent of the data subjects or it must rely on another condition for processing.

Depending on the facts, processing which satisfies this condition may also be permitted under the legitimate interests condition for ordinary data processing in Article 6(1)(f).

Processing relates to personal data which are manifestly made public by the data subject

A controller may process special category personal data where such information has been 'manifestly made public by the data subject'. It may prove difficult to determine what the words 'manifestly made public' actually mean. The same phrase appeared in the Directive, but the UK changed it to 'made public as a result of steps deliberately taken by the data subject' in the 1998 Act. A literal interpretation suggests that publication must be intentional and must be actioned by data subjects themselves. Although an individual who has broadcast information in a television interview can be said to be deliberately making such information public, the same may not be true of an individual who makes a personal announcement to a gathering of friends.

The case of Esch and Others v European Central Bank ((2004) T-320/02) concerned employees of the European Central Bank who had used the bank's internal email system to send emails to different mailing lists with a link to information provided by a trade union. The court decided that by sending these emails the applicants had deliberately revealed their affiliation to this trade union and had themselves made their personal data public.

There is no equivalent condition in Article 6. The circumstances under which the data are manifestly made public by the data subject may evidence an unambiguous and clear affirmative action which amounts to consent and therefore satisfies Article 6(1)(a). However, it is unlikely that posting personal data on a social media page will be enough for another controller to rely on as consent for a specific purpose, in which case another Article 6 condition must be relied upon.

The processing is necessary for the establishment, exercise, or defence of legal claims

Here, by virtue of Article 9(2)(f), the processing of special category personal data must be necessary:

- for the establishment of legal claims;
- for the exercise or defence of legal claims; or
- whenever courts are acting in their judicial capacity.

Most activities of lawyers in carrying out the litigation-related instructions of their clients are covered by this condition, from pre-action through to trial. So too is the processing undertaken by controller clients whilst communicating with their lawyers regarding litigation and in preparing for such communications, for example processing by an employer of employee information with a view to seeking legal advice on an unfair dismissal allegation or redundancy decision.

In the case of *R (on the application of B) v Stafford Combined Court ([2006] EWHC 1645)* an NHS Trust was summoned by the Crown Court to produce the psychiatric medical records of a victim of sexual abuse as evidence in the trial of the man accused of abusing her. The Judicial Review did not comment on whether the processing of the victim's personal data was necessary for the defence of a legal claim, but in the future, with the requirement for greater transparency and record keeping, the controller is more likely to have to evidence a lawful condition for processing such personal data.

This condition is focused on processing in the context of legal disputes and does not give entities any rights to process special category personal data where necessary for the performance of a contract. Although similar to the Directive's wording, the wording in the GDPR is narrower than the equivalent condition under the 1998 Act, as the Regulation is focused on 'legal claims' rather than legal proceedings, legal advice, or legal rights.

The appropriate condition for lawful processing of ordinary personal data under Article 6 depends on the type of controller. A solicitor gathering evidence in defence of a client's claim is performing a contractual obligation (Article 6(1)(b)); a judge delivering a judgment is exercising an official authority vested in him (Article 6(1)(e)); and any of the parties may be acting in reliance on a legal obligation (Article 6(1)(c)).

Processing is necessary for reasons of substantial public interest

This condition has the potential to be very widely interpreted, hence the Regulation specifies a number of caveats to prevent reasons of 'substantial public interest' being a 'soft' option. In the UK, the Bill introduces a list of substantial public interest conditions (Schedule 1, Part 2), one of which must apply in order for the processing to be lawful. In addition the controller (or their representative) must maintain a processing policy and a processing record (for details see the section on processing necessary pursuant to employment law above).

The UK's conditions are specific and detailed and are therefore only summarized here. The controller must prove that the processing is necessary:

- for one of the listed parliamentary, statutory, or government purposes;
- for promoting or maintaining equality of opportunity or treatment;
- for the purpose of prevention or detection of an unlawful act;
- for the protection of the public against dishonesty, malpractice, incompetence, or mismanagement in the administration of a body or association;

- for 'special purposes' (journalism, academic, artistic, or literary purposes) where an unlawful act has been committed or there has been malpractice, incompetence or mismanagement in the administration of a body or association and the controller believes that publication would be in the public interest;
- for the prevention of fraud (in relation to an anti-fraud organization);
- for disclosures in relation to terrorist financing or money laundering;
- for the provision of confidential counselling where the consent of the data subject cannot reasonably be obtained;
- for carrying on certain types of insurance (relating to disclosure of certain health data of relations of an insured);
- for third party data processing for group insurance policies and insurance on the life of another;
- for the administration of an occupational pension scheme;
- for political activities, including campaigning, fundraising, and political surveys (relating to disclosure of political opinions carried out by a registered person or organization);
- to enable an elected representative to respond to requests;
- to enable disclosure to an elected representative if necessary;
- for the purpose of informing an elected representative about a prisoner; or
- for the identification or prevention of doping in sport.

Those practitioners familiar with the old conditions for processing sensitive personal data will recognize a number of these substantial public interest conditions from the 1998 Act. The Regulation did not provide specific exceptions for many of these purposes, so the UK has chosen to exercise its powers of derogation to include them under the umbrella of substantial public interest where they are not provided for elsewhere in Article 9.

The notable new entries are the rights to process special categories of personal data to help prevent the financing of terrorism and money laundering and to prevent the use of performance enhancing drugs by sports men and women. The intent behind the relaxation of privacy in these areas is clear but is likely to be criticized by some.

The specific condition of processing personal data necessary for a third party insurance contract (where the insured is not the one taking out the policy) is also new. The condition for processing pensions is also slightly wider because processing is no longer restricted to processing personal data relating to the family of the pension scheme member.

The journalism exemption is still available as a 'special purpose' where it is in the public interest to expose malpractice. At the time of writing, the controller will be in breach if the personal data are not being processed 'only for the special purposes'

(Section 164 of the Bill). The controller must, therefore, be careful not to use the special category personal data for another purpose.

In 2014 the ICO investigated Global Witness, a not-for-profit, non-governmental organization that campaigns to raise awareness about global environmental issues. The Information Commissioner found that even though Global Witness were not professional journalists they were publishing personal data for the purpose of journalism and that it was in the public interest to uncover the controversial Simandou deal.

The Bill has added 'academic purposes' into the definition of special purposes alongside journalism, art, and literature. This may benefit the likes of Global Witness and academic institutions who wish to expose incompetence by publishing papers which may not qualify as journalism.

The bulk collection of communications data under the Investigatory Powers Act 2016 will no doubt rely on one of the substantial public interest conditions, maybe the necessity to exercise a function conferred by an enactment (Schedule 1, Part 2(6) of the Bill). The UK government believes that this law is proportionate to the aim pursued, which is to tackle terrorism and serious crime, but also safeguards the data protection rights of individuals by the inclusion of oversight mechanisms and a special privacy clause. Not everyone agrees that the correct balance has been struck, but additional protection has been added since the Investigatory Powers Bill was first introduced.

Data sharing for the prevention of fraud could be more limited under the Bill as the processing must be of personal data disclosed by (or in accordance with arrangements made by) an anti-fraud organization (Schedule 1, Part 2(11) of the Bill). Under the 1998 Act private companies carried out checks, for example to prevent the fraudulent use of payment cards or to prevent duplicate applications for 'new customer offers'.

The insurance exemption is contained within the substantial public interest conditions, although the condition itself does not require the controller to evidence any reason of public interest (Schedule 1, Part 2(14) of the Bill). Insurance companies are concerned that this right to process special categories of personal data only applies to certain lines of insurance and does not cover motor or home insurance. Insurers may have relied in the past on implied consent to obtain details of health issues or criminal convictions, but consent will be more difficult in the future given the transparency requirements, the prohibition on making consent conditional to the offer of an insurance policy, and the right of individuals to freely withdraw their consent at any time. Insurance companies may have to do without valuable information which they rely on for underwriting premiums and handling claims.

An example of a case under the 1998 Act in which the court considered the public interest exception in the context of sensitive personal data is *Stone v South East Coast SHA (formerly Kent and Medway SHA) ([2006] EWHC 1668)*. The court concluded that where the public interest required publication in full of a report following an independent inquiry into the care, treatment, and supervision of the claimant prior to his committing two murders and one attempted murder, the decision to publish details from his medical records was justified and proportionate and did not constitute an unwarranted interference with the claimant's rights under the Act or under the European Convention on Human Rights 1950.

If a case for 'substantial public interest' can be made out under this condition, then it should be straightforward to meet the lower threshold for 'public interest' in Article 6(1)(e).

Processing is necessary for the provision of medical or social care or treatment

Here, the controller must show that the processing is necessary for:

- the purposes of preventive or occupational medicine;
- the assessment of the working capacity of the employee;
- medical diagnosis;
- the provision of health care or treatment;
- the provision of social care; or
- the management of health or social care systems or services.

Due to additional safeguards required under Article 9(3), the controller must also establish that the data are processed under the responsibility of a professional under an obligation of professional secrecy. In the UK, according to the Bill, the supervision of a health professional or a social work professional will satisfy this test (Section 10(1)). There is a long list of roles which qualify as health professionals and social work professionals in Section 183 of the Bill, including registered dentists, opticians, and osteopaths, as was the case under the 1998 Act.

The NHS needs some flexibility to process health data without obtaining explicit consent every time. The General Medical Council's confidentiality guidance recognizes the utmost importance of patient confidentiality but also the need to disclose confidential patient data in certain circumstances, for example reporting to the DVLA, reporting gunshot and knife wounds, disclosing information about serious communicable diseases, and information for insurance purposes.

The reference to social care is new alongside health care. This is an important recognition of the services provided to vulnerable people including those with disabilities which may not relate strictly to their health but will involve special category personal data.

Processing under this condition could take many forms so it will depend on the facts which of the Article 6 conditions will be most appropriate to use.

Processing is necessary for reasons of public interest in the area of public health

This is a new condition introduced by the Regulation.

The Bill states that this condition will be met if the processing is:

- necessary for reasons of public interest in the area of public health; and
- carried out under the supervision of a health professional or someone else with a legal duty of confidentiality.

The Regulation cites these specific examples:

- protection against serious cross-border threats to health; and
- ensuring high standards of quality and safety of health care, medicinal products, or medical devices.

In July 2017 the Royal Free Hospital was made to sign an ICO undertaking in respect of unlawful processing of over one million patient records by a third party, DeepMind, for clinical safety testing for a kidney injury detection, diagnosis, and prevention mobile application. The ICO was not satisfied that the Royal Free had evidenced a condition for lawful processing or obtained the consent of the patients whose sensitive personal data had been used in the trial. It is possible that this new public health condition under the Regulation could apply in this scenario, for at least some of the data.

The obligation of professional secrecy is broadly worded to extend beyond doctor–patient confidentiality and could include those bound by the Official Secrets Act or equivalent legislation in relation to cross-border threats. Given that this is a new provision, it remains to be seen how this condition is used in practice.

This condition is focused on public health so any processing of special category personal data should fulfil the criteria for processing necessary in the public interest under Article 6(1)(e).

Processing is necessary for archiving in the public interest, scientific or historical research, or statistical purposes

According to the GDPR, the processing must:

- be necessary for archiving purposes in the public interest, scientific or historical research purposes, or statistical purposes; and
- comply with Article 89(1) of the Regulation.

The Bill goes beyond the GDPR and requires the scientific or historical research and the statistical purposes to also be 'in the public interest'. At the time of writing, lobbying was taking place for the removal of this additional requirement in order to further innovation.

Article 89(1) requires that technical and organizational measures are in place to comply, in particular with the principle of data minimization. This may be achieved by pseudonymization (where the personal identifiers are removed and replaced with ID numbers, for example), even though such data will still be personal data and must still be processed in accordance with the Regulation.

Article 89 stipulates that where possible the archiving or research should be undertaken without identifying data subjects, although if truly anonymized the data would not be personal data and the Regulation would not apply.

Article 89 is concerned with safeguarding the rights and freedoms of individuals and, in the UK, the Bill states that the processing must *not* be 'carried out for the purposes of measures or decisions with respect to a particular data subject' or if 'it is likely to cause substantial damage or distress to an individual' (Section 18).

This condition recognizes the importance of a range of research by the private and public sectors for the benefit of society so long as the necessary safeguards and protections for individuals are in place. As technology advances and the number of internet-enabled devices per household continues to rise, the capture and analysis of 'big data' has become commonplace and more challenging from a privacy perspective.

Archiving must be in the public interest but may be carried out by private bodies according to Recital 158. This Recital also refers to potential legal obligations to 'acquire, preserve, appraise, arrange, describe, communicate, promote, disseminate and provide access to records of enduring value for general public interest' which could be lawfully processed under this condition if other safeguards are met.

Recital 157 refers to potential benefits to society and increased efficiency of social services through the use of information from registries to facilitate research on medical conditions, unemployment, and education. Such scientific research is permitted under the Regulation subject to compliance with the appropriate safeguards.

Recital 159 states that:

processing of personal data for scientific research purposes should be interpreted in a broad manner including for example technological development and demonstration, fundamental research, applied research and privately funded research. In addition, it should take into account the Union's objective under Article 179(1) TFEU of achieving a European Research Area.

One of the objectives of the European Research Area is to encourage the circulation of scientific knowledge and technology.

Medical research was expressly permitted under the 'medical purposes' condition in the 1998 Act. There is no express reference to medical purposes in the Regulation but the 'intelligence services' have the right to process personal data for 'medical purposes' including medical research when undertaken by a health professional under the Bill (Schedule 10). There are also specific laws governing medical research, for example clinical trials, which are highly regulated in the UK.

According to Recital 159, 'Scientific research purposes should also include studies conducted in the public interest in the area of public health'. This creates an overlap for processing in the public interest in the area of public health.

Historical research includes genealogical research (according to Recital 160), although the Regulation does not apply to deceased persons.

Recital 162 helpfully states that statistical purposes means 'any operation of collection and the processing of personal data necessary for statistical surveys or for the production of statistical results'. The compilation and analysis of statistical data is likely to result in 'aggregate data', which is not personal data.

Additional protection applies to confidential information collected by EU and national statistical authorities.

Market research is likely to fall within the meaning of 'statistical purposes' unless the research is of a scientific or historic nature.

Note that there are no grace provisions for research which has already commenced, so all research must comply from 25 May 2018.

As far as Article 6 is concerned, processing under this condition may fall within public interest under Article 6(1)(e) or legitimate interests under Article 6(1)(f). If not, then the data subject's consent may need to be obtained (Article 6(1)(a)). Note that individuals must be permitted to restrict their consent to certain areas of research or parts of research projects (according to Recital 33).

Personal Data Relating to Criminal Convictions and Offences

The balance between the prevention of crime and the privacy of those connected with criminal offences and alleged criminal offences is difficult. Clause 10 of the Bill confirms that personal data relating to criminal convictions and offences or related security measures ('criminal data') includes personal data relating to the *alleged* commission of offences by the data subject, proceedings for the offence, and disposal of such proceedings including sentencing. For example, CCTV footage showing an employee stealing in the workplace would be criminal data.

Under the Regulation, criminal data do not form part of special category personal data. These categories of data are dealt with separately. Article 10 states:

Processing of personal data relating to criminal convictions and offences or related security measures based on Article 6(1) shall be carried out only under the control of official authority or when the processing is authorised by Union or Member State law providing for appropriate safeguards for the rights and freedoms of data subjects. Any comprehensive register of criminal convictions shall be kept only under the control of official authority.

Processing of criminal data under the 'control of official authority' is governed by Part 3 of the Bill which contains a whole raft of provisions regulating the processing of law enforcement data by 'competent authorities'.

Processing of criminal data by anyone else is treated in much the same way as special categories of personal data in Part 2 of the Bill. For example, background checks completed by employers may result in the collection of criminal data. Lawful processing must meet one of the Schedule 1 conditions. Parts 1 and 2 of Schedule 1 are discussed above (conditions relating to employment, health, research, and substantial public interest) but Part 3 contains conditions specifically relating to the processing of criminal data by private sector controllers.

The Schedule 1, Part 3 conditions are met if:

- the data subject has given consent;
- processing is necessary for the protection of an individual's vital interests and the data subject is incapable of giving consent;
- processing is by a not-for-profit body and additional safeguards are met;
- the personal data are already in the public domain;

- processing is necessary to pursue or defend a legal claim or a court is acting in a judicial capacity; or

- processing is necessary for the administration of accounts used in commission of indecency offences involving young children; or

- one of the conditions in Part 2 would be proven 'but for an express requirement for the processing to be necessary for reasons of substantial public interest' and the additional safeguards (including maintenance of a processing policy) are met.

Insurance companies should, therefore, be able to use the insurance condition (in Schedule 1, Part 2 (14)) to process criminal data without consent for underwriting and processing claims in relation to the defined 'insurance business', but this will not be available for motor policies, for which details of motoring convictions are commonly sought.

Processing of any personal data by a 'competent authority' for law enforcement purposes will be governed by Part 3 of the Bill, not just the processing of criminal data.

Competent authorities include UK ministerial government departments, the police, HMRC, SFO, FCA and other UK investigatory authorities, ICO, courts, and various authorities responsible for offender management, for example the Parole Board and private contractors for probation services and prisoner escort arrangements, etc. Any processing of criminal data by an 'intelligence service' is regulated by Part 4 of the Bill.

Law enforcement purposes are widely defined as 'the prevention, investigation, detection or prosecution of criminal offences or the execution of criminal penalties, including the safeguarding against and the prevention of threats to public security'.

The processing of criminal data by a competent authority is *not* 'sensitive processing' (Section 33(8) of the Bill) unless that data reveals the individual's racial origin or details of their health, etc. (as per Article 9 GDPR). Conversely, the processing of criminal data by the intelligence services *is* 'sensitive processing' (Section 84(7) of the Bill).

Part 3, Chapter 2 applies the same six basic data protection Principles to law enforcement processing as to any personal data under Article 5 GDPR, but there are some conditions attached. The controller must be able to demonstrate compliance with the whole of Chapter 2 to be compliant. In all cases the law enforcement purpose must be 'based on law' and the competent authority must either have the consent of the data subject or the processing must be necessary for the performance of that purpose by that competent authority. A higher standard applies where the competent authority is conducting 'sensitive processing'. Where sensitive processing is carried out, either:

- the data subject must have given consent *and* the controller must have an appropriate policy document in place; or

- the processing must be 'strictly necessary' for the law enforcement purpose and must meet one of the Schedule 8 conditions, *and* the controller must have an appropriate policy document in place.

The Schedule 8 conditions, which mirror some of the conditions for lawful processing in Article 9, include:

- judicial and statutory purposes;
- protecting individuals' vital interests;
- personal data already in the public domain;
- pursuing or defending legal claims and courts acting in a judicial capacity;
- preventing fraud; and
- archiving in the public interests, scientific or historical research, or statistical purposes.

As noted above, there is no requirement for competent authorities to prove the consent of the data subject (or that consent has been withheld) for sensitive processing where it is necessary to protect the vital interests of the data subject or another person (Schedule 8 of the Bill). Compliance is harder for the intelligence services because at the very least they must prove that the data subject has unreasonably withheld consent (Schedule 10 of the Bill).

The fourth data protection Principle in Part 3 is accuracy. There are additional requirements for competent authorities in relation to the categorization of personal data and its verification before it is transmitted or made available (Section 36 of the Bill).

Where the competent authority wants to use personal data collected for one law enforcement purpose for another law enforcement purpose (maybe processed by a different controller) it must be 'authorised by law', necessary and proportionate to that other purpose (Section 34(3) of the Bill). The Bill goes further to allow personal data collected for a law enforcement purpose to be processed for a purpose that is not a law enforcement purpose if the processing is 'authorised by law (Section 34(4) of the Bill). These provisions give public bodies more flexibility than their private sector peers.

The processing of personal data for law enforcement purposes will only be permitted for archiving, scientific or historical research, or statistical purposes where it is necessary, does not single out a particular individual, and is unlikely to cause substantial damage or distress to an individual (Section 39 of the Bill).

The appropriate policy document mandated in Part 3 is the same as that required of other controllers processing special categories of personal data in the field of employment, social security, or social protection law under Article 9(2)(b) (see discussion above on processing policies).

Part 3 of the Bill implements the Law Enforcement Directive (2016/6802 see <http://www.dpdocuments.com>). The aim is to harmonize the cross border and domestic regimes for processing of law enforcement data.

Advice on Processing Special Category Personal Data

Controllers and processors should take extra care to understand their new obligations regarding the processing of special category personal data under the Regulation and the Bill in order to minimize the risk of enforcement action.

Research undertaken for publication in *Privacy & Data Protection* (see Volume 12, Issue 8—<http://www.pdpjournal.com>) revealed that unlawful processing of sensitive personal data under the 1998 Act featured in a significant majority of all monetary penalties issued by the ICO. According to the ICO there were 3,615 reported data breaches between April 2015 and December 2016. Of these, by far the highest number (1,551) were in the health sector, which very likely involved sensitive personal data. Although the ICO's fining powers at that time were limited to a maximum of £500,000, the majority of the higher fines issued were for breaches involving sensitive personal data and the frequency of larger fines is increasing.

Some pre-GDPR examples of monetary penalties issued by the ICO in connection with breaches involving sensitive personal data include:

- £200,000 fine in November 2015 against the Crown Prosecution Service after laptops containing videos of police interviews with forty-three victims and witnesses in connection with thirty-one investigations into violent or sexual crimes were stolen from a private film studio.

- £250,000 fine in December 2015 against the Bloomsbury Patient Network after it inadvertently revealed the identities of HIV patients by sending out a newsletter using a list of email addresses in the 'to' field rather than the 'bcc' field.

- £185,000 fine in May 2016 against Blackpool Teaching Hospitals NHS Foundation Trust for inadvertently publishing the private details of 6,574 staff members, including National Insurance numbers, dates of birth, religious beliefs, and sexual orientations.

- £200,000 fine in February 2017 against a private health company, HCA International Ltd, after transcripts of conversations between a doctor and patients about IVF treatment could be accessed online due to a hospital having sent unencrypted audio records of the conversations to a company in India which transcribed them and stored audio files and transcripts on an unsecure server.

- £150,000 fine in May 2017 against Basildon Borough Council for publishing on its web-based planning portal a statement in support of a planning application containing details of a 'traveller family' living on the site including details of their disability requirements and mental health issues. *Please note that this decision was due for an appeal hearing in December 2017.*

- £150,000 fine in May 2017 against Greater Manchester Police for losing unencrypted DVDs containing videos of police interviews with victims of violent or sexual crimes which they had sent to NCA's Serious Crime Analysis Section by Recorded Delivery. The DVDs never arrived and were not recovered. The penalty notice suggests that sending the DVDs by Special Delivery or by courier would have been deemed acceptable but entities must check and comply with any applicable data handling policies in force.

- £100,000 fine in May 2017 against Gloucester City Council after a cyber-attack which gained access to 30 or more email accounts containing sensitive personal data. The Council had failed to implement adequate security measures to protect the personal data and had failed to apply a software patch to prevent the attack even though they were aware of the vulnerability.

In the future, infringements of the data protection Principles or the conditions for processing personal data (Articles 5, 6, and 9) will be subject to the new higher level fines: up to 20 million or up to 4% of total worldwide turnover (whichever is the greater). See Chapter 8 for details of other potential sanctions.

With the increased emphasis on transparency and accountability and the greater focus on documenting the types of data, the purpose of processing, and the conditions relied upon, individuals are likely to be more aware of their rights, which is likely to cause an increase in the number of complaints to the ICO and ICO investigations.

The GDPR states that the controller is responsible for demonstrating compliance with the Article 5 principles relating to processing of personal data but there are many new direct obligations placed on processors by the Regulation. It is not clear whether processors can be directly liable for unlawful processing of special category personal data but the Regulation requires the controller and the processor to enter into a binding processor contract (Article 28(3) under which the processor will be obliged to assist the controller with data protection compliance. According to Article 82(2) a processor shall only be liable where it has not complied with the obligations under GDPR which are 'specifically directed to processors or where it has acted outside or contrary to lawful instructions of the controller'. There is an equivalent provision in the Bill (Section 160(2)). However, if a processor 'infringes [the] Regulation by determining the purposes and means of processing, the processor shall be considered to be a controller in respect of that processing' (Article 28(10)). So, processors should take care not to inadvertently become controllers.

Controllers should undertake a data mapping exercise to review all data processing activities to determine what personal data are processed, and why and how they are processed. The revised GDPR definition of personal data (see Chapter 1) should be borne in mind, as should the new categories of special category personal data, which are genetic and biometric data and data concerning a person's sexual orientation, and the new conditions for processing special category personal data.

Entities should audit IT systems and manual records, and interview key employees about business processes. This exercise will enable controllers (and processors where necessary) to produce processing records required under Article 30 (note that the small company exemption from record keeping does not apply where an organization is processing special category personal data or criminal data (Article 30(5))) and to create the processing policies required under the Bill (Schedule 1, Part 4). The controller must analyse whether each and every instance of special category personal data processing benefits from at least one of the conditions specified above. Should any special category personal data processing not be covered by at least one condition, the controller must determine whether it is able to amend or alter the processing in such a way that it benefits from one of the legitimizing conditions.

The exercise may require some lateral thinking, for example, even if an application or registration form (whether online or in hard-copy format) used by a controller for gathering customer details in its business does not expressly request special category personal data per se, such data may nevertheless be supplied by the customer when completing the form. For this reason, free-form answer boxes should be avoided where possible. Where the data subject does supply special category personal data in a free-form answer, appropriate procedures should be adopted to ensure that the data are not processed (or further processed) by the controller in a manner that constitutes a breach of the Regulation, for example by ensuring that such information is ignored by the keyboard operators when inputting the data into the system, or by deleting the data where they have already been provided in electronic form by the individual, for instance via a web page or app.

Where special category personal data processing is an essential part of the controller's activities, the controller should try to avoid relying on consent for processing; consent is ephemeral as it can be withdrawn by the relevant individual and thus does not constitute a solid foundation on which to build data processing activities.

ICO guidance warns against using consent where another ground exists and the data subject does not have a genuine choice, for example in the health care sector an individual may be misled into believing they have the choice to refuse consent, whereas in reality the processing could be carried out under Article 9(2)(h). Where no ground for lawful processing exists, the processor must rely on consent. Remember that implied consent will not qualify as explicit consent. For best practice, the controller should obtain the signature of the individual or use a tick-box (opt-in) arrangement with a clear explanation of what the individual is consenting to. Controllers should remember that they are expected to keep records relating to all consents obtained.

Article 35 requires a controller to conduct a data protection impact assessment ('DPIA') where the entity processes on a large scale special category personal data or criminal data, prior to commencing the processing (see Chapter 11).

Article 37 requires a controller and a processor to appoint a Data Protection Officer ('DPO') to monitor compliance with the Regulation where their core activities 'consist of processing on a large scale' special category personal data or criminal data. Public authorities must appoint a DPO regardless of the type of processing (see Chapter 12).

The Article 29 Working Party recommends (in their guidelines on DPOs and DPIAs) considering the number of data subjects, the volume of data, and the duration and geographical extent of processing to determine whether processing is carried out on a large scale. They also plan to publish examples of the relevant thresholds for the designation of DPOs, but in the meantime organizations are encouraged to appoint a DPO on a voluntary basis.

Even controllers and processors established outside the EU must comply with the Regulation if they offer goods or services within the EU or where they monitor data subjects in the EU. Private companies processing special category personal data or criminal data on a large scale must designate a representative in each Member State where data subjects are based.

Despite the desire for harmonization of European data protection laws, the GDPR has given member states a significant degree of flexibility to establish their own lawful processing conditions. For example, the UK has chosen to exercise its powers of derogation to implement many of the old conditions for processing special category personal data which existed under the 1998 Act. Controllers and processors must, therefore, be cautious when operating outside of the UK to ensure that they are complying with local laws.

5

Data Security and Breach Notifications

Ann Bevitt and Peter Carey

Introduction	88
Obligations of the Controller and Processor	91
Privacy by Design and Privacy by Default	95
Pseudonymization	96
Privacy Enhancing Technologies	97
ISO 27001	97
Security and Outsourcing	98
Security and Exports	98
Security Breaches	98
Notifying Security Breaches	100
Advice on Breach Notification	104

Introduction

Security of personal data processing is fundamental to data protection law. Controllers and processors should adopt a risk-based approach to the determination of what type of data security measures to implement. In making this determination, they will need to bear in mind the sensitivity (both in a legal and a more general sense) of the personal information that they process, the cost of implementation of relevant measures, as well as the resources that they have available.

Data security is an ongoing responsibility of controllers and processors, since it is applicable to every aspect of processing, and so they should keep up to date with changing technology and security procedures so that the organization remains compliant over time.

The legal requirement to ensure the security of personal data processing derives from Recital 83 and Article 32 of the GDPR, as shown in Box 5.1.

Perhaps it goes without saying, but maximum security can only be achieved by not processing any personal data at all. Indeed, a general principle of data protection is that personal data should be used by an organization only where necessary.

Box 5.1 Data Security

Recital 83 GDPR

In order to maintain security and to prevent processing in infringement of this Regulation, the controller or processor should evaluate the risks inherent in the processing and implement measures to mitigate those risks, such as encryption. Those measures should ensure an appropriate level of security, including confidentiality, taking into account the state of the art and the costs of implementation in relation to the risks and the nature of the personal data to be protected. In assessing data security risk, consideration should be given to the risks that are presented by personal data processing, such as accidental or unlawful destruction, loss, alteration, unauthorised disclosure of, or access to, personal data transmitted, stored or otherwise processed which may in particular lead to physical, material or non-material damage.

Article 32 GDPR

1. Taking into account the state of the art, the costs of implementation and the nature, scope, context and purposes of processing as well as the risk of varying likelihood and severity for the rights and freedoms of natural persons, the controller and the processor shall implement appropriate technical and organisational measures to ensure a level of security appropriate to the risk, including inter alia as appropriate:

    a. the pseudonymisation and encryption of personal data;

    b. the ability to ensure the ongoing confidentiality, integrity, availability and resilience of processing systems and services;

    c. the ability to restore the availability and access to personal data in a timely manner in the event of a physical or technical incident;

    d. a process for regularly testing, assessing and evaluating the effectiveness of technical and organisational measures for ensuring the security of the processing.

2. In assessing the appropriate level of security account shall be taken in particular of the risks that are presented by processing, in particular from accidental or unlawful destruction, loss, alteration, unauthorised disclosure of, or access to personal data transmitted, stored or otherwise processed.

3. Adherence to an approved code of conduct as referred to in Article 40 or an approved certification mechanism as referred to in Article 42 may be used as an element by which to demonstrate compliance with the requirements set out in paragraph 1 of this Article.

4. The controller and processor shall take steps to ensure that any natural person acting under the authority of the controller or the processor who has access to personal data does not process them except on instructions from the controller, unless he or she is required to do so by Union or Member State law.

In other words, consideration should be given, for each instance of personal data processing, as to whether the job could be done without using personal data.

This 'data minimization' principle also applies to the number of copies of personal data in existence in an organization, which should be kept to a minimum. An example of too many copies of personal data being created is where the organization clones a database in order for IT support to be carried out. The risk of information falling into the wrong hands is multiplied for each additional cloned version of the database that is in existence. A further example of too many copies occurs where back-up media are stored in multiples instead of being overwritten.

Organizations should ideally designate a particular individual to have overall responsibility for the day-to-day management of personal data security. As with a Data Protection Officer ('DPO') (in some organizations both jobs will be performed by the same person), this position should report directly to the highest management level of the organization, as he or she will need both the stature and authority necessary to take relevant action. The individual's responsibilities are likely to include ensuring that staff are trained on data security matters, the drafting of procedures and policies for keeping data secure, checking for compliance with those procedures and policies, investigating security incidents including the monitoring of relevant members of staff, making recommendations for change, and dealing with data breaches including making relevant notifications as required (see below).

Although the legal obligations extend only to the processing of 'personal data', in practical terms an organization is likely to want additional information to be held securely, even where it does not amount to information to which data protection law is applicable—examples include trading methods, financial reports, and commercial secrets.

Set out below are examples of security breaches in the UK which resulted in monetary penalties being issued by the Information Commissioner prior to the coming into force of the GDPR. At the time that these monetary penalties were issued, there was a cap of £500,000. Since the cap on administrative fines under the GDPR is significantly higher (see Chapter 8), it is anticipated that similar breaches in future will attract significantly higher penalties.

- A telecoms company received a monetary penalty of £400,000 for security failings that allowed a cyber-attacker to access customer data 'with ease'. The company failed to put in place appropriate technical and organizational measures to ensure that personal data held on a database could not be accessed by an attacker performing an SQL injection attack.

- An insurance company was fined £150,000 following the theft of a hard drive containing the personal information of nearly 60,000 customers. The company did not have appropriate measures in place to prevent the theft by a member of staff or a contractor and the information was not encrypted.

- An NHS Trust received a penalty of £185,000 after inadvertently publishing the private details of 6,574 members of staff, including their National Insurance number, date of birth, religious belief, and sexual orientation. The Trust had no procedure in place governing requests for information from the electronic staff records system and provided no training on the functionality of Excel spreadsheets to staff, or guidance on checking for hidden data before uploading spreadsheets to the website.

- A local police force was ordered to pay a penalty of £100,000 for failing to take appropriate measures to ensure that the basement of a former police station had been cleared of all items before it was sold to a buyer—the buyer discovered copies of interview tapes and other documents on the premises.

- A pregnancy advice service was fined £200,000 for failing to keep online information sufficiently secure—the charity's website had stored the names, addresses, dates of birth, and telephone numbers of people who asked to be telephoned in order to obtain advice on pregnancy issues. The data were not stored securely and a vulnerability in the website's code allowed a hacker to access the system and locate the information.

- A government department was fined £140,000 for failing to provide adequate training for staff in data protection matters—the details of all the prisoners serving time at a prison were emailed to three of the inmates' families.

- A local government body received a monetary penalty of £100,000 for failing to have an effective home-working policy—information relating to the involvement of a social services department with several individuals was published online after a council employee accessed documents, including meeting minutes and detailed reports, from her home computer.

- A bank's monetary penalty of £75,000 resulted from a failure to have adequate staff training procedures in place—a customer's account details were faxed to the wrong recipients.

- An NHS Trust received a penalty of £200,000 when some personal data were sold at an auction—approximately 3,000 patient records were found on a second-hand computer bought through an online auction site.

- A computer company received a penalty of £250,000 for failing to keep online information secure—an entertainment platform was hacked, compromising the personal information of millions of customers, including their names, addresses, email addresses, dates of birth, and account passwords.

Obligations of the Controller and Processor

The first step towards compliance with the security requirements in the GDPR is to make an assessment of the extent of any relevant personal data to be protected. The legal requirement for data security extends to the processing of personal data:

- wholly or partly by automated means; and
- other than by automated means where the personal data form part of a 'filing system' (see the definition in Chapter 1) or are intended to form part of a filing system.

The legal obligation on controllers and processors, under Article 32, is for them to adopt 'appropriate technical and organisational measures to ensure a level of security appropriate to the risk'. Controllers and processors therefore need to take a risk-based approach to security.

Appropriate

When determining what measures are *appropriate*, controllers and processors are required to take into account:

(a) the state of the art;

(b) the costs of implementation;

(c) the nature, scope, context, and purposes of processing; and

(d) the risk of varying likelihood and severity for the rights and freedoms of natural persons.

In addition, controllers and processors may be able to demonstrate, at least in part, their compliance with the data security requirement by their adherence to codes of conduct which cover measures to ensure security of processing, and which have been prepared by associations and other bodies representing categories of controllers or processors and approved by the competent supervisory authority. Similarly, controllers and processors may also be able to rely, again in part, on their adherence to certification mechanisms accredited by the competent supervisory authority. For further information on codes of conduct and certification mechanisms, see Chapter 1.

The GDPR provides a list of security measures which may be considered 'appropriate to the risk' and are designed to integrate the necessary safeguards into the processing of personal data. These are:

(a) the pseudonymization and encryption of personal data;

(b) the ability to ensure the ongoing confidentiality, integrity, availability, and resilience of processing systems and services;

(c) the ability to restore the availability and access to personal data in a timely manner in the event of a physical or technical incident; and

(d) a process for regularly testing, assessing, and evaluating the effectiveness of technical and organizational measures for ensuring the security of the processing.

Although all of these measures may not be appropriate in all circumstances, given that they are listed in the GDPR as examples of appropriate measures, controllers and processors should always consider each of them and have good grounds for rejecting them if they do not implement them in a particular case.

Controllers and processors should carry out a risk assessment to determine what level of expenditure and commitment is appropriate, bearing in mind all of the circumstances of the controller's or processor's processing operations. What will be appropriate for one controller or processor will not necessarily be appropriate for another. For example, a large multinational business will usually have more resources to expend on security measures than a domestic small or medium sized enterprise ('SME'). However, the appropriateness of measures does not just depend on the size of the controller or processor. It may be, for example, that a small controller or processor with limited resources processes personal data that are of a type which merit high levels of protection—examples include local doctors' surgeries in respect of medical data, and travel agents that store records of the periods of time during which people will be absent from their homes.

In determining appropriateness, controllers and processors should also consider the extent of possible damage or loss that might be caused to individuals (e.g. staff or customers) if a security breach occurs, the effect of any security breach on the organization itself, and any likely reputational damage as well as the possible loss of customer trust.

Technical

When assessing what *technical* measures are appropriate to employ, IT expertise should be sought. Examples of technical measures include pseudonymization (see the definition in Chapter 1), secure password protection for computer access, encryption of hard drives, automatic locking of idle terminals, and removal of access rights for USB and other memory media. Appropriate virus-checking software and firewalls should be used to protect the integrity and security of electronically processed data.

Recital 49 of the GDPR recognizes that data processing to ensure network and information security constitutes a legitimate interest. Such processing may be aimed at preventing unauthorized access to electronic communications networks and malicious code distribution and stopping 'denial of service' attacks and damage to computer and electronic communication systems. It also provides some guidance on what such testing of networks and systems is designed to assess, namely the ability to resist, at a given level of confidence, accidental events or unlawful or malicious actions that compromise the availability, authenticity, integrity, and confidentiality of stored or transmitted personal data, and the security of any related services offered by, or accessible via, those networks and systems.

Employees should generally have their access to personal data within the computer systems restricted to that which is necessary for their jobs. This is usually undertaken by establishing hierarchical permissions which apply to each employee as identified by their log-in methodology. Special care should be taken to restrict the access rights of temporary staff.

Where members of staff are to be permitted to take laptops away from the controller's or processor's premises, those laptops must be encrypted, a relatively inexpensive process which safeguards the information stored on the machine's hard drive even where it falls into the wrong hands. However, encryption should not be treated as the 'last word' on security measures for laptops, and other appropriate protections should also be considered.

Where a wireless local area network is used by an organization, steps should be taken to ensure the security of the network.

Organizational

Organizational measures include relevant and appropriate training for all staff members that use, or have access to, personal data in the workplace. What is appropriate will depend on the circumstances. For employees who handle personal data rarely, or in a manner that could have few potentially adverse consequences, a basic training procedure can be adopted. Heads of department or compliance personnel will usually merit more comprehensive training. For larger organizations, a designated person in each relevant department (e.g. Human Resources, Marketing, Customer Services, and Finance) should be well trained on the requirements of data protection law. That person would then act as the initial point of contact for queries within that department, and would often report to a central DPO or Compliance Officer, who may hold a recognized qualification in data protection, such as the Practitioner Certificate in Data Protection (<http://www.dataprotectionqualification.com>).

The legislation obliges controllers and processors to take steps to ensure that their employees only process personal data on instructions from the controller, unless required to do otherwise by law (Article 32(4)). In addition to putting in place relevant staff training procedures, employers should take appropriate references before employment is commenced. Where the organization has a data protection policy, or equivalent, this should be published in the staff handbook or other relevant accessible location. Where a member of staff is found to have breached the policy, appropriate disciplinary action should follow, not least so that employees are aware that such breaches are taken seriously by the organization.

Other examples of appropriate organizational security measures include:

- the monitoring of staff to check for compliance with relevant security standards;
- controlling physical access to IT systems and areas where paper-based data are stored—this can be done by installing appropriate building security measures including card entry or biometric access systems and locked doors;
- adopting a clear desk policy—so that paper-based personal data are not easily accessible to cleaning staff and others who may gain access to relevant areas;
- storing paper-based data in lockable fire-proof cabinets when not in use;
- restricting the use of portable electronic devices outside of the workplace;
- preventing, or restricting, the use of an employee's own personal electronic device for work purposes (see further, Whitcroft O, 'Bring Your Own Device—Protecting Data on the Move', *Privacy & Data Protection*, Volume 13, Issue 4—<http://www.pdpjournal.com>);
- positioning computer screens so that they are not visible to people outside the premises or from corridors within the premises;
- having clear rules about passwords, such as that they must not be written down and stored (or displayed) near the computer equipment to which they relate;
- adopting appropriate techniques for the destruction of both electronically and manually held personal data; and
- making regular back-ups of personal data and storing the media off-site.

Privacy by Design and Privacy by Default

Controllers are required to implement technical and organizational measures to show that they have considered and integrated data compliance measures (including in respect of data security) into their data processing activities. In particular, when designing systems and technologies, controllers should build in privacy from the outset rather than bolting it on at the end—that is, they should adopt a 'privacy by design' (see the definition in Chapter 1) approach. Examples of such an approach include automatically selecting the most privacy-friendly settings where an employer issues devices to employees containing tracking technologies, and automatically minimizing the amount of data collected to that required to provide the service or perform the function.

Privacy by design is a systematic approach to designing any system or technology that embeds privacy into the underlying specifications or architecture of that system or technology. The use of default settings that favour privacy, or 'privacy by default' (see the definition in Chapter 1), is one aspect of the privacy by design approach. An example of such settings is default settings limiting publication on social platforms.

The requirements for privacy by design and privacy by default derive from Recital 78 and Article 25 of the GDPR, as shown in Box 5.2.

Box 5.2 Privacy By Design and By Default

Recital 78 GDPR

The protection of the rights and freedoms of natural persons with regard to the processing of personal data require that appropriate technical and organisational measures be taken to ensure that the requirements of this Regulation are met. In order to be able to demonstrate compliance with this Regulation, the controller should adopt internal policies and implement measures which meet in particular the principles of data protection by design and data protection by default. Such measures could consist, inter alia, of minimising the processing of personal data, pseudonymising personal data as soon as possible, transparency with regard to the functions and processing of personal data, enabling the data subject to monitor the data processing, enabling the controller to create and improve security features. When developing, designing, selecting and using applications, services and products that are based on the processing of personal data or process personal data to fulfil their task, producers of the products, services and applications should be encouraged to take into account the right to data protection when developing and designing such products, services and applications and, with due regard to the state of the art, to make sure that controllers and processors are able to fulfil their data protection obligations. The principles of data protection by design and by default should also be taken into consideration in the context of public tenders.

Article 25 GDPR

1. Taking into account the state of the art, the cost of implementation and the nature, scope, context and purposes of processing as well as the risks of varying likelihood

(continued)

and severity for the rights and freedoms of natural persons posed by the processing, the controller shall, both at the time of the determination of the means for processing and at the time of the processing itself, implement appropriate technical and organisational measures, such as pseudonymisation, which are designed to implement data-protection principles, such as data minimisation, in an effective manner and to integrate the necessary safeguards into the processing in order to meet the requirements of this Regulation and protect the rights of data subjects.

2. The controller shall implement appropriate technical and organisational measures for ensuring that, by default, only personal data which are necessary for each specific purpose of the processing are processed. That obligation applies to the amount of personal data collected, the extent of their processing, the period of their storage and their accessibility. In particular, such measures shall ensure that by default personal data are not made accessible without the individual's intervention to an indefinite number of natural persons.

3. An approved certification mechanism pursuant to Article 42 may be used as an element to demonstrate compliance with the requirements set out in paragraphs 1 and 2 of this Article.

Pseudonymization

Pseudonymization is a privacy-enhancing technique that is an example of a measure which controllers can adopt to meet the principles of privacy by design and privacy by default. It involves the processing of personal data in such a manner that the data can no longer be attributed to a specific data subject without the use of additional information which is kept separately and is subject to technical and organizational measures to ensure that the personal data are not attributed to an identified or identifiable natural person. Data which are key-coded, where the key is kept separately, are an example of pseudonymized data. Other examples include data which have been masked (identifiers are hidden with random characters or other data).

Although pseudonymization can significantly reduce the risks associated with the processing of personal data, pseudonymized data should still be considered personal data and their processing is therefore regulated by the GDPR. However, to incentivize controllers to apply pseudonymization when processing personal data, the GDPR relaxes several requirements on controllers that use the technique. For example, pseudonymization is recognized as an appropriate safeguard for the further processing of personal data which is compatible with the initial purposes of processing, thereby making it easier for controllers to process personal data for a different purpose than the one for which they were initially collected.

Privacy Enhancing Technologies

The use of so-called 'privacy enhancing technologies' ('PETs') can also help achieve the privacy by design goal. PETs are applications or tools with discrete goals that address a single dimension of privacy, such as anonymity, confidentiality, or control over personal information. They originally derived from the notion that an individual's privacy is best protected where his or her personal information is only collected when it is essential to do so.

One example of such technology is software that allows an individual to withhold his true identity from a controller's or processor's electronic systems, or reveals it only when absolutely necessary. Such an approach can help to minimize the information collected about individuals—examples of such tools include anonymous web browsers, specialist email services, and digital cash.

The Information Commissioner takes a wider view of PETs, stating that they include 'any technology that exists to protect or enhance an individual's privacy'. Examples of this wider approach could include:

- encrypted biometric access systems that allow the use of a fingerprint to authenticate an individual's identity, but do not retain the actual fingerprint;
- secure online access for individuals to their own personal data to check its accuracy and make amendments;
- software that allows browsers to detect the privacy policy of websites automatically and compare it to the preferences expressed by the user, highlighting any clashes; and
- 'sticky' electronic privacy policies that are attached to the information itself, preventing it being used in any way that is not compatible with that policy.

ISO 27001

Larger controllers and processors may wish to refer to ISO 27001, the international standard for information security management systems. Whilst it will be too expensive and time-consuming for most controllers and processors to implement fully, the standard effectively provides a useful checklist for the establishment and implementation of any information security management system. It should be noted that compliance with ISO 27001 will not necessarily mean that the organization will not fall foul of the data security requirements in data protection law.

Security and Outsourcing

Where external companies are engaged to carry out functions which involve the processing of personal data, there must be a written contract in place between the controller and the outsourcing company. That contract must contain a provision that obliges the outsourcing company to take appropriate technical and organizational security measures to ensure a level of security appropriate to the risk. The legal requirement to put in place such a contract derives from Recital 81 and Article 28 of the GDPR, as shown in Box 5.3.

The topic of outsourcing (the use of processors to carry out data processing operations on behalf of a controller) is discussed in detail in Chapter 9.

Security and Exports

When transferring personal data to organizations that are located in countries outside the EEA, controllers and processors are subject to the restrictions contained in Chapter V of the GDPR (see Chapter 6).

Whilst such a transfer is no different from any other form of personal data processing in a strictly legal sense, the security obligations will, in practice, be particularly important in this context. In particular, controllers and processors should be aware that the country of the importing organization may have no legal requirements for the security of personal data processing. It may therefore be appropriate to impose contractual obligations on the importing organization to take appropriate security measures and to restrict the importing organization's ability to make onward transfers of the data.

Further, the method of transfer itself should be scrutinized to check that personal data being transferred are adequately protected. It may be that data will need to be encrypted prior to the transfer.

Security Breaches

A 'personal data breach' is defined in Article 4(12) of the GDPR as:

a breach of security leading to the accidental or unlawful destruction, loss, alteration, unauthorised disclosure of, or access to, personal data transmitted, stored or otherwise processed.

A personal data breach can therefore be thought of as any event which results in the integrity or security of personal data being compromised. Such an event can occur for a wide variety of reasons, including loss or theft of electronic equipment on which personal data are stored, equipment failure, human error, and a successful blagging incident or hacking attack.

Box 5.3 Security and Outsourcing

Recital 81 GDPR

To ensure compliance with the requirements of this Regulation in respect of the processing to be carried out by the processor on behalf of the controller, when entrusting a processor with processing activities, the controller should use only processors providing sufficient guarantees, in particular in terms of expert knowledge, reliability and resources, to implement technical and organisational measures which will meet the requirements of this Regulation, including for the security of processing. The adherence of the processor to an approved code of conduct or an approved certification mechanism may be used as an element to demonstrate compliance with the obligations of the controller. The carrying-out of processing by a processor should be governed by a contract or other legal act under Union or Member State law, binding the processor to the controller, setting out the subject-matter and duration of the processing, the nature and purposes of the processing, the type of personal data and categories of data subjects, taking into account the specific tasks and responsibilities of the processor in the context of the processing to be carried out and the risk to the rights and freedoms of the data subject ...

Article 28 GDPR

1. Where processing is to be carried out on behalf of a controller, the controller shall use only processors providing sufficient guarantees to implement appropriate technical and organisational measures in such a manner that processing will meet the requirements of this Regulation and ensure the protection of the rights of the data subject.

   ...

3. Processing by a processor shall be governed by a contract or other legal act under Union or Member State law, that is binding on the processor with regard to the controller and that sets out the subject-matter and duration of the processing, the nature and purpose of the processing, the type of personal data and categories of data subjects and the obligations and rights of the controller. That contract or other legal act shall stipulate, in particular, that the processor:

   a. processes the personal data only on documented instructions from the controller...;

   b. ensures that persons authorised to process the personal data have committed themselves to confidentiality or are under an appropriate statutory obligation of confidentiality;

   c. takes all measures required pursuant to Article 32;

      ...

   f. assists the controller in ensuring compliance with the obligations pursuant to Articles 32 to 36 taking into account the nature of processing and the information available to the processor;

   ...

5. Adherence of a processor to an approved code of conduct as referred to in Article 40 or an approved certification mechanism as referred to in Article 42 may be used as an element by which to demonstrate sufficient guarantees as referred to in paragraphs 1 and 4 of this Article.

   ...

9. The contract or the other legal act referred to in paragraphs 3 and 4 shall be in writing, including in electronic form.

   ...

When a security breach occurs, the relevant controller or processor must, in addition to handling the breach appropriately from both practical and customer service points of view, consider whether the breach gives rise to a legal obligation to notify the breach.

Notifying Security Breaches

The requirements on controllers and processors that arise in the event of a personal data breach derive from Recitals 85–88 and Articles 33 and 34 of the GDPR, as shown in Box 5.4.

The controller has a duty to notify the competent supervisory authority of a personal data breach 'without undue delay' and, where feasible, not later than seventy-two hours after having become aware of it. If notification is not made within seventy-two hours, the controller must when notifying also provide reasons for the delay. However, if a personal data breach is 'unlikely to result in a risk for the rights and freedoms of natural persons', the controller is not required to notify the supervisory authority.

The sorts of risks envisaged vary depending on the type of data that are the subject of the breach and the type of breach, for example a breach disclosing an individual's health or financial information is likely to have a significantly higher risk to the rights and freedoms of a data subject than a breach disclosing only a name. The types of risk covered may therefore include discrimination, identity theft, fraud, financial loss, and damage to reputation or confidentiality. However, there is still some uncertainty as to how controllers should assess this risk and they may wish to err on the side of caution and notify relevant breaches until guidance is issued clarifying how they should approach this issue.

A notification to the supervisory authority must contain certain information, as set out in Article 33(3), namely:

- the nature of the breach including the categories and number of affected data subjects and personal data records;
- details of the DPO or an alternative source of information;
- the likely consequences of the breach; and
- the measures taken or proposed to mitigate the possible adverse effects of the breach.

If not all of this information is available at the time of the initial notification, it should be provided in phases, but again without undue further delay.

If a controller determines that a personal data breach is 'likely to result in a high risk to the rights and freedoms of natural persons', in addition to notifying the relevant supervisory authority, it must also provide these individuals with certain information about the breach (see Article 34(2)), without undue delay. Again, it is unclear how controllers should assess this risk and controllers may wish to err on the side of caution and notify until guidance is issued clarifying how they should approach this issue.

Box 5.4 Notification of Personal Data Breaches

Recitals 85–88 GDPR

(85) A personal data breach may, if not addressed in an appropriate and timely manner, result in physical, material or non-material damage to natural persons such as loss of control over their personal data or limitation of their rights, discrimination, identity theft or fraud, financial loss, unauthorised reversal of pseudonymisation, damage to reputation, loss of confidentiality of personal data protected by professional secrecy or any other significant economic or social disadvantage to the natural person concerned. Therefore, as soon as the controller becomes aware that a personal data breach has occurred, the controller should notify the personal data breach to the supervisory authority without undue delay and, where feasible, not later than 72 hours after having become aware of it, unless the controller is able to demonstrate, in accordance with the accountability principle, that the personal data breach is unlikely to result in a risk to the rights and freedoms of natural persons. Where such notification cannot be achieved within 72 hours, the reasons for the delay should accompany the notification and information may be provided in phases without undue further delay.

(86) The controller should communicate to the data subject a personal data breach, without undue delay, where that personal data breach is likely to result in a high risk to the rights and freedoms of the natural person in order to allow him or her to take the necessary precautions. The communication should describe the nature of the personal data breach as well as recommendations for the natural person concerned to mitigate potential adverse effects. Such communications to data subjects should be made as soon as reasonably feasible and in close cooperation with the supervisory authority, respecting guidance provided by it or by other relevant authorities such as law-enforcement authorities. For example, the need to mitigate an immediate risk of damage would call for prompt communication with data subjects whereas the need to implement appropriate measures against continuing or similar personal data breaches may justify more time for communication.

(87) It should be ascertained whether all appropriate technological protection and organisational measures have been implemented to establish immediately whether a personal data breach has taken place and to inform promptly the supervisory authority and the data subject. The fact that the notification was made without undue delay should be established taking into account in particular the nature and gravity of the personal data breach and its consequences and adverse effects for the data subject. Such notification may result in an intervention of the supervisory authority in accordance with its tasks and powers laid down in this Regulation.

(88) In setting detailed rules concerning the format and procedures applicable to the notification of personal data breaches, due consideration should be given to the circumstances of that breach, including whether or not personal data had been protected by appropriate technical protection measures, effectively limiting the likelihood of identity fraud or other forms of misuse. Moreover, such rules and procedures should take into account the legitimate interests of law-enforcement authorities where early disclosure could unnecessarily hamper the investigation of the circumstances of a personal data breach.

Article 33 GDPR

1. In the case of a personal data breach, the controller shall without undue delay and, where feasible, not later than 72 hours after having become aware of it, notify the personal data breach to the supervisory authority competent in accordance with Article

(continued)

55, unless the personal data breach is unlikely to result in a risk to the rights and freedoms of natural persons. Where the notification to the supervisory authority is not made within 72 hours, it shall be accompanied by reasons for the delay.

2. The processor shall notify the controller without undue delay after becoming aware of a personal data breach.

3. The notification referred to in paragraph 1 shall at least:

   a. describe the nature of the personal data breach including where possible, the categories and approximate number of data subjects concerned and the categories and approximate number of personal data records concerned;

   b. communicate the name and contact details of the data protection officer or other contact point where more information can be obtained;

   c. describe the likely consequences of the personal data breach;

   d. describe the measures taken or proposed to be taken by the controller to address the personal data breach, including, where appropriate, measures to mitigate its possible adverse effects.

4. Where, and in so far as, it is not possible to provide the information at the same time, the information may be provided in phases without undue further delay.

5. The controller shall document any personal data breaches, comprising the facts relating to the personal data breach, its effects and the remedial action taken. That documentation shall enable the supervisory authority to verify compliance with this Article.

Article 34 GDPR

1. When the personal data breach is likely to result in a high risk to the rights and freedoms of natural persons, the controller shall communicate the personal data breach to the data subject without undue delay.

2. The communication to the data subject referred to in paragraph 1 of this Article shall describe in clear and plain language the nature of the personal data breach and contain at least the information and measures referred to in points (b), (c) and (d) of Article 33(3).

3. The communication to the data subject referred to in paragraph 1 shall not be required if any of the following conditions are met:

   a. the controller has implemented appropriate technical and organisational protection measures, and those measures were applied to the personal data affected by the personal data breach, in particular those that render the personal data unintelligible to any person who is not authorised to access it, such as encryption;

   b. the controller has taken subsequent measures which ensure that the high risk to the rights and freedoms of data subjects referred to in paragraph 1 is no longer likely to materialise;

   c. it would involve disproportionate effort. In such a case, there shall instead be a public communication or similar measure whereby the data subjects are informed in an equally effective manner.

4. If the controller has not already communicated the personal data breach to the data subject, the supervisory authority, having considered the likelihood of the personal data breach resulting in a high risk, may require it to do so or may decide that any of the conditions referred to in paragraph 3 are met.

There are a number of exceptions to the requirement to notify individuals, as set out in Article 34(3), including where the high risk is no longer likely to materialize due to measures taken by the controller or because the data are encrypted.

A controller may adopt a number of different means of notifying individuals. Individuals should be contacted directly, unless doing so would involve a disproportionate effort, in which case a public communication, such as prominent website banners or a prominent advertisement in newspapers, may be sufficient. Examples of appropriate direct communication methods include email, SMS, and letters. The most appropriate method of communication is likely to be that which the controller usually employs to communicate with individuals. However, depending on the circumstances, a controller may need to use more than one method of communication. Obviously, a controller should try to avoid using a contact method compromised by the breach as this method could be used by someone impersonating the controller.

The notification should explain to individuals the nature of the breach, in clear and plain language, and should contain, as a minimum, the information set out in Article 34(2), namely:

- a description of the nature of the breach;
- the name and contact details of the DPO;
- a description of the likely consequences of the breach; and
- a description of the measures taken or proposed to be taken by the controller to address the breach, including, where appropriate, measures to mitigate its possible adverse effects.

Measures to mitigate a breach's adverse effects may, depending on the circumstances, include offering services such as credit checking and identity theft protection to assist and support individuals, and forcing individuals to reset their passwords.

The notification should be available in appropriate alternative formats if needed (e.g. braille and large font) and in whichever languages are required to ensure that individuals are able to understand what is being communicated to them.

As noted above, direct notification to individuals is not required if it would involve disproportionate effort. It is unclear how controllers should assess disproportionate effort—although the phrase is used elsewhere in the GDPR (e.g. in the context of providing fair processing notices and in the context of notifying individuals of the rectification or erasure of their personal data), there is no guidance on how to assess disproportionality. Since the controller's actions after the breach to mitigate the likelihood of harm can be taken into account when determining whether to notify individuals, there is a strong incentive for controllers to take prompt and effective action to avoid having to notify individuals.

A controller is also required to document in a breach register the facts surrounding the personal data breach, its effect and any remedial action taken. The purpose of the register is to enable the supervisory authority to verify compliance with Article 33.

If a processor experiences a personal data breach it must notify the controller without undue delay. However, it is not required to make any further notifications.

Advice on Breach Notification

In light of the notification requirements, controllers and processors need to ensure that they have in place effective ways of detecting breaches, and controllers need to have in place a strategy for dealing with personal data breaches. This strategy should be documented in a breach management plan which should focus on steps that can be taken in the immediate aftermath of a breach to mitigate the risk of harm to individuals.

In guidance issued in the UK prior to the GDPR coming into force, the Information Commissioner stipulated that there should be four elements to any breach management plan:

- containment and recovery;
- assessment of ongoing risk;
- notification of breach; and
- evaluation and response.

Regarding containment, the ICO suggests deciding who should take the lead on investigating the breach and ensuring they have the appropriate resources, and also establishing who needs to be made aware of the breach and informing them of what they are expected to do to assist in the containment exercise. As regards recovery, the ICO recommends establishing whether there is anything that can be done (such as the physical recovery of equipment or the use of backup tapes to restore lost or damaged data) to recover any losses and limit the damage the breach can cause.

The Article 29 Data Protection Working Party has also issued guidelines on personal data breach notification (WP 250). As well as providing guidance on issues such as what a breach is and when a controller becomes aware of a breach, the guidelines also give examples of data breaches and whom should be notified in different situations.

A failure to notify either the supervisory authority or affected individuals can result in an administrative fine of up to 2 per cent of annual worldwide turnover for the preceding financial year or 10 million euros (whichever is greater) (see Chapter 8), and affected individuals can also claim compensation under Article 82 (see Chapter 7).

6

International Data Transfers

Eduardo Ustaran

Introduction	105
Examples of International Transfers	107
Scope of Data Transfers	108
Adequate Level of Protection	108
Transfers to the United States—Privacy Shield	110
Providing Adequacy Safeguards	114
The Contractual Route	115
Codes of Conduct and Certification Mechanisms	116
Binding Corporate Rules	117
The Derogations	119
Non-repetitive Transfers	121
Advice for Organizations	121

Introduction

European data protection law has restricted the free flow of personal data from locations within Europe to locations outside Europe for more than twenty years. The reasoning behind the legislation in relation to the export restriction is simple: if controllers are permitted, without restriction, to transfer personal data to countries without adequate data protection regimes, then the protection afforded by EU law will be lost. This approach has been justifiably criticized by multinational organizations and others who say that it creates an intolerable global trading environment and is effectively a restriction on global free trade.

The GDPR continues the tradition: transfers of personal data to any country outside the European Economic Area ('EEA') (which consists of the EU Member States together with Iceland, Liechtenstein, and Norway) may only take place subject to the requirements of Chapter V of the Regulation, namely that:

- the third country ensures an adequate level of protection for the personal data as determined by the European Commission; or

- in the absence of that adequate level of protection, the controller or processor wishing to transfer the data provides appropriate safeguards on condition that enforceable data subject rights and effective legal remedies for data subjects are available; or

- in the absence of an adequate level of protection or of appropriate safeguards, a transfer or a set of transfers of personal data fits within one of the derogations for specific situations covered by the Regulation.

Interestingly, the restriction on cross-border data transfers is specifically extended, in Article 44 (see Box 6.1), to transfers of personal data to 'international organisations'. Article 4(26) defines an international organization as:

an organisation and its subordinate bodies governed by public international law, or any other body which is set up by, or on the basis of, an agreement between two or more countries.

Examples of such international organizations include the United Nations, the World Bank, the World Trade Organization, the International Monetary Fund, the World Health Organization, the International Atomic Energy Agency, and the International Committee of the Red Cross.

That the Regulation maintains, and arguably extends somewhat, the restrictions on international transfers of personal data has been baffling to some commentators. They point to the obvious difficulties that are caused to international trade. Recital 101 of the Regulation goes some way to explaining the reasoning behind the restrictions—whilst it recognizes that cross-border flows of personal data are necessary for the expansion of international trade, it states that the level of protection of natural persons ensured in the EU by the Regulation should not be undermined.

To understand the basis for this approach, it is necessary to bear in mind that the European institutions responsible for drafting and adopting the Regulation have tried to preserve the effect of the new regime by preventing any attempts to weaken the protection afforded to individuals. In practice, this creates a situation that effectively imposes EU data protection standards in jurisdictions outside Europe (see

---

Box 6.1 Restrictions on Data Exports

Article 44 GDPR

Any transfer of personal data which are undergoing processing or are intended for processing after transfer to a third country or to an international organisation shall take place only if, subject to the other provisions of this Regulation, the conditions laid down in this Chapter are complied with by the controller and processor, including for onward transfers of personal data from the third country or an international organisation to another third country or to another international organisation. All provisions in this Chapter shall be applied in order to ensure that the level of protection of natural persons guaranteed by this Regulation is not undermined.

below). In practical terms, for some large multinational organizations, this issue has meant the adoption of EU data protection practices across their operations irrespective of where the data processing activities actually take place.

This chapter considers the data export restriction, its implications, and the methods and practices that might be employed to satisfy its provisions. Consideration is also given to certain arrangements and agreements that exist to allow the international flow of personal data, such as using specified contractual clauses, the 'Privacy Shield', and binding corporate rules. Despite the focus of the chapter on the issue of data exports per se, it should be remembered that the transfer of personal data overseas is an aspect of 'processing' and therefore that each of the remaining data protection rules must be complied with in respect of each and every such transfer.

Examples of International Transfers

Although many international transactions obviously involve transfers of personal data overseas, there are some situations where it is less obvious that an international transfer of personal data is taking place. In some instances, organizations may perceive that they make no international transfers of personal data, when in fact the reality is otherwise.

The following examples of international transfers are offered to hopefully widen the reader's perception of the types of circumstances in which the GDPR's provisions on data exports will become relevant:

(a) A multinational organization, based in the United States, with offices in the UK and other European countries, maintains a computer network that connects all its sites. Considerable quantities of information (including personal data) are regularly transferred between various points on the network.

(b) A UK company engages in cross-border list rental whereby lists of customers or marketing data are transferred to organizations abroad.

(c) A German company's entire database is transferred to Switzerland as a result of the purchase of the company by a Swiss organization.

(d) The forwarding of an email containing customer details by a person in the UK to a person in Hong Kong.

(e) The transfer to India of files containing digital voice dictation for the purpose of such data being converted to Word documents (e.g. letters) before being returned to the UK by email (cross-border digital dictation outsourcing).

(f) The human resources department of a global organization with offices in the UK is to be moved from Ireland to Singapore.

(g) A UK company publishes the names, home addresses, and mobile telephone numbers of its staff in an internal directory, which is made available to branches of the company located in third countries.

Scope of Data Transfers

The concept of transfer is not defined by the Regulation. However, transfer is not the same as mere transit. Therefore, the fact that personal data may be routed through a third country on the way from an EEA country does not bring such transfer within the scope of the restriction of the Regulation unless some substantive processing operation is conducted on the personal data in the third country.

In practice, there are two common situations that have been a source of concern in the past, but that are not subject to the restrictions on data exports:

- technical routing of packet-switch technology (such as internet email and web pages), which may involve random transfers of personal data between computer servers located anywhere in the world; and
- electronic access to personal data by travellers who happen to be physically located for a short period of time in a place that does not afford an adequate level of protection—for example, a person who logs on to a computer system based in the EU to access data from a foreign airport.

In addition, following the European Court of Justice decision in the Swedish case of *Bodil Lindqvist* (C-101/01 [2003]), where an individual in a Member State merely loads personal information onto a website that is hosted in that state or another Member State so that the information can be accessed by anyone who connects to the internet, this does not necessarily constitute a transfer of data to a third country.

However, where there is an international exchange of information about individuals with the intention of automatically processing that personal information after it has been exchanged, that should be regarded as a transfer for the purposes of the Regulation, even if the original exchange does not qualify as processing of personal data. An example of this would be where information is provided by someone in the EU over the telephone to someone in a third country who then enters the information on a computer.

Adequate Level of Protection

Article 45(1) of the Regulation states that:

[a] transfer of personal data to a third country or an international organisation may take place where the Commission has decided that the third country, a territory or one or more specified sectors within that third country, or the international organisation in question, ensures an adequate level of protection.

When assessing the adequacy of the level of protection, the European Commission must, in particular, take account of the following elements:

(a) the rule of law, respect for human rights and fundamental freedoms, relevant legislation, both general and sectoral, including concerning public security, defence, national security and criminal law, and the access of public authorities to personal data, as well as the implementation of such legislation, data protection rules, professional rules. and security measures, including rules for the onward transfer of personal data to another third country or international organization which are complied with in that country or international organization, case law, as well as effective and enforceable data subject rights and effective administrative and judicial redress for the data subjects whose personal data are being transferred;

(b) the existence and effective functioning of one or more independent supervisory authorities in the third country or to which an international organization is subject, with responsibility for ensuring and enforcing compliance with the data protection rules, including adequate enforcement powers, for assisting and advising the data subjects in exercising their rights, and for cooperation with the supervisory authorities of the EU Member States; and

(c) the international commitments the third country or international organization concerned has entered into, or other obligations arising from legally binding conventions or instruments as well as from its participation in multilateral or regional systems, in particular in relation to the protection of personal data.

After assessing the adequacy of the level of protection, the European Commission may decide, by means of an implementing act, that a third country, a territory or one or more specified sectors within a third country, or an international organization ensures an adequate level of protection within the meaning given by the law, as described above.

The Commission's implementing act must provide for a mechanism for a periodic review, at least every four years, which must take into account all relevant developments in the third country or international organization. The implementing act must specify its territorial and sectoral application and, where applicable, identify the supervisory authority or authorities with responsibility for ensuring and enforcing compliance with the data protection rules.

In addition, the European Commission must, on an ongoing basis, monitor developments in third countries and international organizations that could affect the functioning of any adequacy decisions adopted, including those that were adopted under the original Data Protection Directive. As a result, where available information reveals that a third country, a territory or one or more specified sectors within a third country, or an international organization no longer ensures an adequate level of protection, the European Commission is entitled and required to repeal, amend, or suspend the decision as appropriate.

For completeness, the Regulation confirms that any adequacy decisions adopted by the European Commission on the basis of the Data Protection Directive will remain in force until amended, replaced, or repealed by another European Commission decision. Under the Directive, the European Commission recognized Andorra, Argentina, Canada, Faroe Islands, Guernsey, The Isle of Man, Israel, Jersey, New Zealand, Switzerland, and Uruguay as providing adequate protection. Table 6.1 lists these countries/territories together with their relevant laws,

Table 6.1 Adequate countries/territories and Opinions and Decisions

Country	Name/description of data protection law	Article 29 Working Party Opinion	Commission Decision
Switzerland	Federal Data Protection Law and the legislation in several cantons	7 June 1999; Opinion 5/99	26 July 2000; Commission Decision 2000/518/EC
Canada	Canadian Personal Information Protection and Electronic Documents Act 2000 (PIPED Act)	26 January 2001; Opinion 2/2011	20 December 2001; Commission Decision 2002/2/EC
Argentina	Personal Data Protection Act No. 25.326 and related legislation	3 October 2002; Opinion 4/2002	30 June 2003; Commission Decision 2003/490/EC
Guernsey	Data Protection (Bailiwick of Guernsey) Law 2001	13 June 2003; Opinion 5/2003	21 November 2003; Commission Decision 2003/821/EC
Isle of Man	Data Protection Act 2002	21 November 2003; Opinion 6/2003	28 April 2004; Commission Decision 2004/411/EC
Jersey	Data Protection (Jersey) Law 1987 and ancillary laws	9 October 2007; Opinion 8/2007	8 May 2008; Commission Decision 2008/393/EC
Faroe Islands	Act No 73 of 8 May 2001 on Processing of Personal Data	9 October 2007; Opinion 9/2007	5 March 2010; Commission Decision 2010/147/EU
Andorra	Qualified Law 15/2003 of 18 December on the protection of personal data	1 December 2009; Opinion 7/2009	19 October 2010; Commission Decision 2010/625/EU
Israel	Privacy Protection Act 5741-1981	1 December 2009; Opinion 6/2009	31 January 2011; Commission Decision 2011/61/EU
Uruguay	Act No 18.331 on the Protection of Personal Data and 'Habeas Data' Action and related legislation	12 October 2010; Opinion 6/2010	21 August 2012; Commission Decision 2012/484/EU
New Zealand	Privacy Act 1993	4 April 2011; Opinion 11/2011	19 December 2012; Commission Decision 2013/65/EU

the Article 29 Working Party's Opinions of the laws, and the relevant European Commission Decision.

Transfers to the United States—Privacy Shield

Considering the large volume of data transfers carried out between the EU and the United States, the US Department of Commerce and the European Commission originally developed a mechanism, known as Safe Harbor, as a self-regulatory framework that would allow organizations to satisfy the requirements of EU data protection law in respect of transatlantic data transfers. On 26 July 2000, following extensive negotiations, the Commission issued a decision stating that the Safe Harbor Privacy Principles provided adequate protection for personal data transferred from the EU. This decision enabled EU personal data to be transferred to US-based companies that agreed to abide by the Safe Harbor Privacy Principles.

However, since its adoption, the Safe Harbor Framework was fraught with challenges. Although the data protection requirements set out in the Safe Harbor Privacy Principles were meant to match the adequacy standards of the EU Data Protection Directive, its self-certification nature and the non-European style of its provisions attracted much criticism over the years. Perceived weaknesses included that participants did not perform required annual compliance checks and the lack of active enforcement by the Federal Trade Commission compared to other domestic cases. These factors led some EU data protection authorities to question the validity of the Safe Harbor framework as an adequacy mechanism.

The Snowden effect

The disclosures by Edward Snowden in June 2013 about the mass surveillance operations carried out by the US National Security Agency had a very visible knock-on effect on the way in which the EU regulates international transfers of personal data. In light of the existing criticisms of the Safe Harbor framework and amid allegations that companies that participated in the scheme might have been involved in US surveillance activities, calls for the revocation of the Safe Harbor framework from activists and some of the data protection authorities led the European Parliament to adopt a resolution seeking its immediate suspension.

The European Commission rejected doing so because of concerns that suspending the Safe Harbor framework would adversely affect EU business interests and the transatlantic economy. However, it agreed that there were a number of weaknesses in the Safe Harbor framework and it had no choice but to reopen the dialogue with the US government in order to find a way of strengthening the framework and restoring its credibility.

The Commission announced this renegotiation on 27 November 2013 through two communications to the European Parliament and the Council of the EU, entitled 'On the Functioning of the Safe Harbor from the Perspective of EU Citizens and Companies Established in the EU' and 'Rebuilding Trust in EU–US Data Flows'. In these communications, the European Commission stressed that the EU and US were strategic partners and that transatlantic data flows were critical to commerce, law enforcement, and national security on both sides of the Atlantic. However, it also recognized that the Snowden revelations had damaged the EU's trust in this partnership, and that this trust needed to be rebuilt.

Towards 'Safe Harbor II'

The European Commission began discussions with US authorities aimed at updating the Safe Harbor framework in January 2014. The original aim was to identify remedies by the summer of that year and to implement them as soon as possible thereafter.

The European Commission had provided thirteen specific recommendations aimed at addressing the Safe Harbor's weaknesses and ensuring that the framework remained an effective mechanism for facilitating commercial transatlantic data flows. These recommendations focused on four broad priorities, namely transparency, redress, enforcement, and access to data by US authorities. In June 2014, the then Commissioner for Justice, Viviane Reding, provided an update on the negotiations, reporting that the US Department of Commerce had agreed to twelve of the Commission's thirteen recommendations. However, the sticking point was the final recommendation, that the national security exception was only to be applied when strictly necessary and proportionate.

At the same time, the validity of Safe Harbor was questioned by Austrian law student Maximillian Schrems, who lodged a complaint with the Irish Data Protection Commissioner requesting the termination of any transfers of personal data by Facebook Ireland to the United States. Mr Schrems claimed that Facebook Ireland—the data controller for Facebook's European users' data—could no longer rely on the Safe Harbor framework to legitimize the transfers of his data to the US because of the wide access that US intelligence agencies had to such data as revealed by Snowden.

The complaint was then escalated to the Irish High Court, which in turn referred the matter for decision by the Court of Justice of the European Union ('CJEU'), the highest judicial authority on the interpretation of EU law. On 6 October 2015, the CJEU issued its judgment and declared the Safe Harbor adequacy decision invalid. This ruling increased the pressure on the European Commission to agree a more robust alternative mechanism for transfers of data from the EU to the US.

Birth of the Privacy Shield

On 29 February 2016, and after more than two years of negotiations with the Department of Commerce, the European Commission released its much-awaited draft decision on the adequacy of the new EU–US Privacy Shield framework, accompanied by information on how the framework will work in practice. The Privacy Shield framework's documentation is significantly more detailed than that associated with its predecessor, imposing more specific and exacting measures on organizations wishing to join the framework.

Crucially, the Privacy Shield framework also includes additional checks and balances designed to make sure that the privacy rights of EU individuals can be exercised when their data are being processed in the United States, as well as various official letters from US government officials providing assurances regarding the legal limitations affecting access to personal data by US government agencies.

Following the European Commission's announcement, the Article 29 Working Party issued a preliminary statement on 3 February 2016 (before the relevant documentation had been publicly disclosed) welcoming the conclusion of the negotiations between the EU and the US on the introduction of the Privacy Shield. However, on 13 April 2016 the Working Party published an Opinion setting out its detailed analysis of the framework. In this Opinion, the Working Party set out its concerns on the commercial aspects of the Privacy Shield and the ability of US public authorities to access data transferred under the Privacy Shield.

In particular, the Working Party considered that the Privacy Shield did not include certain key data protection principles from EU law. The Working Party also expressed concern about the protection for onward data transfers and that the redress mechanism for individuals could prove too complex. Finally the Working Party noted that the documentation did not exclude massive and indiscriminate collection of personal data originating from the EU by US intelligence agencies and that the new Ombudsperson was not sufficiently independent or powerful. The Opinion concluded by urging the European Commission to resolve these concerns and improve the Privacy Shield.

Operation of the Privacy Shield

Following further negotiations to address the Article 29 Working Party's concerns, on 12 July 2016 the European Commission finally issued its adequacy decision concerning the Privacy Shield framework for the transfer of personal data from the EU to the US. The Privacy Shield formally entered in operation on 1 August 2016, and US businesses subject to the jurisdiction of the Federal Trade Commission or Department of Transportation could, from that date, join the Privacy Shield by filing an online registration with the Department of Commerce. This covers most US for-profit businesses, but excludes a number of banks, financial services companies, and other businesses that are not subject to the jurisdiction of those regulatory agencies.

The seven principles (set out in Box 6.2) with which Privacy Shield organizations must comply are similar to the principles under Safe Harbor. However, each of them was strengthened in important ways, especially the principle of recourse, enforcement, and liability. To see the full text of the Privacy Shield Principles, see <http://www.dpdocuments.com>.

Box 6.2 The Privacy Shield Principles

1. Notice
2. Choice
3. Accountability for Onward Transfer
4. Security
5. Data Integrity and Purpose Limitation
6. Access
7. Recourse, Enforcement, and Liability

The Privacy Shield requires companies that self-certify compliance to take certain steps to demonstrate that they can comply. They must:

- Conduct an internal compliance assessment to determine the company's ability to comply with the principles with respect to information that will be covered by the certification. To the extent that there are any gaps in its ability to comply, the company should adopt internal controls, policies, and procedures to come into compliance.

- Register with a third-party arbitration provider to handle any complaints from EU individuals about the handling of their information that the company is unable to fully resolve, and pay any relevant registration fees.

- Adopt a Privacy Shield notice that contains thirteen specified details about the company's privacy practices, and publish the notice online.

From the public statements made by a number of privacy activists—including Max Schrems himself—it is very likely that the Privacy Shield will be put to the test in the CJEU. Ongoing concerns about government surveillance have been cited as the main reasons for a potential legal challenge. If so, it will take several years before the CJEU makes a final decision. However, it is important to note that the negotiations between the European Commission and the US Department of Commerce were specifically aimed at addressing the issues that affected Safe Harbor, so it is by no means certain that the CJEU would rule against the Privacy Shield unless the US government changed its commitments under the framework.

Providing Adequacy Safeguards

In reality, and given the low number of countries that qualify as 'adequate', in the majority of cases, controllers or processors wishing to transfer personal data internationally (especially to countries other than the US) will need to deploy a mechanism that provides appropriate safeguards for the data. The Regulation addresses this situation by listing several possible mechanisms that may be suitable for these purposes, namely:

- A legally binding and enforceable instrument between public authorities or bodies.

- Binding corporate rules in accordance with Article 47.

- Standard data protection clauses adopted by the European Commission.

- Standard data protection clauses adopted by a supervisory authority and approved by the Commission.

- An approved code of conduct pursuant to Article 40 together with binding and enforceable commitments of the controller or processor in the third country to apply the appropriate safeguards, including as regards data subjects' rights.

- An approved certification mechanism pursuant to Article 42 together with binding and enforceable commitments of the controller or processor in the third country to apply the appropriate safeguards, including as regards data subjects' rights.

- Contractual clauses between the controller or processor and the controller, processor, or the recipient of the personal data in the third country or international organization, or provisions to be inserted into administrative arrangements between public authorities or bodies, that are specifically approved for that purpose by the competent data protection supervisory authority.

This menu of options represents an improvement compared to the Directive as it provides greater choice and flexibility for both exporters and importers of personal data.

The Contractual Route

Traditionally, the most frequently used mechanism to legitimize international data transfers to countries that are not deemed to provide an adequate level of protection has been the so-called 'standard contractual clauses' or 'model clauses'. Under the Directive, this was a contract pre-approved by the European Commission and establishing certain obligations applicable to both exporters and importers aimed at safeguarding the personal data in accordance with EU standards.

In this regard, on 15 June 2001, the European Commission adopted a Decision setting out standard contractual clauses ensuring adequate safeguards for personal data transferred by controllers in the EU to controllers in 'non-adequate' jurisdictions. This Decision obliged Member States to recognize that companies or organizations using these standard clauses in contracts concerning personal data transfers to countries outside the EEA were offering adequate protection to the data.

Similarly, on 27 December 2001, the European Commission adopted a second Decision setting out standard contractual clauses for the transfer of personal data to processors established in non-EEA countries that were not recognized as offering an adequate level of data protection.

In 2003, the European Commission stated in its First Report on the implementation of the Directive, that it intended to adopt further Decisions so that economic operators would have a wider choice of standard contractual clauses. Accordingly, the Commission issued a new Decision on 27 December 2004 amending its Decision of June 2001 and adding a second version to the sets of standard contractual clauses that could be used to legitimize international transfers between controllers. This second version was based on an alternative draft pioneered by the International Chamber of Commerce ('ICC').

The inflexible nature of the original 2001 controller to processor clauses led to a further proposal by the ICC and, on 5 February 2010, the European Commission notified its Decision updating and replacing the original controller to processor standard clauses with a new set of model clauses. Since 2010, EEA-based controllers wishing to rely on standard contractual clauses to legitimize international data transfers to processors outside the EEA have had to use the updated controller to processor clauses for new processing operations.

These following sets of standard contractual clauses (which are available at <http://www.dpdocuments.com>) remain valid until they are replaced or amended by new versions which match the more prescriptive framework under the Regulation:

- the 2001 controller to controller clauses;
- the 2004 alternative controller to controller clauses; and
- the 2010 controller to processor clauses.

Whilst the European Commission approved model contracts will indeed continue to be a suitable mechanism to legitimize international data transfers, the ability of data protection authorities to either adopt standard contractual clauses themselves or to authorize transfers based on ad-hoc contracts presented to them by the parties is likely to play an important role in the development of the contractual route for transfers.

Some technology companies, such as Microsoft, Amazon Web Services, and Google have already pioneered the idea of obtaining the approval of the data protection authorities for their own versions of data transfer agreements. The advantage of this approach is that companies may enjoy greater flexibility as regards how they contractually commit to the protection of personal data in a way that is more realistic and less likely to cause breach of the contractual obligations.

The key practical advantages of the contractual route are:

- To the extent that an agreement is based on the standard contractual clauses adopted by the European Commission or the European data protection authorities, in principle it will be regarded as a valid mechanism to legitimize data transfers.
- From a resources perspective, drafting and entering into an agreement is not very time-consuming.

However, the key practical disadvantages of relying on an agreement are:

- Given the static nature of a contractual document, it is likely to be unworkable for multiple and evolving transfers.
- In order to meet the standards sought by the European Commission or the data protection authorities, the contract must include very strict requirements affecting the use and sharing of personal information by the parties.

Codes of Conduct and Certification Mechanisms

One of the novelties of the Regulation in the area of international data transfers is the express addition of codes of conduct and certification mechanisms as adequacy methods. Both of these methods are yet to be tested, so it remains to be seen whether they provide a practical and effective solution to legitimize international data transfers.

Codes of conduct and certification are defined in Chapter 1.

Binding Corporate Rules

The most significant development in the area of international data transfers under the Regulation is the inclusion of Binding Corporate Rules ('BCR') as a mechanism available to both controllers and processors to legitimize such transfers within their corporate groups.

In 2003, the EU data protection authorities developed the concept of BCR to allow multinational corporations and groups of companies to make intra-organizational transfers of personal data across borders in compliance with EU data protection law. Its express inclusion in the Regulation confirms both the commitment by the EU policy makers to it and the increasingly important role that intra-group global privacy programmes have in ensuring compliance with EU data protection law.

BCR concept

Data exports within a multinational corporate group are subject to the same rules as exports outside the group. And using contractual arrangements is hardly a cost-effective way of legitimizing international transfers for data-reliant organizations operating on a worldwide basis. For many global companies, using personal data is all about sharing information beyond national borders and jurisdictional differences. Therefore, a flexible, tailor-made solution that does away with the impracticalities of having to enter into innumerable contracts among subsidiaries is likely to be the only practical option.

Over the years, the EU data protection authorities have acknowledged the role of BCR as a mechanism to legitimize data exports within a corporate group. In essence, a set of BCR is a global set of rules based on European privacy standards, which multinational organizations draw up and follow voluntarily and national regulators approve in accordance with their own legislations.

The idea of using BCR to create adequate safeguards for the purposes of the Directive was originally devised by the Article 29 Working Party in its Working Document WP 74. Since then, the EU data protection authorities have increased their level of cooperation to streamline the BCR approval process. This cooperation led to the adoption of a 'mutual recognition' process which was effectively incorporated into the Regulation.

BCR requirements

According to the Regulation, data protection authorities must approve a set of BCR following the so-called consistency mechanism (see Chapters 8 and 11) provided that it is legally binding and expressly confers enforceable rights on data subjects. A full and valid set of BCR must specifically include the following elements:

1. the structure and contact details of the corporate group and of each of its members;

2. the data transfers or set of transfers, including the categories of personal data, the type of processing and its purposes, the type of data subjects affected, and the identification of the third country or countries in question;

3. their legally binding nature, both internally and externally;

4. the application of the general data protection principles, in particular purpose limitation, data minimization, limited storage periods, data quality, data protection by design and by default, legal basis for processing, processing of special categories of personal data, measures to ensure data security, and the requirements in respect of onward transfers to bodies not bound by the BCR;

5. the rights of data subjects in regard to processing and the means to exercise those rights, including the right not to be subject to decisions based solely on automated processing, including profiling, the right to lodge a complaint with the competent supervisory authority and before the competent courts, and to obtain redress and, where appropriate, compensation for a breach of the BCR;

6. the acceptance by the controller or processor established on the territory of a Member State of liability for any breaches of the BCR by any member concerned not established in the Union;

7. how the information on the BCR is provided to the data subjects;

8. the tasks of any DPO or any other person or entity in charge of monitoring compliance with the BCR;

9. the complaint procedures;

10. the mechanisms for ensuring the verification of compliance with the BCR;

11. the mechanisms for reporting and recording changes to the rules and reporting those changes to the supervisory authority;

12. the cooperation mechanism with the supervisory authority to ensure compliance;

13. the mechanisms for reporting to the competent supervisory authority any legal requirements to which a member of the corporate group is subject in a third country which are likely to have a substantial adverse effect on the guarantees provided by the BCR; and

14. the appropriate data protection training to personnel having permanent or regular access to personal data.

In summary, the key practical advantages of BCR are:

- Flexibility: once in place, BCR enable the unrestricted sharing of data between all companies within a corporate group with minimum contractual documentation. Further, the organization can tailor the rules applicable to intra-group data transfers to fit its business requirements.

- Legal certainty: BCR constitute a firm legal basis for international transfers, which is supported by all data protection authorities.
- Efficient management and exploitation of information: in this respect, BCR assists to:
  - proactively regulate data processing operations and avoid a fire-fighting approach;
  - implement business processes lawfully, in particular in relation to offshore data centres, international outsourcing of data processing operations, and global data sharing within the group; and
  - maximise the value of data and the benefits of information sharing.
- Consistency: BCR further facilitate the implementation of privacy and security policies in a consistent way across the corporate group by:
  - providing an umbrella framework for data processing operations;
  - enabling a uniform approach to compliance;
  - enabling compliance policies to be better tailored to fit business requirements; and
  - making it easier to minimize the risk of non-compliance.
- Reduced regulatory scrutiny: approval of a BCR programme will effectively constitute a delegation of compliance and supervision by the data protection authorities to the organization itself.

However, BCR have the following key practical disadvantages:

- The process of looking in detail into data processing operations for the purpose of a BCR application may result in flushing out data protection issues which are unknown (although obviously there are also positive elements in this from a compliance point of view).
- Despite the progress, BCR remain a relatively novel and still evolving concept. This means that it will not always be possible to fully anticipate the position that data protection authorities will take in relation to certain matters.

The Derogations

In the absence of an adequate level of protection or of appropriate safeguards, a transfer or a set of transfers of personal data may still take place if it fits within one of the derogations for specific situations covered by the Regulation. The following, which largely reproduce those contained in the Directive, are the derogations under the GDPR.

Consent

Data exports can lawfully be made with the explicit consent of the individual. Consent must still be specific and informed. This means that the individual must be informed of the possible risks of such transfers due to the absence of an adequacy decision and appropriate safeguards.

Contract performance

The Regulation allows data transfers in cases where specific types of contracts are in place or being contemplated. In the case of a contract between the exporter and the individual to whom the data relates, a transfer may be carried out if such transfer is necessary for performance of the contract or is a necessary part of pre-contractual measures taken by the exporter at the request of the individual.

In the case of a contract between the exporter and someone other than the individual, the transfer will be lawful if the contract is entered into at the individual's request or in her interests and the transfer is necessary for the performance or conclusion of the contract.

The contracts covered by these provisions are not restricted to the supply of goods or services, and may apply in the case of employment contracts. However, whether a transfer is necessary for the performance of a contract will depend on the nature of the goods or services provided under the contract rather than the way in which the exporter's operations are organized. In other words, a transfer is not necessary if the only reason for it is the fact that the exporter has chosen to structure its operations in a way that involves transferring data overseas.

Therefore, if a customer books a holiday abroad through an EEA-based travel agent, the travel agent must transfer the booking details to the foreign hotel in order to fulfil the contract with the customer. However, if for pure efficiency or cost-cutting reasons that travel agent decides to place its customer database in a computer based outside the EEA, it cannot be said that the transfer of personal data to the computer located overseas is necessary for the performance of the contract with the customer.

Substantial public interest

Transfers can be carried out where necessary for reasons of substantial public interest. This case is most likely to apply in situations where the transfer is necessary for reasons of crime prevention and detection, national security, and tax collection.

Legal claims

Transfers can be made where they are necessary for establishing, exercising, or defending legal claims.

Vital interests

Exports of personal data can lawfully be carried out where necessary to protect the vital interests of the data subject or other persons. In practice, this relates to matters of life and death, such as the transfer of medical records of an individual who has become seriously ill or been involved in a serious accident abroad.

Public registers

Exports of personal data can also be made from information available on a public register provided that the person to whom the information is transferred complies with any restrictions on access to, or use of, the information in the register. This allows transfers of extracts from a public register of directors, shareholders, or professional practitioners, for example, but would not allow transfers of the complete register. In addition, if there are conditions of use imposed by the body or organization responsible for compiling the register, they must be honoured by the importer and any further recipients.

Non-repetitive Transfers

Finally, and as a last resort, a transfer may take place if the transfer is not repetitive, concerns only a limited number of data subjects, is necessary for the purposes of compelling legitimate interests pursued by the controller (which are not overridden by the interests or rights and freedoms of the data subjects), and the controller has assessed all the circumstances surrounding the data transfer and has on the basis of that assessment provided suitable safeguards with regard to the protection of personal data.

In these situations, the controller must inform the supervisory authority and the data subject of the transfer. The individual must also be informed of the compelling legitimate interests pursued by the controller.

Advice for Organizations

Overcoming the restrictions on international data transfers is one of the most difficult compliance challenges faced by global organizations operating in the EU. As described above, finding and implementing the right mechanism to ensure an adequate level of protection in every case is likely to be onerous and time-consuming. However, in the face of technological developments, greater globalization, and surveillance threats, the appetite of the EU institutions for a softer approach in the foreseeable future is likely to be low.

Accordingly, and to ensure compliance, organizations are strongly advised to develop a viable global data protection compliance programme in line with the adequacy criteria devised by the European Commission and commit to abiding by it through either a contractual mechanism or a set of BCR.

7

The Rights of Individuals

Heledd Lloyd-Jones and Peter Carey

Introduction	122
Responding to Individuals	123
Exemptions	125
The Right of Access	126
Data Portability	137
Rectification	139
Rights to Object	140
The Right to Object to Direct Marketing	140
Right to Erasure	143
Right to Restriction of Processing	147
Automated Decision-taking	149
Compensation	151
Right to a Judicial Remedy	153
Complaints to the Commissioner	154

Introduction

The GDPR confers several distinct rights on individuals. These rights are exercisable only against controllers. Processors do not have to comply (unless they are under a contractual obligation with a controller to do so).

The rights of individuals (also known as data subject rights) are subject to certain exemptions enacted for the benefit of controllers. In addition to these exemptions, controllers should remember that personal data processed by individuals in the course of a purely personal or household activity fall outside the scope of the GDPR and that such information is therefore also effectively exempt from the data subject rights.

Whenever a request is received from an individual seeking to exercise any of the rights, controllers are expected to follow the procedural rules set out in Article 12 of the GDPR. These rules (which are discussed in this chapter), deal with timescales for

---

Box 7.1 Rights of Individuals

- Access to personal data and to information regarding processing
- Data portability
- Rectification
- Erasure ('right to be forgotten')
- Restriction
- Objection
- Prevention of automated decision-making
- Compensation
- Complaints to the Commissioner

---

responding to requests, requirements when communicating with individuals, and the circumstances when a fee may be charged.

Children are able to exercise their own rights under data protection law provided that they are of a sufficient age to understand the nature of what they are requesting. There is a general presumption in the UK that children aged thirteen years and above have sufficient maturity to exercise their own data protection rights. Below that age, the presumption is that parents and guardians are able to exercise the rights on behalf of children.

Controllers should be cautious where a person seeks to exercise a data protection right on behalf of another. In most cases it is advisable for the controller to ask to see some written evidence that the person making the request has been authorized by the data subject to act on his or her behalf in the exercise of the data protection right in question.

Finally, by way of introductory material, the GDPR is silent on the question as to whether it is possible to exclude any or all of the rights by way of contractual provision. Whilst the answer remains unsettled, it is likely that both the courts and the Commissioner would be cautious about allowing variation of the rights by contract, although the courts may, as a separate matter, be willing to enforce a promise by an individual to not exercise those rights. Further, consumer protection law could render void an attempt by a controller to exclude data protection rights in a consumer contract since such exclusion would likely be 'unfair'.

In describing the rights (which are listed in Box 7.1), this chapter makes reference to terminology that arises frequently in the context of data protection law. Readers are referred to Chapter 1 for an explanation of the meaning of many of these terms.

Responding to Individuals

Article 12 of the GDPR sets out a number of procedural requirements that controllers should follow whenever they receive a request from an individual seeking to exercise one or more of the rights.

Before responding to such a request, controllers should ensure they are satisfied as to the individual's identity. It is not necessary in every case to require *evidence* of identity—Article 12(4) provides that the controller may request the provision of information necessary to confirm the identity of the data subject where the controller has reasonable doubts concerning the identity of the person making the request. An email or signed letter from the individual will often be sufficient, especially if the controller has had previous dealings with the individual. Where the request comes from a solicitors' firm, which states that it is instructed by the data subject to make the access request, there will ordinarily be no need to check this assertion of authority (see *Gurieva and Another v Community Safety Development (UK) Ltd* [2016] EWHC 643 (QB)). Where appropriate, however, the controller should ask for more formal evidence. The controller could for example ask the requester to supply:

- information which the controller has on file and which will be known to the individual (e.g. a customer account number, date of birth, or relevant password);
- a document which shows an original signature of the individual as witnessed by a competent person; and/or
- a document that only the relevant individual would be likely to have access to (e.g. copy utility bill, passport, or driving licence).

When responding to individuals who are exercising their GDPR rights, controllers should usually provide the requested information in writing—this can include email. If a request is made by email, the controller should respond by email where possible, unless the individual has requested otherwise. However, Article 12 provides that, at the request of an individual, information may be provided verbally, provided the controller has evidence of the data subject's identity. It is advisable for controllers who do agree to provide information verbally to keep a record of the information that has been provided in case the individual subsequently complains.

Responses to requests from individuals to exercise any of their rights must be issued 'without undue delay' and ordinarily within one month of receipt of the request. However, in the case of complex requests or multiple requests, it is open to the controller to extend the time by two further months. If the controller wishes to extend time on this basis, the individual should be informed, within one month of receipt of the request, of the extension and the reasons that the extension is necessary.

Data subjects are entitled to exercise each of their GDPR rights free of charge. However, where requests are 'manifestly unfounded or excessive' (e.g. because of their repetitive nature), controllers may either charge a reasonable fee (to reflect the controller's administrative costs), or may refuse to comply with the request altogether. The GDPR does not define what is meant by 'manifestly unfounded or excessive' but it is possible that requests that will require disproportionate effort on the part of controllers will fall into this category. The burden of demonstrating that a request is manifestly unfounded or excessive falls on the controller.

As a result of Article 11(2), a controller is able to reject a request if it concerns data that are no longer held by the controller in a manner that allows the requester to be identified—this might be because the controller has diligently complied with its obligations under Article 5 of the GDPR to keep personal data in a form which permits identification of data subjects for no longer than is necessary for the purposes for which the personal data are processed (see Chapter 2). Such a request would, however, have to be dealt with if the data subject provides additional information that enables the controller to identify him or her.

If the controller declines to deal with a request from an individual in relation to any of the rights, the individual should be informed of this, together with the controller's reasons, within one month of receipt of the request. Data subjects should also be informed of their rights to complain to the Commissioner and their rights to challenge the controller's refusal in the courts.

Finally, controllers should note that Article 12(1) imposes an obligation on controllers to take appropriate measures to ensure that any communications sent to data subjects in connection with the exercise of their rights should be made in a concise, transparent, intelligible, and easily accessible form, using clear and plain language, especially when communicating with children.

Exemptions

There are a considerable number of exemptions from the rights conferred on individuals by the GDPR. Each Member State is empowered to restrict the operation of each of the data subject rights to the extent necessary to safeguard:

- national security;
- defence;
- public security;
- the prevention, investigation, detection, or prosecution of criminal offences or the execution of criminal penalties, including the prevention of threats to public security;
- other important objectives of general public interest, for example monetary, budgetary and taxation matters, public health, and social security;
- the protection of judicial independence and judicial proceedings;
- the prevention, investigation, detection, and prosecution of breaches of professional ethics;
- certain monitoring, inspection, and regulatory functions;
- the protection of the data subject or the rights and freedoms of others; and
- the enforcement of civil law claims.

In the UK, exemptions from obligations imposed by the GDPR in relation to data subject rights are set out in Schedules 2–4 of the Bill.

The Right of Access

The right of access to information, sometimes called the 'data subject access right', applies to controllers that carry out data processing that falls within the scope of the GDPR (see Chapter 1). It obliges controllers to provide individuals with access to their data and with additional prescribed information regarding the processing of their data.

This right often results in a significant burden, both administratively and financially, to controllers. It can also be a powerful tool enabling individuals to gain access to vast quantities of information held about them by organizations of all kinds.

The right of subject access is set out in Article 15 of the GDPR, as shown in Box 7.2. It entitles individuals, upon request, to be informed by a controller without undue delay whether personal data relating to them are being processed by or on behalf of that controller. If such data are being processed then, unless an exemption applies, the individual is entitled to access to the personal data and to be provided with additional information regarding the processing of the data. As in the case of all data subject rights, when responding to subject access requests, controllers should comply with the procedural requirements set out in Article 12 (see above).

Box 7.2 The Right of Subject Access

Article 15 GDPR

1. The data subject shall have the right to obtain from the controller confirmation as to whether or not personal data concerning him or her are being processed, and, where that is the case, access to the personal data and the following information:

    (a) the purposes of the processing;

    (b) the categories of personal data concerned;

    (c) the recipients or categories of recipient to whom the personal data have been or will be disclosed, in particular recipients in third countries or international organisations;

    (d) where possible, the envisaged period for which the personal data will be stored, or, if not possible, the criteria used to determine that period;

    (e) the existence of the right to request from the controller rectification or erasure of personal data or restriction of processing of personal data concerning the data subject or to object to such processing;

    (f) the right to lodge a complaint with a supervisory authority;

    (g) where the personal data are not collected from the data subject, any available information as to their source;

    (h) the existence of automated decision-making, including profiling, referred to in Article 22(1) and (4) and, at least in those cases, meaningful information about the logic involved, as well as the significance and the envisaged consequences of such processing for the data subject.

2. Where personal data are transferred to a third country or to an international organisation, the data subject shall have the right to be informed of the appropriate safeguards pursuant to Article 46 relating to the transfer.

3. The controller shall provide a copy of the personal data undergoing processing. For any further copies requested by the data subject, the controller may charge a reasonable fee based on administrative costs. Where the data subject makes the request by electronic means, and unless otherwise requested by the data subject, the information shall be provided in a commonly used electronic form.

4. The right to obtain a copy referred to in paragraph 3 shall not adversely affect the rights and freedoms of others.

The nature and extent of the right

Individuals have the right to know whether or not their personal data are being processed by, or on behalf of, the controller, and, where that is the case, to be given access to the data, as well as additional specified information regarding the processing of the data. This additional information mirrors the information that must be included in privacy notices issued to individuals at the time their data are first obtained (see Chapter 3). Specifically, individuals who exercise the right of access are entitled to be supplied with the following information:

(a) the purposes of the processing;

(b) the categories of personal data concerned;

(c) the recipients or categories of recipient to whom their data have been or will be disclosed, in particular recipients in third countries or international organizations;

(d) where possible, the envisaged period for which the personal data will be stored, or, if not possible, the criteria used to determine this period;

(e) the existence of the rights to request rectification, erasure, restriction, and to object (see later in this chapter);

(f) the right to lodge a complaint with the Commissioner;

(g) in cases where personal data have not been collected directly from the controller, any available information as to their source;

(h) the existence of automated decision-making, and, in cases where automated decision-making is taking place, meaningful information about the logic involved, as well as the significance and potential consequences of any such automated decision-making (see later in this chapter); and

(i) in cases where the data subject's personal data are transferred to a third country or to an international organization, the safeguards that apply (see Chapter 6).

Where the individual makes a request by electronic means, and unless otherwise requested by the data subject, Article 12(3) indicates that this information should be provided in a 'commonly used electronic form'. Where the requested information includes personal data provided by the data subject herself, there may also be an obligation, as a result of the right to data portability, to supply this particular data in a structured, commonly used, and machine-readable format (see later in this chapter).

The 'purpose' of subject access requests

According to Recital 63 of the GDPR, rights of access are conferred on data subjects 'in order to be aware of, and verify, the lawfulness of the processing'. This echoes a corresponding recital in the former Data Protection Directive which indicated that individuals should have rights of subject access 'in order to verify in particular the accuracy of the data and the lawfulness of the processing'.

The proposition that the purpose of the right of subject access is to enable data subjects to check the accuracy of their data and to check their data are otherwise being processed in accordance with the controller's obligations might, on the face of it, suggest that requests made for other purposes are invalid, or even that such requests could be rejected pursuant to Article 12(5) as manifestly unreasonable.

However, controllers that are tempted to adopt this position should do so with caution. It is true that a series of cases (decided under the former Data Protection Directive) has emphasized that the proper purpose of a subject access request is to enable a data subject to check the accuracy of the data and to see that they are being processed lawfully (see *Johnson v MDU* [2007] EWCA Civ 282; *Durant v FSA* [2003] EWCA Civ 1746; *College van burgemeester en wethouders van Rotterdam v Rijkeboer* (C-553/07 [2009]); *YS v Minister voor Immigratie* (C-141/12 and C-372/12 [2014]). Giving judgment in the Court of Appeal in *Durant*, Auld LJ famously opined that in entitling an individual to have access to his data, the purpose of the subject access right 'is to enable him to check whether the controller's processing of it unlawfully infringes his privacy and, if so, to take such steps … to protect it. It is not an automatic key to any information, readily accessible or not, of matters in which he may be named or involved. Nor is to assist him, for example, to obtain discovery of documents that may assist him in litigation or complaints against third parties'.

However, the UK courts have more recently arrived at a position whereby motive and purpose are firmly considered to be largely irrelevant to the validity of subject access requests (see *Dunn v Durham County Council* [2012] EWCA Civ 1654; *Iesni v Westrip Holdings* [2011] 1 BCLC 498; *Southern Pacific Personal Loans Ltd* [2013] EWHC 2485 (Ch); *Elliott v Lloyds TSB Bank plc and Another* [2012] EW Misc 7; *Gurieva and Another v Community Safety Development (UK) Ltd* [2016] EWHC 643 (QB); *Kololo v Commissioner of Police for the Metropolis* [2015] EWHC 600 (QB); *Lin v Commissioner of Police for the Metropolis* [2015] EWHC 2484 (QB)). Indeed, in *Dawson Damer and Others v Taylor Wessing LLP* [2017] EWCA Civ 74, the Court of Appeal held that Auld LJ's observations in *Durant* regarding the purpose of the subject access right had been misunderstood, concluding that 'arguments … as to why there should not be a "no other purpose rule" are compelling'.

Despite these developments, where organizations are responding to an access request from a person who is contemplating litigation against the organization, the organization will (as in all cases) be able to use the 'legal professional privilege' exemption to restrict access to personal data contained in any documents to which legal professional privilege attaches. Other exemptions, including the rule against supplying third party information, may also be used where appropriate.

Searches

Following an access request, controllers are obliged to search all of their electronic and relevant paper-based filing systems for personal data relating to the requester. This can be both time-consuming and expensive for controllers. Nevertheless, controllers may take some comfort from the fact that the GDPR makes provision, in cases where requests are 'excessive', for controllers to extend time for the response, or alternatively, to refuse to act altogether. The GDPR does not, however, define the meaning of 'excessive' in this context.

In determining whether a request is 'excessive', decided cases under the 1998 Act regarding proportionality and the extent of the controller's search obligations are likely to be relevant. In the case of *Ezsias v Welsh Ministers* [2007] All ER (D) 65, the High Court held that, in order to comply with the duty to respond to a subject access request, controllers are obliged to carry out a 'reasonable and proportionate' search for the information requested but that searches need not be exhaustive; it is not necessary to 'leave no stone unturned'.

This finding was cited with approval by the Court of Appeal in *Ittihadieh v 5-11 Chene Gardens RTM Company Ltd and Others* [2017] EWCA Civ 121, which held that 'the mere fact that a further and more extensive search reveals further personal data relating to that individual does not entail the proposition that the first search was inadequate'. In order to satisfy requirements of proportionality when planning searches, controllers should take into account all relevant considerations including the value and potential benefit of the request for the data subjects. In *Dawson-Damer and Others v Taylor Wessing LLP* [2017] EWCA Civ 74, the Court of Appeal found that, in relation to searches, 'what is weighed up in the proportionality exercise is the end object of the search, namely the potential benefit that the supply of the information might bring to the data subject, as against the means by which that information is obtained'.

Controllers are not required to carry out searches where it is clear that a requested search will not yield any personal data, or will reveal only personal data that are exempt from disclosure. However, where it is not possible to know with any degree of certainty whether information is exempt from disclosure without first reviewing the information in question, the search obligation cannot be avoided. In *Dr Cécile Deer v The University of Oxford* [2017] EWCA Civ 121, the controller's reasons for not carrying out a search for data falling within specific categories included that relevant data were covered by legal professional privilege, or were already in the possession of the data subject. However, Lewison LJ expressed the following view:

Unless it is clear from a SAR that carrying out a requested search will not yield any personal data, or it is clear that any personal data retrieved by such a search will be exempt from disclosure, I do not think that in principle a controller complies with a duty to carry out a reasonable and proportionate search by not carrying out any search at all.

The information that must be supplied

Controllers should appreciate that rights of access under Article 15 apply only to personal data, as that term is defined in Article 4 (see Chapter 1).

Other than in the case of public authorities (which have additional disclosure obligations under UK law), there is no obligation to supply information held in unstructured manual filing systems (see Chapter 1) in response to a subject access request. In *Johnson v Medical Defence Union* [2004] EWHC 347 and *Smith v Lloyds TSB* [2005] EWHC 246 the applicants were denied a remedy by the courts where they claimed access to paper-based information which had originally been produced in electronic form, but which, at the time of the request, existed merely in paper (printed out) form. The court held that the time of the request was the key moment for determining the existence of 'personal data' for the purposes of complying with the request. This was so despite an intriguing argument by Ashley Roughton, barrister for the claimants in each case, that if data had once been processed electronically in an organization, then the same data should be processed in compliance with data protection law for the remainder of their existence in that organization (for more on the so-called 'once processed, always processed' argument, see Roughton A, 'Once Processed, Always Processed—Issues Explained', *Privacy & Data Protection*, Volume 5, Issue 4—<http://www.pdpjournal.com>).

Information cannot be withheld from data subjects on the grounds that it is already known to them, or, indeed, on the grounds that the data were originally supplied by them in the first place (see *Dr Cécile Deer v The University of Oxford* [2017] EWCA Civ 121). The logic here is that it is wholly reasonable for individuals to seek to check that information held by a controller accurately records information supplied to the controller by the data subject. In practice many individuals who submit subject access requests do not, however, require the disclosure of either personal data supplied by them to the controller or personal data contained in communications between themselves and the controller. In appropriate circumstances, it can be useful to check with requesters whether they require this category of information before the response is issued.

It should be noted that, when dealing with requests for access, controllers are obliged to provide access to the personal data that are being processed rather than copies of documents containing the data (and also that although information about a data subject may be held in multiple different documents, e.g. contact details or transaction records, the information need be provided only once). Although it is common for controllers to respond to access requests by supplying copies of documents, it is certainly open to controllers to supply the personal data in a different form, for example by preparing a summary or by compiling extracts from relevant records.

Although this method of supplying the information can be more time-consuming than simply providing copies of relevant documents, the ability to supply a summary or extract can be useful to controllers in certain circumstances. When adopting this approach, controllers should take care to ensure that the 'summary' of personal data does in fact contain all non-exempt personal data and that sufficient detail is included to ensure summaries or extracts are intelligible to the individual. In the case of *R v Secretary of State for the Home Department, ex p Lord* [2003] EWHC 2073, a prisoner applied for subject access in order to see reports which had been prepared on him by prison staff and other professionals. It was the policy of the prison, when dealing with such requests, to summarize the information contained in the reports rather than to supply copies of the reports. The applicant prisoner successfully argued that the summary he was given did not fully reflect the content of the reports and the court granted him access to the original documents.

Controllers should appreciate that Schedules 2–4 of the Bill make detailed provision for exemption from the right of subject access. These exemptions largely replicate the exemptions afforded by the 1998 Act.

Subject access and emails

For the purpose of responding to subject access requests, emails are no different from any other type of information: personal data contained in emails must be supplied unless the data concerned are exempt from disclosure. However, dealing with requests for personal data contained in emails can give rise to particular difficulties in practice.

Personal data of a particular requester may be located in emails sent and received by multiple users, and may be stored in disparate parts of information technology systems as well as on local devices (which may, or may not, be directly managed by the controller—an example of the latter is where an employee is permitted to use his or her own mobile phone for sending and receiving work emails). Identifying and recovering such emails can present particular challenges.

Because emails falling within the scope of a subject access request may be sent or received by employees of the controller using personal devices or personal email accounts, controllers should ensure they have systems in place that either prohibit the use of personal devices and personal email accounts for business communications or that allow them to access relevant data or enable them to compel employees to conduct relevant searches where necessary.

An additional challenge that can arise in the case of requests seeking to access personal data contained in emails is that central searches of email systems that use the requester's name as a search criteria will usually generate large numbers of false positive results, especially where the requester is also a user of the system. Considerable care should therefore be taken when designing searches of email systems in order to minimize the retrieval of irrelevant records.

In particular, controllers should bear in mind that many emails originally sent or received by a requestor, or copied to them, on business systems will often be about matters other than the requestor; it will often therefore be the case that such emails do not include the requestor's personal data. More targeted searches of emails sent or received by individuals who are known to have had specific dealings with the requester may, depending on the circumstances, satisfy proportionality requirements and be more productive. Controllers should, however, be alive to the possibility that some routine emails sent or received by individuals will include their personal data. This could readily be true of emails sent in relation to HR matters, including, for example, proposed redundancy or disciplinary matters; emails the contents of which permit inferences or conclusions to be made regarding the requestor's opinions, knowledge, or expertise; or emails establishing the presence of the requestor at a meeting held at a particular location and on a particular date. It may even be that the time and date that an email is sent by a data subject constitutes his or her personal data and will need to be produced in response to a subject access request.

Finally, when devising electronic searches in order to respond to a subject access request, controllers should bear in mind that even where relevant data have been deleted from live systems, personal data held in archive or back-up systems will still be disclosable. Controllers should therefore ensure searches are carried out across all relevant IT systems and back-up media. There is, however, no requirement to search for data that have been actively deleted and which cannot readily be accessed or restored by system users. The UK Information Commissioner's view is that data which, following deletion, continue to be held in such a way that they cannot be used to make decisions about individuals, but which could technically be reconstituted by those with relevant technical expertise, can be treated as falling outside the scope of a subject access request (see ICO Subject Access Code of Practice, 2014).

In practice, emails are notoriously challenging for controllers to handle when managing subject access requests. They can often contain information, including opinions, about individuals that the controller would prefer not to be disclosed to the individual. A robust 'Use of Emails' policy within the organization, plus appropriate training on the policy and on data protection matters generally, may reduce the instances of embarrassment or legal exposure.

The logic behind automated decisions

A data subject who makes an access request is entitled to be given meaningful information about the logic involved in any automated decision-making that takes place based solely on automated processing and which produces legal effects or similarly significant effects concerning him or her. The data subject also has a right to be told about the significance and the envisaged consequences for him or her of such decision-making.

A common example of an automated decision-making process is credit scoring. Where a computer programme, as a result of information keyed in, effectively makes the 'decision' concerning whether to extend a loan to an individual, then the individual concerned is entitled on request to a meaningful description of the logic involved—that is, the method by which the decision was reached. This is in addition to the right under Articles 13 and 14 (see Chapter 3) to be supplied with this information at the time the personal data are collected by either the controller or the processor. Controllers may be able to comply with this requirement by supplying a general statement of the purpose and operation of the relevant software, provided this statement is readily intelligible and in clear and plain language.

In addition to forming part of the material that must be forwarded to an individual upon a subject access request being made, automated decisions form the basis of a separate right for individuals—see 'Automated Decision-taking' later in this chapter for further discussion on the right not to be subject to decision-making based solely on automated processing.

Rights in relation to data transfers

An individual who makes a subject access request also has the right, pursuant to Article 15(2) of the GDPR, to be informed about the safeguards relied on by the controller in relation to the transfer of personal data to any country outside the European Economic Area or to any international organization (see Chapter 6). The right does not apply to transfers to countries or organizations where the European Commission has made a finding that the country or organization in question ensures an adequate level of privacy protection.

Access requests to public authorities in the UK

Public authorities are under the same obligations as other organizations to respond to subject access requests. However, public authorities may be obliged to go one step further than other organizations in searching for and disclosing relevant information. This is because, as regards public authorities, UK legislation extends specified data subject rights (including the right of access) not only to personal data processed by electronic means and personal data forming, or intended to form, part of a filing system (see Chapter 1), but also to unstructured paper records.

Rights of access to such unstructured personal data are, however, limited. Public authorities are not obliged to comply with a request for access to such data unless the request contains a description of the data. Furthermore, even where a request includes a description of the unstructured personal data that the data subject wishes to receive, a public authority is not obliged to comply with the request if it estimates that the cost of compliance would exceed an 'appropriate limit' designated in regulations made under the Freedom of Information Act 2000. If compliance with the request would exceed the appropriate limit, the authority must nevertheless inform the data subject as to whether such data are being processed, unless the cost of doing so would itself exceed the 'appropriate limit'.

Third party information

In certain cases, the controller will be unable fully to comply with a request for information without also disclosing information relating to another individual who can be identified from the information requested (e.g. where data relate to two or more people and only one of them has made a subject access request).

Examples include information relating to joint tenants of a property, a report written by one person about another person, and a workplace complaint made about the behaviour of two people acting together. In such cases controllers are entitled to withhold the requested personal data to the extent that this is necessary in order to protect the rights and freedoms of other individuals.

In determining whether another person can be identified from personal data that are otherwise disclosable to the data subject, the controller is entitled to take into account, not only the information that would otherwise be supplied to the requestor, but also any information that the controller reasonably believes is likely to be in the requestor's possession (or is likely to come into his or her possession). In the event that another person is identifiable, the controller is entitled to refuse to comply with the data subject's request (to the extent that doing so would involve the disclosure of information about that person) unless:

(a) the other person has consented to the disclosure of the information to the person making the request; or

(b) it is reasonable in all the circumstances to comply with the request without the consent of the other person.

It should be noted that the information that may be withheld by a controller under this provision is that which relates to an 'individual'. Information concerning a company or other organization will thus generally not be covered by the provision—this means that, for example, a controller would be unable to withhold information concerning the source of personal data processed by the controller where the source is a company or other organization.

In determining whether it is 'reasonable in all the circumstances' to comply with the request without the consent of the other individual who may be identified, particularly relevant considerations set out in the Bill are:

(a) the type of information that would be disclosed;

(b) any duty of confidentiality owed to the individual;

(c) any steps taken by the controller with a view to seeking the consent of the individual;

(d) whether the other individual is capable of giving consent; and

(e) any express refusal of consent by the individual.

In considering whether it is reasonable to disclose third party information without consent, the type of information concerned is clearly relevant; it is suggested that the less 'personal', intrusive, or extensive the third party information, the more likely it is to be reasonable to disclose the information without consent.

While Article 23(1)(i) of the GDPR provides that Member States may adopt legislative measures to protect the 'rights and freedoms of others', the reference, in (b), to confidentiality, is a feature of UK legislation that does not have a direct counterpart in the GDPR. The UK law of confidence and the data subject access right do not, particularly in the context of third party information, sit well together. As far as point (b) is concerned, controllers often maintain that they are entitled to withhold third party information on the basis that the information is confidential. There are two reasons why controllers may need to be cautious about this approach. The first is that the existence of a 'duty of confidentiality' is merely one factor to be taken into account in determining whether it is reasonable to disclose—it may still be reasonable to disclose third party data even where a duty of confidentiality clearly exists. The second is the general principle, enshrined in the constitution of the EU, that domestic law (including the common law duty of confidence) must be interpreted to comply, so far as is possible, with EU law. The data subject access provisions in the GDPR (Article 15) make no reference to the law of confidence as such.

It is unclear whether the lack of any steps (in (c)) taken by the controller to gain the consent of the relevant individual will make it more or less reasonable to comply with the request in the absence of such consent—the courts might take the view, on the one hand, that the individual is deserving of more protection where he is unaware of any proposed provision of his information or, on the other hand, that the controller should be unable to hide behind a lack of any attempt on its part to contact the third party and that the information should therefore be disclosed. Interestingly, the controller is under no obligation to seek the consent of any relevant third party.

Amendments to data

It is usual for personal data to be amended over time in the ordinary course of business (e.g. by addition, deletion, or correction). The GDPR is silent as to the steps controllers should take where amendments to personal data are due to take place between the time of receipt of a subject access request and the date upon which the response will be issued. It is suggested that in the event that an access request is received, all relevant data should be preserved so that all personal data falling within the scope of the request and held at the date of receipt can be reviewed and all non-exempt personal data supplied to the data subject. Controllers and all employees involved in the management of requests should be aware that it is a criminal offence to alter, deface, block, erase, destroy, or conceal information with the intention of preventing disclosure of all or part of the information that the person making the request would have been entitled to receive.

Access requests and legal proceedings

Increasingly commonly, organizations receive access requests from persons who are engaged in, or who are contemplating, legal proceedings against the organization. As discussed above, an individual does not need a 'reason' to make an access request, and so his motive in so doing will usually be irrelevant.

However, the courts do have a discretion as to whether to grant an order for subject access. Following the judgment of Mumby J in *R v Secretary of State for the Home Department, ex p Lord* [2003] EWHC 2073 (Admin), this discretion is generally understood to be 'wide and untrammeled'. It follows that it is open to the UK courts, when exercising discretion in subject access cases, to have regard to the motives of an individual in making subject access requests and in pursuing litigation. In *Dr Cécile Deer v The University of Oxford* [2017] EWCA Civ 121, the Court of Appeal noted that even though a collateral purpose of assisting in litigation is not an absolute bar to seeking to enforce an access request in the courts, 'if an application is an abuse of rights, for example where litigation is pursued merely to impose a burden on the controller, that would be a relevant factor' in relation to the exercise of the court's discretion. Other relevant factors would be whether the application to the court was procedurally abusive and whether the requested data was of real value to the data subject. In the absence of any such factors, however, the court found that if there is a valid request and a failure on the part of the controller to comply with its obligations 'then the discretion will ordinarily be exercised in favour of the data subject'.

Where organizations are responding to an access request from a person who is contemplating litigation against the organization, the organization will (as in all cases) be able to use the 'legal professional privilege' exemption to restrict access to personal data contained in any documents to which legal professional privilege attaches. Other exemptions, and the rule against supplying third party information, may also be used where appropriate.

Fees and time limits

In most cases controllers are required to respond to subject access requests within one month and free of charge. There are, however, some exceptions to this general rule. As indicated above, controllers may extend time by two further months in the case of complex requests or multiple requests. Controllers that wish to extend time on this basis should, however, inform recipients of the time extension and the reasons why the extension is necessary within one month of receipt of the request. More specifically, in relation to examination results that have yet to be announced, the Bill provides that the deadline for compliance with a subject access request is five months from the date of receipt or, if earlier, before the end of a period of forty days from the date the results are announced.

Controllers that can demonstrate that a request is 'manifestly unfounded or excessive' are entitled to either decline to comply with the request altogether or, alternatively, may agree to comply with the request for a reasonable fee that reflects the controller's administrative costs. The Bill makes provision for the making of regulations specifying limits on the fees that may be charged by controllers.

Example of a simple subject access request
Luisa receives the brochure from Bathrooms Galore but notices something odd about the address label on the packaging. Her name appears as 'Mrs Luisa P. Bailey'. She feels sure that she did not tell the telephone operator her middle name, nor that she was married. She writes a letter to Bathrooms Galore asking for a copy of all the information it holds on her and details of the source of that information. Bathrooms Galore must supply Luisa with the information she has requested and must do so within one month of receiving her request.

Data Portability

The right of data portability, conferred by Article 20 of the GDPR, is closely related to the right of subject access. It entitles individuals to receive personal data that they have provided to a controller in a 'structured, commonly used and machine-readable format', and to transmit or have those data transmitted to another controller. The right is intended to facilitate the ability of data subjects to move, copy, or transmit their personal data from one IT system to another and to switch between different service providers.

Scope of the right

The right applies only to personal data that have been provided by the data subject and are processed by automated means where the legitimizing ground for processing (see Chapter 3) is either that the data subject consents, or that the processing is necessary for the performance of a contract with the data subject (or in order to take steps prior to entering into such a contract). This would include personal data processed by a utility provider or online services provider in the course of providing contracted services but could also extend to data processed by an employer in order to enter into a contract with an employee (e.g. CV and application form) or in connection with an employee's pay and compensation.

The right does not apply where processing is legitimized on other grounds, for example because it is necessary for the purpose of the controller's legitimate interests or for the purposes of complying with a legal obligation or discharging public functions.

Where the right applies, a data subject is entitled to receive relevant data in a structured, commonly used, and machine-readable format and to share the data with another controller 'without hindrance'. Controllers who supply data subjects with their personal data pursuant to Article 20 should not therefore seek to impose legal or technical restrictions on the further disclosure of the personal data concerned or put in place arrangements that will impede access or disclosure on costs grounds.

Data subjects also have the right to ask controllers to transmit relevant personal data directly to another controller. However, compliance with this right is limited to what is 'technically feasible'. Controllers are encouraged to develop interoperable formats that will facilitate the exercise of the portability right (see Recital 68), but the GDPR does not impose any legal obligation on controllers to adopt or maintain systems which ensure that the transfer of data to other controllers will be technically feasible.

The right to data portability clearly applies to personal data knowingly and actively supplied by data subjects when signing up for a contract, or provided by them in the course of receiving services. In cases where personal data are not directly supplied by data subjects, there is, however, a degree of uncertainty regarding the scope of the right to data portability. Personal data generated by a controller as a result of the controller's analysis of raw data regarding the data subject's use of a service, or as a result of a risk assessment conducted using data provided by an individual data subject or observed by the controller ('inferred data'), cannot reasonably be described as data 'provided by' the data subject and are therefore excluded from the scope of the portability right. But the position in relation to personal data generated as a direct result of an individual's use of the controller's service ('observed data') is less clear.

The Article 29 Working Party (in its Guidelines on the right to data portability of 5 April 2017, WP 242) has expressed the firm view that, for the purposes of the data portability right, personal data that record a data subject's use of a service or device (i.e. 'observed data') should be treated as data 'provided by' the data subject. For the full text of the Working Party's Guidelines, see <http://www.dpdocuments.com>.

The Working Party's view, that the phrase 'provided by the data subject' should be interpreted broadly to include all data observed about the data subject in the course of the controller's dealings with the data subject (e.g. usage data, transaction history, access log, health data collected by app recordings), is understandable given that benefits of data portability are considered to include empowering data subjects by preventing 'lock- in', fostering opportunities for innovation, and enriching services and customer experiences.

However, controllers should note that the precise scope of the portability right is controversial; the view that 'observed data' falls within the scope of the right to data portability has been criticized by some, including the European Commission, as exceeding what was agreed during the legislative process.

Advice for controllers

As in the case of all data subject rights, when responding to portability requests, controllers should comply with the obligations set out in Article 12 (see above).

The portability right requires controllers to supply relevant data to data subjects in a 'structured commonly used and machine-readable format'. According to the Working Party Opinion referred to above, for the purposes of data portability, data are 'machine readable' if they are in a data format that can be automatically read and processed by a computer. This includes CSV, JSON, and XML data formats but excludes PDF documents and scanned images.

When responding to portability requests, controllers have no specific obligation to check the quality or accuracy of relevant data prior to transmission and are not responsible for subsequent processing of the data by the data subject or by any third party recipient; receiving controllers are responsible for ensuring that their subsequent processing of any ported data complies in full with the GDPR.

Transmitting controllers are, however, responsible for ensuring that they act strictly in accordance with the data subject's instructions and that the data that are transferred are limited to data which the data subject wishes to be transferred. Where possible, data subjects should therefore be asked to specifically identify the data they wish the controller to transmit. Transmitting controllers are also responsible for implementing appropriate security measures necessary to ensure the secure transmission of relevant data to the correct destination.

Article 20(4) of the GDPR provides that the right to data portability should not adversely affect the rights and freedoms of others. According to the Article 29 Working Party's 2017 Guidelines, this restriction is intended to avoid the transmission of information that includes personal data relating to individuals other than the requester, in circumstances where such transmission would adversely affect the rights of these other individuals. Such adverse impact could arise where, for example, ported data includes information relating to contacts of the individual who has requested the transmission of his or her data, and the receiving controller is able to use data relating to these other individuals for its own commercial purposes.

Receiving controllers should therefore ensure any personal data relating to third parties which is transmitted to them as a result of a portability request is retained only to the extent strictly necessary and is processed at all times in accordance with the rights of these other individuals under the GDPR.

For further comments and insights on the right to data portability, see Fulford N, 'The New Right to Data Portability', *Privacy & Data Protection*, Volume 17, Issue 3 (<http://www.pdpjournal.com>).

Rectification

Article 16 of the GDPR entitles individuals to have personal data rectified if they are inaccurate or incomplete. The right is closely linked to the controller's obligation pursuant to Article 5(1)(d) of the GDPR to take all reasonable steps to ensure that personal data are accurate.

Where the right is exercised, the controller is also required, by virtue of Article 19, to inform any recipient (including employees of the controller, processors, and third parties) to whom the personal data have been disclosed of the rectification, unless this proves impossible or involves disproportionate effort. The data subject is entitled on request to be informed about these recipients.

As in the case of all data subject rights, when responding to requests for rectification, controllers should comply with the obligations set out in Article 12 (see above).

The main challenges for controllers are likely to arise where there is disagreement as to whether relevant personal data are inaccurate or incomplete. If, contrary to the data subject's claims, the controller is satisfied that personal data are in fact accurate or complete, the controller may decline to take action in response to a request and notify the data subject accordingly. In the event of dispute, it would then be open to the data subject to refer the matter to the national data protection regulator or to the courts (see later in this chapter). As a practical measure, in cases of such disagreement, the data subject may be prepared to agree that the contested data may be retained on file by the controller provided it is held on a restricted basis (see further below) and/or is supplemented with a statement recording the data subject's view.

The duty under Article 19 to inform each recipient to whom the data have been disclosed of any rectification also presents potential challenges. Recipients do not have to be informed of rectification where this proves impossible or would involve a disproportionate effort, but controllers should nevertheless take steps wherever possible to keep track of and record all personal data disclosures. This will not only assist controllers to comply with the obligation to notify third party recipients but will also enable controllers to comply with the distinct obligation under Article 19 to inform data subjects on request about the recipients of data that the controller has been required to correct.

It is worth noting that the obligation to notify third party recipients about rectification appears to apply irrespective of the data subject's wishes. As it is conceivable that data subjects who succeed in making a request for rectification to one controller will not always wish other controllers to be made aware that they have made a rectification request, controllers should therefore ensure that data subjects are made aware that successful rectification requests may be notified to third party recipients and should be ready to deal with data subject objections to such notification.

Rights to Object

Article 21 of the GDPR entitles individuals to object to the processing of their data in a range of specified circumstances.

In cases where personal data are processed for direct marketing purposes (see below), the right is absolute; controllers that receive objections from individuals regarding the use of their data for direct marketing purposes are required to cease processing for these purposes and there are no exceptions.

Individuals also have more limited rights of objection to the processing of their personal data in cases where the legitimizing grounds for processing (see Chapter 3) are that processing is necessary for the controller's legitimate interests or the performance of a task in the public interest or the exercise of official authority, or that the data are processed for purposes of scientific or historical research or for statistical purposes. In these cases the right of objection is subject to certain limitations, so that, notwithstanding the data subject's objection, a controller is not required to cease processing relevant personal data where there is an overriding justification for the processing concerned (see further below).

The Right to Object to Direct Marketing

This right gives individuals the power to require controllers to stop using their data for any direct marketing purposes. This includes the right to prevent profiling carried out for the purpose of direct marketing as well as the right to prevent the sending of unwanted marketing messages by any means.

The right to require the cessation of processing for the purposes of direct marketing applies to all media used for marketing, for example postal marketing, email marketing, fax marketing, text message marketing, telephone marketing, and online behavioural advertising. The right can be exercised only against a controller that uses relevant personal data for direct marketing purposes.

A general objection to the use of personal data for direct marketing purposes will impact on a controller's ability to conduct direct marketing by any means. It is, however, reasonable to assume that a specific request for the cessation of a particular type of marketing (e.g. 'please do not send me any more brochures by post') would allow the controller to continue to carry out marketing using other media.

Example of a request to cease direct marketing

This example follows on from that used in 'subject access requests'. Some months after Luisa has placed an order for bathroom equipment, she receives a colour brochure from Bathrooms Galore, which provides information on its new bathroom ranges. She writes to the company requesting that she be 'taken off the mailing list'. Following receipt of this request, the company must ensure that it does not send marketing materials to Luisa in the future.

It should be noted that the right to prevent direct marketing is different from the question as to whether any particular direct marketing is conducted lawfully under the legislation. In other words, the absence of any objection to the receipt of direct marketing materials by a particular individual does not necessarily mean that the sending of such materials to that individual will be lawful. Direct marketing by email (which includes marketing communications sent by text message), telephone, or fax must additionally comply with the E-Privacy Regulation, considered in Chapter 10.

Scope of the right

The right applies to all personal data processed for direct marketing purposes. Although direct marketing is not defined in the GDPR, it is understood to refer to advertising and marketing material that is directed at specific recipients. Direct marketing certainly includes the transmission of commercial advertising material to specific individuals by a range of means including post, fax, email, and SMS/text message. Direct marketing is not, however, restricted to the promotion of commercial goods, services, and businesses. Historically, the Commissioner has taken a very broad approach to the definition of direct marketing, considering it to include any targeted communication by an organization to an individual which informs the individual about the 'aims and ideals' of the organization. The definition therefore extends to political canvassing as well as to communications by charities that inform potential donors of their activities.

It is important to appreciate that the right extends beyond the right to prevent the sending of direct marketing materials. All other activities associated with direct marketing that occur prior to the actual sending of a marketing communication—such as gathering and sorting data, performing profiling, filtering, and mining activities—will also be caught. Mere storage of data, if such data are held only for the purposes of direct marketing, will also amount to processing for the purposes of direct marketing.

Advice for controllers

The right to object to the use of personal data for direct marketing purposes is absolute; there are no exemptions. Provided the controller is satisfied as to the identity of the data subject, a request that the data subject's personal data should no longer be processed for direct marketing purposes should therefore be actioned in full. As in the case of all data subject rights, when responding to objections to the processing of personal data for marketing purposes, controllers should comply with the obligations set out in Article 12 (see above).

Following receipt of a marketing objection from a data subject, data held concerning that individual should be flagged in some way so that the data are not used for future direct marketing. Rather than deleting the contact details of the requesting individual altogether, it may be advisable for the controller to retain these details (or a pared down version of them), together with the suppression information, so that the controller can ensure that even if the individual's details are reacquired in the future, they will not receive any unwanted marketing. Even if a related request for erasure is received from the data subject (see later in this chapter), in most cases it is likely that the controller will be entitled to retain a record of action taken in response to the marketing objection because this information will be held, not for direct marketing purposes, but for the purpose of the controller's legitimate interests in preventing unlawful direct marketing. Such records will therefore be outside the scope of most erasure requests.

There are obvious advantages in ensuring that relevant information technology systems and software (e.g. customer relationship management products) incorporate functions that allow for the suppression of customer details from future marketing initiatives.

Objections not related to direct marketing

Articles 21(1) and 21(6) also confer rights on data subjects to object to the use of their personal data in certain circumstances.

Article 21(1) of the GDPR applies where the conditions legitimizing processing (see Chapter 3) are that processing is necessary for the performance of a task carried out in the public interest or for the exercise of public functions. It also applies to personal data processed on the grounds that processing is necessary for the legitimate interests of the controller or of a third party. Article 21(6) applies to personal data processed for the purposes of scientific and historical research or for statistical purposes.

Individuals whose personal data are processed on any of these grounds have the right at any time to object to the processing of their data. This right to object is not, however, unqualified. In all cases, objections must be based 'on grounds relating to the data subject's particular situation'. In the case of objections made pursuant to Article 21(1) the right will not apply where the processing is necessary for the establishment, exercise, or defence of legal claims, or where the controller demonstrates compelling legitimate grounds for the processing which override the interests, rights, and freedoms of the data subject.

The Bill sets out a series of additional exemptions that may operate in certain circumstances to limit the exercise of the right of objection under Article 21(1). For example, in relation to data processed for the purposes of preventing or detecting crime or fraud, there is no obligation to comply with the right of objection under Article 21(1) to the extent that doing so would be likely to prejudice these purposes.

In the case of data processed for purposes of scientific and historical research or for statistical purposes, the right of objection pursuant to Article 21(6) does not apply where the processing is necessary for the performance of a task carried out for reasons of public interest. The Bill further limits the right of objection in the case of personal data processed for these purposes by creating an exemption which can be relied on provided that: processing is not carried out for the purpose of measures or decisions with respect to a particular data subject; technical and organizational measures are deployed to ensure respect for data minimization; and processing is not likely to cause substantial damage or substantial distress.

Advice for controllers

As in the case of all data subject rights, when responding to objection requests, controllers should comply with the obligations set out in Article 12 (see above). Controllers should be aware that in cases where a data subject makes a valid objection to the processing of his or her data pursuant to Article 21(1), he or she may also be entitled to seek the erasure of this data under Article 17 (see below).

Right to Erasure

Article 17 confers a right on data subjects to have personal data erased in certain circumstances. The right of erasure, sometimes described as 'the right to be forgotten', is intended to ensure that data subjects can insist on the deletion of their personal data in circumstances where the continued processing of the data is inconsistent with the requirements of the GDPR or is otherwise unlawful. This right can be exercised by data subjects even if the processing is not causing the data subject any damage or distress.

Scope of the right

Individuals have the right to have their personal data erased and to prevent the processing of their data in the following circumstances:

- Personal data are no longer necessary in relation to the purpose for which they were collected or otherwise processed.

As set out in Chapter 3, by virtue of Article 5(e) personal data may be processed in identifiable form for no longer than is necessary for the purposes for which the personal data are processed. A data subject who becomes aware that his or her data are held in breach of this obligation is entitled to insist on the erasure of such data, unless an exemption applies (see later in this chapter).

- The only legal basis for processing the personal data is that the data subject consents, but the data subject's consent has been withdrawn.

As set out in Chapter 3, personal data may be processed only where one of the conditions listed in Article 6 of the GDPR applies. The processing of special categories of data (discussed in Chapter 4) is permitted only where one or more of the conditions in Article 9(2) of the GDPR (or any of the further conditions specifically provided for in UK legislation) also apply. The right to erasure applies in cases where the only lawful ground for processing is the consent of the data subject. Therefore, where a controller processes some personal data relating to a particular data subject on the basis of consent but also processes other personal data on a different basis, for example in order to perform a contract with the data subject, the right to erasure may apply to some, but not all personal data relating to the data subject.

- The data subject objects to the processing pursuant to Article 21(1) and there are no overriding legitimate grounds for the processing.

Article 21(1) of the GDPR confers certain rights on data subjects to require controllers to cease processing their personal data. For further information on rights to object under Article 21(1) see above. In cases where the right to objection under Article 21(1) applies to require a controller to cease processing an individual's personal data, the controller can also be required to erase the data on request unless there is an overriding legitimate reason for retaining the data.

- The data subject objects to the processing pursuant to Article 21(2) of the GDPR.

Article 21(2) of the GDPR confers rights on data subjects in relation to data processed for direct marketing purposes, entitling them to object to the processing of their personal data for these purposes (see above for more information on the right to object to direct marketing). Data subjects who exercise the right of objection to the use of personal data for marketing purposes have a corresponding right to require the erasure of the data concerned. However, it is important to appreciate that although the right to object to the use of one's personal data for marketing purposes under Article 21(2) is absolute, this does not trigger an absolute right to erasure. There may be circumstances where the right to erasure does not apply (e.g. where retention is necessary for the defence of a legal claim), or alternatively it may be the case that personal data held for direct marketing purposes are also held for an additional purpose, in relation to which the right of erasure does not apply; an individual could not compel the erasure of personal contact details held both for marketing purposes and for the purpose of performing a contract with him or her.

The right of erasure will extend both to records of marketing communications sent to data subjects and also to any underlying personal data that are held for direct marketing purposes, including personal data used for profiling purposes (i.e. to identify a subject as a marketing target). As direct marketing is considered to include any targeted communications that promote the 'aims and ideals' of an organization, data held for the purposes of political canvassing and for charitable fundraising purposes may therefore be caught by the right of erasure.

- The personal data are unlawfully processed (i.e. otherwise than in breach of the GDPR).

Article 17 entitles data subjects to seek the erasure of their personal data that have been unlawfully processed by a controller. This might be the case where, for example, personal data have been processed in breach of an enforceable duty of confidentiality, or personal data are being processed by a public authority ultra vires.

- The personal data have to be erased in order to comply with a legal obligation.

Individuals are entitled to require the erasure of their personal data in circumstances where the controller is under a legal obligation to erase the data.

- The personal data have been collected in connection with the provision of online services to a child.

One of the specific aims of the GDPR is the protection of the personal data of children who engage with online services. The right to erasure ensures that children who consent to the processing of their personal data by online service providers at a time when they may not be fully aware of the risks involved may subsequently insist on the erasure of their data (and may do so even after they have become adults).

Exemption from the right to erasure

The right to erasure does not apply to the extent that processing is necessary:

- to exercise the right of freedom of expression and information;
- to comply with a legal obligation or for the performance of a public interest task or exercise of official authority;
- for public health purposes in the public interest;
- for archiving purposes in the public interest, scientific research, historical research, or statistical purposes; and
- for the exercise or defence of legal claims.

The right of erasure is further limited in the UK by the Bill. For example, the right does not apply to personal data processed for the purposes of preventing or detecting crime, apprehending or prosecuting offenders, or assessing or collecting taxes, to the extent that compliance would prejudice any of these purposes.

Informing recipients

A controller that is required by Article 17 to erase personal data that the controller has made public, for example as a result of online publication, is also required to take reasonable steps to notify other controllers that are processing the personal data of the erasure request. Furthermore, Article 19 of the GDPR obliges controllers to inform any recipient to whom personal data have been disclosed (including employees of the controller, processors, and third parties) of any erasure carried out pursuant to Article 17, unless this proves impossible or involves disproportionate effort. The data subject is entitled on request to be informed about any such recipients.

The obligations to notify recipients, and controllers who are processing the data as a result of its having been made public, about an erasure request give rise to a number of challenges for controllers.

Firstly, these obligations are not absolute and it is not entirely clear when they will apply. The duty under Article 19 to inform recipients about a successful erasure request arises only where notification does not involve 'a disproportionate effort'; the duty under Article 17(2) to notify controllers processing personal data that have been made public is limited to a duty to take 'reasonable steps'.

Secondly, it is not clear from the legislation what steps, if any, third party controllers are required to take once they have been notified about the erasure of data pursuant to an erasure request. The imposition on the controller of notification obligations is clearly intended to ensure that rights of erasure can be extended to third party controllers who process personal data that have been the subject of a successful erasure request (see Recital 66). However, Article 19 is silent as to the steps that recipients are expected to take when notified of an erasure. While Article 17(2) does provide that controllers should take reasonable steps 'to inform controllers which are processing the personal data that the data subject has requested the erasure by such controllers of any links to, or copy or replication of, those personal data', it will not necessarily be the case that a data subject who exercises the right of erasure against one controller either wishes other controllers to be informed of the erasure or intends the erasure request to apply also to third party controllers. It is also entirely possible that a third party controller that has obtained personal data as a result of their having been made public by another controller will process those data on the basis of processing grounds that do not allow for erasure requests, or will be able to rely on exemptions to the right of erasure that are not available to the controller that made the data public.

Advice for controllers

The right of erasure is not an absolute right. It does not apply to the extent that any of the exemptions set out at Article 17(3) or in the Bill is applicable. Neither does the right apply in cases where a request for erasure relates to an objection made pursuant to Article 21(1) where there are nevertheless overriding legitimate grounds for the processing. Accordingly it will sometimes be necessary for controllers to carry out a balancing exercise between, on the one hand, the data subject's interest in erasure and, on the other, competing legitimate interests of the controller and others.

When carrying out this balancing exercise, controllers may be assisted by the judgment of the Court of Justice of the European Union ('CJEU') in the case of *Google Spain SL & Google Inc. v Mario Costeja Gonzalez* (C-131/12 [2014]). The *Gonzalez* case (which was considered under the Data Protection Directive) concerned a request submitted to Google for removal, from the list of results displayed following a search made on the basis of the claimant's name, of links to web pages that reported details of a repossession order made against the claimant some sixteen years previously. The CJEU held that reports of the claimant's property repossession were excessive and no longer relevant, and that search engine links from the claimant's name to these online reports should therefore be removed. In reaching this conclusion, the CJEU identified a non-exhaustive list of considerations that could be relevant when balancing the individual's right to erasure against other competing factors, including the impact of publication on the data subject, and the impact of erasure on the commercial interests of the controller and, in the case of search engine publication, on the rights of the controller and others to freedom of expression.

Guidelines published by the Article 29 Working Party on the implementation on the CJEU's judgment in *Gonzalez* are also likely to be of assistance to controllers in receipt of requests for erasure where a balancing exercise between competing interests needs to be carried out. They are likely to be relevant not only in cases where a controller has to consider whether to reject an erasure request because processing is necessary for exercising rights of freedom of expression (see Article 27(3)(a)), but also where an erasure request is linked to an objection made under Article 21(1) and the controller considers there to be overriding legitimate grounds for the processing (see Article 17(1)(c)). For the full text of the Article 29 Working Party's Guidelines see <http://www.dpdocuments.com>.

As in the case of all data subject rights, when responding to erasure requests, controllers should comply with the obligations set out in Article 12.

Right to Restriction of Processing

The GDPR entitles data subjects to require controllers to process their data on a restricted basis in certain circumstances. Where the right applies, controllers may store affected personal data, but may not use the data in any way without the data subject's consent unless an exemption applies. The right operates to ensure that data subjects who have objections to the processing of their data are able to insist that their data be retained, but not otherwise processed by the controller, pending the resolution of their objections. The right to restriction applies in the following circumstances:

- The data subject contests the accuracy of the personal data.

Data subjects who contest the accuracy of their personal data are entitled to insist that their data be retained but not otherwise processed without consent, pending verification of the accuracy of the data.

- The processing is unlawful and the data subject opposes erasure.

Under Article 17, data subjects have the right to require the erasure of personal data that have been processed unlawfully. Article 18 entitles data subjects whose personal data are processed unlawfully to require the processing of their data to be restricted as an alternative to erasure.

- The controller no longer needs the personal data for the purpose of the processing.

Data subjects are entitled to require controllers to retain data that are no longer required by the controller (and which ought therefore to be deleted by the controller) on a restricted basis where the data are required by the data subject for the establishment, exercise, or defence of legal claims.

- The data subject has objected to processing pursuant to Article 21(1).

As explained above, where the legitimizing basis of processing is that processing is necessary for legitimate interests, data subjects are entitled, as a result of Article 21(1), to object to the processing of their data. Article 18 entitles data subjects who have objected to the processing of their data under Article 21(1) to restrict the processing of their data for so long as is necessary to enable the controller, in order to resolve the data subject's objection, to determine whether the legitimate processing grounds of the controller override the interests, rights, and freedoms of the data subject.

The right to restriction of processing is subject to a number of exemptions set out in the UK Bill. For example, the right will not apply where personal data are processed for specified regulatory purposes to the extent that restriction would be likely to prejudice these purposes. Similarly the right will not apply in the case of personal data processed for the purposes of preventing or detecting crime, apprehending or prosecuting offenders, or assessing or collecting taxes, to the extent that compliance would prejudice any of these purposes.

Informing the data subject and third parties

Where the right to restriction applies, controllers are required by Article 19 to inform all recipients to whom the data have been disclosed of the restriction, unless this is impossible or involves disproportionate effort. Data subjects are also entitled to be informed of any such recipients, presumably so that they can contact these recipients directly. Article 19 does not, however, compel third party controllers to take action when they are notified by another controller that personal data held by them have been the subject of a successful request for restriction. Neither does it take account of the possibility that the data subject may not wish other controllers to be notified of a restriction. In practice, and depending on the circumstances, controllers may wish to consider checking with the data subject before contacting any third party regarding a restriction request.

Controllers should also note that if they agree to a restriction request, the data subject has the right to be informed before any restriction on processing is lifted.

As in the case of all data subject rights, when responding to requests for restriction, controllers should comply with the obligations set out in Article 12.

Automated Decision-taking

Article 22 of the GDPR restricts the ability of controllers to make decisions by wholly automated means where the decisions being taken will have a significant impact on individuals.

Compared with other data subject rights, the right not to be subject to decision-making of this kind is unusual in that it imposes restrictions on controllers but does not confer specific rights on data subjects to require controllers to take action on request. Data subjects who have been subject to relevant automated decision-taking in breach of Article 22 are able to enforce their rights by complaining to the Commissioner or by bringing a claim in the courts (see below).

The GDPR does not spell out what is meant by 'significant effects'. However, Recital 72 gives a number of examples of the kind of decision-making that is restricted by Article 22. These include online credit decisions and e-recruiting and any automated profiling carried out to assess a person's 'performance at work, economic situation, health, personal preferences or interests, reliability or behaviour, location or movements', where this produces legal effects or a similarly significant impact. Automated decision-taking which is subject to some human oversight or intervention, or which could only have a minimal impact on data subjects (e.g. an online competition with a low value prize), is not restricted by Article 22.

There are three sets of circumstances in which the general prohibition on the use of wholly automated decision-making that will have significant effects can be disregarded.

Provided appropriate measures have been put in place by the controller to safeguard the data subject's rights, freedoms, and legitimate interests, controllers may carry out automated decision-taking that will have significant effects on data subjects if they have the data subject's explicit consent (see Chapter 3) or if this decision-making is necessary for entering into or performing a contract between the data subject and the controller. The protective measures that controllers would reasonably be expected to put in place will include:

- ensuring that the decision-taking is carried out in a fair and transparent way by providing meaningful information about the logic involved, as well as the envisaged consequences and their significance for data subjects;

- using reliable and appropriate mathematical or statistical processes;

- implementing appropriate technical or organizational measures to minimize inaccuracies and enable inaccuracies to be corrected;

- securing personal data in a way that is proportionate to the risks posed to the interests and rights of relevant data subjects and prevents discriminatory effects.

Automated decision-taking that will have significant effects on data subjects is also permitted where this is authorized by EU or Member State law which also lays down suitable measures to safeguard the data subject's rights and freedoms and legitimate interests. The Bill sets out safeguards that must be deployed when controllers engage in automated decision-making required or authorized by UK law.

It should be noted that the use of special category personal data for automated decision-taking is subject to additional restrictions. Special category personal data may be used for significant automated decision-taking only if suitable measures are in place to safeguard the data subject's rights, freedoms, and legitimate interest, and either the data subject consents, or the decision-taking is necessary for reasons of substantial public interest and is provided for by law.

Advice for controllers

Controllers should identify whether any of their processing operations constitute significant automated decision-making for the purposes of Article 22. To the extent that such decision-making is taking place, controllers may wish to consider the benefits of introducing a degree of human oversight in the decision-making process in order to remove the decision-making from the scope of Article 22. If this is impracticable, however, then unless the automated decision-taking is authorized by law or is necessary for the purpose of a contract, controllers should ensure that appropriate mechanisms are in place for obtaining explicit consent from data subjects before any significant automated decision-taking is carried out. Having regard to the standards required by the GDPR in relation to consent, controllers should bear in mind, however, that consent to automated decision-taking can be relied on only where individuals have a genuine choice (i.e. where an alternative form of decision-taking is available) and where the controller and the data subject are on an even footing. This is likely to present particular challenges for employers seeking consent from employees in order to carry out automated decision-taking that will have a significant impact on them.

In all cases where automated decision-taking is used in order to make significant decisions, controllers should ensure that appropriate safeguards are in place. As set out in Article 22(3), these safeguards should as a minimum include making provision for data subjects to request human intervention in relation to relevant decision-taking and to express a point of view and to complain about an automated decision that has affected them in a significant way.

Right to know 'logic'

Individuals are entitled to be informed of the 'logic' behind any automated decision-making about them which will have significant effects. This right arises as a result of the controller's obligation under Article 13 to inform data subjects about the handling of their personal data (see Chapter 3) and the right of access under Article 15 (see above).

Example of an automated decision

A recruitment company, Jobs'R'us offers jobs on its website. Applications are made online by individuals who fill in answers to certain questions about themselves. A computer program then determines whether the candidate will be invited for an interview. James applies for a job online but is rejected. In these circumstances, James must be informed, at the time he makes the application, that the decision concerning his suitability for the job will be taken by automated means. He should also be told about the logic involved. Jobs'R'us must also ensure that appropriate safeguards are in place to safeguard James' interests, for example by offering James an opportunity to seek a review of the decision to reject his application.

Compensation

Article 82 of the GDPR entitles any person who suffers damage as a result of a breach of the GDPR by either a controller or a processor to receive compensation.

Who can be sued?

Both controllers and processors can be liable for compensation claims. Their exposure to liability differs, however, in that controllers can be held liable for any damage caused by processing that breaches the GDPR, whereas processors can be held liable only where damage is caused by a breach of the obligations that are specifically imposed on processors by the GDPR or where they act outside, or contrary to, the lawful instructions of the controller. Both controllers and processors are exempt from liability for compensation if they can establish that they are not in any way responsible for the processing giving rise to the damage claimed.

As obligations in relation to data subject rights are imposed exclusively on controllers, processors' liability to compensate data subjects whose GDPR rights are breached will, in practice, be limited to cases where the processor has acted contrary to, or beyond the scope of, the controller's instructions. However, in order to ensure that data subjects are able to receive effective compensation, the GDPR provides that controllers and processors who are involved in the same processing are deemed jointly liable for damage caused by such processing. Irrespective of fault, data subjects may therefore bring a claim for compensation against any controller or processor that has been involved in processing which, in breach of the GDPR, has given rise to damage. A controller or processor that is held liable in this way is, however, entitled to recover from other relevant controllers or processors that part of the compensation paid out by them to a data subject that corresponds to the responsibility of these other processors or controllers for the damage caused. Because of the potential for deemed joint liability for claims and the risk of disputes regarding allocation of responsibility for such claims, organizations that are involved in processing personal data with other organizations should ensure that deemed joint liability for claims and mechanisms for allocating respective responsibility for any such claims are considered before any relevant processing takes place. These issues could usefully be included in the agreements that controllers and processors are required to enter into for the purposes of Articles 26 and 28.

Who can bring a claim?

Any person who has suffered damage (or distress) as a result of a breach of the GDPR may sue a relevant controller or processor for compensation. It is not necessary for the claimant to be the data subject in relation to the relevant processing. Additionally, in relation to compensation claims that are made by data subjects, the GDPR makes provision for claims to be brought on their behalf by suitably designated representative bodies. Court proceedings may be brought in the courts of any country in which the controller has an establishment, or in the courts of the country in which the data subject is habitually resident (unless the controller or processor is a public authority acting in the course of exercising public functions). Controllers and processors that are involved in processing personal data relating to individuals living in other EU Member States could therefore face compensation proceedings in foreign courts as a result of their handling of personal data in the UK.

Compensation claims

Claims for compensation may be brought for financial, physical, and psychological damage as well as for distress caused by an infringement of the GDPR. Any such compensation should be 'full and effective' (see Recital 146 of the GDPR).

In the UK, the assessment of damages in data protection cases is very much an evolving area. Cases decided under the 1998 Act (particularly cases decided following the judgment of the Court of Appeal in *Google Inc. v Vidal Hall and Others* [2014] EWHC 13(QB) which held that, notwithstanding the wording of Section 13(2) of the 1998 Act, damages were recoverable for non-pecuniary losses) give some indication of the approach the courts are likely to take when determining compensation claims, but it should be appreciated that these cases are small in number and damages awards are often highly fact-dependent.

In *Halliday v Creation Finance Ltd* [2013] EWCA Civ 33 the Court of Appeal awarded damages of £750 in respect of distress suffered by a claimant who said he had suffered distress when the defendant's actions resulted in incorrect entries being made in his credit records. In determining this modest award, the court had regard to the fact that the inaccuracy was due to a single technical error, rather than multiple breaches, was not attributable to any fraudulent or malicious intent, and did not have any damaging consequences for the claimant (e.g. in relation to his reputation or ability to access goods and services).

In *AB v Ministry of Justice* [2014] EWHC 1847 (QB) the claimant recovered a slightly more generous award in respect of emotional distress suffered as a result of extended delays on the part of the Ministry of Justice ('MoJ') when responding to subject access requests made following the death of the claimant's wife and his subsequent exchange of correspondence with the MoJ as to whether a full post mortem was required. The MoJ's response to AB's subject access request was issued some seventeen months late; some data falling within the scope of the request was not disclosed for a further six years. The court held that the claimant had suffered distress as a result of this delay and awarded compensation in the sum of £2,500.

More recently, in the case of *Andrea Brown v Commissioner of Police for the Metropolis and Chief Constable of Greater Manchester Police* (2016) Claim Nos. 3YM09078 & A53YP250 (CC at Central London), the claimant, a police officer with the Metropolitan Police, was awarded damages for distress occasioned when the defendant, contemplating disciplinary action against her, used its policing powers to gather intelligence regarding her movements (and those of her child) over a six-year period. The Metropolitan Police (which took no formal action against the claimant following the collection of this data) was ordered to pay to the claimant compensation in the sum of £9,000. This award included damages for loss of dignity and control over one's private information. In setting the level of the award, the court took account of the fact that there had been multiple contraventions which were not inadvertent or technical and which had involved the use of private information about a child.

In *TLT and Others v Secretary of State for the Home Department* [2016] EWHC 2217 (QB) the High Court considered a number of joint claims arising from the inadvertent online publication of details of 1,598 lead applicants for asylum or leave to remain. The information related to the family returns process (the means by which those with children who have no right to remain in the UK are returned to their country of origin). It was accepted that the disclosure of information regarding these asylum claims was likely to result in distress both for the affected data subjects and, in some cases, for relatives still living in their countries of origin. The court awarded damages of between £2,500 and £12,500, taking into account a range of relevant factors including evidence of distress suffered in each case, the reasonableness of beliefs regarding the consequences of publication for each claimant, and claimants' loss of control over their personal data and confidential information.

Right to a Judicial Remedy

In addition to the right to seek compensation, the GDPR confers a right on data subjects to apply to the courts for a remedy in any case where they consider that their data are being processed contrary to GDPR requirements. Proceedings brought to enforce the rights conferred under Chapter III of the GDPR may be issued in the courts of the country where the data subject has his or her habitual residence (unless the controller is a public authority exercising its public functions), or in the courts of the country where the controller has an establishment.

Complaints to the Commissioner

The GDPR confers responsibility on supervisory authorities to deal with complaints made by or on behalf of data subjects and others—see Chapter 8 for further information on the role and duties of the UK Information Commissioner.

Article 57(1)(f) of the GDPR indicates that one of the tasks of supervisory authorities is to:

(f) handle complaints lodged by a data subject, or by a body, organization or association in accordance with Article 80, and investigate, to the extent appropriate, the subject matter of the complaint and inform the complainant of the progress and the outcome of the investigation within a reasonable period, in particular if further investigation or coordination with another supervisory authority is necessary.

Supervisory authorities are specifically required to put in place measures (e.g. standard complaint forms) to facilitate the making of complaints.

On receiving a data subject complaint, supervisory authorities are required to carry out an investigation to the extent appropriate, and to inform data subjects about the progress and outcome of any such investigation.

Article 77 of the GDPR confers a corresponding right on any data subject who believes that the processing of personal data relating to him infringes the GDPR to lodge a complaint with the Information Commissioner. Complaints about GDPR infringements may also be submitted by representative bodies (constituted in accordance with Article 80(1) of the GDPR) acting either on behalf of affected data subjects or independently.

It is significant that complaints may be brought by individuals who believe themselves to be the subject of unlawful processing, whether or not such belief is reasonable; in this way the GDPR makes generous provision for the making of complaints by data subjects. The Commissioner is, however, required to investigate complaints only to the extent appropriate and is thus afforded a degree of discretion in relation to the investigation of complaints that are misfounded or otherwise unmeritorious.

For further detail in relation to the Commissioner's powers, including the power to impose an administrative fine in cases where a finding is made to the effect that processing has resulted in a breach of a data subject right, see Chapter 8.

8

Enforcement and the Role of the Regulator

Alison Deighton and Peter Carey

Introduction	155
Supervisory Authority Enforcement Role	156
Other Remedies	162
Consistency Mechanism	162
Cross-border Processing and Appointing a Lead Authority	163
UK Enforcement Action	166
UK Enforcement Procedures	166
Request for Assessment	166
Information Notice	167
Assessment Notice	169
Enforcement Notice	170
Monetary Penalty Notices	171
Appeals	173
Powers of Entry and Inspection	173

Introduction

Enforcement of data protection law in Member States is primarily the task of the national supervisory authorities.

The GDPR provides supervisory authorities with a wide array of enforcement powers, ranging from powers to conduct investigations, request information, and issue warnings, to the ability to impose significant fines for breaches of data protection rules, which is generally regarded as the most compelling motivator of compliance activity.

Supervisory authorities also have the power to impose a ban on data processing activities and order suspension of data flows, both of which can stop an organization from functioning effectively and, ultimately, could put an organization out of business.

In order to harmonize regulatory activity across Europe, supervisory authorities are required to cooperate with one another and to comply with a consistency mechanism under the GDPR to ensure a consistent approach to key decisions. Controllers and processors can also benefit from appointing a lead supervisory authority in relation to cross-border data processing, which facilitates communication with regulators across multiple jurisdictions and enables approvals to be sought in a streamlined manner.

Part 6 of the Data Protection Bill (which will become the UK's Data Protection Act once passed) sets out the methods by which the Information Commissioner can seek to ensure compliance with data protection requirements. The Information Commissioner's formal enforcement activities consist mostly of serving notices on organizations and imposing fines (monetary penalties).

Information Notices require controllers and processors to supply information to the Commissioner, Assessment Notices require controllers and processors to provide access to premises, equipment, and staff to enable the Information Commissioner to make a compliance assessment, while Enforcement Notices require controllers to comply with measures which are listed in the notice. It is a criminal offence to fail to respond to an Information Notice and failures to comply with Assessment Notices or Enforcement Notices may attract a monetary penalty.

A notice is unlikely to be served on organizations in the UK unless the Commissioner has received some information concerning a potential compliance issue. This may occur in a number of ways. An investigation could be triggered by a complaint by an individual or could relate to a sector investigation that the Information Commissioner is carrying out.

In addition to the powers of enforcement given to the Information Commissioner under the legislation, an individual who is the subject of loss or distress may bring court proceedings against the controller for compensation—this topic is discussed in Chapter 7. However, the Commissioner has no power to award compensation to an individual.

The Commissioner is also responsible for enforcing the Privacy and Electronic Communications (EC Directive) Regulations 2003 ('PECR'), as amended by the Privacy and Electronic Communications (EC Directive) (Amendment) Regulations 2011 (considered in Chapter 10). The Commissioner's powers in relation to PECR are substantially similar to her powers under the GDPR, including an ability to fine organizations.

The sections below examine, firstly, the role of supervisory authorities under the GDPR and, secondly, the procedures that the Information Commissioner in the UK follows when taking enforcement action.

Supervisory Authority Enforcement Role

Article 57 of the GDPR tasks supervisory authorities with (amongst other things) monitoring and enforcing the Regulation, promoting awareness, handling complaints, and conducting investigations.

In order to enable supervisory authorities to carry out these tasks effectively, they are provided with significant enforcement powers, which range from issuing warnings and reprimands at the lower end of the scale to imposing fines of up to 20 million euros or 4 per cent of annual worldwide turnover (whichever is higher) at the more severe end.

Article 58 of the GDPR lists all of the powers of supervisory authorities and splits them into three categories: (i) investigative; (ii) corrective; and (iii) authorization and advisory. The scope of each of these powers is examined in turn below.

It is important to note that, under Article 31 of the Regulation, controllers and processors are required to cooperate with supervisory authorities in the performance of their tasks. Therefore, when a supervisory authority is exercising any of its powers to request information, perform audits, or access premises for the purposes of monitoring and enforcing the Regulation, controllers and processors are obliged to comply with supervisory authority requests or face regulatory action for failing to do so.

Investigative powers

Supervisory authorities are granted extensive investigative powers under the GDPR. These include the power to order the provision of information, to carry out investigations in the form of data protection audits, to review data protection certifications granted to organizations under Article 42(7), to obtain from controllers and processors 'all information necessary for the performance of its tasks', and to access premises and equipment of controllers and processors.

Investigations are usually commenced following a complaint lodged by a data subject. However, this does not have to be the case. If a supervisory authority has particular concerns about a sector or particular practice, an investigation can be launched even if no complaints have been received.

Obviously receiving a request for information from a supervisory authority or notification of an audit is a cause for concern. Controllers and processors should ensure that they involve their Data Protection Officer ('DPO') or other data protection advisors at the earliest opportunity so that analysis of potential concerns can be commenced, with a view to mitigating or reducing the risk of strict enforcement action.

It is worthwhile monitoring supervisory authority enforcement actions on a regular basis, as investigation and enforcement activity will often focus on a particular sector or processing theme, where the supervisory authority is receiving a high number of complaints or has its own concerns about data protection practices. Where enforcement action is being taken against organizations in a particular sector or in relation to specific activities, this should act as a prompt to review data processing operations in the relevant area.

It is important to note that the power to access premises and equipment must be exercised in accordance with Member State procedural law. In many countries, this will require some form of judicial authority or warrant. It is therefore advisable to check the scope of any warrant or authority granted to ensure that the supervisory authority does not seek access to any information or systems that are not covered by the scope of the warrant.

It is also crucial to ensure that all staff, particularly those in the front line such as reception staff, are aware that the supervisory authority has 'dawn raid' powers, and that they know what to do and who to contact if the supervisory authority turns up unannounced.

Usually the supervisory authority will be willing to wait until legal advisors and/or the DPO are present (provided that advisors can make themselves available within a reasonable period of time). It will also be important to keep a note and copy of all information and systems viewed, accessed, or copied by the supervisory authority. These records will prove invaluable when carrying out an analysis of any likely enforcement action and steps that the controller or processor can take to prepare a defence or mitigate any risk.

Corrective powers

The corrective powers of supervisory authorities under the GDPR are significant and include:

- issuing warnings that *intended* processing operations are likely to infringe the Regulation (in which case continuing with the proposed processing is likely to attract further regulatory attention);
- issuing reprimands where processing has infringed the Regulation;
- ordering a controller or processor to comply with a data subject's request to exercise his or her rights;
- ordering processing operations to be brought into compliance, which could include requiring specified steps to be taken within a specified period;
- ordering data subjects to be informed of a breach;
- issuing a temporary or permanent ban on data processing;
- ordering the rectification or erasure of personal data;
- withdrawing a data protection certification;
- imposing fines; and
- ordering the suspension of international data transfers.

Often supervisory authorities will work behind the scenes with controllers and processors to agree how processing activities can be brought into line with the GDPR before taking formal enforcement action. This may result in no formal enforcement action being taken at all if the supervisory authority is satisfied that the controller or processor in question has corrected the breach. Alternatively, voluntary undertakings may be provided by the controller or processor.

However, where serious breaches have occurred or where the supervisory authority is not satisfied with the steps that a controller or processor is proposing to take, then formal action should be expected.

Fines

Where serious breaches of the Regulation occur, supervisory authorities will consider whether an administrative fine is appropriate. Fines may be imposed on the controller and/or (in certain circumstances) any processors involved in a breach. Article 83 of the GDPR sets the upper limits for fines and is split into two broad categories. Within the first category are the types of infringements that can result in a fine of up to 10 million euros, or 2 per cent of worldwide annual turnover (whichever is the higher), as set out in Table 8.1 below.

Table 8.1 Infringements that can result in fines of up to 10 million euros or 2 per cent of worldwide annual turnover

Article	Nature of infringement
8	Failure to obtain parental consent when offering information society services to a child and failure to make reasonable efforts to verify consent
11	Failure to notify a data subject who is seeking to exercise his or her rights that the controller is not in a position to identify the data subject from the information held
25	Failure to implement data protection by design and by default measures, including failing to minimize personal data collected, failing to minimize access to personal data, and failing to get rid of data when no longer required
26	Where acting as a joint controller, failing to allocate respective responsibility for complying with the Regulation in a transparent manner (ideally such allocation will be in a documented form to rebut any claim that responsibilities have not been effectively allocated)
27	Failure to appoint a representative in the European Union for a controller or processor who is not established in the European Union but who is caught by the application of the Regulation by virtue of Article 3(2)
28	Failure to take adequate measures when appointing a data processor, including failing to choose a processor offering adequate guarantees in relation to data protection measures and failing to have in place a written contract including the mandated data processing clauses
29	A processor processing personal data other than on the instruction of a controller (except if required to do so by Union or Member State law)
30	Failure to comply with record keeping requirements in relation to data processing activities
31	Failure to cooperate with the supervisory authority
32	Failure to take adequate security measures to protect personal data
33	Failure to notify data protection breaches to the supervisory authority
34	Failure to notify high risk data protection breaches to the data subject(s)
35	Failure to carry out an adequate data protection impact assessment where processing is likely to result in a high risk to the rights and freedoms of data subjects
36	Failure to consult the supervisory authority where a data protection impact assessment has shown that data processing will result in high risks to the data subjects which it is not possible to mitigate
37	Failure to designate a DPO when required to do so

(continued)

Table 8.1 Continued

Article	Nature of infringement
38	Failure to involve the DPO in all relevant data protection matters; failure to provide the DPO with adequate resources necessary to fulfil their tasks and maintain their expert knowledge; failure to ensure the independence of the DPO; failure to ensure reporting by the DPO to the highest management level; or dismissal or penalizing the DPO merely for performing his or her tasks
39	Failure to appoint a DPO to carry out the designated tasks or failure to enable the DPO to complete those tasks
42	Where a controller or processor has submitted its processing to a certification mechanism, failure to provide the relevant certification body with all information and access to its processing activities necessary to conduct the certification procedure

The second category contains the types of infringements that can result in a fine of up to 20 million euros, or 4 per cent of worldwide annual turnover (whichever is the higher), as set out in Table 8.2 below.

Table 8.2 Infringements that can result in fines of up to 20 million euros or 4 per cent of worldwide annual turnover

Article	Nature of infringement
5	Failure to comply with the processing principles relating to lawfulness, fairness and transparency; purpose limitation; data minimization; accuracy; storage limitation; integrity and confidentiality; or accountability
6	Failure to have a lawful basis for processing
7	Where relying on consent, failure to obtain valid consent which meets GDPR requirements
9	Processing special categories of data (see Chapter 4) without meeting one of the conditions set out in Article 9
12–22	Failure to comply with individuals' rights, including transparency requirements, rights of access, right to rectification, right to erasure, right to restriction of processing, right to data portability, right to object, and rights in relation to automated decision-making
44–49	Transfer of personal data outside the European Union without adequate protection
Chapter IX	Breach of any national laws made under Chapter IX, which includes exemptions related to freedom of expression and processing for journalistic purposes or for the purposes of academic, artistic, or literary expression; additional rules relating to processing of national identification numbers; additional rules relating to processing in the context of employment; and exemptions relating to processing for archiving, research, or statistical purposes
58	Failure to comply with a supervisory order or failure to provide access to premises or equipment where a supervisory authority has power to enter

Where the relevant percentage of worldwide annual turnover exceeds the fixed sum, the maximum fine will be the higher amount. When calculating turnover it appears that the turnover of the controller's or processor's whole group will be within scope and not solely the relevant company that has committed the infringement. This is the approach taken under competition law, although at the time of writing this has yet to be tested by the supervisory authorities.

Certification bodies (organizations that assess whether a controller or processor organization is data protection compliant) and monitoring bodies can also be subject to fines if they breach their respective obligations under the Regulation.

Traditionally the highest fines imposed by supervisory authorities have related to breaches of security obligations. However, under the GDPR it is clear that breaching individuals' rights, failing to ensure a lawful basis for processing, and transferring personal data outside of the European Union without adequate protection take just as much importance from an enforcement perspective. Organizations will therefore do well to ensure that these elements of their data protection compliance programmes receive just as much prominence as their information security practices.

Article 83 sets out the factors that supervisory authorities will take into account when determining whether to impose a fine and the amount of the fine. Such factors include the nature, gravity, and duration of the breach; the nature and scope of the processing; the number of data subjects affected; and the level of damage suffered by them.

The actions of the controller or processor both prior to and after the breach will also be taken into account, including whether the breach was intentional or negligent, actions taken to mitigate damage suffered by the data subjects, the measures that the controller or processor has in place to ensure security and compliance with the Regulation, adherence to approved codes of conduct or certification mechanisms, any relevant prior breaches, and the degree of cooperation offered by the controller or processor with the regulatory investigation.

These factors demonstrate that it is possible for controllers and processors to take proactive steps to reduce the likelihood and severity of administrative fines being imposed by ensuring that they have in place robust privacy governance programmes. If a controller or processor can demonstrate that they have appropriate policies, training, and procedures in place, and that these have been communicated effectively to staff members, this will assist enormously in reducing the likelihood or severity of a fine. Similarly, signing up to a recognized code of conduct or achieving a recognized data protection certification will be helpful to demonstrate that compliance with the Regulation is taken seriously, which will be a mitigating factor when a supervisory authority is considering imposing a fine.

Supervisory authorities will also consider whether an organization has made any financial gain as a result of a breach when making decisions about fines. If a business has gained additional commercial advantage (e.g. by carrying out targeted advertising using profiling without notifying individuals) or avoided costs (e.g. by taking short cuts when implementing technical security measures), then fines will be increased accordingly.

Member States are permitted to bring in their own laws to regulate whether and to what extent public authorities are subject to fines. At the time of writing no such national legislation has been implemented, but this position should be checked in the relevant jurisdiction where a breach by a public authority has occurred.

Authorization and advisory powers

In addition to monitoring and enforcing compliance with the Regulation, supervisory authorities also have powers to issue guidance and authorizations and to adopt standard contract clauses to meet data processing and overseas transfer requirements.

These powers also extend to approving binding corporate rules, overseas transfer clauses, and codes of conduct; accrediting certification bodies; and issuing certifications. These powers are explored in more detail in other chapters of this book and are not therefore examined in detail here.

Other Remedies

In addition to regulatory enforcement action, the GDPR specifies a number of other remedies that are available to individuals who consider that a breach of the Regulation has occurred.

These include a right to a judicial remedy against a controller or processor, a right to mandate a not-for-profit body to lodge a complaint or exercise remedial rights on behalf of the data subject, and a right to compensation for any damage suffered as a result of a breach.

Consistency Mechanism

In order to ensure a consistent approach to regulatory activities the GDPR sets out a consistency mechanism, which requires supervisory authorities to consult with the European Data Protection Board ('EDPB') before taking certain decisions. Decisions that require EDPB consultation are as follows:

- adoption of a list of processing operations which require data protection impact assessments;
- approval of codes of conduct;
- approval criteria for accreditation and certification bodies;
- adoption of standard data processing clauses or standard data transfer clauses;
- authorization of data transfer clauses proposed by a controller or data processor; and
- approval of binding corporate rules.

The EDPB is made up of representatives from the supervisory authorities of each Member State and the European Data Protection Supervisor. In the ordinary course, the EDPB is required to respond to consultation requests within eight weeks. However, this can be extended by a further six weeks for complex cases. If a supervisory authority does not agree with an EDPB decision, the supervisory authority may escalate the matter through the dispute resolution procedure set out in Article 65 of the GDPR. The deadline for resolution is a further one-month period, which may be extended to two months for complex cases.

This means that for a controller or processor awaiting regulatory approval for data transfer agreements or binding corporate rules there could be a delay of up to six months in cases where the EDPB does not agree with the decision proposed by the supervisory authority. In any event, the shortest possible timeframe for EDPB approval is likely to be eight weeks. Controllers and processors should build these timeframes into their planning processes when implementing binding corporate rules or seeking approval for bespoke data transfer agreements.

Cross-border Processing and Appointing a Lead Authority

In relation to cross-border processing activities, an organization may appoint a lead authority to act as the principal point of contact for cross-border processing matters. This is useful for controllers and processors to ensure consistency of regulatory action and to minimize the number of supervisory authorities with which they have to liaise in relation to cross-border matters.

What is cross-border processing?

The GDPR defines cross-border processing in Article 4(23). There are two types of processing that will be caught by the definition (and therefore in connection with which a lead authority has competency to act):

(i) processing which takes place in the context of multiple offices, branches or other 'establishments' of a company in multiple Member States; and

(ii) processing which takes place in the context of the activities of a single establishment of a controller or processor in the European Union but which substantially affects or is likely to substantially affect data subjects in more than one Member State.

Cases where a lead authority cannot be appointed

There are a number of circumstances where, even though data processing is carried out across multiple Member States, it is not possible to designate a lead authority to regulate those activities.

Where a controller or processor is established in one Member State and carries out processing of data relating to data subjects in multiple Member States but the nature of that processing is unlikely to have any substantial effect on the data subjects, the lead authority principle will not apply. It is hard to define exactly what will constitute a 'substantial effect'. However, the regulators have indicated that the following factors are relevant:

- any damage or negative impact on data subjects caused by the processing;
- effects on health, wellbeing, and financial or economic status;

- potential limitation of rights or denial of opportunity;
- analysis of special categories of data;
- any actions likely to influence the behaviour of individuals in a significant way; and
- embarrassment, or processing which will have an effect on reputation.

If the controller or processor does not have an establishment in the European Union then it will not be possible to designate a lead authority. For example, an online services provider based solely in the United States that targets data subjects across Europe would be subject to the GDPR regime but would have to liaise individually with each relevant supervisory authority, rather than liaising with a lead authority.

If the legal basis for processing under Article 6 is compliance with a legal obligation or carrying out a task in the public interest, the supervisory authority in the state concerned has competency to act and not the lead authority.

There has been much debate about whether a multinational group of companies is able to appoint a lead authority to act in relation to the processing activities of multiple companies which are established as separate legal entities and not solely as branch offices. The wording in Article 56 of the Regulation talks about cross-border processing carried out by 'that controller or processor', which would seem to suggest that where there are multiple companies, each of which is a controller in its own right, then it will not be possible to designate a single lead authority. However, the Article 29 Data Protection Working Party's Guidelines for establishing a controller or processor's lead supervisory authority (adopted on 13 December 2016, as revised on 5 April 2017) indicate that it is possible for a single lead authority to be designated for a group of companies. Specifically, the guidance states at Section 2.1.2:

[T]he decision system of [a] group of companies could be more complex, giving independent making powers relating to cross border processing to different establishments. The criteria set out above should help groups of undertakings to identify their main establishment.

It is therefore clear that a lead authority can be designated for multiple controllers or processors, provided that the decision-making in relation to the data processing activities of the group is made from a central location.

Which authority is the lead authority?

The lead authority is the supervisory authority in the jurisdiction where the controller's or processor's main establishment is located (or where the single establishment is located if the controller or processor is only physically located in one Member State). Often it will be obvious which establishment is the 'main establishment'. However, in other cases, where there is no centralized decision-making it may be more difficult to determine where the main establishment is.

For controllers, the starting position is the place within the European Union where the central administration for the controller is located. However, if decisions about data processing activities take place and are implemented in a different jurisdiction, the latter jurisdiction will count as the main establishment for lead authority purposes.

For processors, the main test is also the place of central administration. If there is no place of central administration in the Union, then the jurisdiction where the main processing activities occur will be the place of main establishment.

For organizations where the main establishment is in the UK, this poses an interesting question post-Brexit. If decisions regarding data processing activities continue to be made in the UK, it seems unlikely that it will be possible to designate a lead authority in the European Union. However, if data processing decision-making is delegated to an establishment within Europe, then it will be possible to designate that establishment as the main establishment for lead authority purposes.

The designation of the lead authority is made by the controller or processor themselves. However, this is subject to scrutiny by the supervisory authorities and may be challenged if the supervisory authorities do not agree with the analysis of the controller or processor. It will be up to the relevant organization to provide sufficient evidence to the supervisory authorities of where decision-making happens so as to convince them that the correct designation has been made.

Cooperation between supervisory authorities

Article 60 of the GDPR requires the lead supervisory authority to cooperate with other concerned supervisory authorities when taking regulatory enforcement action. The lead authority may request mutual assistance from other authorities, which may take the form of information sharing, investigations, or monitoring implementation of a remedial measure.

The lead authority is also required to submit draft decisions to other concerned supervisory authorities and take due account of their views when finalizing its decision. If a supervisory authority raises a reasoned objection to a draft decision and the lead authority does not intend to follow the objection, the matter is referred to the EDPB and the consistency mechanism will apply (see above).

In exceptional circumstances it is possible, under Article 66, for a supervisory authority to take action in relation to cross-border data processing activities without consulting other authorities. This will be the case where a supervisory authority considers that urgent action is required to protect the rights and freedoms of data subjects.

Where an organization has multiple establishments across Europe but a particular complaint relates solely to data subjects in one Member State, the supervisory authority in that Member State may notify the lead authority that this is the case and the lead authority will then decide whether to act. This could apply, for example, to local employment-related data processing where processing is directed at local level and not through any centralized HR function. If the lead authority decides to act, the lead authority must cooperate with the other supervisory authority and take into account representations made by that authority.

UK Enforcement Action

At the time of writing, the position of the UK regulator (the Information Commissioner) post-Brexit has yet to be determined. It seems likely that the Commissioner will not be part of the EDPB, nor will the UK be bound by the consistency mechanism under the GDPR. Assuming that this is the case (the remainder of this chapter is written on this assumption), there will therefore be scope for the Information Commissioner in the UK to take a different approach to enforcement than that adopted across the European Union.

In practice, however, it seems unlikely that the Commissioner will take any marked departure from the historic approach to enforcement taken by that office. Moreover, in order to maintain any adequacy decision for cross-border data transfers, it will be necessary for the UK to be able to demonstrate that data protection laws are enforced robustly and with remedies available to individuals that are 'essentially equivalent' to the remedies available under the GDPR.

It is therefore expected that the approach taken to enforcement by the Information Commissioner under the GDPR will continue in the UK post-Brexit. It is also expected that the Commissioner will continue to cooperate closely with supervisory authorities in the European Union. Article 50 of the GDPR requires the European Commission and EU supervisory authorities to take appropriate steps to develop international cooperation mechanisms to facilitate effective enforcement and to provide mutual assistance for enforcement purposes, including through complaint referrals, investigative assistance, and information exchange. It will be in the interests of both the Information Commissioner and European supervisory authorities to facilitate such mutual assistance where cross-border data processing is concerned.

UK Enforcement Procedures

In the UK, the data protection regime is enforced by the Information Commissioner through a range of powers set out in Part 6 of the Data Protection Bill. These powers will apply both to enforcement of the GDPR while the UK remains part of the European Union and also post-Brexit.

The remainder of this chapter looks at the procedural mechanisms followed by the Information Commissioner when taking enforcement action.

Investigation of complaints

Any person who believes that he or she is being directly affected by the processing of personal data may lodge a complaint with the Information Commissioner pursuant to Article 77 of the Regulation. Such a request will usually be made where the person concerned feels that the processing is being carried out in contravention of the Regulation, although the requester does not have to allege or prove such contravention. The Information Commissioner must respond to complaints within three months, either to notify the complainant of the outcome or update them on progress.

The Information Commissioner encourages individuals to address their concerns directly to the relevant organization in order to attempt to resolve them before raising a complaint with the Information Commissioner. The Information Commissioner's website indicates that individuals should raise a complaint within three months of their last contact with the organization in question.

In determining the appropriate manner in which to carry out an assessment, as to which the Information Commissioner has absolute discretion, the Commissioner will consider all relevant information including:

(a) the extent to which the request appears to her to raise a matter of substance;

(b) any undue delay in making the request; and

(c) whether or not the person making the request is entitled to make a subject access request.

There are a range of possible actions that the Commissioner can take, from simply sending a letter to the controller requesting written details of the processing operations in question to a full-blown investigation involving Information Commissioner's Office ('ICO') personnel attending the offices of the controller.

Information Notice

The Information Commissioner may serve a document, known as an Information Notice, on any controller or processor, requiring them to furnish certain information to the Information Commissioner within a time limit specified in the notice. The purpose of the notice is to allow the Commissioner to gather sufficient information to determine whether the controller is processing in contravention of the statutory provisions.

The Information Commissioner may serve an Information Notice in order to obtain information that the Commissioner reasonably requires to enable fulfilment of the Commissioner's functions under the data protection legislation.

An Information Notice must specify the reasons why the Information Commissioner requires the requested information and may also specify a time limit for compliance and the format in which the information must be provided. The Information Notice must also notify the controller or processor of their rights of appeal against the notice.

See below for further information on the appeal process.

Time limit for compliance

The time limit imposed by the Information Commissioner for compliance with the Information Notice starts to run from the day the notice is served. In most cases it cannot expire before the day on which the rights of appeal against the notice elapse (see below) and, where an appeal is brought, will not expire until the determination or withdrawal of the appeal. Exceptionally, where the Information Commissioner requires the information as a matter of urgency, the time limit specified in the notice can be shorter than the above but must not be less than seven days. In this event the Information Commissioner must make a statement as to why the Commissioner considers the matter to be urgent. There is a right of appeal to the tribunal against the Commissioner's decision to include such a statement and against its effect.

The Commissioner may withdraw (in writing) an Information Notice. Compliance is not required after such a withdrawal.

Exemptions from compliance

A person may choose not to comply with an Information Notice where compliance would reveal one or more of the following:

(a) the content of any communication between a lawyer and his or her client where the subject of such communication is advice in respect of the client's rights, obligations, or liabilities under the data protection legislation;

(b) the content of any communication between a lawyer and his or her client, or between a lawyer or his or her client and any other person, made in connection with or in contemplation of proceedings (including proceedings before the Tribunal) under the Act; or

(c) the commission by that person of an actionable criminal offence (except a criminal offence under the Act or perjury laws).

Special purposes

The Bill prevents the Information Commissioner from serving an Information Notice on a controller which relates to processing for the special purposes (the purposes of journalism, academic, artistic, or literary purposes) unless the Commissioner has made a determination that:

(a) the personal data are not being processed only for the special purposes;

(b) the personal data are not being processed with a view to the publication by any person of any journalistic, academic, literary, or artistic material which has not previously been published by the controller; or

(c) carrying out processing of the personal data in compliance with a provision of the data protection legislation specified in the determination is not incompatible with the special purpose.

Special purposes determination by the Commissioner

The Commissioner may, at any time, make a special purposes determination in writing. The purpose of such a determination is to allow the Commissioner to serve an

Enforcement Notice (for further detail see 'Enforcement Notice—Special purposes' below).

Notice of such a determination must be given to the controller together with a statement of the rights of appeal. The determination will not take effect until the end of the period in which an appeal can be brought. Where an appeal is brought the determination will have no effect until after the conclusion or withdrawal of the appeal.

Criminal offences

It is an offence to fail to comply with an Information Notice. It is a defence to show that the accused exercised all due diligence to comply with the notice.

Further, it is an offence to make a false statement (knowingly or recklessly) in response to an Information Notice.

Assessment Notice

The Information Commissioner may serve an Assessment Notice on a controller or processor to enable the Commissioner to carry out an assessment of whether the controller or processor has complied with or is complying with data protection legislation. The Assessment Notice may require the controller or processor to do any of the following:

(a) permit the Information Commissioner to enter specified premises;

(b) provide access to and copies of specified documents;

(c) permit the Information Commissioner to inspect or examine documents, information, and equipment and to observe data processing on the premises; and

(d) make people available to be interviewed who process personal data on behalf of the controller.

The Assessment Notice must specify time periods for compliance with each requirement and the rights of appeal. The time limits for compliance must not expire before the end of the period within which an appeal can be brought against the notice. In urgent cases the Commissioner may specify in the Assessment Notice that shorter time periods apply. In such cases the Commissioner must give the reason for reaching this opinion and a minimum time period of seven days from the date on which the Assessment Notice is served will apply.

Where the Information Commissioner serves an Assessment Notice on a processor, the Commissioner must also give a copy of the notice to each controller for whom the processor processes personal data so far as reasonably practicable.

An Assessment Notice does not have effect where compliance would result in disclosure of a communication which is subject to legal advice privilege or litigation privilege in connection with obligations, liability, or rights under data protection legislation.

Nor is the Information Commissioner empowered to serve an Assessment Notice where personal data are being processed for the special purposes.

Enforcement Notice

Where the Information Commissioner is satisfied that a controller or processor has contravened or is contravening data protection legislation, the Commissioner may serve on the controller an Enforcement Notice requiring the controller or processor to take specific steps to rectify the contravention or to refrain from processing certain specified personal data. An Enforcement Notice is more likely to be served in cases where the contravention in question is causing (or is likely to cause) a person damage or distress.

The Commissioner may also serve Enforcement Notices on monitoring bodies that are failing to monitor approved codes of conduct and on certification providers that are failing to comply with certification requirements.

An Enforcement Notice must state the relevant failure and give reasons for reaching that opinion. An Enforcement Notice may impose a ban on all processing of personal data or a particular type of processing.

Where an Enforcement Notice relates to a failure to comply with accuracy requirements or individuals' rights of erasure, rectification, or restriction of processing, the Enforcement Notice may also require rectification or erasure of information that contains an expression of opinion which the Commissioner considers is based on inaccurate personal data.

Where a controller or processor has accurately recorded personal data but the data are inaccurate, the Enforcement Notice may require the controller or processor to take specified steps to ensure the accuracy of data, to flag that the data subject considers that the data are inaccurate, or to supplement the data with a statement of true facts approved by the Commissioner.

Where the Enforcement Notice requires the controller or processor to rectify or erase any personal data, the Commissioner may require the controller or processor to notify third parties of that rectification or erasure. The requirement to notify third parties will not be imposed where this is not reasonably practicable (e.g. where there are a large number of such persons).

Every Enforcement Notice must contain a time limit for compliance, along with a statement of the rights of appeal.

An Enforcement Notice may be cancelled or varied by the Information Commissioner in writing to the controller or processor. A controller or processor that has received an Enforcement Notice may apply in writing to the Commissioner for the cancellation or variation of the notice. This may be done only where a change of circumstances means that some or all of the requirements of the notice need not be complied with to ensure compliance with data protection legislation and only where the time limit for the bringing of an appeal has expired. An appeal is available against the decision of the Information Commissioner not to allow such an application.

Time limit for compliance

The time limit imposed on a controller or processor by the Information Commissioner for compliance with an Enforcement Notice starts to run from the day the notice is served. Subject to the limited exception below, it cannot expire before the day on which the rights of appeal against the notice elapse and, where an appeal is brought, will not expire until the determination or withdrawal of the appeal.

Where the Information Commissioner requires the information as a matter of urgency, the time limit specified in the notice can be shorter than the above but must not be less than seven days. In this event the Information Commissioner must state why the Commissioner considers the matter to be urgent. There is a right of appeal to the Information Tribunal against the Information Commissioner's decision to include such a statement and against its effect.

Special purposes

The Information Commissioner is prevented from serving an Enforcement Notice which relates to processing for the special purposes unless the court has granted leave for the notice to be served and the Information Commissioner has made a relevant determination (see above).

The court will not grant leave for this purpose unless it is satisfied that the Information Commissioner has reason to suspect that the contravention of data protection legislation in question is of substantial public importance. Additionally, the court must be satisfied that the controller or processor (as applicable) has been given notice of the application for leave, which will not be necessary where the case is one of urgency.

Monetary Penalty Notices

Unlike several European Member States pre-GDPR (e.g. Ireland), the UK data protection regulator has had the power to issue Monetary Penalty Notices since 2010. The value of potential monetary penalties has, however, increased significantly under the GDPR.

A Monetary Penalty Notice is an order addressed to a particular controller or processor to pay a sum of money, essentially a fine, by a certain date. The maximum sum that a controller or processor can be required to pay is the greater of 20 million euros or 4 per cent of the undertaking's total annual worldwide turnover in the preceding financial year. The money paid is not retained by the ICO, but instead goes into the Consolidated Fund (i.e. the UK government's bank account).

A monetary penalty can be served on an individual or an organization in respect of specific provisions of data protection legislation.

It should be noted that other UK regulators can impose fines for activities which essentially amount to data protection breaches. In particular, the Financial Conduct Authority, which has a regulatory function in connection with banks, insurance companies, and other financial services bodies, has a significant power to impose unlimited fines (in 2010, Zurich Insurance was fined £2.28 million for losing a disk containing records of 46,000 customers) for a wide range of misdeeds. However, this chapter is concerned only with the powers of the Information Commissioner.

Formalities

The Information Commissioner may serve a Monetary Penalty Notice on a controller or processor where the Commissioner is satisfied that:

(a) there has been a contravention of any of the data protection principles by the controller or processor;

(b) the controller or processor has failed to comply with the rights of a data subject;

(c) there has been a failure to comply with the obligations of a controller or processor in Articles 25 to 39 of the GDPR (which include obligations to notify personal data breaches to the Information Commissioner and to individuals, privacy by design and by default obligations, and requirements in relation to data protection impact assessments);

(d) there has been a breach in relation to overseas transfer requirements;

(e) a controller or processor has failed to comply with an Assessment Notice or an Enforcement Notice.

Before a Monetary Penalty Notice can be served, the Commissioner must issue a Notice of Intent, informing the relevant person that it may make written representations within a specified time in relation to the Information Commissioner's proposal to serve such a notice. The notice must also contain the amount of the proposed penalty. The controller may then make written (and in some cases oral) representations, which the Commissioner will take into account before making a final decision.

Monetary penalties to date

The Information Commissioner has not been shy in exercising the power to serve monetary penalties. Both the number of penalties issued, and the amount of the fines imposed, surpassed many expectations in the pre-GDPR period. At the time of writing, the highest penalty that had been issued against a private sector controller was £400,000 (October 2016). This involved TalkTalk Telecom Group plc, who failed to have adequate security arrangements in place and enabled a cyber attacker to access customer data.

The highest penalty in the public sector was £325,000, involving an NHS Trust that disposed of computer hard-drives inappropriately. The level of fines will inevitably increase with the introduction of much higher upper limits under the GDPR.

Trends from previous monetary penalties indicate that the Information Commissioner will impose fines in circumstances where significant numbers of complaints from data subjects are received. Thus a large number of fines have been imposed under PECR in relation to unsolicited marketing communications, including fines for sending spam email and texts, cold calling, and use of automated calls (see Chapter 10).

In addition, data security breaches involving special categories of personal data or which put data subjects at risk of identity theft or fraud have historically been more likely to attract a fine.

Appeals

Safeguards on the operation of powers by the Information Commissioner allow a controller or processor to appeal against the issue of all notices including monetary penalties.

Appeals are heard in the first instance by the First Tier Tribunal (Information Rights). Appeals from decisions of the First Tier Tribunal may be made to the Upper Tribunal and from there (in exceptional cases) to the Court of Appeal.

As an initial consideration the Tribunal must dismiss the appeal from the controller or processor unless it considers that one of the following two factors is true:

(i) that the notice against which the appeal is brought does not accord with some legal provision; or

(ii) that the Information Commissioner ought to have exercised her discretion (if any) differently.

If either factor is made out by the appellant, then the Tribunal must allow the appeal or substitute the notice with any other notice which the Information Commissioner could have served.

Powers of Entry and Inspection

For the Information Commissioner to be lawfully entitled to enter premises and inspect records without consent, the Commissioner must obtain a warrant from a judge. The judge must be satisfied, by information on oath supplied by the Information Commissioner, that there are reasonable grounds for suspecting that a controller or processor has contravened, or is contravening, data protection legislation or that an offence under the Act has been, or is being, committed. In each case there must be grounds to believe that evidence of the breach will be found on relevant premises.

Unless the judge is satisfied that the matter is urgent or that advance warning would defeat the objective of the search (in which case a no-notice search warrant may be issued) the Commissioner must have given seven days' notice in writing to the occupier of the premises in question demanding access to the premises and must show that:

1. the occupier has been notified by the Information Commissioner of the application for the warrant and has had an opportunity of being heard by the judge on the question of whether or not a warrant should be issued; and

2. either:

   (a) access was demanded at a reasonable hour and was unreasonably refused, or

   (b) although entry to the premises was granted, the occupier unreasonably refused to comply with a request by the Information Commissioner or any of the Information Commissioner's officers, for example to search, inspect, or examine equipment.

A warrant will permit the Information Commissioner and ICO staff, within seven days of the date of the warrant, to search the relevant premises and to inspect, examine, operate, and test any equipment found there which is used, or intended to be used, for the processing of personal data. It also permits him to inspect and seize any documents or other material which provide evidence of the offence or breach of the GDPR requirements or PECR. Reasonable force may be used in the execution of a warrant.

Certain matters are exempt from the powers of inspection and seizure conferred by a warrant. These include legally privileged material and personal data processed for national security purposes. A warrant cannot be issued in relation to personal data processed for the 'special purposes' unless the Information Commissioner has issued a relevant determination (see above).

Offence

It is an offence to intentionally obstruct the Information Commissioner in exercising this power. It is also an offence to fail, without reasonable excuse, to give the Commissioner any assistance that he or she may reasonably require, or to make a false statement in response to a query raised by the Information Commissioner during a visit under warrant.

9

Outsourcing Personal Data Processing

Suzanne Rodway and Peter Carey

Introduction	175
The Nature of a Processor	177
Obligations on Processors	178
Choice of Processor	179
Ongoing Assurance	179
The Written Contract	180
Pre-GDPR Arrangements	181
Sub-processors	181
Processor Versus Controller	182
Cloud Services	183
Foreign Processors	183

Introduction

Organizations frequently use third party businesses to perform one or more functions of their day-to-day activities—examples include payroll administration, the use of mailing houses, confidential waste management, data storage, IT management, website hosting, and debt collection. Where such 'outsourcing' arrangements involve the processing of personal data, certain specific legal obligations arise.

In many outsourcing arrangements, in data protection terminology, the outsourcing organization (the customer) is known as the 'controller' and the third party processing business (the supplier) is known as the 'processor'. Under the Directive and the 1998 Act, processors were not subject to any direct statutory obligations. However, a key change under the GDPR is that both controllers and processors have direct obligations under the law. In particular the GDPR:

- makes processors jointly and severally liable with controllers;

- makes processors directly subject to regulatory enforcement and action, civil litigation, criminal penalties (where applicable under Member State law), damages, and compensation claims; and

- increases the number of mandatory data protection clauses required in vendor contracts.

Under the old rules, suppliers would often argue that they were processors to ensure they had no strict liability under the law. As the GDPR now imposes direct obligations on processors, suppliers may be more willing to reassess whether they are a controller or processor going forward and aligning the contractual terms accordingly. However, in practice, under both the old and new legal regimes, it is ultimately a matter of fact as to whether a supplier is a processor or a controller in its own right (irrespective of what the contract may state). The new direct obligations imposed on processors may generally lead to a more active negotiation of data protection clauses by both parties.

The liability for compliance as between controllers and processors has also changed under the GDPR, as both parties now have direct joint and several statutory liability, and this will likely impact the negotiation of liability clauses and indemnities in outsourcing agreements. 'Joint and several liability' means that either party can be held fully liable for all damages irrespective of that party's actual level of responsibility for the action/inaction leading to the damage.

Controllers ultimately remain responsible for the processing undertaken by their processors. This means that they can remain liable for any breaches of data protection law which are caused by the actions or inactions of their processors. A processor will only be directly liable for damage caused by any processing that has been carried out in contravention of the processor's obligations under the GDPR, or where the processor has acted outside the instructions of the controller (Article 82(2)). However, as stated above, whilst there is a theoretical split in terms of liability to the data subject, the GDPR makes it clear that each controller or processor can be held liable for the entire damage in order to ensure that the data subject is always adequately compensated. Contractual arrangements between controllers and processors will therefore need to address the contractual liability between the parties to ensure a fair allocation of liability for non-compliance.

Furthermore, in relation to the contractual arrangements between controllers and processors, it has to be noted that the processor will generally have certain minimum contractual obligations to the controller (these are discussed in greater detail in the 'Written Contracts' section below).

The outsourcing arrangement may or may not involve the transfer of personal data from the controller to the processor; yet such a transfer is not a necessary aspect of the controller–processor relationship. For example, in the case of website hosting, the initial recipient of the data provided by users to the site will be the processor; here the data will commonly move from the processor to the controller, but not necessarily vice versa. In other outsourcing arrangements—for example the outsourcing of marketing functions to a mailing house—there will be a transfer of personal data from the controller to the processor. Some outsourcing arrangements—for example payroll administration—will involve transfers in both directions between the controller and the processor.

Where the company that is to perform the outsourced function is located outside the European Economic Area ('EEA'), and where the outsourcing involves a transfer of personal data from the EU-based (or UK-based) controller to that processor, there is an additional requirement to legitimize the foreign transfer prior to it taking place. Methods of legitimizing foreign transfers are discussed in Chapter 6. Where the exporting controller uses the set of model contractual clauses for overseas transfers to processors, those clauses can simultaneously address the data security and contractual requirements for processors as well as satisfying the restrictions on data exports.

In order to comply with the fair collection obligations in Articles 12–14 of the GDPR (see Chapter 3), it will usually be necessary for the controller to have made available to its customers and other relevant data subjects brief details of the outsourcing arrangements.

The Nature of a Processor

Processors take a variety of forms and perform a variety of different functions, but all have one common element: the fact that they process personal data *on behalf of* a controller.

The definition of 'processor' in the GDPR is almost identical to the previous definition in the Directive, and appears in Box 9.1.

The reference to 'person' in this context includes a corporation as well as an individual (however, in the vast majority of cases processors will be corporations as opposed to sole traders). Thus a processor will always be a separate legal entity to the controller, although the controller and processor do not necessarily need to be 'at arms' length'—it is possible for a processor to be a company which is part of the same group of companies as the controller.

A processor may only process the personal data of a controller on the instructions of said controller. In addition, the GDPR now directly addresses the role of a processor who acts outside the instructions of the controller and confirms that if a processor infringes the Regulation by determining the purposes and means of processing then it will be considered a controller in its own right in respect of those data and directly subject to all obligations under the GDPR.

Box 9.1 Processor—Definition

Article 4(8) GDPR

A natural or legal person, public authority, agency or other body which processes personal data on behalf of the controller.

Box 9.2   Pre-contractual Checks on the Processor

Article 28(1) GDPR

The controller shall only use processors providing sufficient guarantees to implement appropriate technical and organisational measures in such a manner that processing will meet the requirements of this Regulation and ensure the protection of the rights of the data subject.

The Information Commissioner's Office has issued helpful guidance on processors (see <http://www.dpdocuments.com>). Whilst the guidance requires updating in terms of the governance responsibilities between controllers and processors, the section on whether an organization is a controller or a processor remains useful.

Obligations on Processors

The GDPR imposes a number of direct obligations on processors for the first time. These obligations include requirements to:

- Appoint an EU representative where the processor is based outside of the EEA but is subject to the GDPR.
- Maintain processing inventories which include the following information:
  - name and contact details of the processor;
  - details of the controller(s) the processing is on behalf of;
  - the categories of personal data processed for each controller;
  - any cross-border transfers of the personal data (including recipient details and the safeguards in place to legitimize the transfer);
  - a general description of the technical and organizational measures in place to protect the personal data.
- Cooperate with data protection authorities.
- Implement appropriate technical and organizational security measures.
- Notify security breaches to the controller without undue delay.
- Comply with the restrictions on transfers of personal data to third countries (see Chapter 6).
- Obtain the consent of the controller before subcontracting processing of personal data and entering into written contracts with sub-processors.
- Appoint a Data Protection Officer ('DPO'), where applicable (see Chapter 12).

A significant change under the GDPR is that supervisory authorities are now able to impose sanctions directly on processors (see Chapter 8). In addition, processors, like controllers, can be subject to claims for compensation by data subjects through the courts.

Choice of Processor

When choosing a processor to carry out personal data processing operations on its behalf, a controller must take into account the ability of the processor to take appropriate care of personal data and must choose a processor that provides 'sufficient guarantees in respect of the technical and organisational security measures governing the processing to be carried out'—see Box 9.2.

There is no guidance in the legislation as to how these checks should be made or what constitutes 'sufficient' in this context. It is suggested that the outsourcing organization should make enquiries of potential processors and should take account of the responses to such enquiries in making its choice of processor. Going forward, codes of conduct and certification schemes may assist in enabling a processor to demonstrate these sufficient guarantees (see Chapter 1).

The controller should look for an indication of specific measures that the prospective processor has implemented, including physical and electronic measures, as well as adequate provision for staff training in both data protection and data security matters. The processor should supply the controller with a copy of its information security policy as well as copies of references from other controllers (its customers) in appropriate circumstances.

In cases where the outsourcing arrangements involve either significant quantities of personal data, or include special categories of personal data, the pre-contractual checks should be rigorous, and may involve the use of data security specialists who may need to enter the premises of the prospective processor in order to vet its systems. Copies of relevant correspondence regarding pre-contractual checks should be retained in case the Information Commissioner or a court investigates the controller's appointment of a particular processor at some future stage.

Ongoing Assurance

In addition to choosing a processor that is able to comply with relevant security standards and the need to impose certain contractual obligations on the processor, the controller is required to monitor the processor's activities regularly in order to ensure that it is meeting its GDPR compliance obligations on an ongoing basis. The GDPR requires the processor to be able to evidence its compliance with its obligations under the GDPR and the controller is entitled to audit the processor's processing activities (Article 28(h)).

It is unclear from the legislation how often checks should be made and what form the checks should take. Much will depend on the circumstances of the processing arrangements and the type of data being processed. It would not be necessary for the controller itself to have the expertise to carry out the checks—the checking process could be outsourced where appropriate. In order for checks to be carried out effectively, appropriate contractual rights of inspection (including the right of access to relevant premises) should form part of the contract with the processor. As part of these contractual rights, controllers should also consider checking a processor's ongoing compliance with any applicable codes of conduct and/or certification schemes.

The Written Contract

The GDPR makes it clear that the controller will not be treated as complying with its obligations under the Regulation in respect of its arrangements with a processor unless the transaction is 'governed by a contract' (see Article 28(3)), and that contract must be in writing, which can include electronic form (Article 28(9)).

Further, the contract must contain certain obligations on the processor. It should be noted that it is the responsibility of the outsourcing business (the controller) to ensure compliance with this provision of the legislation—reliance by the controller on the processor's standard contractual terms of trade will be insufficient to satisfy this obligation where the terms do not include these mandatory data protection clauses. Bearing this in mind, and the renegotiation of any agreements pre-dating the GDPR that will inevitably be required, it may be sensible for processors to amend their standard contractual terms to include the relevant provisions.

The contract must set out:

- the subject-matter and duration of the processing;
- the nature and purpose of the processing;
- the type of personal data and categories of data subjects; and
- obligations and rights of the controller.

The Directive and the 1998 Act stipulated that the contract contain only two mandatory provisions. The GDPR extends these requirements substantively. The contract must now stipulate that the processor will:

- process the personal data only in accordance with the written instructions of the controller (including instructions regarding transfers to third countries);
- ensure its employees who will be undertaking processing operations on the personal data are subject to confidentiality obligations (either by contract or statute);
- take all measures to comply with the security obligations under the Regulation;
- not engage another processor (i.e. a sub-processor) without the prior specific or general written consent of the controller and will inform the controller of any additions to or replacements of sub-processors;
- flow down these contractual obligations to any sub-processors;
- assist the controller by appropriate technical and organizational measures to meet its obligations with respect to the rights of data subjects (e.g. assist in responding to subject access requests);

- assist the controller with its obligations relating to breaches, data protection impact assessments, and consultations with data protection authorities;

- delete or return all personal data at the end of the provision of the services at the controller's choice (unless Member State or Union law prevents deletion); and

- evidence compliance with these requirements and permit audits by the controller (or its third party auditors).

In most cases the controller–processor relationship will be governed by a written contract in any event, and it will be a relatively simple matter to include the above additional data protection provisions in new contracts. The controller may also want to include additional data protection related rights and obligations such as a warranty and indemnity regarding breach of the provisions and obligations on the processor to train its staff in data protection and data security.

As stated above, it is likely that clauses will be needed to specifically address apportionment of liability for data protection breaches. Similarly, contracts will need to specifically address allocation of responsibilities in joint-controller outsourcing arrangements.

For a detailed consideration of the mandatory contractual clauses, how compliance could be demonstrated, and the practicalities of doing so, see Nissim J, 'Practicalities of Managing the Controller–Processor Relationship', *Privacy & Data Protection*, Volume 17, Issue 4 (<http://www.pdpjournal.com>).

Pre-GDPR Arrangements

It is important to remember that the GDPR has retrospective effect and that it therefore applies to pre-existing processing activities at the GDPR's commencement date (25 May 2018).

All controllers should, therefore, review their pre-existing contractual arrangements with processors. Those that do not meet the above requirements will require attention, either by entering into a new contractual arrangement or by amending the existing one.

Sub-processors

The question often arises as to the legal position of a company that is engaged by a processor to perform some of the data processing operations.

As noted above, the GDPR directly addresses this issue in a way which the Directive and the 1998 Act previously did not. Often the controller will wish to be a party to the sub-processing agreement and/or will want to vet the choice of sub-processor. In any event, the sub-processing agreement must now carry equivalent terms to those in the main controller–processor agreement. The controller would be well advised to require the head processor to provide the controller with a copy of the contractual provisions upon which all sub-processors are engaged.

Processor Versus Controller

It is not always easy to determine whether a particular company or organization is a 'controller' or 'processor' of personal data (and it should be remembered that there can be more than one joint controller of personal data). The distinction will be crucial going forward because the liabilities an organization is subject to and its responsibilities under the GDPR vary depending on whether it is a controller or a processor. As a result, parties will be more conscious of their obligations and liabilities and are likely to be more willing to challenge proposed contractual clauses.

Historically some businesses preferred to be classed as processors as this meant that they did not have any direct data protection liability. However, that is less of an issue now that there is joint and several liability between controllers and processors, although they should bear in mind the potential downside: as processor, they will be unable to use the relevant personal data for their own purposes, for example in the marketing of their own products or services. However, as stated above it will be a question of fact as to whether a supplier is a controller or a processor and any permitted uses of the personal data should be clearly spelt out in the contract.

The crucial distinguishing feature between a processor and a controller is the degree of autonomy that the entity exercises over the relevant personal data processing operations. Whilst the operations may be complex and extensive, the real question is whether they are performed *on behalf of* a third party (i.e. the controller). This is true whether or not the outsourcing controller is capable of performing the operations itself. It may of course be that the reason for the outsourcing is the very expertise that characterizes the nature of, and the need for, the relationship between the two organizations.

It is possible for any given personal data processing to be performed by a number of controllers jointly, and it should not be assumed that the transfer of personal data from one business to another for a certain specified purpose will always give rise to the controller–processor relationship. For example, two businesses may undertake to pool their client or customer database with a view to a joint marketing operation. In this scenario each business will be a controller in respect of the amalgamated database.

The GDPR introduces a new definition of joint data controller, set out in Box 9.3.

Box 9.3   Joint Data Controllers—Definition

Article 26(1) GDPR
Where two or more controllers jointly determine the purposes and means of processing, they shall be joint controllers.

Joint controllers are required to determine 'in a transparent manner' (Article 26(1)) their respective roles and responsibilities for compliance with the Regulation, especially in relation to the rights of data subjects and the obligation to provide privacy notices. This relationship, and the allocation of responsibilities, should be made clear to data subjects and addressed in contractual arrangements. It is important to note that irrespective of the relationship and the agreed allocation of responsibilities, data subjects are able to exercise any of their rights against either controller.

Cloud Services

Cloud service providers, which will usually be processors, are not treated differently from a GDPR compliance perspective than any other supplier. As such, it is the controller's responsibility to ensure that the contractual provisions meet the requirements of data protection law. The usual data protection compliance issues regarding the use of cloud service providers (see the concerns of the Article 29 Working Party in Opinion 05/12 on Cloud Computing—WP 196—<http://www.dpdocuments.com>) will have to be assessed during vendor selection and due diligence.

Although most such arrangements are undertaken on the basis of the cloud supplier's own written standard terms of business, it will be no defence for the controller to complain that it had 'no choice' but to agree to those standard terms. Thus controllers would be well advised to either negotiate new terms with the cloud provider or to select an alternate provider whose terms meet the legal requirements.

Cloud services often involve the storage and further processing of personal data on servers that are located in non-EEA countries, in which case the controller must ensure that the arrangements meet the requirements of Chapter V of the GDPR (Articles 44–50) on data transfers (see Chapter 6 and the next section).

Foreign Processors

The extra-territorial application of the GDPR (see Chapter 1) means that processors that were previously not subject to European data protection rules could now find themselves so subject (e.g. vendors in third countries that undertake monitoring of the behaviour of EU citizens on behalf of controllers).

Where a processor is located outside the EEA, and not in a country that has been designated as adequate for data exports by the European Commission, an additional hurdle is the export ban contained in Chapter V of the GDPR (Articles 44–50). The outsourcing of a telephone call centre to a company located in India or South Africa is one common example.

Chapter 6 looks at the methods that can be used to legitimize the transfer of personal data to third countries. In the context of outsourcing, the most practical method for the legitimization of the transfer is the use of the model contractual clauses. Where a processor is part of the same corporate group as the controller, Binding Corporate Rules can also be considered.

10

Electronic Communications

Peter Given and Peter Carey

Introduction and Historical Background	184
Definitions	186
Email Marketing	189
Text Message Marketing	194
Telephone Marketing	195
Fax Marketing	196
Location Data	197
Cookies and Similar Devices	198
Limitations on Processing of Traffic Data	200
Calling and Connected Line Identification	200
Telephone Directories	202
Non-itemized Bills	202
Termination of Unwanted Call Forwarding	202
Security	202
Breach Notification	203
Enforcement	203

Introduction and Historical Background

As a direct result of the explosion in the provision and availability of telecommunications services in the final two decades of the last millennium, concerns arose over the privacy of individuals regarding the use and operation of telephones and related devices. Such concerns became multiplied with the advent of digital technology, the availability of calling line identification, the rise of internet trading, mobile telephony, and new services and technologies such as text messaging, instant messaging, social media, location data, and cookies.

Although mainstream data protection legislation applied to the electronic communications sector in the same way as it did in other industries, the European Union considered that extra safeguards were required for electronic communications. The Directive concerning the processing of personal data and the protection of privacy in the electronic communications sector (2002/58/EC) ('the E-Privacy Directive') was designed to provide those safeguards.

The UK implemented the E-Privacy Directive by way of secondary legislation, namely the Privacy and Electronic Communications (EC Directive) Regulations 2003 (SI 2003/2426) ('PECR'), which came into force on 11 December 2003. Both the E-Privacy Directive and PECR were updated by Directive 2009/136/EC and the Privacy and Electronic Communications (EC Directive) (Amendment) Regulations 2011 (SI 2011/1208) respectively.

The continuing (and in some areas accelerating) pace of technological development in the second decade of the current millennium has required a further review and overhaul in relation to issues covered by the E-Privacy Directive. The EU Commission chose to do this by way of Regulation rather than a Directive. A draft of the new E-Privacy Regulation, which is tabled to come into effect on 25 May 2018, was published in January 2017. In this chapter and unless otherwise indicated, references to the E-Privacy Regulation are to the draft of the Regulation published in January 2017. While the chapter is focused on the E-Privacy Directive and PECR (the law in force at the time of writing), salient provisions of the E-Privacy Regulation are referred to where appropriate.

Unlike Directives, which require implementing legislation in each Member State, Regulations have direct effect throughout the EU. From the perspective of the EU Commission, effecting reforms by way of Regulation promotes greater legal certainty and harmonization by avoiding potentially divergent legislation and interpretation in Member States. Regulations therefore promise an equal level of protection for users and subscribers throughout the EU, and lower compliance costs for businesses operating across borders. In the UK, it is anticipated that the European Union (Withdrawal) Act will create legislation in the UK in identical terms to that contained in the enacted version of the E-Privacy Regulation.

The E-Privacy Regulation is intended to operate as *lex specialis* to the GDPR. The GDPR sets out the general law relating to the protection of personal data. The E-Privacy Regulation, on the other hand, sets out particular rules relating to privacy and electronic communications.

It should be noted, though, that like the E-Privacy Directive and PECR, the E-Privacy Regulation applies to electronic communications per se, and therefore will apply even where the organization sending a communication or providing a communications service is not a data controller (e.g. due to the fact that the organization does not have sufficient information on individuals to amount to personal data). Further, the legislation is designed to be technologically neutral; in other words, the E-Privacy Directive and PECR, and the E-Privacy Regulation once in force, apply to all electronic communications technologies.

The E-Privacy Regulation stems from an ex post Regulatory Fitness and Performance Programme 'REFIT evaluation' of the E-Privacy Directive. The EU Commission concluded that the Directive's objectives and principles remained sound, but that the Directive had not kept pace with technological developments. In particular, recently developed or expanded internet-based services were found not to be subject to the EU electronic communications framework, including the

Directive. Concern focused on 'Over-the-Top' or 'OTT' services such as Voice over IP ('VoIP'), instant messaging and web-based email services, now widely used by consumers as substitutable for traditional services but not subject to the same rules. A further concern related to the development of new techniques for tracking the online behaviour of end-users, which were not covered by the Directive. Consequently, the EU Commission concluded that the Directive should be repealed and wholly replaced by the E-Privacy Regulation.

As with the GDPR, the E-Privacy Regulation is designed to have extra-territorial effect and to be supported by significantly enhanced penalties and sanctions for breach. Among other things, the E-Privacy Regulation applies to electronic communications data processed in connection with the provision and use of electronic communications services in the EU, regardless of whether that processing itself takes place within the EU. It also applies to electronic communications data processed in connection with the provision of electronic communications services from outside the EU to end-users in the EU.

PECR created rights for individuals, as well as companies and organizations, over and above those under mainstream data protection law. The rules also make compulsory the supply to telephone subscribers of certain services or facilities and allow telecommunications providers to make a reasonable charge for some of those services or facilities. They restrict the processing of location data to certain specified circumstances and they provide restrictions on the use of cookies without consent. Possibly of most significance to many organizations, PECR prevented the sending of marketing electronic mail (the definition of electronic mail includes emails, text messages, multimedia messaging services ('MMS'), and video messages) to individual subscribers without prior consent unless there is an existing relationship between the sender and the recipient.

PECR also extended the powers of the Information Commissioner under the DPA, including the ability to serve monetary penalties, to cover breaches of PECR, and to make breach notification (to both the Information Commissioner's Office ('ICO') and affected individuals) mandatory in certain circumstances. Similarly, Article 23 of the E-Privacy Regulation directly imports and adopts the general conditions for imposing administrative fines set out in Chapter VII of the GDPR. Accordingly, fines of up to 20 million euros or (if higher) 4 per cent of an organization's total worldwide annual turnover for the previous financial year might be imposed for certain infringements of the Regulation.

Definitions

The E-Privacy Directive (and PECR in the UK), the key provisions of which are listed in Box 10.1, provides a legal regime for the protection of the privacy of individuals (and in certain cases corporate subscribers) when using electronic communications equipment. It can be seen as being complementary to the provisions of the DPA and, pending the adoption of the E-Privacy Regulation, the GDPR. Indeed, much of the terminology is similar to that contained in mainstream data

---

Box 10.1 Key Provisions of the Directive/PECR

- Restrictions on the use of emails for marketing purposes
- Restrictions on the processing of traffic data
- Restrictions on the processing of location data
- Withholding of calling or called line identification (CLI)
- Unsolicited direct marketing telephone calls and faxes
- Higher security standards
- Compulsory breach notification
- Right of subscribers to receive non-itemized bills
- Entries in telephone directories
- Extension of the Commissioner's powers

---

protection law. However, certain additional words and phrases require additional explanation. Several terms in PECR are imported from other statutes, notably the Broadcasting Act 1990, the Communications Act 2003, and the Electronic Commerce (EC Directive) Regulations 2002. Some of those definitions will be amended or replaced by the E-Privacy Regulation. Key prospective changes are highlighted in Table 10.1.

The definitions in Table 10.1, essential to an understanding of the content of this chapter, are as they appear in PECR and related legislation.

Table 10.1 Definitions

Bill	Includes an invoice, account, statement, or other document of similar character.
Call	A connection established by means of a telephone service available to the public allowing two-way communication in real time.
Communication	Any information exchanged or conveyed between a finite number of parties by means of a public electronic communications service, but does not include information conveyed as part of a programme service, except to the extent that such information can be related to the identifiable subscriber or user receiving the information. The proposed E-Privacy Regulation distinguishes between (a) electronic communications content and (b) electronic communications metadata. Electronic communications content means the content exchanged by means of electronic communications services, such as text, voice, videos, images, and sound. Electronic communications metadata is defined to replace the Directive/PECR term 'Traffic Data'. In essence, the new definitions provide the basis for different rules governing the processing of communications content (what was said) and communications metadata (who said it, when, where and how).

(continued)

Table 10.1 Continued

Communications provider	A person who provides an electronic communications network or an electronic communications service.
Corporate subscriber	A subscriber who is: (a) a company within the meaning of Section 735(1) of the Companies Act 1985 (this Act was repealed on 1 October 2009 and replaced with the Companies Act 2006); (b) a company incorporated in pursuance of a Royal Charter or letters patent; (c) a partnership in Scotland; (d) a corporation sole; or (e) any other body corporate or entity which is a legal person distinct from its members.
Electronic communications network	(a) a transmission system for the conveyance, by the use of electrical, magnetic, or electro-magnetic energy, of signals of any description; and (b) such of the following as are used, by the person providing the system and in association with it, for the conveyance of the signals: (i) apparatus comprising the system; (ii) apparatus used for the switching or routing of the signals; (iii) software and stored data; and (iv) other resources, including network elements which are not active.
Electronic communications service	A service consisting in, or having as its principal feature, the conveyance by means of an electronic communications network of signals, except in so far as it is a content service.
Electronic mail	Any text, voice, sound, or image message sent over a public electronic communications network which can be stored in the network or in the recipient's terminal equipment until it is collected by the recipient and includes messages sent using a short message service (SMS).
Individual	A living individual and includes an unincorporated body of such individuals.
Information society service	Any service normally provided for remuneration, at a distance, by means of electronic equipment for the processing (including digital compression) and storage of data, and at the individual request of a recipient of a service.
Location data	Any data processed in an electronic communications network or by an electronic communications service indicating the geographic position of the terminal equipment of a user of a public electronic communications service, including data relating to the: (a) latitude, longitude, or altitude of the terminal equipment; (b) direction of travel of the user; or (c) time the location information was recorded. The proposed E-Privacy Regulation includes the concept of location data within the definition of electronic communications metadata.
Personal data breach	A breach of security leading to the accidental or unlawful destruction, loss, alteration, unauthorized disclosure of, or access to, personal data transmitted, stored, or otherwise processed in connection with the provision of a public electronic communications service.

Table 10.1 Continued

Programme service	Any of the following services (whether or not it is, or it requires to be, licensed), namely—
	(a) any service which is a programme service within the meaning of the Communications Act 2003 (i.e. a television programme service; the public teletext service; an additional television service; a digital additional television service; a radio programme service; or a sound service provided by the BBC); and
	(b) any other service which consists in the sending, by means of an electronic communications network, of sounds or visual images or both either—
	(i) for reception at two or more places in the UK (whether they are so sent for simultaneous reception or at different times in response to requests made by different users of the service), or
	(ii) for reception at a place in the UK for the purpose of being presented there to members of the public or to any group of persons.
Public communications provider	A provider of a public electronic communications network or a public electronic communications service.
Public electronic communications network	An electronic communications network provided wholly or mainly for the purpose of making electronic communications services available to members of the public.
Public electronic communications service	Any electronic communications service that is provided so as to be available for use by members of the public.
Subscriber	A person who is a party to a contract with a provider of public electronic communications services for the supply of such services.
Traffic data	Any data processed for the purpose of the conveyance of a communication on an electronic communications network or for the billing in respect of that communication and includes data relating to the routing, duration, or time of a communication. In the proposed E-Privacy Regulation this term is replaced by 'electronic communications metadata'. The expanded definition reads: 'data processed in an electronic communications network for the purposes of transmitting, distributing or exchanging electronic communications content; including data used to trace and identify the source and destination of a communication, data on the location of the device generated in the context of providing electronic communications services, and the date, time, duration and the type of communication'.
User	Any individual using a public electronic communications service.
Value-added service	Any service which requires the processing of traffic data or location data beyond that which is necessary for the transmission of a communication or the billing of that communication.

Email Marketing

Whilst the GDPR governs the use of email addresses for marketing purposes in the same way as other personal data processing, PECR represents the first specific legislative restriction in the UK on the use of electronic communications for marketing purposes. Article 13 of the E-Privacy Directive provides that:

1. The use of . . . electronic mail for the purposes of direct marketing may only be allowed in respect of subscribers who have given their prior consent.

2. Notwithstanding paragraph 1, where a natural or legal person obtains from its customers their electronic contact details for electronic mail, in the context of the sale of a product or a service, in accordance with Directive 95/46/EC, the same natural or legal person may use these electronic contact details for direct marketing of its own similar products or services provided that customers clearly and distinctly are given the opportunity to object, free of charge and in an easy manner, to such use of electronic contact details when they are collected and on the occasion of each message in case the customer has not initially refused such use.

3. Member States shall take appropriate measures to ensure that, free of charge, unsolicited communications for purposes of direct marketing, in cases other than those referred to in paragraphs 1 and 2, are not allowed either without the consent of the subscribers concerned or in respect of subscribers who do not wish to receive these communications, the choice between these options to be determined by national legislation.

Regulation 22 of PECR, which is designed to implement Article 13 above, provides that:

(1) This regulation applies to the transmission of unsolicited communications by means of electronic mail to individual subscribers.

(2) Except in the circumstances referred to in paragraph (3), a person shall neither transmit, nor instigate the transmission of, unsolicited communications for the purposes of direct marketing by means of electronic mail unless the recipient of the electronic mail has previously notified the sender that he consents for the time being to such communication being sent by, or at the instigation of, the sender.

(3) A person may send or instigate the sending of electronic mail for the purposes of direct marketing where—

(a) that person has obtained the contact details of the recipient of that electronic mail in the course of the sale or negotiations for the sale of a product or service to that recipient;

(b) the direct marketing is in respect of that person's similar products or services only;

(c) the recipient has been given a simple means of refusing (free of charge except for the costs of the transmission of the refusal), the use of his contact details for the purposes of such direct marketing, at the time that the details were initially collected, and, where he did not initially refuse the use of the details, at the time of each subsequent communication.

(4) A subscriber shall not permit his line to be used in contravention of paragraph (2).

Thus, the sending of unsolicited direct marketing emails (including text and other electronic messages) without consent is unlawful, except in certain specified circumstances. There is no definition of 'direct marketing' in the E-Privacy Directive or PECR. However, the term is defined in the DPA, Section 11(3), which provides that direct marketing is the 'communication (by whatever means) of any advertising or marketing material which is directed to particular individuals'. This is a wide definition that has been interpreted to include messages by non-profit-making entities (such as charities and political parties) that promote their aims and objectives. The proposed E-Privacy Regulation also contains a broad definition of what constitutes direct marketing.

Under the E-Privacy Directive and PECR, organizations wishing to send marketing communications by email or text to individual subscribers must obtain the prior consent of the intended recipient of the email or text unless the so-called 'soft opt-in' provisions apply—that is, the contact details have been obtained in the context of the sale or negotiations for the sale of a product or service between the sender and the recipient, the email relates to the 'similar' products or services of the sender, and the recipient is given the opportunity, free of charge, to opt out (or 'unsubscribe') from receiving further marketing emails both at the time of collection of the data and in every subsequent communication.

Where consent does need to be obtained (i.e. where the soft opt-in provisions above do not apply), such consent will need to meet the standard of consent required by the GDPR (see Chapter 3). Although the E-Privacy Directive merely provides that consent must be obtained from the intended recipient of emails, PECR state that the consent must have been given to the sender of the emails—this has a detrimental effect on the 'list rental' business in the UK as, in the case of list rental, the sender of the emails is not the person to whom consent has been given, even where such consent exists. In this scenario (and bearing in mind the requirements of the GDPR), the consent should specifically refer to the sender (although this raises practical issues). Similarly, 'host mailing' services will be adversely affected due to the requirement of the soft opt-in exemption that the products or services be those of the sender of the marketing emails (i.e. consent will be required to send marketing emails concerning a third party's products and services).

It should be noted that Regulation 22 applies only to 'individual subscribers' and, therefore, excludes corporate subscribers. The exclusion of corporate subscribers means that the sending of marketing communications to them is not restricted by Regulation 22, hence such marketing communications will be lawful if they comply with the GDPR (and, in the UK, other requirements of PECR—specifically Regulation 23).

The E-Privacy Regulation defines 'direct marketing communications' as 'any form of advertising, whether written or oral, sent to one or more identified or identifiable end-users of electronic communications services, including the use of automated calling and communication systems, with or without human interaction, electronic mail, SMS, etc'. Article 16 states that:

1. Natural or legal persons may use electronic communications services for the purposes of sending direct marketing communications to end-users who are natural persons that have given their consent.

2. Where a natural or legal person obtains electronic contact details for electronic mail from its customer, in the context of the sale of a product or a service, in accordance with Regulation (EU) 2016/679 (GDPR), that natural or legal person may use these electronic contact details for direct marketing of its own similar products or services only if customers are clearly and distinctly given the opportunity to object, free of charge and in an easy manner, to such use. The right to object shall be given at the time of collection and each time a message is sent.

These provisions are similar to those in the E-Privacy Directive and PECR. To promote legal certainty and to ensure that the rules protecting against unsolicited electronic communications remain future-proof, the E-Privacy Regulation sets out a single set of rules that do not vary according to the technology used to convey those unsolicited communications.

The Article 29 Working Party (the forerunner of the European Data Protection Board) has, however, expressed concern that the scope of the direct marketing definition is too limited (see Opinion 01/2017). Specifically, the relevant definition refers only to communications that are 'sent'. While this clearly catches email, it arguably does not catch advertising on the web or through social media platforms which may not involve 'sending'.

Exception for 'existing customer relationship'

Article 13(2) of the E-Privacy Directive refers, in the derogation from the requirement for prior consent, to the concept of a person as a 'customer'. Concern was expressed, notably in the UK, that this provision would exclude the use of the contact details of persons who had submitted their data outside of a contractual relationship—for example, where a *prospective* customer submits her details on a website to register her interest in a product or service. There is no definition of 'customer' in the E-Privacy Directive, but some meaning can be gathered from Recital 41, which refers to the concept of an 'existing customer relationship', as follows:

Within the context of an existing customer relationship, it is reasonable to allow the use of electronic contact details for the offering of similar products or services, but only by the same company that has obtained the electronic contact details in accordance with Directive 95/46/EC. When electronic contact details are obtained, the customer should be informed about their further use for direct marketing in a clear and distinct manner, and be given the opportunity to refuse such usage. This opportunity should continue to be offered with each subsequent direct marketing message, free of charge, except for any costs for the transmission of this refusal.

It is interesting to note that PECR make no reference to 'customer' in this context. Instead, Regulation 22(3)(a) refers to the contact details of a person that have been obtained 'in the course of the sale or negotiations for the sale of a product or service'. The provisions of PECR are thus somewhat wider than the equivalent provision in the E-Privacy Directive.

The ICO, in its guidance on direct marketing, has provided further detail on the scope of the existing customer relationship derogation in PECR. The guidance states that the customer does not actually have to have bought anything. It is sufficient if negotiations for a sale took place. This means that the customer should have actively expressed an interest in buying the organization's products or services. This could manifest itself by the customer requesting a quote, or asking for more details of a product the organization offers. However, merely logging into the company's website to browse its range of products would not be enough to amount to negotiations.

The above provision effectively constitutes a significant disadvantage for charities, political parties, and other not-for-profit entities. Such organizations will be unable to use the soft opt-in approach unless they are promoting actual goods or services.

The E-Privacy Regulation follows the E-Privacy Directive by referring only to a 'customer' of the natural or legal person who obtains electronic contact details for electronic mail in the context of the sale of a product or service. Under the new rules, therefore, the derogation may apply narrowly to existing customers, and not to prospective customers who have yet to conclude a purchase.

Similar products and services

In the existing customer relationship derogation, both the E-Privacy Directive, PECR, and the E-Privacy Regulation refer to the concept of 'similar products and services'. There is no definition of this phrase in any of these pieces of legislation. In the absence of such a definition, the ordinary meanings of the words should be relied on. We could surmise that a water utility company that commences a new venture in the provision of telecommunications services would need prior consent when contemplating the sending of emails about the new services to existing customers. However, a law firm that had acquired clients for the purpose of performing a conveyancing service could probably send emails to such clients about the firm's probate services, as such services are likely to be 'similar' to those for which the firm has already provided advice.

In the absence of specific legislative guidance, the ICO has adopted a relatively flexible subjective test for the 'similarity' of products and services: the question that should be asked is, 'Would the customer reasonably expect messages about the product or service in question?' The ICO notes that whether this is the case or not will be context specific and may depend on the type of business in question and the category of product. The onus is thus on marketers to ensure that customers are alerted to their full range of products and services at the outset.

Compliance with existing law

One further difference between the E-Privacy Directive and PECR is the reference in the E-Privacy Directive to compliance with mainstream data protection law as being a necessary prerequisite to the exception from the need to obtain consent for electronic direct marketing. Thus the E-Privacy Directive requires the marketer to obtain the contact details of existing customers in accordance with applicable EU data protection law for the exception to apply.

PECR, on the other hand, does not explicitly require compliance with existing legislation as a prerequisite. This means that, for example, a failure to make readily available a fair processing notice at the point of data collection, as required by the GDPR, would not necessarily breach PECR or preclude reliance on the existing customer relationship derogation. This is largely an academic point, though, as the failure to comply with the GDPR would be potentially actionable under that legislation.

The E-Privacy Regulation follows the approach taken in the E-Privacy Directive rather than PECR.

Identity of the sender and return address

By virtue of Regulation 23 of PECR, it is unlawful to send a marketing email where the identity of the sender is disguised or concealed. Further, it is unlawful to send a marketing email where a valid return address, to which the recipient can respond requesting the cessation of such marketing, is not provided. It is important to note that these rules apply to marketing messages sent to corporate subscribers as well as those sent to individual subscribers.

Article 16 of the E-Privacy Regulation makes similar provision and, in this regard, also makes no distinction between individual and corporate recipients. However, the Article 29 Working Party has observed that there is no explicit prohibition on the use of false identities. Recital 34 to the draft E-Privacy Regulation suggests that there would be such a prohibition, but the operative provision in Article 16(6) merely states that end-users must be informed of the identity of the legal or natural person on behalf of whom the communication is transmitted, with no clear statement prohibiting disguised or concealed identities.

Text Message Marketing

The sending of short message service (SMS or text) messages for marketing purposes is regulated in the EU in the same way as the sending of emails for marketing purposes—the definition of 'email' in the E-Privacy Directive and PECR includes SMS messages.

See the section on 'Email Marketing' above for further detail on the use of SMS messages for marketing purposes.

The sending of SMS messages to individuals based on their geographical location falls within the definition of 'value-added services'—for further detail see the section below, 'Location Data'.

Telephone Marketing

Telephone marketing, whether by voice or fax, has proved to be a highly success-ful sales technique. But it has also led to considerable numbers of complaints in many countries of the EU and elsewhere. Directive 97/66/EC (which is no longer in force) sought to address this concern by regulating the use of telecommunications equipment for direct marketing. The E-Privacy Directive, reproducing many of the original restrictions and obligations in Directive 97/66/EC using new, technologic-ally-neutral language, contains provisions concerning unsolicited calls, automated calling, and fax machines. In the UK, Regulations 19–21 of PECR contain the relevant provisions.

Unsolicited calls for direct marketing

It is unlawful for a person to use, or instigate the use of, a public electronic com-munications service for the purposes of making unsolicited live (i.e. voice to voice) calls for direct marketing purposes where the number called either is that of a subscriber who has previously notified the caller that such calls should not be made to that number, or has been entered on a specific register maintained for that purpose.

In the UK, the operation of the register of numbers (commonly referred to as the Telephone Preference Service or TPS) was previously the responsibility of the Office of Communications ('OFCOM'). From 30 December 2016, the ICO took over responsibility for the register. Numbers must be entered on the register at least twenty-eight days prior to the date of the call for the call to be unlawful. An entry of a number on the register will not render a direct marketing call unlawful where the relevant subscriber has notified the particular caller that he does not object to receiving direct marketing calls on that number—in other words, the bar on calling a number that has been entered on the register will be ineffective against a caller who has received permission from the subscriber to whom that number relates, whether the number was entered on the register before or after that permission was given.

As previously stated, it should be remembered that PECR applies to anyone who uses a publicly available electronic communications service for direct marketing, not just to data controllers.

Organizations making telephone marketing calls are also required, when making such calls, to present their telephone number. This will enable individuals to more easily refuse or report unwanted calls and will assist the ICO in investigating and taking action against non-compliance.

Under the E-Privacy Regulation, the default position is that live (i.e. voice to voice) direct marketing calls may only be made with the consent of the recipient of the call. However, the Regulation permits Member States to provide by law that calls can be made without consent provided the recipient of the call has not objected to the call (essentially this would be a similar regime to that which currently exists under PECR). If this provision is a feature of the final version of the E-Privacy Regulation, it will be for the UK government to enact legislation to maintain the status quo.

Use of automated calling systems

Under PECR, it is unlawful to use an automated calling or communications system to call a number and communicate a pre-recorded (i.e. non-live) direct marketing message, unless the called line is that of a subscriber who has notified the caller that he consents to receiving such messages. This provision of the legislation outlaws automated voice calls without prior permission having been obtained. As with voice-to-voice calls, organizations making automated telephone marketing calls are also required to present their telephone number.

The TPS or Telephone Preference Service

Regulation 26 of PECR obliges the ICO to maintain and keep up to date the register of numbers that have been allocated to subscribers who do not wish to receive unsolicited direct marketing calls and have notified that wish to the ICO (or, prior to 30 December 2016, OFCOM). The ICO is obliged to remove a number from the register where it has reason to believe that the number is no longer allocated to the subscriber that requested entry on the register. The ICO may (as has been the case) outsource the function of keeping the register to a third party organization.

Marketers are expected to pay a fee to the ICO for access to the register. The fee that is chargeable must not exceed the sum that, when aggregated with other fees within a particular period, equals the cost to the ICO of performing its statutory duties in relation to the register in that period.

Fax Marketing

Under PECR, it is unlawful to send a direct marketing fax to:

(a) an individual subscriber unless the individual has notified the caller that he or she consents to such communications;

(b) a corporate subscriber who has previously notified the caller that such unsolicited communications should not be sent; or

(c) any subscriber where that subscriber's number has been registered on the Fax Preference Service run by the ICO for at least twenty-eight days prior to the sending of the fax.

Location Data

Location data is information processed in an electronic communications network or by an electronic communications service that describes the geographical location of a user's device. It is a very useful aspect of mobile technology since there is a vast array of possible marketing initiatives that thereby become available—a simple example is where a user requests a service provider to send him the telephone number of (or show him a map from his current location to) his 'nearest Italian restaurant'. In addition to the potential provision of such useful information (referred to in the legislation as 'value-added services'), the pinpointing of a mobile device's location carries with it significant privacy risks. The law, therefore, restricts the use of location data to certain defined circumstances. Article 9 of the E-Privacy Directive provides that:

1. Where location data other than traffic data, relating to users or subscribers of public communications networks or publicly available electronic communications services, can be processed, such data may only be processed when they are made anonymous, or with the consent of the users or subscribers to the extent and for the duration necessary for the provision of a value-added service. The service provider must inform the users or subscribers, prior to obtaining their consent, of the type of location data other than traffic data which will be processed, of the purposes and duration of the processing and whether the data will be transmitted to a third party for the purpose of providing the value-added service. Users or subscribers shall be given the possibility to withdraw their consent for the processing of location data other than traffic data at any time.

2. Where consent of the users or subscribers has been obtained for the processing of location data other than traffic data, the user or subscriber must continue to have the possibility, using a simple means and free of charge, of temporarily refusing the processing of such data for each connection to the network or for each transmission of a communication.

3. Processing of location data other than traffic data in accordance with paragraphs 1 and 2 must be restricted to persons acting under the authority of the provider of the public communications network or publicly available communications service or of the third party providing the value-added service, and must be restricted to what is necessary for the purposes of providing the value-added service.

Regulation 14 of PECR provides that:
(2) Location data relating to a user or subscriber of a public electronic communications network or a public electronic communications service may only be processed—
(a) where that user or subscriber cannot be identified from such data; or
(b) where necessary for the provision of a value added service, with the consent of that user or subscriber.

(3) Prior to obtaining the consent of the user or subscriber under paragraph (2)(b), the public communications provider in question must provide the following information to the user or subscriber to whom the data relate—

(a) the types of location data that will be processed;

(b) the purposes and duration of the processing of those data; and

(c) whether the data will be transmitted to a third party for the purpose of providing the value added service.

(4) A user or subscriber who has given his consent to the processing of data under paragraph (2)(b) shall—

(a) be able to withdraw such consent at any time, and

(b) in respect of each connection to the public electronic communications network in question or each transmission of a communication, be given the opportunity to withdraw such consent, using a simple means and free of charge.

Thus, location data (as defined) of a person may only be processed if it is anonymized or where necessary in the context of the provision of a value-added service with the consent of the relevant person (there are limited exemptions to this restriction where location data is required to facilitate responses to emergency calls (Regulation 16) or to send emergency alerts (Regulation 16A)). In addition, the communications provider must furnish the relevant person with certain information prior to the obtaining of consent from that person. The information that must be provided is similar to that specified under the 'fair collection' provisions in the GDPR (see Chapter 3). Any person who gives his or her consent for the processing of his or her location in connection with the provision of a value-added service must be given the means to withdraw that consent at any time. That person must also be given a free and simple means to withdraw their consent each time they connect to the public electronic communications network or send a communication. Regulation 14 also provides that location data can only be processed under Regulation 14 by a public communications provider, a provider of a value added service, or a person acting on the authority of either of them.

It is interesting to note that the UK government has chosen to create a considerably more comprehensive definition of 'location data' than that which appears in the E-Privacy Directive. The operative provisions of the Directive merely refer to the 'geographic position of terminal equipment', whereas PECR additionally include 'latitude, longitude, altitude, direction of travel and time the location information was recorded', thus incorporating some of the wording from the recitals to the Directive. The proposed E-Privacy Regulation follows the Directive rather than PECR, referring only to the location of the device.

Cookies and Similar Devices

Although using technologically neutral terminology, Regulation 6 of PECR directly impacts the use of devices known as cookies. A cookie is a text file commonly placed on a user's computer by website operators. A cookie is often used for saving settings on the user's system and for sending those settings back to the server that originally created them, thus allowing a website to 'recognize' a revisiting user. Cookies may be temporary (session) or permanent. Temporary cookies are used to pass information between web pages in a single visit (e.g. for use with an online shopping cart) and the user's browser will delete temporary cookies when it is shut down. Permanent cookies are stored on the user's device for a defined period, for example one year, and can be used to save a user's personal choices and preferences between visits. More controversially, cookies can be used to record information about a user's activities online—profiles on surfing habits and other information can thus be accumulated for behavioural analysis and marketing purposes.

The E-Privacy Directive and PECR prohibit the use of cookies (and similar devices) unless the consent of the subscriber or user of the device on which the cookie is set is obtained and that person is provided with certain information. This prohibition does not apply where the cookie is:

- for the sole purpose of carrying out the transmission of a communication over an electronic communications network; or
- strictly necessary to provide an information society service requested by the subscriber or user.

An Article 29 Working Party Opinion (Opinion 04/2012) on cookies attempted to clarify the situations where consent for cookies does not need to be obtained. The Opinion notes that some cookies can be exempted from informed consent under certain conditions if they are not used for additional purposes. These cookies may include (a) cookies used to keep track of a user's input when filling in online forms over several web pages or cookies used to keep track of items placed in a shopping cart; (b) multimedia player session cookies (cookies used to store technical data needed to play back video or audio content); and (c) user interface customization cookies (e.g. language preference cookies to remember the language selected by the user across web pages), provided these are session cookies.

It should be remembered that there will inevitably be occasions when a cookie's usage will fall within the definition of personal data, in which case the provisions of the GDPR must be complied with. In particular, controllers should remember the requirement to avoid excessive processing—see Chapter 2.

The information requirement provides that users must be furnished with clear and comprehensive information about the purposes of the storage of and function of cookies. This information should ideally be located in a cookies policy.

The proposed E-Privacy Regulation builds upon the notice and consent requirements of the E-Privacy Directive and PECR. It requires the provider of browsers or similar software to build functionality into the browser or software allowing users to consent to (or reject) the setting of cookies on their device. This proposal reflects the GDPR-derived requirement for consent to be specific, and to be an affirmative act.

The Article 29 Working Party has expressed a strong preference for blocking cookies by default as the approach most in line with GDPR protections. However, the draft E-Privacy Regulation published in January 2017 represented a move away from blocking by default, which was the approach taken in an earlier, leaked, draft.

Limitations on Processing of Traffic Data

PECR places restrictions on the processing of traffic data. Traffic data are defined as 'any data processed for the purpose of the conveyance of a communication on an electronic communications network or for the billing in respect of that communication and includes data relating to the routing, duration, or time of a communication'.

In addition to the specific restrictions detailed below, traffic data may only be processed for the following purposes:

(a) the management of billing or traffic;

(b) customer enquiries;

(c) the prevention or detection of fraud;

(d) the marketing of telecommunications services; and

(e) the provision of a value-added service.

Subject to two exceptions (other than 'national security', which is a general exemption under PECR), traffic data must be erased or depersonalized by the public communications provider when no longer required for the purpose of the transmission of a communication. Depersonalization of traffic data will occur where the personal or identifying details of the individual (or corporate subscriber) concerned are removed from such data. Thus, by way of example, a communications provider may keep figures relating to call duration and billing for statistical purposes.

The exceptions, which allow the storage of non-depersonalized traffic data in respect of both individual and corporate subscribers, are contained in Regulations 7(2) and 7(3) of PECR. The first relates to the payment of charges or interconnection payments. The second, which concerns the marketing of electronic communications services or the provision of value-added services, may be undertaken only with the consent of the subscriber or user and the processing of the traffic data must not exceed the duration necessary for the marketing or service in question. There is a further limited exemption to the restriction on using traffic data where the data is required to send emergency alerts (Regulation 16A).

Under the proposed E-Privacy Regulation, electronic communications metadata cannot be processed without consent, unless it is necessary for fulfilment of quality of service requirements, for billing or interconnection payments, or for stopping fraud or abuse. Processing for other purposes is permitted with consent, provided those purposes could not be achieved by processing information that is made anonymous.

Calling and Connected Line Identification

In several European countries it has been possible for some time to identify the telephone number of a person making a call. Calling Line Identification ('CLI') provides a number of benefits, including allowing a called person the freedom to choose whether to accept a particular call before it is answered and giving information to emergency services on the location of distressed callers who may not be able to give such information.

Outgoing calls

Under PECR, a user is entitled to be able to prevent CLI attaching to her *outgoing* call whether or not she is the subscriber to the line from which she is calling. In the UK, this is possible by dialling 141 immediately prior to the number of the person being called. Additionally, a subscriber has the right to block CLI on all outgoing calls on her line or on individual calls on a call-by-call basis. Both services must be made available free of charge by the relevant electronic communications service provider. This would be replicated by the proposed E-Privacy Regulation, with an ability to override CLI blocking in order to trace malicious or nuisance calls.

Incoming calls

A person is entitled to prevent his equipment from providing information identifying any *incoming* call. Such identification may be made available in two ways—by a display device or by a call return service. Further, where equipment makes details of the telephone number of a subscriber being called available to the caller, the subscriber must be able to prevent presentation of his number. Both services must be made available free of charge.

Where incoming caller identification is available, it must be possible for the person being called to reject any call, where the caller has withheld his number, before it has been answered.

999 or 112 calls

In order to facilitate responses to emergency calls, both 999 (UK emergency services) and 112 (the single European emergency call number) calls are subject to the following rules:

(a) no prevention of CLI shall be permitted for these calls; and

(b) the identity of the calling line cannot be prevented from being presented on the called line.

Further, the restrictions on processing location data under PECR do not apply to emergency calls.

Malicious or nuisance calls

Regulation 15 of PECR permits a communications provider to override any attempt by a person who makes malicious or nuisance calls to withhold the identity of the calling line where:

(a) a subscriber has requested the tracing of such calls received on his line; and

(b) the provider is satisfied that the action is necessary and expedient for the purposes of tracing such calls.

Telephone Directories

PECR gives certain rights to individual and corporate subscribers in relation to entries in publicly available telephone directories (whether available in paper or electronic form). Both an individual and a corporate subscriber are entitled to request that no entry of their telephone number appear in a directory (i.e. ex-directory status). Further, the personal data of an individual subscriber must not be included in any such directory unless he has been given a statement of the purposes of the directory and he has been given the opportunity to decide whether his personal data is included in the directory.

Article 15 of the E-Privacy Regulation requires providers of public directories to obtain the consent of end-users to include their personal data in the directory.

Reverse search directories

Where personal data of an individual subscriber are to be included in a directory with facilities which enable users of that directory to obtain access to those data solely on the basis of a telephone number (a reverse search directory), the subscriber must be informed of that facility and his 'express' consent must be obtained. Thus, reverse search directories will be unlawful unless each and every person listed has consented to the use of their information by way of opt-in device.

Non-itemized Bills

Any subscriber is entitled to receive bills that are not itemized. This provision is designed to protect the privacy of a person in relation to other members of his or her household.

Termination of Unwanted Call Forwarding

Where calls are automatically forwarded to a subscriber's number, the subscriber is entitled to the termination of that forwarding at no cost and without delay.

Security

A provider of a public electronic communications service is under a duty to take appropriate technical and organizational measures to ensure the security of the service provided. The provider of an electronic communications network must comply with any reasonable request of the service provider in this regard.

Breach Notification

The E-Privacy Directive and PECR require the compulsory reporting of breaches for parts of the electronic communications sector. When a 'personal data breach' (see Table 10.1) occurs within an organization that provides a service which allows members of the public to send electronic messages (e.g. telecommunications companies and internet service providers), the ICO must be informed. The notification, which must be communicated to the ICO within twenty-four hours of the organization becoming aware of the breach, must include the following information:

- name and contact details;
- date and time of the breach;
- date and time the breach was detected;
- information as to the type of breach;
- information about the personal data concerned.

Organizations that fail to comply with this breach notification provision can be fined up to £1,000. This, relatively low, fine is in addition to the power of the Commissioner to fine the communications provider for breaching the GDPR or other provisions of PECR.

In addition to notifying the regulator, PECR impose an obligation on the provider to inform its subscribers about the data breach if the breach is likely to adversely affect them. Providers should inform relevant individuals about any steps that they can take in order to mitigate any possible adverse impact on themselves.

The E-Privacy Regulation alters this position. There is no provision for data breach notification under the E-Privacy Regulation, meaning there will be no unnecessary overlap with the requirements of the GDPR (which itself contains general breach notification requirements).

Enforcement

The rules in PECR are enforceable by the Information Commissioner and most of the Commissioner's powers and functions under mainstream data protection legislation, including the powers of entry and inspection and to issue a fine, are extended to the provisions of PECR. The ICO also has the power to require an audit to be conducted of the activities of service providers in certain circumstances. In addition, OFCOM may request the Commissioner to exercise the Commissioner's enforcement function in respect of any contravention of any of the requirements of PECR.

The ICO has become increasingly focused on enforcing the requirements of PECR, particularly in relation to infringements of PECR's requirements concerning electronic direct marketing. At the time of writing, the largest fine imposed to date is £400,000 (note that this pre-dates the fine regime under the GDPR). This fine was imposed on a company that made 99.5 million automated calls to individuals without their consent (in breach of PECR). The calls were made over an 18-month period and led to over 1,000 complaints.

Enforcement and penalties under the proposed E-Privacy Regulation draw largely upon, and specifically import many provisions from, the GDPR. This includes fines of up to 20 million euros or (if higher) 4 per cent of an organization's total worldwide annual turnover for the previous financial year, which can be imposed for certain infringements of the E-Privacy Regulation.

11

Data Protection Impact Assessments

Olivia Whitcroft

Introduction	205
What Is a DPIA?	206
When to Carry Out a DPIA	207
Identifying Whether a DPIA Is Required	210
Who Should Carry Out a DPIA	211
How to Conduct a DPIA	212
Reporting and Publication of the DPIA	221

Introduction

Article 35 of the GDPR requires data protection impact assessments ('DPIAs') to be carried out on processing activities which are likely to result in a high risk for individuals.

Whilst the GDPR has introduced them as a new legal requirement, they are not a new concept. DPIAs (or the similar concept of privacy impact assessments) have been promoted by the Information Commissioner's Office (ICO) and other European data protection authorities for many years as a useful, good-practice tool to help organizations ensure compliance with key data protection obligations, and to manage data protection risk proactively. Therefore, in addition to the high risk activities for which DPIAs are *required* under the GDPR, organizations may *choose* to conduct DPIAs when considering other new data processing activities.

The output (result) of DPIAs can assist in demonstrating compliance with data protection principles in accordance with the GDPR's accountability requirement, which is discussed in Chapter 12. Additionally, DPIAs can also play a key role in achieving 'data protection by design' and 'data protection by default' (see Chapter 1), which are required under Article 25 of the GDPR. In accordance with the requirements of 'data protection by design', compliance measures must be implemented at the time that the means for processing is determined and during the processing itself. 'Data protection by default' requires that only those personal data which are necessary for each specific purpose are processed—this applies to the amount of data collected, the extent of data processing, the period of storage, and accessibility.

Conducting DPIAs may therefore avoid legal penalties for non-compliance, and the potential costs and associated reputational damage of having to halt or reverse implementation or launch of a new project.

In April 2017, the Article 29 Working Party published Guidelines on DPIAs and on determining whether processing is likely to result in a high risk under the GDPR (WP 248). A revised version was published in October 2017—see <http://www.dpdocuments.com>. Further, the ICO published a Code of Practice on 'Conducting Privacy Impact Assessments' in February 2014; although this pre-dates the GDPR, it contains useful guidance on different elements of the DPIA process. For the full text of the ICO Code of Practice, see <http://www.dpdocuments.com>.

What Is a DPIA?

A DPIA is a process that enables data protection risk to be identified and managed. The Working Party Guidelines describe it as a 'process for building and demonstrating compliance' and emphasize that it is 'a continual process, and not a one-time exercise'.

DPIAs encourage a structured assessment of a data processing activity to identify data protection risks inherent in the activity, and to determine whether it is legally compliant. Organizations can then take appropriate steps to mitigate and manage the identified risks.

There is no single way in which to conduct a DPIA, but the process involves the following stages, as set out in Article 35(7) of the GDPR, and consistent with the ICO's Code of Practice:

(i)   describe the data processing activities and the purposes of the processing;

(ii) assess the necessity and proportionality of the processing activities in relation to the purposes;

(iii) assess the data protection risks; and

(iv) determine the measures to address the risks, including measures to ensure the protection of personal data and compliance with the GDPR.

Other key elements of a DPIA are:

(v)   obtain the advice of the Data Protection Officer ('DPO'), where one has been designated (this is required under Article 35(1) of the GDPR);

(vi) where appropriate, seek the views of data subjects or their representatives on the intended processing (required under Article 35(9) of the GDPR);

(vii) consult with the relevant supervisory authority (the ICO in the UK) where the DPIA indicates that the processing activities would result in a high risk (required under Article 36 of the GDPR); and

(viii) conduct a review to assess if the processing of personal data is performed in compliance with the DPIA, at least where there is a change in the risks involved (required under Article 35(11) of the GDPR).

Organizations may find it helpful, where possible, to integrate the DPIA process into existing project management and risk assessment procedures. This may create less of a burden on project teams than carrying out the DPIA as a wholly separate exercise or new process.

Nevertheless, it will be important that such procedures incorporate the key requirements for DPIAs. Annex 2 of the Working Party Guidelines provide some common criteria for DPIAs to clarify the basic requirements of the GDPR, and which can be used to show that a particular DPIA methodology meets the standards required by the GDPR.

When to Carry Out a DPIA

The first step in a DPIA process is to determine whether a DPIA is needed. Organizations should ensure that relevant people within the organization are equipped to identify when a DPIA is required, and know how to initiate a DPIA. Article 35(1) of the GDPR states:

Where a type of processing in particular using new technologies, and taking into account the nature, scope, context and purposes of the processing, is likely to result in a high risk to the rights and freedoms of natural persons, the controller shall, prior to the processing, carry out an assessment of the impact of the envisaged processing operations on the protection of personal data. A single assessment may address a set of similar processing operations that present similar high risks.

In short, this requires DPIAs to be carried out for potentially high risk data processing activities.

Several similar projects could be covered by the same DPIA. The Working Party DPIA Guidelines provide the following examples:

- a group of municipal authorities each setting up a similar CCTV system; and
- a railway operator with video surveillance at all its train stations.

Article 35(3) lists specific circumstances where a DPIA shall, in particular, be required:

(a) a systematic and extensive evaluation of personal aspects relating to natural persons which is based on automated processing, including profiling, and on which decisions are based that produce legal effects concerning the natural person or similarly significantly affect the natural person;
(b) processing on a large scale of special categories of data referred to in Article 9(1), or of personal data relating to criminal convictions and offences referred to in Article 10; or
(c) a systematic monitoring of a publicly accessible area on a large scale.

Point (a) of Article 35(3) captures data analytics, including profiling, which result in decisions significantly affecting individuals. In April 2017, the ICO published a discussion paper (called a 'feedback request') on profiling and automated decision-making, which gives examples of activities falling within this point:

- profiling and scoring for purposes of risk assessment (e.g. for credit scoring, insurance premium setting, fraud prevention, detection of money laundering);
- location tracking, for example by mobile apps, to decide whether to send push notifications;
- loyalty programmes;
- behavioural advertising; and
- monitoring of wellness, fitness, and health data via wearable devices.

The ICO also notes that point (a) applies in the case of partially automated processing, and therefore some human involvement in the process would not preclude the need for a DPIA. For the full text of this discussion paper, see <http://www.dpdocuments.com>. In October 2017, the Article 29 Working Party published Guidelines on automated individual decision-making and profiling (WP 251)—see <http://www.dpdocuments.com>.

Point (b) of Article 35(3) captures processing on a large scale of special categories of data or data relating to criminal convictions and offences. Recital 91 of the GDPR provides some guidance on what this covers:

large-scale processing operations which aim to process a considerable amount of personal data at regional, national or supranational level and which could affect a large number of data subjects and which are likely to result in a high risk, for example, on account of their sensitivity.

It goes on to state:

The processing of personal data should not be considered to be on a large scale if the processing concerns personal data from patients or clients by an individual physician, other health care professional or lawyer.

The Article 29 Working Party's Guidelines on Data Protection Officers (WP 243) (see <http://www.dpdocuments.com>) provide guidance on the meaning of 'large scale'. They indicate that it should take into account the number of data subjects, the volume of data and/or range of data items, the duration of the activity, and the geographical extent of the activity. They also give examples of large-scale processing, including processing of patient data in the regular course of business by a hospital or processing of personal data for behavioural advertising by a search engine. The meaning of 'special categories of data' is discussed further in Chapter 4.

Point (c) of Article 35(3) captures systematic monitoring of publicly accessible areas on a large scale. Recital 91 of the GDPR adds 'especially when using optic-electronic devices'. The Working Party's guidance on the meaning of 'large scale' (as referred to above) is also useful here. The same document also discusses the meaning of 'systematic', which is considered to mean one or more of the following:

- occurring according to a system;
- pre-arranged, organized, or methodical;
- taking place as part of a general plan for data collection; and
- carried out as part of a strategy.

The Guidelines suggest that a piazza, shopping centre, street, or public library are examples of a 'publicly accessible area', which indicates a physical space. However, monitoring online may also be considered high risk for which a DPIA is needed.

Points (a) to (c) of Article 35(3) are not an exhaustive list of high risk activities. The Working Party Guidelines on DPIAs seek to provide a more concrete set of activities, and indicate that the criteria below should be considered. As a rule of thumb, if a processing operation meets at least two of these criteria, the Guidelines suggest that a DPIA will be required:

- Evaluation or scoring—including profiling and predicting. Examples include a bank screening its customers against a credit reference database, a biotechnology company offering genetic tests to assess and predict health risks, and a company building behavioural or marketing profiles based on use of its website.

- Automated decision-making with legal or similar significant effect—this covers, for example, where the processing may lead to exclusion or discrimination against individuals.

- Systematic monitoring—processing used to observe, monitor, or control data subjects. This is wider than (but includes) monitoring of publicly accessible areas listed in Article 35(3).

- Sensitive data—as well as use of special categories of data and data relating to criminal convictions specified in Article 35(3), this includes other data which can increase the risks to individuals, such as electronic communications data, location data, financial data, and information produced for personal activities when using online services (such as email or document management services).

- Data processed on a large scale—again, this is wider than the specific large-scale activities listed in Article 35(3).

- Datasets that have been matched or combined—this covers, for example, combining data used for different purposes or from different organizations.

- Data concerning vulnerable data subjects—such data subjects may include employees, children, the mentally ill, asylum seekers, the elderly, patients, and other individuals where there is an imbalance in the relationship between them and the organization.

- Innovative use or applying technological or organizational solutions—examples include combining use of finger print and face recognition for improved physical access control, and 'Internet of Things' applications.

- Processing which prevents data subjects from exercising a right or using a service or a contract—for example where a bank screens its customers against a credit reference database in order to decide whether to offer them a loan.

Article 35(4) of the GDPR requires supervisory authorities (including the ICO in the UK) to publish a list of processing operations for which a DPIA is required. Further, Article 35(5) provides that the ICO may also publish a list of processing operations for which no DPIA is required, for example where activities comply with other conditions specified by the ICO under specific rules or guidelines. At the time of writing, these lists are not yet available.

Whilst they give some scope for variance between EU Member States on the specific projects for which a DPIA is required, the criteria listed in the Working Party Guidelines seek to promote the development of common EU lists of processing operations for which DPIAs are, or are not, required. Further, they are subject to a consistency mechanism involving the EU Data Protection Board where they involve processing activities in several Member States (relating to offering goods or services, or monitoring of behaviour) or may substantially affect the free movement of data within the European Union.

Article 35(10) contains an exception to the requirements for regulated activities carried out pursuant to a legal obligation or public interest. An organization does not need to carry out a DPIA if one has already been carried out as part of setting the legal basis for those activities.

DPIAs should not be reserved exclusively for new projects or technologies. The need for a DPIA should also be considered where existing data processing activities are to be altered or upgraded. Frequently the potential data protection impact of these projects is overlooked, yet seemingly innocuous tweaks to existing data processing can have a significant impact on data protection compliance and risk. Further, the Guidelines recommend that organizations carry out DPIAs as part of general accountability obligations, even for high risk processing operations that were already underway before the application of the GDPR in May 2018.

In summary, DPIAs should be considered whenever new technologies or processes are developed that will involve the collection, use, or sharing of personal data, or when significant changes are made to existing data processing activities, even though only a portion of these projects will *require* a DPIA under the GDPR.

A DPIA should be carried out in cases where it is not clear whether a DPIA is required under the GDPR, and organizations may also wish to carry out DPIAs on a wider range of projects given the additional benefits of a DPIA in addressing data protection risks and ensuring compliance.

Identifying Whether a DPIA Is Required

The GDPR requires DPIAs to be carried out 'prior to the processing', and therefore organizations will need to ensure that new projects are not launched before a DPIA has been considered and, where necessary, carried out. Assessment of whether a DPIA is needed should therefore be carried out early on as part of project management procedures. Organizations that include a series of basic data protection screening questions in their internal project initiation documents find that the question of whether a DPIA is required becomes a routine consideration. Whether a DPIA is actually conducted will depend on the results of the screening questions.

To ensure data protection issues are considered seriously during product development, some organizations require the completion of a DPIA or privacy review in order to secure project funding. In addition, even where a DPIA is not required, the GDPR (Article 30(1)) requires organizations to maintain a record of processing activities, and questions within project initiation procedures can be a useful way to capture this information.

It is important that DPIAs do not become meaningless box-ticking exercises. Using a short series of screening questions to determine the extent to which a DPIA is actually required can help to prioritize projects and use limited resources to best effect. Some organizations automate this process, requiring project teams to provide a high-level description of their proposed data processing activities, and answer several key screening questions, online. The sequencing and number of questions to be answered will be determined by answers provided to previous questions. These tools do not need to be sophisticated and can be created in-house, whether they are automated or utilize a simple spreadsheet or decision tree.

The types of screening questions that are utilized will vary from one organization to another, and will depend on the nature of the organization's activities and their approach to DPIAs. Those that wish to focus on the GDPR's DPIA requirements may limit screening questions to high risk areas identified within the GDPR, the ICO's lists, and associated guidance. Questions may centre on the matters raised in the Working Party Guidelines (such as evaluation and scoring, automated decision-making, systematic monitoring, and use of sensitive data), but tailored to be relevant to the organization's activities.

As well as screening questions, it can be useful for project initiation documents to request basic details of the context of the project and who is involved. This information can form the foundation for descriptions of processing activities, consultations with stakeholders, and assessments of proportionality and risk.

Who Should Carry Out a DPIA

The obligation to carry out a DPIA is on the controller. Processors involved in the relevant processing activities should assist in accordance with their contract with the controller (see Chapter 9), but have no direct obligations to conduct DPIAs.

Further, a DPIA can be useful for assessing the data protection impact of a technology product which may be used by several different controllers. A DPIA carried out by the provider of the product could inform its customers (as controllers) of the relevant risks and solutions, and assist with such customers' own DPIAs (whether or not the provider is involved with the processing operations in practice).

The controller's DPO should be involved with the DPIA. The Working Party Guidelines raise other potential roles and responsibilities, such as business units of the organization, independent experts, the chief information security officer, and the IT department. The role of the DPO and internal stakeholders are discussed later in this chapter.

How to Conduct a DPIA

There are a number of stages to conducting a DPIA, and each of them is discussed in turn in this section.

Describe the data processing activities and the purposes of the processing

In order to assess whether a particular type of processing or technology is compliant with data protection requirements, it is crucial to understand what the data processing activities comprise. Article 35(7)(a) of the GDPR requires:

a systematic description of the envisaged processing operations and the purposes of the processing, including, where applicable, the legitimate interest pursued by the controller.

The project team should be asked to describe the data processing activities in some detail. Preparation of information flow diagrams may also be useful. Posing a series of questions can aid the process, and it can be helpful to structure these questions on the basis of the data lifecycle, as follows:

- What are the objectives of the project and why does it require the processing of personal data?
- What types of data will be collected or processed? Will any sensitive personal data be included?
- How will the data be collected? From whom?
- What will the data be used for? What are the purposes?
- Describe how the data will be processed.
- Where will the data be processed? How will it be stored?
- What hardware, software, networks, and/or paper systems will be used?
- By whom will the data be processed or accessed?
- Will the data be anonymized or pseudonymized? Collated with other data?
- If the data have already been collected, how will the new use/processing/location/processor differ from the current position?
- With which third parties will the data be shared?
- For how long will the data be kept?
- How will the data be destroyed?

Assess the necessity and proportionality of the processing activities in relation to the purposes

The benefits and aims of the project and the relevant data processing activities should be identified as part of project management procedures and the descriptions prepared during the 'Describe the data processing activities and the purposes of the processing' stage above.

Organizations should also consider whether there are alternative solutions which meet their goals without creating the same data protection risks. These will assist in assessing necessity and proportionality. For example, a high risk data processing activity which carries minimal benefit for individuals or significantly affects their data protection rights may not be proportionate. Further, if there is a feasible alternative which is of lower risk (e.g. one that makes less use of personal data), such activity may also not be necessary. Alternative solutions may also be considered as part of measures to address the risks at the 'Determine the measures to address the risks' stage below.

As raised in the Working Party DPIA Guidelines, specific GDPR requirements contribute to necessity and proportionality, such as identification of the purposes and the legal basis for processing, data minimization, data retention, and the rights of data subjects.

Assess the data protection risks

This stage requires identification and assessment of specific risks to the rights and freedoms of data subjects. This aspect lies at the heart of the DPIA process. Recital 84 of the GDPR reminds us that a DPIA is required for high risk activities 'to evaluate, in particular, the origin, nature, particularity and severity of that risk'.

Many organizations will be familiar with assessing risk in other areas—for example financial, operational, or legal risks—and may wish to use a similar risk assessment methodology for assessing data protection risks. However, it is important that the focus of the DPIA is in assessing risks to individuals (and not solely risks to the organization), and that the categorization of risks must be consistent with the requirements of data protection law. For example, the activities listed in Article 35(3) (as set out above) should be considered a potentially high risk (although this may be reduced based on the particular circumstances or the measures taken to address such risk at the 'Determine the measures to address the risks' stage below).

An assessment of risk includes a review of compliance with the GDPR, and such compliance is one of the required outcomes of the DPIA. However, it goes beyond a mere legal compliance review. Organizations should also consider the expectations of individuals and the practical impact on them of the processing operations. Organizations should seek to view the processing activity from the individual's perspective. Consultation with data subjects may assist to identify the risks (and proposed solutions), as discussed at 'Seek the views of data subjects or their representatives' below.

It is also important to discuss the risks with the project team and others involved with design and implementation. Examples of these internal stakeholders include the project management team, developers, technology teams, procurement, processors, communications and customer-facing roles, governance and compliance teams, researchers, and senior management. It also includes the DPO, and the GDPR of course requires the involvement of the DPO, where designated, as discussed at 'Advice of the DPO' below. It may be helpful to go through risk registers at project meetings attended by representatives from different stakeholder groups.

Guidance and codes of conduct on specific topics from regulators or industry bodies may also assist in identifying privacy risks. Article 35(8) of the GDPR provides that compliance with Codes of Conduct approved under the GDPR (see Chapter 1) should be taken into account in assessing the impact of processing operations. In addition, whilst the focus of DPIAs under the GDPR is the protection of personal data, organizations may wish to consider wider privacy risks, including additional compliance risks (e.g. under privacy and electronic communications rules—see Chapter 10—or human rights laws), and invasion of physical privacy of individuals (e.g. through surveillance or bodily testing).

The Working Party DPIA Guidelines remind us that, as well as privacy, the rights and freedoms of data subjects may involve other fundamental rights, such as freedoms of speech, thought and movement, prohibition of discrimination, and 'right to liberty, conscience, and religion'.

Examples of specific data protection and privacy risks include misuse or overuse of personal data, loss or unauthorized modification of data, loss of anonymity, intrusion into private life through monitoring or tracking, and a lack of transparency. Expanding on the initial screening questions discussed above, organizations should seek to identify the elements of a new project or processing activity which may lead to such privacy risks.

Useful areas for inquiry are as follows.

- Will personal data be processed for new purposes?
- Is new or untested technology being used which handles personal data?
- Does the project involve activities relating to an increased number of individuals or particularly vulnerable individuals?
- Are data subjects able to exercise their rights in relation to the relevant processing activities?
- Does the data processing extend beyond the reasonable expectations of an individual? Would an individual be surprised to learn of the data processing?
- Are controls in place to limit the likelihood of inappropriate disclosure or sharing of data?
- Will third parties access or process personal data?
- Is data which is sensitive to individuals being processed?
- What is the impact of the relevant processing on the organization's other data processing activities? Are data sets being changed or combined, giving them new meaning?
- Will there be a change to the way in which individuals can be identified?
- Might data be inaccurate or incomplete?
- Are activities of individuals being monitored or tracked?
- Will decisions affecting individuals be made based on profiling or scoring?

- Are individuals subjected to any surveillance, testing, or other intrusion of the person?
- What is the impact over time of the changing context within which data are used?
- Does the volume of data or length of data retention present an increased security risk?
- Is data protection effectively managed for the relevant processing operations?

In order to determine the level of risk, organizations should take into account both the severity of the potential data protection impact and the likelihood of such impact arising. Recital 90 of the GDPR states that the DPIA should assess the 'likelihood and severity of the high risk, taking into account the nature, scope, context and purposes of the processing and the sources of the risk'. For example, if the potential impact was loss of personal data, the severity may depend on how much harm the loss would cause, and the likelihood may depend on the security measures in place to prevent such a loss.

The measures discussed at 'Determine the measures to address the risks' below may reduce the level of risk by changing either the severity or the likelihood of the impact. It is common to assign a number to each of these factors, and then multiply them together for the overall level of risk. Less mathematical methods include colour coding the level of risk, or designating a rating of high, medium, or low.

In deciding the overall risk rating, as well as risks to individuals, organizations may wish to consider other risks to the organization, such as failure of the project and associated costs, legal penalties or claims, damage to reputation, and loss of trust of customers or the public.

The results of the risk assessment can be recorded in a risk register. An example risk register is shown in Table 11.1. Appendices to the risk register can describe how to assign risk ratings for different issues, taking into account GDPR requirements and associated guidance.

Determine the measures to address the risks

Having identified data protection risks, effort should be invested in determining appropriate ways in which to address those risks, including measures to ensure the protection of personal data and compliance with the GDPR. Frequently, it will not be possible to eliminate risks, and the focus should instead be on managing or mitigating the risk to a level that is acceptable to the organization.

It can be useful to adopt a broad approach to identifying possible mitigation strategies, listing a wide array of steps that might be taken to manage or reduce risk. The list can be recorded in the risk register, and refined with the relevant project team and other stakeholders, taking into account feedback on whether the risks are effectively mitigated, and what modifications might be possible without compromising the technology or what the project is intended to deliver. The cost of proposed remediation will also need to be considered and weighed against the identified risks.

Table 11.1 Risk register

Ref.	Issue	Description of risk and source of risk	Potential data protection impact	Likelihood of impact (Rate 0–3)	Severity of impact (Rate 0–3)	Overall risk rating (Rate 0–9)	Recommendations	Accepted/ rejected and further action
1.	**Fair Processing Notice—insufficient information available to data subjects.**	*Describe the issue, e.g. stakeholder consultation revealed lack of understanding of proposed data processing; DPO compliance review of existing privacy notice indicates it does not contain sufficient information to cover proposed new processing activities.*	*Describe the nature of the impact and associated compliance concerns, e.g. lack of transparency for data subjects on use of their data; associated breach of Article 13 GDPR.*	☐ N/A (0) *(explain why)* ☐ Low risk (1) ☐ Medium risk (2) ☐ High risk (3) *(Tick one)*	☐ No impact (0) *(explain why)* ☐ Low impact (1) ☐ Medium impact (2) ☐ High impact (3) *(Tick one)*	*Calculate the overall risk rating by multiplying the likelihood of impact by the severity of impact.*	*Describe proposed steps to address the risk, e.g. amend the fair processing notice; draft new, specific fair processing notices; improve presentation and availability of the notices.*	*Specify if recommendations have been accepted or rejected by the project team and next steps (where applicable).*

	Describe the issue, e.g. DPO compliance review:	Describe nature of the impact and associated compliance concerns, e.g.		Calculate the overall risk rating by multiplying the likelihood of impact by the severity of impact.	Describe proposed steps to address the risk, e.g.	Specify if recommendations have been accepted or rejected by the project team and next steps (where applicable).
2.	Collection of health data—sensitive personal data carries high risks. (Continue with other issues and risks).	(a) concern in ensuring relevance and proportionality of data to project purposes; (b) need to satisfy specific processing condition under Article 9 GDPR; (c) ensuring transparency (see issue 1 above); (d) ensuring appropriate security measures to protect the data.	unjustified use or other misuse of special categories of data; breach of Articles 5(1)(c), 9, and 32 GDPR. ☐ N/A (0) (explain why) ☐ Low risk (1) ☐ Medium risk (2) ☐ High risk (3) (Tick one)	☐ No impact (0) (explain why) ☐ Low impact (1) ☐ Medium impact (2) ☐ High impact (3) (Tick one)		limit the amount of health data collected; obtain data subject explicit consent; build in appropriate consent mechanism; keep health data separate from other data with enhanced security.

The focus of mitigation strategies should be on reducing the risk of the data protection impact on individuals, either by reducing the severity of the impact, or reducing the likelihood of such impact occurring. For example, useful considerations are:

- whether it is necessary to collect and process all of the proposed data fields, or whether the severity of the impact could be minimized by using less data, fewer (or less intrusive) data fields, or even to pseudonymize or anonymize the data; and

- whether strong security controls, governance procedures (including access controls) and staff training would reduce the likelihood of data being misused, and therefore the likelihood of the impact arising.

To the extent that proposed processing activities do not require a DPIA (e.g. elements of the project which do not present a high risk), organizations will still need to ensure all proposed activities involving personal data comply with the principles of the GDPR. Organizations may therefore find it helpful to incorporate a wider compliance review into their DPIA process, or to carry out a standalone compliance review for lower risk projects.

Some risks or compliance matters may already be addressed as part of business as usual (e.g. existing procurement procedures, security assessments, or privacy notices), in which case no additional solutions may be required as part of the DPIA. These existing measures can be cross-referenced within the DPIA to ensure they continue to address the relevant risk effectively throughout design and implementation of the project.

Proposed solutions should be discussed with the project team, not least to determine whether the mitigating steps are realistic and capable of being implemented.

Documenting the agreed solutions is an important part of the DPIA process. The findings will need to be communicated internally. Checklists, template charts, heat maps, and dashboards can be created in-house and utilized as efficient ways to communicate key findings and any proposed remediation.

A plan for agreeing how the recommendations will be integrated into the project should also be agreed. In addition, it will be important to follow up with the project team and ensure that agreed modifications are implemented, and that they have the desired effect. Organizations may find it useful to record the agreed measures in a solutions table, which can be used as a checklist throughout the project implementation process. It can also be used as a post-implementation tool for future data protection audits and updates to the DPIA (see 'Review to assess if the processing of personal data is performed in compliance with the DPIA' below). An example solutions table is shown in Table 11.2.

Advice of the DPO

Seeking the advice of the DPO (where one has been designated) when carrying out a DPIA is required under Article 35(1). The DPO is likely to have a significant role in a DPIA, with central knowledge of the data protection framework within the

Table 11.2 Solutions table

Ref.	Issue/ processing activity	Purpose of processing activity	Data protection risk(s)	Agreed solution	Risk avoided, mitigated, accepted?	Next steps and responsibilities
1.	Collection of health data from data subjects	*Describe the purpose/benefits of the processing activity (as it can be helpful to record the reasons for the risk arising as well as how the risk is being addressed), e.g. collection of health data will assist in providing tailored services and ensuring health and safety.*	*Summary of the risk(s) being addressed; cross-reference to risk register if appropriate, e.g.:* *(a) Relevance and proportionality of data to project purposes.* *(b) Sensitive personal data condition under Article 9 GDPR.* *(c) Transparency of processing activities for data subjects.* *(d) Security of health data.*	*Details of the solution, e.g.:* *(a) Limit the amount of health data collected and concerning only relevant data subjects (specify data categories and individuals here or separately).* *(b) Obtain explicit consent of data subjects using specified mechanism.* *(c) Separate notification about use of health data; specify how this will be communicated.* *(d) Specify security measures, e.g. encryption, location of storage, access controls.*	*Extent to which risks have been addressed, e.g. mitigated to bring risk level to low.*	*Describe next steps to implement the solution, how it will be implemented, and whose responsibility it is to take it forward, e.g. measures for obtaining consent and drafting/ presenting information; involvement of security specialists.*

organization, and being well placed to identify compliance obligations, risks, and solutions.

In particular, the Article 29 Working Party's Guidelines on Data Protection Officers (WP 243) (see <http://www.dpdocuments.com>) recommend that advice should be sought from the DPO on whether to carry out a DPIA, what methodology to follow, whether to outsource it, what safeguards to apply to mitigate the risks, whether the DPIA has been correctly carried out, and whether its conclusions comply with the GDPR. These tasks should be clearly outlined, both in the DPO's contract and within information provided to employees, management, and other stakeholders.

Seek the views of data subjects or their representatives

Organizations are required, as part of the DPIA, to seek the views of data subjects or their representatives on the intended processing. Such consultation can enable an organization to understand the concerns and expectations of the individuals, test proposed solutions, and improve transparency in relation to the project and proposed uses of personal data.

The obligation is, however, qualified; it is only required 'where appropriate' and 'without prejudice to the protection of commercial or public interests or the security of the processing operations'. Therefore, it may not always be needed, for example to the extent that it would not affect the outcome of the risk assessment, or when protecting overriding interests to keep aspects of the proposed project confidential. The extent to which an organization consults on any particular issue should be proportionate to the risks involved. The Working Party DPIA Guidelines consider that an organization should document its justification for not seeking the views of data subjects if it decides that this is not appropriate.

The method of seeking views may include informal discussions, as well as more formal written consultation exercises. The approach taken may vary between public and private sector organizations. The ICO's Code of Practice encourages the use of existing consultation mechanisms, such as focus groups, user groups, public meetings, and consumer or citizen panels. For employee data, existing consultation mechanisms with trade unions may be appropriate.

The Code of Practice also provides that effective external consultations should follow the following principles:

- Timely—at the right stage and allowing enough time for responses.
- Clear and proportionate—in scope and focus.
- Reach and representative—ensure those likely to be affected have a voice.
- Ask objective questions and present realistic options.
- Feedback—ensure that those participating get feedback at the end of the process.

Results of consultation with data subjects will feed into the risk assessment, and key outcomes can be recorded in the risk register.

Consultation with the supervisory authority

Article 36 of the GDPR requires organizations to consult with the supervisory authority (the ICO in the UK) where a DPIA indicates that the processing activities would result in a high risk, in the absence of measures taken to mitigate the risk.

The Working Party DPIA Guidelines indicate that this arises when the 'residual risks' are high, in other words where high risks remain notwithstanding the steps taken by the organization to address the risks. An example is where the individuals may encounter significant consequences which they may not overcome. In addition, the GDPR allows UK law to require organizations to consult with or obtain prior authorization from the ICO in relation to a task carried out in the public interest, including processing relating to social protection and public health.

The ICO must give advice to the organization where it considers that activities would not comply with the GDPR, in particular where the risk assessment has been insufficient. Advice must generally be given within eight weeks, although this may be extended by six weeks in complex circumstances. As consultation must take place prior to the relevant processing activities, the additional time must be factored into project timetables, as it could cause delays to the launch of new systems and activities.

Organizations must provide the ICO with information about the processing activities, including the responsibilities of controllers and processors, the purposes and means of the processing, the measures to protect the rights of individuals under the GDPR, the contact details of the DPO (where applicable), and the DPIA itself.

Review to assess if the processing of personal data is performed in compliance with the DPIA

Following implementation of a project, organizations should carry out regular reviews of the processing activities to ensure the data protection risks are being and continue to be appropriately addressed in accordance with the DPIA. Article 35(11) of the GDPR requires such reviews 'at least where there is a change in the risks involved'. Changes in the risks could arise, for example, from changes to the processing activities or their purpose, or from external factors, such as the expectations or concerns of individuals, or legal decisions, and guidance.

The Working Party Guidelines provide further examples of such changes: the effects of certain automated decisions have become more significant, or new categories of individuals become vulnerable to discrimination. Changes could also lower the risks as well, meaning that a DPIA is no longer required. The consequences of Brexit within the UK may also impact the risk profile.

Regular risk reviews or audits, or continuous monitoring and updating of the DPIA, can be used to assess whether risks have changed and ensure that appropriate solutions are in place. Organizations should therefore set an appropriate review date for each DPIA.

Reporting and Publication of the DPIA

As well as recording the measures to address the risks, there can be benefits in producing a more detailed DPIA report. This can assist with accountability (see Chapter 12) and transparency (Chapter 3), capture lessons learnt, and assist with communication of the DPIA to interested parties. A DPIA report would commonly include background to the project and the DPIA, a summary of the DPIA process and outcomes, and details of the findings and solutions from the risk assessment.

Both the Article 29 Working Party and the ICO encourage organizations to publish DPIA reports to improve transparency and individuals' understanding of the ways in which their personal data are used. It is particularly good practice where members of the public are affected by the processing activities.

Public authorities should consider including DPIA reports in their publication schemes under the Freedom of Information Act 2000.

Most organizations have typically been reluctant to publish reports given the fact that commercially sensitive information may be included, and due to concerns that the DPIA may later be used to provide evidence of known shortcomings in data processing systems. Some DPIAs will indeed be sensitive, and it may be possible to assert a claim of legal professional privilege where the DPIA is conducted under the supervision of lawyers.

Certainly, care should be taken when documenting the DPIA process, and careful consideration given to recommending how the identified risks may be mitigated. DPIAs represent an important internal process, and their objectivity and value may be reduced when drafted for external consumption. Nevertheless, organizations should consider publishing extracts from or summaries of a DPIA report.

Even if a DPIA report is not published, organizations will need to communicate the outcomes to appropriate stakeholders. As well as the project team and those responsible for signing off the project, this may include those who were consulted during the DPIA process, and people with a role in applying or monitoring the data protection measures once the processing activities are underway.

12

Accountability and the Role of the Data Protection Officer

Jenai Nissim

Introduction	223
The Accountability Requirement	224
The Role of the DPO	226
When Is a DPO Mandatory?	226
Accessibility	231
Expertise and Skill of the DPO	233
Involvement of the DPO	234
Necessary Resources	235
Independence	236
Security of Tenure	236
Conflict of Interest	237
Data Protection Impact Assessments	238
Record Keeping	238
Policies and Procedures	239

Introduction

Although the GDPR entrenches the concept of 'accountability', it is not a new concept in data protection law and practice. Regulators, such as the UK Information Commissioner's Office ('ICO'), have for many years required organizations to demonstrate how they were compliant. Such evidence was usually provided in the form of data protection policies, privacy notices, the content and methodology of training courses for individuals responsible for the processing activities of the organization, and in some cases the existence and content of an appropriate compliance programme.

The UK Data Protection Bill (see <http://www.dpdocuments.com>) seeks to incorporate and supplement the GDPR to include specific requirements in relation to data processing in the UK and additionally encompasses the provisions of Directive (EU) 2016/680 (the Law Enforcement Directive) (see <http://www.dpdocuments.com>) particularly in relation to the processing of personal data for law enforcement purposes. Accordingly, references in this chapter and in Chapter 13 to the GDPR are also to the Data Protection Bill, unless stated otherwise. In relation to accountability and the role of the Data Protection Officer ('DPO'), changes are introduced by the Data Protection Bill in relation to the appointment of a DPO by 'competent authorities', meaning a person specified in the list contained in Schedule 7 of the Data Protection Bill, and any other person if and to the extent that the person has statutory functions for any of the law enforcement purposes. Therefore, if any authorities meet such criteria then, unless the controller is a court or other judicial authority acting in its judicial capacity, they will need to consider the requirement to appoint a DPO. Any differences between the GDPR and the Data Protection Bill in relation to the role of the DPO are discussed in more detail where relevant in this chapter.

This chapter looks at accountability under the GDPR and the role that the DPO plays in ensuring compliance with both the accountability requirement and the data protection Principles generally.

The Accountability Requirement

The overarching requirement to demonstrate compliance under the GDPR is set out under Article 5(2):

The Controller shall be responsible for, and be able to demonstrate compliance with [the principles relating to the processing of personal data].

Article 5(2) makes explicit reference to 'controllers', and therefore 'processors' are not required to comply with the accountability provisions per se, albeit controllers will want processors to demonstrate to them how they comply with contractual obligations imposed upon them regarding compliance with data protection legislation (see Chapter 9).

The GDPR features several references to controllers (and in some cases processors) needing to demonstrate compliance with the GDPR, as well as references to measures which should be taken for compliance purposes. Examples include the requirement on a controller to 'maintain a record of processing activities under its responsibility' (Article 30).

The main GDPR Articles and Data Protection Bill sections that directly reference the need to demonstrate compliance are set out in Table 12.1 for ease of reference.

As may be gathered from Table 12.1, accountability is a wide concept, and covers a number of processing activities of organizations. Demonstrating compliance with the GDPR, which is the heart of accountability, can be achieved in a variety of ways, which are discussed in more detail throughout this chapter.

Table 12.1 GDPR Articles and Data Protection Bill sections referencing accountability requirements

Reference	Subject matter	Requirement
Article 7	Consent	'Where processing is based on consent, the controller shall be able to demonstrate that the data subject has consented to processing of his or her personal data.'
Article 21 GDPR	Right to object	'The controller shall no longer process the personal data unless the controller demonstrates compelling legitimate grounds for the processing which override the interests, rights and freedoms of the data subjects or for the establishment, exercise or defence of legal claims.'
Article 24 GDPR	Appropriate technical and organizational measures	'The controller shall implement appropriate technical and organisational measures to ensure and to be able to demonstrate that the processing is performed in accordance with this Regulation.'
Article 25 GDPR	Data protection by design and default	An approved certification mechanism pursuant to Article 42 may be used as an element to demonstrate compliance with the requirements set out in paragraphs 1 and 2 of Article 25.
Article 28 GDPR	Using processors	[The processor shall] make available to the controller all information necessary to demonstrate compliance with the obligations laid down in this Article and allow for and contribute to audits, including inspections, conducted by the controller or another auditor mandated by the controller.
Article 30 GDPR	Record keeping	'Each controller and, where applicable, the controller's representative, shall maintain a record of processing activities under its responsibility.'
Article 33 GDPR	Data breaches	'The controller shall document any personal data breaches, comprising the facts relating to the personal data breach, its effects and the remedial action taken. That documentation shall enable the supervisory authority to verify compliance with this Article.'
Article 35 GDPR	Data Protection Impact Assessments	'The assessment shall contain at least (a) a systematic description of the envisaged processing operations and the purposes of the processing, including, where applicable, the legitimate interest pursued by the controller; (b) an assessment of the necessity and proportionality of the processing operations in relation to the purposes; (c) an assessment of the risks to the rights and freedoms of data subjects referred to in paragraph 1 [of Article 35]; and (d) the measures envisaged to address the risks, including safeguards, security measures and mechanisms to ensure the protection of personal data and to demonstrate compliance with this Regulation taking into account the rights and legitimate interests of the data subjects and other persons concerned.'
Article 37 GDPR	Designation of the DPO	The controller and the processor shall designate a DPO in certain cases.
Section 67 Data Protection Bill	Designation of the DPO	'The controller must designate a data protection officer, unless the controller is a court, or other judicial authority, acting in its judicial capacity.'
Section 69(2) Data Protection Bill	Tasks of the DPO	'In relation to the policies mentioned in subsection (1)(e), the data protection officer's tasks include (a) assigning responsibilities under those policies; (b) raising awareness of those policies; (c) training staff involved in processing operations; and (d) conducting audits required under those policies.'

First and foremost, national data protection regulators and the European Data Protection Board ('EDPB') have both emphasized that the appointment of a DPO or other individual responsible for compliance with data protection will be key not only to achieving compliance with the GDPR, but also to demonstrating how compliance has been achieved.

Accountability can be demonstrated in a number of ways, including by creating a data protection compliance programme and monitoring the organization's compliance with data protection requirements; implementing robust pre-contractual and ongoing due diligence arrangements on third party processes; and ensuring that data protection policies and procedures are created and adhered to within the organization. Accountability can also be demonstrated through training and awareness-raising mechanisms throughout an organization to ensure that those individuals with responsibility for processing personal data are aware of the requirements under the GDPR.

The Role of the DPO

One of the key changes introduced by the GDPR is the requirement to appoint a DPO in certain circumstances.

The Article 29 Working Party (the forerunner of the EDPB) guidance states that 'DPOs will be at the heart of this new legal framework for many organisations, facilitating compliance with the provisions of the GDPR'—see WP 243, 5 April 2017 at <http://www.dpdocuments.com>.

Even if an organization is not mandated to appoint a DPO, regulators encourage voluntary appointment. In the event that an individual is appointed as DPO on a voluntary basis, guidance issued by the Article 29 Working Party indicates that those individuals must still comply with the provisions of Articles 37–39 of the GDPR (see below). Furthermore, unless it is obvious that a DPO does not need to be designated under the GDPR:

1. the decision not to appoint a DPO must be documented to demonstrate that the relevant factors have been considered; and

2. the decision must be reviewed as an organization's processing activities change over time to ensure that the processing activities undertaken by a controller or processor do not subsequently trigger the requirement to appoint a DPO under Article 37.

When Is a DPO Mandatory?

The requirement to designate (or appoint) a DPO, which applies to both controllers and processors, is governed by Article 37 of the GDPR and section 67 of the Data Protection Bill. It involves the organization making a determination as to whether it is required to make the appointment. This is not always an easy determination, and it involves a number of factors. Some organizations will already have one or more DPOs on staff, in which case they do not need to make the determination. Therefore the remainder of this section concerns only those organizations that have yet to appoint a DPO. It is suggested that if, after full consideration, there is any doubt regarding the need to appoint a DPO, organizations should make the appointment.

Article 37(1) of the GDPR requires that:

the controller and the processor shall designate a DPO in any case where;
(a) the processing is carried out by a public authority or body except for courts acting in their judicial capacity;
(b) the core activities of the controller or the processor consist of processing operations which, by virtue of their nature, their scope and/or their purposes, require regular and systematic monitoring of data subjects on a large scale; or
(c) the core activities of the controller or the processor consist of processing on a large scale of special categories of data pursuant to Article 9 and personal data relating to criminal convictions and offences referred to in Article 10.

Section 67 of the Data Protection Bill requires that:
(1) The controller must designate a data protection officer, unless the controller is a court, or other judicial authority, acting in its judicial capacity.
(2) When designating a data protection officer, the controller must have regard to the professional qualities of the proposed officer, in particular:
  (a) the proposed officer's expert knowledge of data protection law and practice, and
  (b) the ability of the proposed officer to perform the tasks mentioned in section 69.

Public authority or body

Sub-paragraph (a) in the definition above refers to a 'public authority or body'. There is no definition of this phrase in the GDPR. However, the Data Protection Bill defines 'competent authority' in Section 28 as '(a) a person specified in Schedule 7 [of the Bill], and (b) any other person if and to the extent that the person has statutory functions for any of the law enforcement purposes'. In reality both definitions cover all public sector controllers and processors (except the court system or other judicial authority, acting in its judicial capacity). Therefore all such bodies must designate a DPO.

It should be borne in mind that some private sector bodies carry out public sector-type processing. Examples include public transport services, energy suppliers, and processors working on behalf of organizations in the public sector. In the opinion of the Article 29 Working Party, these organizations should designate a DPO and such appointments should cover all processing activities, not just those limited to public tasks.

What are 'core activities'?

The phrase 'core activities', referred to in sub-paragraphs (b) and (c) of Article 37(1), is not defined in the GDPR. However, Recital 97 states that core activities are:

primary activities and do not relate to the processing of personal data as ancillary activities.

Such activities should therefore be thought of as key operations necessary to achieve the processor's or controller's goals. This should not be interpreted as excluding activities which form an intrinsic part of such goals. For example (according to the Article 29 Working Party), although the provision of health care is the core activity of a hospital, the hospital could not provide the health care without processing medical records and health care data. Similarly, while the provision of groceries is the core activity of a supermarket, the supermarket could not provide online groceries without processing the personal data of its customers.

On the other hand, paying employees or having standard IT support services, whilst deemed essential to the operation of such organizations, is likely to be deemed to be a support function rather than a function related to the 'core activities' of a processor or controller.

Systematic monitoring of data subjects on a large scale

Sub-paragraph (b) of Article 37(1) requires an organization to appoint a DPO where its core activities involve the regular and systematic monitoring of data subjects on a large scale.

There is limited guidance in the GDPR as to the definition of 'large scale'. However, Recital 91 states that large-scale processing operations are:

operations which aim to process a considerable amount of personal data . . . and which could affect a large number of data subjects and which are likely to result in a high risk.

An organization should therefore consider the number of data subjects concerned in the processing activity, the volume and/or type of the data processed, the duration or permanence of the data processing activity, and the geographical extent of the processing when determining whether or not the processing is likely to constitute 'large scale' processing.

The Article 29 Working Party guidance provides a number of examples such as processing:

- patient data in the regular course of business by a hospital;
- travel data of individuals using a city's public transport system (e.g. tracking individuals via the use of travel cards);
- real time geolocation data of customers of an international fast food chain for statistical purposes by a processor who specializes in providing such services;
- personal data for behavioural advertising by search engines; and
- customer data in the regular course of business by an insurance company or bank.

However, the size of the controller or processor should also be borne in mind. As the guidance states, the 'processing of patient data by an individual physician' or the 'processing of personal data relating to criminal convictions and offences by an individual lawyer' do not constitute processing on a large scale.

When assessing whether or not processing activity is carried out on a large scale, organizations should document these considerations and whether or not the criteria of Article 37 have been met. This document should be retained in order to demonstrate compliance with the GDPR, and should be reviewed periodically or as the organization's processing activities change.

Although 'regular and systematic monitoring' is not defined in the GDPR, Recital 24 refers to monitoring the behaviour of data subjects as including tracking and profiling of individuals on the internet in order to take decisions concerning them, to predict their personal preferences, behaviours, and attitudes, and to use the personal data for data-driven marketing activities. Article 29 Working Party guidance states that the notion of monitoring is not restricted to the online environment and therefore that online tracking is just one example of the type of monitoring which could be undertaken.

According to the Article 29 Working Party, monitoring will be 'regular' when it is:

- ongoing or occurring at particular intervals for a particular period;
- recurring or repeated at fixed times; or
- constantly or periodically taking place.

Monitoring will be 'systematic' when it is:

- occurring according to a system;
- pre-arranged, organized, or methodical;
- taking place as part of a general plan for data collection; or
- carried out as part of a strategy.

Examples of regular and systematic monitoring include placing tracking devices in employee work vehicles, operating a telecommunications network, profiling for the purposes of risk assessment (e.g. credit scoring or the calculation of insurance premiums), location tracking, gathering data for loyalty programmes, monitoring of fitness and health-related data via wearable devices, behavioural advertising, and using data from smart meters.

Special categories of data on a large scale

Finally, a DPO must be designated where an organization processes special categories of data (see Chapter 4) or any information relating to criminal convictions and offences on a large scale as part of its core activities.

An assessment will need to be made to ascertain whether or not such processing activities meet the 'core activities' and 'processing on a large scale' criteria, and the decision and rationale should be documented, regularly reviewed, and made available to regulators (if requested) in order to demonstrate compliance with the GDPR.

Processor DPOs

The Article 29 Working Party points out that where a controller's activities do not meet the requirement to appoint a DPO, this does not necessarily mean that the processor is not required to make a DPO appointment. For example, a small business distributor of household appliances uses a processor whose core activity is to provide website analytical services and assistance with targeted advertising and marketing. Although the small business does not process personal data on a large scale, due to the number of similar small business customers that the processor has, when all of the processing is taken together, the processor will process personal data on a large scale and therefore must designate a DPO.

Tasks/functions of the DPO

There are a number of obligations that relate to a DPO under the GDPR. Whilst some of these requirements do not apply to voluntary DPOs (e.g. protected employment status), many of the DPO's tasks can and should be carried out by a voluntary DPO where this is appropriate based on the personal data processed and the manner in which the personal data are processed. The tasks and expectations of the DPO are set out in Figure 12.1 and will be discussed in the remainder of this chapter.

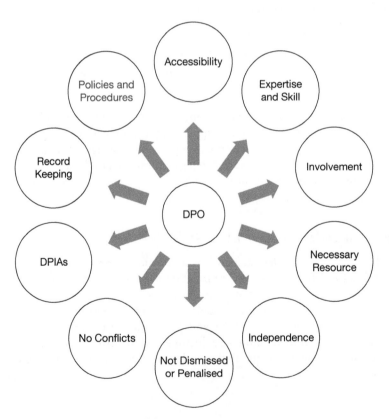

Fig. 12.1 Tasks and expectations of the DPO

Accessibility

A group of undertakings is permitted to appoint a single DPO provided that the DPO is 'easily accessible from each establishment'. Whilst there is no definition of this phrase, it is clear that it does not mean that the DPO will have to be co-located in a number of different offices or branches of an organization.

However, provision should be made for how individuals, employees, regulators, and other third parties may confidentially contact the DPO. Furthermore, the Article 29 Working Party guidance states that the DPO 'should be located within the European Union, whether or not the controller or processor is established in the EU'. Such a requirement may mean that some organizations not established in the EU (but still caught by the extra-territorial applicability of the GDPR) have to appoint not only a representative in the EU, but also a DPO.

Public authorities or bodies can also appoint a single DPO for a number of separate entities 'taking into account their organisational structure and size'. If one DPO is appointed for a number of public authorities or bodies, those public authorities or bodies will need to assess whether or not a DPO could perform duties for them collectively based on the way that the public authorities or bodies are set up and their size. For example, if there are a number of small public authorities and bodies with similar organizational structures and the processing of personal data is not complex, there is no reason why a single DPO could not be appointed for more than one public authority. If, however, a public authority processes a vast amount of personal data using complex systems and/or processes sensitive personal data or performs monitoring of individuals on a systematic scale, such that a large amount of time needs to be dedicated to the role of a DPO, then the public authority in question should appoint a DPO solely for that public authority.

It is recommended that decisions, and the rationale behind them, to appoint a 'group' DPO are appropriately documented and reviewed as the processing activities of the public authorities or bodies evolve over time.

Key requirements on accessibility of the DPO

The following factors should be borne in mind:

1. The DPO should be a contact point for individuals, employees, regulators, and third parties.

2. The DPO should be provided with the resources to enable them to fulfil their tasks effectively, especially if they are responsible for several public authorities and bodies.

3. The DPO should ensure that their contact details are published so that they can be contacted easily. A generic email address could be used, for example dpo@xyz.com, provided that such email address is regularly monitored, emails are responded to promptly, and the confidentiality of the email address is guaranteed given the sensitivity of the information that could be received

not only from data subjects but also from employees. The DPO may also wish to set up internal and external data protection sections of an organization's website to communicate their contact details.

4. The DPO should ensure that communications take place in the language of the data subjects and supervisory authorities concerned. It will therefore be necessary for organizations to consider having versions of key privacy documentation, for example privacy policies, data protection training, and privacy notices translated into local languages, and interpreters on hand should any data protection complaints be received. This does not necessarily mean that if an organization is established in a number of EU countries, the DPO will be expected to speak twenty different languages to communicate with individuals in all relevant countries. However, if the DPO has a team, consideration must be given to ensuring that individuals and regulators can communicate with the DPO in their local language.

5. The DPO must be bound by obligations of confidentiality and secrecy. It goes without saying that by the very nature of the role of the DPO, the DPO will be provided with confidential information about individuals and the organization for which it acts as DPO. In many cases the DPO will need to ensure that employees feel that they can trust the DPO with data protection matters if they need to be escalated to them. The Article 29 Working Party guidance explicitly picks up on this very point, stating that 'employees may be reluctant to complain to the DPO if the confidentiality of their communications is not guaranteed'. It is therefore recommended that any such communications are afforded the utmost confidentiality, for example by ensuring that calls are not recorded and emails are maintained by specifically authorized delegates or members of the DPO's team. Furthermore, the DPO's employment or service contract should contain appropriate confidentiality provisions which extend beyond termination to ensure any confidential information is safeguarded.

6. The DPO should be contactable regardless of whether or not the DPO is in the same place as employees. There are a number of ways that the DPO could be contacted, for example a dedicated 'hotline', email address, or online portal could be established. However, in all cases, as referred to above, the organization should ensure that such methods of communication are secure, that the confidentiality of the communications is guaranteed at all times, and that such communications are responded to promptly. Whilst all these methods of communication are great in theory, it is important that individuals (data subjects and employees) and regulators know these exist, otherwise the DPO is unlikely to receive many communications through these methods. From another practical point of view, consideration will need to be given to situations where one individual is appointed as the DPO for an international organization. Unless the DPO is able to deploy a team of individuals who report into the DPO, the DPO may struggle to make themselves available to, for example US and Indian employees if they are based in the UK, especially given the time difference practicalities, let alone the potential resource issues.

Expertise and Skill of the DPO

Article 37(5) of the GDPR states that a DPO shall be designated on the basis of their professional qualities, and in particular their expert knowledge of data protection law and practice and the ability to fulfil the tasks referred to in the GDPR.

According to Recital 97, expert knowledge should be gauged by taking into account the data processing operations carried out by the relevant organization and the level of protection required for the personal data processed by the controller or the processor.

In practice, expertise should be proportionate to the sensitivity, complexity, and amount of personal data processed by the controller or processor and whether personal data are systematically transferred outside the EU. For example, a small business with straightforward processing activities, such as a company undertaking marketing tasks as a processor on behalf of organizations based solely in the UK, will not require a DPO who has extensive medical or financial services experience of cross-border processing of special categories of personal data.

Whilst it is not necessary for DPOs to be qualified lawyers or legally trained as such, the DPO must have expert knowledge of national and European data protection laws and practices and an in-depth understanding of the GDPR. In this regard, a suitable qualification such as the Practitioner Certificate in Data Protection (<http://www.dataprotectionqualification.com>) is desirable.

Whilst knowledge of the relevant business sector and the organization concerned is useful, this is not essential. However, a sufficient understanding of the processing operations undertaken by an organization as well as the information systems and data protection and security needs of the organization are useful.

When recruiting a DPO from outside of the organization, controllers and processors should implement a suitable vetting process to guarantee that the individual appointed meets the requirements of the GDPR.

A DPO must have the 'ability to fulfil their tasks'. Although there is no definition of this phrase, guidance suggests that a DPO should have personal qualities which include integrity and excellent professional ethics. The DPO's primary concern should be compliance with the GDPR at all times, and the DPO should play a key role in fostering a culture of data protection within the organization.

Additionally, whilst an ability to 'influence' is not listed as a criterion for the DPO in the GDPR or in any guidance, given the seniority of the role of the DPO and the DPO's overarching objective to ensure compliance with data protection legal requirements, the DPO will often find themselves involved in difficult conversations regarding business requirements versus compliance. The ability to influence effectively in such conversations can therefore be paramount to the success of the DPO's role.

Key requirements and characteristics of a DPO

The following factors should be borne in mind:

1. The DPO should have expert knowledge of national and European data protection legislation, and in-depth knowledge of the GDPR.
2. The DPO should have knowledge of an organization's processing activities or sector-specific requirements to enable them to provide appropriate advice.
3. The DPO should have experience of overseas data transfers and experience of working with global organizations (if applicable).
4. The DPO must have the ability to act with integrity and professional ethics and to be able to bring influence to bear at all levels of the business to ensure that data protection requirements are understood and buy-in from management obtained.

Involvement of the DPO

In order for a DPO to perform their obligations effectively, they must be engaged in all issues relating to data protection at the earliest stage possible (Article 38(1)) and in particular the DPO must be consulted and their advice sought when data protection impact assessments are undertaken (Article 35(2)).

It is recommended that when a DPO is appointed, relevant communications are cascaded throughout the organization at all levels to ensure that all individuals regardless of level within the organization understand the role of the DPO and when and how the DPO can and should be consulted.

The following factors should be borne in mind:

1. Organizations must ensure that the DPO is invited to senior and middle management meetings and to sit on working groups involved in the processing of data to enable the DPO to have early visibility of data protection matters.
2. The DPO should be present when decisions with data protection implications are taken and all relevant information should be provided to the DPO in a timely manner in order to enable them to provide adequate data protection advice.
3. The DPO's opinion must be given due weight when discussing data processing activities and, in the event of a disagreement, the rationale for not following the DPO's advice must be documented. The record of such decision may be required to be given to a regulator in the event of non-compliance with data protection legal requirements.
4. The DPO must be promptly consulted once a personal data breach or non-compliance with data protection legislation occurs and the DPO should play an active role in advising the organization on how to respond to the breach.
5. In order to ensure that the DPO can effectively fulfil their tasks and that they are consulted in a timely manner on all things related to data protection, job descriptions should be updated (or where these do not exist, created) to provide specific requirements in terms of what the DPO is expected to do.

6. Internal guidelines setting out when to escalate matters to the DPO should be documented, reviewed, and updated where necessary, and all relevant staff members should be trained to enable them to understand when and how matters should be escalated to the DPO.

7. When the DPO is appointed, communications should be publicized detailing the appointment of the DPO and the importance of their role in the organization to ensure there is 'buy-in' and support at all levels of the organization.

8. The DPO should make themselves available to all individuals in the organization and attend local team meetings (if appropriate) so that individuals feel able to engage actively with the DPO.

Necessary Resources

Controllers and processors must provide the resources necessary to enable their DPOs to carry out their tasks under the GDPR.

Such resources include providing the DPO with access to personal data and processing operations in order to enable them to understand the processing activity, and supporting the DPO in maintaining his or her expert knowledge of data protection legislation (Article 38(2)).

The Article 29 Working Party guidance also states that the role of the DPO must be effectively and sufficiently well-resourced in relation to the data processing activities carried out. There must be active support of the DPO's functions by senior management; sufficient time for the DPO to fulfil their duties; adequate support in terms of financial resources, infrastructure, and staff; and necessary access to other services and departments such as human resources, the legal department (if any), information technology (IT), and security.

Organizations are encouraged to set up open lines of communication with the DPO and it is recommended that the DPO considers setting up a team of data protection specialists within the organization, a dedicated page on a company's internal and external websites, a dedicated email address for individuals within and outside the organization and for regulators to use to escalate concerns relating to data protection, and that the DPO's contact details are published on internal and external websites.

Key organizational tasks as regards the DPO's resources include:

1. assessing the roles and responsibilities of the DPO and considering whether the DPO is able to perform their tasks with existing resource(s);

2. considering the extent of the DPO's remit and, if this covers a number of offices or locations (within or outside a number of countries), assessing whether the DPO needs to appoint a DPO team;

3. if a DPO team needs to be appointed, considering what training and experience the team needs; and

4. ensuring that the DPO has a personal development plan and that a log of all training and development is recorded to demonstrate that the DPO is up to date on data protection law and developments.

Independence

Controllers and processors must ensure that the DPO does not receive any instructions regarding the exercise of their tasks. Regardless of whether the DPO is an employee of the organization or is an external appointment, the DPO should be in a position to perform their tasks and duties in an independent manner (Article 38(3) and Recital 97).

In particular a DPO must not be instructed:

1. as to what results should be achieved when providing any data protection advice;
2. how to investigate any complaints into an allegation of non-compliance or otherwise relating to data protection matters;
3. whether or not to consult a supervisory authority; and
4. to take a view regarding an issue related to data protection, for example a particular interpretation of the law.

It should be remembered that controllers and processors must follow the requirements of data protection law. In doing so, they should usually follow the advice of their DPO. If they do not follow such advice, the DPO must be permitted to voice their dissenting opinion, and a record of such advice must be retained (as well as the reasons for not following the advice).

The following are suggested guidelines for controllers and processors relating to the independence of the DPO:

1. set out the roles and responsibilities of the DPO clearly and ensure that these are known and understood by those engaging with the DPO;
2. ensure that where pressure is put on the DPO or where individuals attempt to influence the DPO's decision, appropriate action is taken, for example reminding relevant individuals that such behaviour may cause compliance issues for the organization; and
3. ensure that the DPO is supported and empowered to undertake their role and that the DPO is not penalized for undertaking their tasks (e.g. refusing to amend advice on a matter).

Security of Tenure

Controllers and processors must not dismiss or penalize the DPO for performing his or her tasks (Article 38(3)).

Penalties against the DPO may only be permitted if they are imposed in relation to the role of the DPO carrying out their duties. Penalties may include the absence or delay of promotion, prevention of career advancement, or denial from benefits which other employees receive. It is unlawful to impose such penalties on the basis that an organization does not agree with the advice of the DPO. The mere threat of penalties is also unlawful if the threat is used in relation to the proper exercise of the DPO's activities.

Although the GDPR does not specify how and when a DPO may be dismissed or replaced, the Article 29 Working Party guidance suggests that the DPO's employment contract should address these issues and should contain guarantees against unfair dismissal as a result of the DPO exercising their duties. Furthermore, it is advisable to ensure that the DPO's contract contains sufficiently clear detail about the tasks of the DPO and their reporting lines.

Conflict of Interest

The DPO may fulfil other tasks and duties provided that any such tasks and duties do not result in a conflict of interest (Article 38(6)).

This can be difficult to demonstrate for organizations that appoint an individual to undertake two roles, for example as the DPO on the one hand and the chief operating officer, chief executive officer, chief financial officer, chief medical officer, head of IT, marketing, or human resources on the other. These roles have been listed by the Article 29 Working Party as being non-compatible with the role of the DPO if such positions are likely to involve the DPO determining the means and purposes of the processing of personal data. Whilst the examples provided are senior roles, the titles of the roles are less important than the actual responsibilities and tasks of the role itself.

Additionally, the Article 29 Working Party's view is that if the DPO is also a data protection lawyer (i.e. providing advice to an organization on other data protection matters), then this could lead to a conflict of interest and therefore it may not be appropriate for both roles to be filled by one person.

In the event that undertaking additional tasks for an organization is likely to result in a conflict of interest with the DPO role, the individual concerned should not be permitted to undertake the role of a DPO or the DPO should decline taking on such tasks.

Key action points to bear in mind regarding conflicts of interest are the following:

1. Identify positions which would be incompatible with the function of a DPO. This determination should be based on the size of the organization and the responsibilities of relevant individuals, not only their role title. For example, the head of human resources may simply deal with employment advice in one organization, but in another they could play a more operational role and therefore determine the means for processing and the manner in which the personal data are processed.

2. Draw up internal rules regarding conflicts of interest and include a general explanation about conflicts of interest and how these can arise, as well as what to do if there is a suspicion or a likelihood of a conflict arising.

3. Create a document declaring that the DPO has no conflicts of interest and require them to notify the board or senior management immediately if any conflicts arise in the future. Make sure such declaration is renewed regularly, implement periodic attestations of such declarations, and retain documentary evidence to demonstrate compliance.

4. Ensure that any vacancy notice for the position of a DPO or a service contract is sufficiently precise and detailed to avoid a conflict of interest situation.

Data Protection Impact Assessments

Data protection impact assessments ('DPIAs') are discussed in Chapter 11. However, in the context of the role of the DPO it is important to note that DPOs must provide advice where requested with regard to the DPIA and must monitor its performance pursuant to Article 35.

Additionally, Article 35(2) requires the advice of the DPO to be sought when carrying out a DPIA. The Article 29 Working Party guidance recommends that the DPO's advice should be sought on:

- whether or not to carry out a DPIA;
- what methodology to follow when carrying out a DPIA;
- whether to carry out the DPIA in-house or to outsource it;
- what safeguards to apply to mitigate any privacy risks;
- whether the DPIA has been correctly carried out; and
- whether its conclusions (e.g. whether or not to go ahead with the processing and what safeguards to apply) are in compliance with the GDPR, as well as whether or not the DPIA needs to be submitted to a supervisory authority for any prior approval as part of the consultation process.

DPOs should therefore create and help to facilitate processes and procedures for dealing with DPIAs pursuant to Article 36 of the GDPR.

Record Keeping

Article 30(1) and Article 30(2) of the GDPR require controllers and processors to maintain records of processing activities under their responsibility.

Although record keeping is not specifically included in the list of tasks that a DPO is required to undertake (see Article 39), that list is not exhaustive. It is therefore suggested that one of the additional tasks in which the DPO should be involved is the creation and maintenance of records in accordance with Article 30. As will be seen in Chapter 13, the record keeping function is invaluable to the DPO to help him or her monitor and ensure compliance with the GDPR. It therefore makes sense that the DPO should be centrally involved with the record keeping function.

Policies and Procedures

Section 69(2) of the Data Protection Bill imposes additional obligations on a DPO appointed by a competent authority as follows:

(2) In relation to the policies mentioned . . . , the data protection officer's tasks include:
    (a) assigning responsibilities under those policies,
    (b) raising awareness of those policies,
    (c) training staff involved in processing operations, and
    (d) conducting audits required under those policies.

The creation of data protection policies, allocation of responsibility for compliance under the policies, and monitoring compliance with the policies are discussed in more detail in Chapter 13.

13

Creating a Data Protection Compliance Programme

Jenai Nissim

Introduction	240
Stage 1—Assessing Data Processing Activities	241
Stage 2—Creating Data Protection Policies	242
Stage 3—Data Protection Training and Raising Awareness	244
Stage 4—Implementing Controls to Reduce and Monitor Risk	246
Stage 5—Monitoring Compliance	248
Stage 6—Reporting	249
Stage 7—Annual Review Process	249

Introduction

Creating a data protection compliance programme is at the heart of data protection compliance. It is the subject of the final chapter in the book because it is necessary to understand how data protection law applies to the activities of organizations before a compliance programme can be created. Some organizations will already have a programme and therefore need to consider whether it will be necessary to update the programme in light of the GDPR and the Data Protection Bill. Other organizations will need to consider creating a compliance programme for the first time.

References in this chapter to the Data Protection Officer ('DPO') include not only a formal DPO appointee (as described in Chapter 12) but also anyone who has responsibility within an organization for data protection compliance. This might include a Compliance Officer, a Company Secretary, an in-house lawyer, the Head of Human Resources, the Head of the IT Department, or any other role that has been designated to include the function of ensuring the organization's data protection compliance.

A compliance programme should be based on consideration of a number of factors, which are discussed in Stage 1 below. Although there is no 'one size fits all'

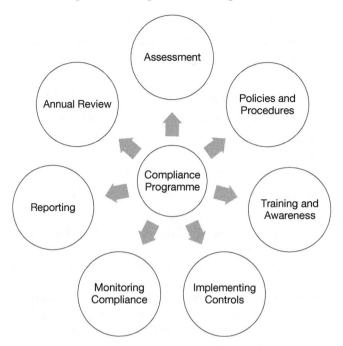

Fig. 13.1 The stages of compliance programme creation

compliance programme as such (as each organization will have its own unique issues and ways of operating), the DPO should have responsibility for determining the core elements of the compliance programme and the activities to be covered. It is useful to divide the creation of the compliance programme into seven stages—these are shown in Figure 13.1 and are discussed below in more detail.

Stage 1—Assessing Data Processing Activities

The first task of the DPO (or if one has yet to be appointed, the person in the organization with responsibility for data protection matters) in connection with creating a compliance programme is to assess the data processing activities of the organization.

This can best be done by reviewing existing records of processing activities, existing data protection procedures and documentation, and privacy notices. However, if these do not already exist, the DPO should consider how they can obtain the information required to build these documents and procedures. Data mapping or data audit questionnaires distributed to specific areas of the organization are a useful starting point and should be used to gather as much information about data processing activities as possible. Any such exercise should yield answers to show:

1. the types of personal data that are processed;
2. the categories of data subjects whose personal data are processed;
3. why the personal data are processed (in order to determine the lawful basis for processing);
4. how the personal data are processed;
5. which locations the personal data are processed in or sent to;
6. details of the third parties to whom the personal data are sent to or the personal data is shared with;
7. how long personal data are retained for; and
8. details of safeguards in place to protect the personal data.

For a useful guide on how to undertake data mapping, see Fulford N, 'People, Processes, Technology—A How To Guide to Data Mapping', Privacy & Data Protection, Volume 16, Issue 8.

Once this information is obtained, the DPO should review the responses provided and make an initial assessment of the risks of the data processing activities and what further action is necessary. For example, does the organization need to create any new data protection procedures to ensure compliance, update any privacy notices, or review its data sharing arrangements to ensure these contain adequate data protection clauses (see Chapter 9).

Senior management and the DPO should then agree a benchmark to demonstrate how good the organization's compliance with data protection laws currently is and how 'risky' the data processing activities currently are. This should be the baseline for the compliance programme and the documentation and activities prepared as part of the compliance programme.

Stage 2—Creating Data Protection Policies

Article 24 of the GDPR provides that the controller 'shall implement appropriate technical and organisational measures to ensure and be able to demonstrate that processing is performed in accordance with the Regulation' and that, 'where proportionate in relation to the processing activities', appropriate data protection policies shall be implemented by the controller. Once the data protection profile of an organization has been assessed, the DPO can consider what, if any, additional data protection policies are required. For example, most organizations will at a minimum require a general data protection policy to be in place and may have more detailed and specific policies relating to using personal data for marketing, data subject rights, breach management and notification, and other relevant activities. However, if an organization undertakes high risk processing or processing on a large scale, then it may require several further policies, for example relating to access control to the special categories of information or information security and outsourcing policies when allowing third parties to have access to the same.

Any data protection policies created should reflect the processing undertaken by the controller or processor. 'Off-the-shelf' data protection policies should be amended and updated to reflect what actually happens in the organization as opposed to what organizations think they should be doing. This is of paramount importance, as the data protection policies form the foundation of an organization's data protection compliance programme. If they are not a true reflection of the reality on the ground, any training or subsequent business operating procedures based on the policies are likely to be ineffective and may expose the organization to unnecessary risk of non-compliance. For example, in the event of a data breach, regulators will usually ask for a copy of the data protection policies and procedures that are in place and will additionally ask individuals if they were aware of these policies and procedures and followed the same.

It is certainly possible for an organization to have just one data protection policy. However, given the requirements of the GDPR, it is advisable for an organization to have a main overarching data protection policy followed by a small number of key polices, for example in relation to data breach management and notification, information security, data protection impact assessments, and subject access rights. Of course, the more data protection policies an organization has, the harder it can be to find information quickly. Therefore, the key data protection policy and all other associated policies should be linked and cross-referred to enable easy access to relevant information. This could be achieved by the organization having a well publicized privacy page which contains links to these policies.

Each area of an organization is likely to require its own data protection procedures which implement the requirements of the main data protection policies into operational processes. The data protection procedures should adhere to the principles set out in Chapter 12 regarding ownership of roles and responsibilities for compliance with data protection requirements and review periods, and must be documented. It is advisable for the DPO to undertake checks to ensure that each area of an organization (where appropriate) has documented data protection procedures that are being adhered to. This can be achieved by an annual review of the policies. Part of the review could involve the interviewing of key personnel involved in the processing activities and benchmarking the results against the policy content.

When drafting data protection policies, consideration should be given to the global footprint of an organization. If the organization is located in one country only, then drafting a country-specific data protection policy will be appropriate. However, if the organization operates globally, both within and outside of the European Economic Area ('EEA'), the DPO must consider how local data protection laws are taken into account. Having country-specific schedules with key differences in data protection laws and requirements is often helpful and can be used to clearly identify differences in data protection legislation applicable across an organization. Furthermore, highlighting these differences on an internal privacy page is also useful for raising awareness of these requirements.

Compliance as regards the data transfers themselves may be achieved in a number of ways, for example entering into binding corporate rules, using model contractual clauses, having a global data protection policy in which the strictest data protection standards apply, or having a standard global data protection policy with local data protection policies deviations—these options were discussed in Chapter 6. Monitoring compliance with all data protection laws within a global organization is discussed further at Stage 5 below.

Once the data protection policies have been drafted, they must be embedded into the culture of an organization as opposed to being placed in a policy repository to gather dust—see Stage 3 below for more details of how this can be achieved.

The policies should be reviewed periodically, especially when the organization's data processing activities change significantly or when there is any allegation of non-compliance. This is to ensure that the policies reflect the most accurate methods and purposes for an organizations processing of personal data and to ensure that individuals who process personal data understand their obligations clearly. Old versions of data protection policies should be retained to demonstrate that they were in place at the time of, for example, a data security breach and how they have been updated and reviewed over time.

'Ownership' for certain actions and responsibilities within the data protection policies should also be defined. For example, the HR department may be required to ensure that all employees are background-checked, and the Audit department may monitor compliance with data retention procedures to ensure that personal data are deleted from systems when no longer required. By assigning ownership (after consultation with the impacted owners), the DPO will be able to encourage relevant key individuals within the organization to step up to their new obligations.

Finally, data protection policies should be made available to all individuals who process personal data. As discussed above, these can be uploaded to a dedicated data protection page on an internal website or stored in an organization's policy repository. If a policy repository does not exist, one should be created to enable the data protection policies to be located and shared easily, including with regulators upon request.

Stage 3—Data Protection Training and Raising Awareness

Whilst creating a suite of data protection policies is an essential first step, it is also necessary to ensure that they are available where needed.

Ideally the DPO should upload new data protection policies to the data protection section of the organization's internal website. This will ensure that they are readily available for anyone who wishes or needs to read them.

Additionally, appropriate training on the policies (including any amendments) must be rolled out where appropriate, for example in relation to high-risk processing activities or high-volume processing, such as responding to subject access requests or processing large amounts of sensitive personal data. This is to ensure that relevant individuals are fully aware of the requirements under the data protection policies and the organization's approach in relation to compliance with the data protection legislation generally.

In addition, running appropriate training on the policies is of paramount importance under the GDPR. Training should be mandatory on induction (the Information Commissioner's Office ('ICO') has recommended, as a rule of thumb, that at least 15 per cent of the time spent by new staff members in induction programmes should be devoted to data protection matters) and should be provided at regular periods thereafter. Such training should take place before individuals have access to an organization's personal data.

Whilst there is no set timeframe laid out by the GDPR in terms of how often data protection training should be undertaken, annual data protection refresher training is advisable. More frequent data protection training may be required in relation to high-risk processing or where issues of non-compliance frequently arise. Furthermore, in the event of any data security breach or non-compliance with the GDPR, it is recommended that the individuals involved in the breach or incident are provided with additional data protection refresher training as soon as possible thereafter.

Where an organization appoints a processor (see Chapter 9), it is important to ensure that the processor requires its personnel to undertake regular data protection training. Such assurance can be provided to the controller by way of attestation from the processor, or through the controller reviewing the content of the processor's training materials.

It is not enough to provide an 'option' for individuals to undertake data protection training. Optional training courses do not meet the requirements of the GDPR. Instead, data protection training must be mandatory and must be monitored for compliance. Whilst it should be the responsibility of the DPO to ensure that relevant data protection training is provided or made available, individuals within the organization and those in management roles should ensure that the training is completed. It is advisable for the DPO to implement a process to monitor the completion of data protection training, with action being taken to fix new appointments for any staff members who did not undertake the training. The mandatory nature of training is something which regulators will look at when undertaking any audits or enforcement action.

Where staff members who were scheduled to undertake training were unable to complete the training for good reason, for example where the employee is on maternity leave or has now left the organization, the rationale for non-completion should be documented and retained to demonstrate compliance at a later date. If individuals habitually do not complete data protection training as required, it is recommended that relevant action is taken and that such action includes disciplinary measures where appropriate.

Finally, it is worth noting that data protection training should be provided to all persons within the organization who work with, or have access to, personal data. This includes all levels of staff members within the organization. It therefore follows that data protection training should be provided to both receptionists and the chief executive officer alike, as well as to individuals on a shop floor (if relevant). Of course the *type* of, and *duration* of, such training will be different according to job roles. Whilst junior administrative staff may require an hour's session once per year, senior members of the HR team are likely to require one or two days of in-depth training on a regular basis.

Raising awareness of data protection generally within an organization is one of the key factors which can make or break the success of any compliance programme. It is therefore recommended that this aspect is discussed with senior management at an early stage to enable them to have visibility of any compliance activities forming part of the compliance programme. This is important for gaining buy-in from the organization when implementing any data protection audits or testing of procedures, and is also a useful way of sharing the vision that the DPO has for compliance within the organization. Holding face-to-face workshops or seminars for individuals responsible for the management of teams that process personal data can be a useful way to highlight the aims of the DPO as they establish the compliance programme.

Given the seniority of a DPO and the fact that they may currently sit within other functions, for example legal or audit, junior employees can feel intimidated or cautious about approaching them. It is therefore vital that the DPO not only raises awareness of the importance of data protection within the organization but also of their own profile to enable all employees to feel empowered to talk to the DPO if they have any issues regarding compliance.

Meetings with junior employees can often yield significant insight into the day-to-day processing activities of an organization, so implementing an open door policy and fostering a friendly and approachable environment can be very useful. A weekly 'get together' where individuals can come to talk about data protection issues freely is not only likely to empower employees to do the right thing when it comes to data protection compliance but also to break down any barriers which may exist or which may be perceived due to hierarchy.

Clearly, the culture of an organization will play an important part in whether or not junior employees engage with the DPO, which is why communication of the DPO's role and objectives, as well as their importance within the organization, should ideally come from the top.

Stage 4—Implementing Controls to Reduce and Monitor Risk

Once an organization has established the data processing activities it undertakes and where it may potentially be carrying additional privacy risks, the DPO should establish minimum regulatory requirements which must be met.

For example, Article 5(1)(f) of the GDPR requires that personal data must be processed in a manner that ensures appropriate security of the personal data. If a risk is identified in allowing individuals to bring their own devices to work in order to access company email, there should be certain minimum security requirements that must be adhered to before this happens. These requirements should be written down and communicated to ensure they are followed.

It is not necessarily the DPO's duty to specify what those requirements will be, as this may be something which is outside the DPO's area of expertise and could also potentially cause a conflict of interest situation. However, the DPO should work with the relevant departments such as the IT and security teams to ensure that individuals understand the legal requirements, so they in turn can ensure that appropriate controls are put in place to protect the personal data. These controls should be monitored for compliance.

Another example of a potential control could be that all individuals have to undertake data protection training annually. The DPO should measure whether or not training is undertaken by all employees and report back to senior management, who in turn should take action if the data protection training has not been undertaken. These are simple examples of controls.

Any requirements that the DPO mandates should relate to the full life cycle of the personal data in question, for example from collection, to processing, storage, and deletion of the personal data. It is important therefore that the DPO considers exactly what the organization is doing with the personal data to ensure that the organization is aware of its obligations from the moment the personal data are collected (e.g. to ensure privacy by design and minimization), to how they are used (e.g. the processing is based on a lawful condition and the purposes of processing have been clearly communicated to the individuals) and shared (e.g. with third parties), to how they are destroyed or deleted when they are no longer required.

The controls and requirements that an organization implements should also deal with the outsourcing of its data processing activities. For example, a separate compliance programme could be set up to monitor a third party's compliance with the relevant data protection provisions. Such a programme should cover the following factors:

1. undertaking appropriate checks on potential processors to ensure they meet the requirements of the GDPR before they are chosen;

2. ensuring that data processing contracts contain adequate data protection provisions at the contracting stage;

3. ensuring that suppliers adhere to the provisions of the contract (e.g. in relation to sub-processing or the transfer of personal data outside of the EEA);

4. verifying the scope of any third party data audits and what the controller will check as part of an audit; and

5. establishing what happens on termination of the relationship.

Controls as regards processors are particularly important since enforcement action from regulators in this area has been rigorous. For example, the ICO has been very clear that all organizations that outsource data processing operations must ensure that they carry out their own due diligence and make rigorous checks to satisfy themselves that, for example in the case of a processor being used to conduct marketing operations, the processor has obtained the personal data it is using fairly and lawfully and that it has the necessary consent to use the data for those purposes.

Throughout Stage 4—Implementing Controls to Reduce and Monitor Risk—we have talked about 'controls' and discussed some simple examples. For those taking

Example risk and/or requirement	Example proposed control
All individuals must be aware of their obligations under data protection legislation	All individuals undertake annual training
Only the individuals who need to process personal data have access	All access to systems is monitored and reviewed to ensure this is still relevant and necessary. Access controls are reviewed every 12 months
Marketing emails must only be sent to individuals who have consented to receive the same	Run a suppression list against all marketing lists for all campaigns and opt people out of marketing and maintain suppression lists

Fig. 13.2 Example controls

on the role of the DPO for the first time, the purpose of implementing controls is to help the controller or processor manage the risks of data processing. Some examples of risks and controls are set out in Figure 13.2.

Stage 5—Monitoring Compliance

Once the DPO has set up a standard set of requirements against which it wishes to measure an organization's compliance, he or she should implement the monitoring procedures.

There is no hard and fast rule as to the time frame for monitoring any particular controls implemented by an organization, as some may be dependent upon the activity in question. For example, annual data protection training would be monitored for completion annually, whereas a review of all access controls by the IT department may be undertaken more frequently, such as every six months or when an individual leaves the organization.

The DPO should familiarize themselves with the data protection requirements and controls of the organization and choose a number of requirements to monitor in order to provide meaningful reporting information and to enable an assessment of the organization's compliance with data protection generally. The monitoring of controls can also be used as a way to ensure that any small issues of non-compliance do not become larger ones, for example laptops being frequently left unlocked or letters being sent to the wrong recipients—whilst these may not be very serious and may occur infrequently, they can help identify more significant issues of non-compliance.

Monitoring the number of complaints from individuals in relation to the processing of their personal data and the areas to which the complaints relate, as well as any regulatory letters or correspondence in relation to an organization's data processing activities, gives a good indication of whether or not relevant data protection requirements are being met. For example, if an organization receives a number of complaints that data subject access requests are not being responded to within the relevant time period, the department responsible for fulfilling the requests should review its processes to ensure that any issues of non-compliance are rectified immediately and do not become a larger issue.

The DPO should also undertake their own targeted testing and audits where they have concerns that data protection procedures are not being followed.

Stage 6—Reporting

It is recommended that the DPO create a data protection report to summarize activities and any compliance issues discovered. The report should be prepared based on the information that the DPO has gathered as part of the compliance programme and should be circulated to the board and senior and middle management.

The data protection report should cover enough information to enable the board to have visibility of any key data protection issues, for example the number of potential data protection breaches occurring in a given month and/or the number of complaints received from individuals relating to data processing.

Whilst technical and information security are not always part of the role of the DPO, the DPO should work closely with the IT team to ensure that any issues are resolved. The DPO should also obtain information from other areas of the organization to ensure that those areas are safeguarding personal data and have their own quality assurance checks and controls.

Remember, the role of the DPO is to 'facilitate compliance' with data protection legislation. Responsibility for compliance with the GDPR remains with the controller and/or processor.

It can be useful to prepare an annual data protection report setting out the work the DPO has undertaken in the preceding year together with any issues which may have or may impact compliance and the work that is anticipated for the forthcoming year. This can be used by the DPO to ensure that they have the necessary resources and support over the coming months.

Stage 7—Annual Review Process

It is recommended that the compliance programme is reviewed on an annual basis, as well as in the following instances:

1. where there has been a potential issue of non-compliance, for example a data security breach or other non-compliance with the GDPR, or any regulatory action;

2. where there has been a specific change in law which impacts on the processor or controller processing activities;

3. where there has been a change in the data processing activities carried out by the organization, for example where the controller and/or processor has commenced processing biometric personal data via a mobile app.

As regards the compliance programme generally, the DPO will need to be supported by all areas of an organization as he or she assists the organization and its employees (at all levels) on their journey to achieving and demonstrating data protection compliance. The journey of developing an effective and rigorous data protection compliance programme can be a lonely and challenging one. It is therefore useful for the DPO to establish a network of data protection and privacy colleagues in relevant departments throughout the organization. These individuals should be an invaluable resource to the DPO as he or she navigates the compliance aspects of the GDPR.

APPENDIX 1

Regulation (EU) 2016/679 of the European Parliament and of the Council

of 27 April 2016

on the protection of natural persons with regard to the processing of personal data and on the free movement of such data, and repealing Directive 95/46/EC (General Data Protection Regulation)

(Text with EEA relevance)

THE EUROPEAN PARLIAMENT AND THE COUNCIL OF THE EUROPEAN UNION,

Having regard to the Treaty on the Functioning of the European Union, and in particular Article 16 thereof,

Having regard to the proposal from the European Commission,

After transmission of the draft legislative act to the national parliaments,

Having regard to the opinion of the European Economic and Social Committee [1],

Having regard to the opinion of the Committee of the Regions [2],

Acting in accordance with the ordinary legislative procedure [3],

Whereas:

(1) The protection of natural persons in relation to the processing of personal data is a fundamental right. Article 8(1) of the Charter of Fundamental Rights of the European Union (the 'Charter') and Article 16(1) of the Treaty on the Functioning of the European Union (TFEU) provide that everyone has the right to the protection of personal data concerning him or her.

(2) The principles of, and rules on the protection of natural persons with regard to the processing of their personal data should, whatever their nationality or residence, respect their fundamental rights and freedoms, in particular their right to the protection of personal data. This Regulation is intended to contribute to the accomplishment of an area of freedom, security and justice and of an economic union, to economic and social progress, to the strengthening and the convergence of the economies within the internal market, and to the well-being of natural persons.

(3) Directive 95/46/EC of the European Parliament and of the Council [4] seeks to harmonise the protection of fundamental rights and freedoms of natural persons in respect of processing activities and to ensure the free flow of personal data between Member States.

---

[1] OJ C 229, 31.7.2012, p. 90.   [2] OJ C 391, 18.12.2012, p. 127.

[3] Position of the European Parliament of 12 March 2014 (not yet published in the Official Journal) and position of the Council at first reading of 8 April 2016 (not yet published in the Official Journal). Position of the European Parliament of 14 April 2016.

[4] Directive 95/46/EC of the European Parliament and of the Council of 24 October 1995 on the protection of individuals with regard to the processing of personal data and on the free movement of such data (OJ L 281, 23.11.1995, p. 31).

(4) The processing of personal data should be designed to serve mankind. The right to the protection of personal data is not an absolute right; it must be considered in relation to its function in society and be balanced against other fundamental rights, in accordance with the principle of proportionality. This Regulation respects all fundamental rights and observes the freedoms and principles recognised in the Charter as enshrined in the Treaties, in particular the respect for private and family life, home and communications, the protection of personal data, freedom of thought, conscience and religion, freedom of expression and information, freedom to conduct a business, the right to an effective remedy and to a fair trial, and cultural, religious and linguistic diversity.

(5) The economic and social integration resulting from the functioning of the internal market has led to a substantial increase in cross-border flows of personal data. The exchange of personal data between public and private actors, including natural persons, associations and undertakings across the Union has increased. National authorities in the Member States are being called upon by Union law to cooperate and exchange personal data so as to be able to perform their duties or carry out tasks on behalf of an authority in another Member State.

(6) Rapid technological developments and globalisation have brought new challenges for the protection of personal data. The scale of the collection and sharing of personal data has increased significantly. Technology allows both private companies and public authorities to make use of personal data on an unprecedented scale in order to pursue their activities. Natural persons increasingly make personal information available publicly and globally. Technology has transformed both the economy and social life, and should further facilitate the free flow of personal data within the Union and the transfer to third countries and international organisations, while ensuring a high level of the protection of personal data.

(7) Those developments require a strong and more coherent data protection framework in the Union, backed by strong enforcement, given the importance of creating the trust that will allow the digital economy to develop across the internal market. Natural persons should have control of their own personal data. Legal and practical certainty for natural persons, economic operators and public authorities should be enhanced.

(8) Where this Regulation provides for specifications or restrictions of its rules by Member State law, Member States may, as far as necessary for coherence and for making the national provisions comprehensible to the persons to whom they apply, incorporate elements of this Regulation into their national law.

(9) The objectives and principles of Directive 95/46/EC remain sound, but it has not prevented fragmentation in the implementation of data protection across the Union, legal uncertainty or a widespread public perception that there are significant risks to the protection of natural persons, in particular with regard to online activity. Differences in the level of protection of the rights and freedoms of natural persons, in particular the right to the protection of personal data, with regard to the processing of personal data in the Member States may prevent the free flow of personal data throughout the Union. Those differences may therefore constitute an obstacle to the pursuit of economic activities at the level of the Union, distort competition and impede authorities in the discharge of their responsibilities under Union law. Such a difference in levels of protection is due to the existence of differences in the implementation and application of Directive 95/46/EC.

(10) In order to ensure a consistent and high level of protection of natural persons and to remove the obstacles to flows of personal data within the Union, the level of protection of the rights and freedoms of natural persons with regard to the processing of such data

should be equivalent in all Member States. Consistent and homogenous application of the rules for the protection of the fundamental rights and freedoms of natural persons with regard to the processing of personal data should be ensured throughout the Union. Regarding the processing of personal data for compliance with a legal obligation, for the performance of a task carried out in the public interest or in the exercise of official authority vested in the controller, Member States should be allowed to maintain or introduce national provisions to further specify the application of the rules of this Regulation. In conjunction with the general and horizontal law on data protection implementing Directive 95/46/EC, Member States have several sector-specific laws in areas that need more specific provisions. This Regulation also provides a margin of manoeuvre for Member States to specify its rules, including for the processing of special categories of personal data ('sensitive data'). To that extent, this Regulation does not exclude Member State law that sets out the circumstances for specific processing situations, including determining more precisely the conditions under which the processing of personal data is lawful.

(11) Effective protection of personal data throughout the Union requires the strengthening and setting out in detail of the rights of data subjects and the obligations of those who process and determine the processing of personal data, as well as equivalent powers for monitoring and ensuring compliance with the rules for the protection of personal data and equivalent sanctions for infringements in the Member States.

(12) Article 16(2) TFEU mandates the European Parliament and the Council to lay down the rules relating to the protection of natural persons with regard to the processing of personal data and the rules relating to the free movement of personal data.

(13) In order to ensure a consistent level of protection for natural persons throughout the Union and to prevent divergences hampering the free movement of personal data within the internal market, a Regulation is necessary to provide legal certainty and transparency for economic operators, including micro, small and medium-sized enterprises, and to provide natural persons in all Member States with the same level of legally enforceable rights and obligations and responsibilities for controllers and processors, to ensure consistent monitoring of the processing of personal data, and equivalent sanctions in all Member States as well as effective cooperation between the supervisory authorities of different Member States. The proper functioning of the internal market requires that the free movement of personal data within the Union is not restricted or prohibited for reasons connected with the protection of natural persons with regard to the processing of personal data. To take account of the specific situation of micro, small and medium-sized enterprises, this Regulation includes a derogation for organisations with fewer than 250 employees with regard to record-keeping. In addition, the Union institutions and bodies, and Member States and their supervisory authorities, are encouraged to take account of the specific needs of micro, small and medium-sized enterprises in the application of this Regulation. The notion of micro, small and medium-sized enterprises should draw from Article 2 of the Annex to Commission Recommendation 2003/361/EC [5].

(14) The protection afforded by this Regulation should apply to natural persons, whatever their nationality or place of residence, in relation to the processing of their personal data. This Regulation does not cover the processing of personal data which concerns

---

[5] Commission Recommendation of 6 May 2003 concerning the definition of micro, small and medium-sized enterprises (C(2003) 1422) (OJ L 124, 20.5.2003, p. 36).

legal persons and in particular undertakings established as legal persons, including the name and the form of the legal person and the contact details of the legal person.

(15) In order to prevent creating a serious risk of circumvention, the protection of natural persons should be technologically neutral and should not depend on the techniques used. The protection of natural persons should apply to the processing of personal data by automated means, as well as to manual processing, if the personal data are contained or are intended to be contained in a filing system. Files or sets of files, as well as their cover pages, which are not structured according to specific criteria should not fall within the scope of this Regulation.

(16) This Regulation does not apply to issues of protection of fundamental rights and freedoms or the free flow of personal data related to activities which fall outside the scope of Union law, such as activities concerning national security. This Regulation does not apply to the processing of personal data by the Member States when carrying out activities in relation to the common foreign and security policy of the Union.

(17) Regulation (EC) No 45/2001 of the European Parliament and of the Council [6] applies to the processing of personal data by the Union institutions, bodies, offices and agencies. Regulation (EC) No 45/2001 and other Union legal acts applicable to such processing of personal data should be adapted to the principles and rules established in this Regulation and applied in the light of this Regulation. In order to provide a strong and coherent data protection framework in the Union, the necessary adaptations of Regulation (EC) No 45/2001 should follow after the adoption of this Regulation, in order to allow application at the same time as this Regulation.

(18) This Regulation does not apply to the processing of personal data by a natural person in the course of a purely personal or household activity and thus with no connection to a professional or commercial activity. Personal or household activities could include correspondence and the holding of addresses, or social networking and online activity undertaken within the context of such activities. However, this Regulation applies to controllers or processors which provide the means for processing personal data for such personal or household activities.

(19) The protection of natural persons with regard to the processing of personal data by competent authorities for the purposes of the prevention, investigation, detection or prosecution of criminal offences or the execution of criminal penalties, including the safeguarding against and the prevention of threats to public security and the free movement of such data, is the subject of a specific Union legal act. This Regulation should not, therefore, apply to processing activities for those purposes. However, personal data processed by public authorities under this Regulation should, when used for those purposes, be governed by a more specific Union legal act, namely Directive (EU) 2016/680 of the European Parliament and of the Council [7]. Member States may entrust competent authorities within the meaning of Directive (EU) 2016/680 with tasks which are not necessarily carried out for the purposes of the prevention, investigation, detection

---

[6] Regulation (EC) No 45/2001 of the European Parliament and of the Council of 18 December 2000 on the protection of individuals with regard to the processing of personal data by the Community institutions and bodies and on the free movement of such data (OJ L 8, 12.1.2001, p. 1).

[7] Directive (EU) 2016/680 of the European Parliament and of the Council of 27 April 2016 on the protection of natural persons with regard to the processing of personal data by competent authorities for the purposes of prevention, investigation, detection or prosecution of criminal offences or the execution of criminal penalties, and the free movement of such data and repealing Council Framework Decision 2008/977/JHA (see page 89 of this Official Journal).

or prosecution of criminal offences or the execution of criminal penalties, including the safeguarding against and prevention of threats to public security, so that the processing of personal data for those other purposes, in so far as it is within the scope of Union law, falls within the scope of this Regulation.

With regard to the processing of personal data by those competent authorities for purposes falling within scope of this Regulation, Member States should be able to maintain or introduce more specific provisions to adapt the application of the rules of this Regulation. Such provisions may determine more precisely specific requirements for the processing of personal data by those competent authorities for those other purposes, taking into account the constitutional, organisational and administrative structure of the respective Member State. When the processing of personal data by private bodies falls within the scope of this Regulation, this Regulation should provide for the possibility for Member States under specific conditions to restrict by law certain obligations and rights when such a restriction constitutes a necessary and proportionate measure in a democratic society to safeguard specific important interests including public security and the prevention, investigation, detection or prosecution of criminal offences or the execution of criminal penalties, including the safeguarding against and the prevention of threats to public security. This is relevant for instance in the framework of anti-money laundering or the activities of forensic laboratories.

(20) While this Regulation applies, inter alia, to the activities of courts and other judicial authorities, Union or Member State law could specify the processing operations and processing procedures in relation to the processing of personal data by courts and other judicial authorities. The competence of the supervisory authorities should not cover the processing of personal data when courts are acting in their judicial capacity, in order to safeguard the independence of the judiciary in the performance of its judicial tasks, including decision-making. It should be possible to entrust supervision of such data processing operations to specific bodies within the judicial system of the Member State, which should, in particular ensure compliance with the rules of this Regulation, enhance awareness among members of the judiciary of their obligations under this Regulation and handle complaints in relation to such data processing operations.

(21) This Regulation is without prejudice to the application of Directive 2000/31/EC of the European Parliament and of the Council [8], in particular of the liability rules of intermediary service providers in Articles 12 to 15 of that Directive. That Directive seeks to contribute to the proper functioning of the internal market by ensuring the free movement of information society services between Member States.

(22) Any processing of personal data in the context of the activities of an establishment of a controller or a processor in the Union should be carried out in accordance with this Regulation, regardless of whether the processing itself takes place within the Union. Establishment implies the effective and real exercise of activity through stable arrangements. The legal form of such arrangements, whether through a branch or a subsidiary with a legal personality, is not the determining factor in that respect.

(23) In order to ensure that natural persons are not deprived of the protection to which they are entitled under this Regulation, the processing of personal data of data subjects who are in the Union by a controller or a processor not established in the Union should be

---

[8] Directive 2000/31/EC of the European Parliament and of the Council of 8 June 2000 on certain legal aspects of information society services, in particular electronic commerce, in the Internal Market ('Directive on electronic commerce') (OJ L 178, 17.7.2000, p. 1).

subject to this Regulation where the processing activities are related to offering goods or services to such data subjects irrespective of whether connected to a payment. In order to determine whether such a controller or processor is offering goods or services to data subjects who are in the Union, it should be ascertained whether it is apparent that the controller or processor envisages offering services to data subjects in one or more Member States in the Union. Whereas the mere accessibility of the controller's, processor's or an intermediary's website in the Union, of an email address or of other contact details, or the use of a language generally used in the third country where the controller is established, is insufficient to ascertain such intention, factors such as the use of a language or a currency generally used in one or more Member States with the possibility of ordering goods and services in that other language, or the mentioning of customers or users who are in the Union, may make it apparent that the controller envisages offering goods or services to data subjects in the Union.

(24) The processing of personal data of data subjects who are in the Union by a controller or processor not established in the Union should also be subject to this Regulation when it is related to the monitoring of the behaviour of such data subjects in so far as their behaviour takes place within the Union. In order to determine whether a processing activity can be considered to monitor the behaviour of data subjects, it should be ascertained whether natural persons are tracked on the internet including potential subsequent use of personal data processing techniques which consist of profiling a natural person, particularly in order to take decisions concerning her or him or for analysing or predicting her or his personal preferences, behaviours and attitudes.

(25) Where Member State law applies by virtue of public international law, this Regulation should also apply to a controller not established in the Union, such as in a Member State's diplomatic mission or consular post.

(26) The principles of data protection should apply to any information concerning an identified or identifiable natural person. Personal data which have undergone pseudonymisation, which could be attributed to a natural person by the use of additional information should be considered to be information on an identifiable natural person. To determine whether a natural person is identifiable, account should be taken of all the means reasonably likely to be used, such as singling out, either by the controller or by another person to identify the natural person directly or indirectly. To ascertain whether means are reasonably likely to be used to identify the natural person, account should be taken of all objective factors, such as the costs of and the amount of time required for identification, taking into consideration the available technology at the time of the processing and technological developments. The principles of data protection should therefore not apply to anonymous information, namely information which does not relate to an identified or identifiable natural person or to personal data rendered anonymous in such a manner that the data subject is not or no longer identifiable. This Regulation does not therefore concern the processing of such anonymous information, including for statistical or research purposes.

(27) This Regulation does not apply to the personal data of deceased persons. Member States may provide for rules regarding the processing of personal data of deceased persons.

(28) The application of pseudonymisation to personal data can reduce the risks to the data subjects concerned and help controllers and processors to meet their data-protection obligations. The explicit introduction of 'pseudonymisation' in this Regulation is not intended to preclude any other measures of data protection.

(29) In order to create incentives to apply pseudonymisation when processing personal data, measures of pseudonymisation should, whilst allowing general analysis, be possible

within the same controller when that controller has taken technical and organisational measures necessary to ensure, for the processing concerned, that this Regulation is implemented, and that additional information for attributing the personal data to a specific data subject is kept separately. The controller processing the personal data should indicate the authorised persons within the same controller.

(30) Natural persons may be associated with online identifiers provided by their devices, applications, tools and protocols, such as internet protocol addresses, cookie identifiers or other identifiers such as radio frequency identification tags. This may leave traces which, in particular when combined with unique identifiers and other information received by the servers, may be used to create profiles of the natural persons and identify them.

(31) Public authorities to which personal data are disclosed in accordance with a legal obligation for the exercise of their official mission, such as tax and customs authorities, financial investigation units, independent administrative authorities, or financial market authorities responsible for the regulation and supervision of securities markets should not be regarded as recipients if they receive personal data which are necessary to carry out a particular inquiry in the general interest, in accordance with Union or Member State law. The requests for disclosure sent by the public authorities should always be in writing, reasoned and occasional and should not concern the entirety of a filing system or lead to the interconnection of filing systems. The processing of personal data by those public authorities should comply with the applicable data-protection rules according to the purposes of the processing.

(32) Consent should be given by a clear affirmative act establishing a freely given, specific, informed and unambiguous indication of the data subject's agreement to the processing of personal data relating to him or her, such as by a written statement, including by electronic means, or an oral statement. This could include ticking a box when visiting an internet website, choosing technical settings for information society services or another statement or conduct which clearly indicates in this context the data subject's acceptance of the proposed processing of his or her personal data. Silence, pre-ticked boxes or inactivity should not therefore constitute consent. Consent should cover all processing activities carried out for the same purpose or purposes. When the processing has multiple purposes, consent should be given for all of them. If the data subject's consent is to be given following a request by electronic means, the request must be clear, concise and not unnecessarily disruptive to the use of the service for which it is provided.

(33) It is often not possible to fully identify the purpose of personal data processing for scientific research purposes at the time of data collection. Therefore, data subjects should be allowed to give their consent to certain areas of scientific research when in keeping with recognised ethical standards for scientific research. Data subjects should have the opportunity to give their consent only to certain areas of research or parts of research projects to the extent allowed by the intended purpose.

(34) Genetic data should be defined as personal data relating to the inherited or acquired genetic characteristics of a natural person which result from the analysis of a biological sample from the natural person in question, in particular chromosomal, deoxyribonucleic acid (DNA) or ribonucleic acid (RNA) analysis, or from the analysis of another element enabling equivalent information to be obtained.

(35) Personal data concerning health should include all data pertaining to the health status of a data subject which reveal information relating to the past, current or future physical or mental health status of the data subject. This includes information about the natural

person collected in the course of the registration for, or the provision of, health care services as referred to in Directive 2011/24/EU of the European Parliament and of the Council[9] to that natural person; a number, symbol or particular assigned to a natural person to uniquely identify the natural person for health purposes; information derived from the testing or examination of a body part or bodily substance, including from genetic data and biological samples; and any information on, for example, a disease, disability, disease risk, medical history, clinical treatment or the physiological or biomedical state of the data subject independent of its source, for example from a physician or other health professional, a hospital, a medical device or an in vitro diagnostic test.

(36) The main establishment of a controller in the Union should be the place of its central administration in the Union, unless the decisions on the purposes and means of the processing of personal data are taken in another establishment of the controller in the Union, in which case that other establishment should be considered to be the main establishment. The main establishment of a controller in the Union should be determined according to objective criteria and should imply the effective and real exercise of management activities determining the main decisions as to the purposes and means of processing through stable arrangements. That criterion should not depend on whether the processing of personal data is carried out at that location. The presence and use of technical means and technologies for processing personal data or processing activities do not, in themselves, constitute a main establishment and are therefore not determining criteria for a main establishment. The main establishment of the processor should be the place of its central administration in the Union or, if it has no central administration in the Union, the place where the main processing activities take place in the Union. In cases involving both the controller and the processor, the competent lead supervisory authority should remain the supervisory authority of the Member State where the controller has its main establishment, but the supervisory authority of the processor should be considered to be a supervisory authority concerned and that supervisory authority should participate in the cooperation procedure provided for by this Regulation. In any case, the supervisory authorities of the Member State or Member States where the processor has one or more establishments should not be considered to be supervisory authorities concerned where the draft decision concerns only the controller. Where the processing is carried out by a group of undertakings, the main establishment of the controlling undertaking should be considered to be the main establishment of the group of undertakings, except where the purposes and means of processing are determined by another undertaking.

(37) A group of undertakings should cover a controlling undertaking and its controlled undertakings, whereby the controlling undertaking should be the undertaking which can exert a dominant influence over the other undertakings by virtue, for example, of ownership, financial participation or the rules which govern it or the power to have personal data protection rules implemented. An undertaking which controls the processing of personal data in undertakings affiliated to it should be regarded, together with those undertakings, as a group of undertakings.

(38) Children merit specific protection with regard to their personal data, as they may be less aware of the risks, consequences and safeguards concerned and their rights in relation

[9] Directive 2011/24/EU of the European Parliament and of the Council of 9 March 2011 on the application of patients' rights in cross-border healthcare (OJ L 88, 4.4.2011, p. 45).

to the processing of personal data. Such specific protection should, in particular, apply to the use of personal data of children for the purposes of marketing or creating personality or user profiles and the collection of personal data with regard to children when using services offered directly to a child. The consent of the holder of parental responsibility should not be necessary in the context of preventive or counselling services offered directly to a child.

(39) Any processing of personal data should be lawful and fair. It should be transparent to natural persons that personal data concerning them are collected, used, consulted or otherwise processed and to what extent the personal data are or will be processed. The principle of transparency requires that any information and communication relating to the processing of those personal data be easily accessible and easy to understand, and that clear and plain language be used. That principle concerns, in particular, information to the data subjects on the identity of the controller and the purposes of the processing and further information to ensure fair and transparent processing in respect of the natural persons concerned and their right to obtain confirmation and communication of personal data concerning them which are being processed. Natural persons should be made aware of risks, rules, safeguards and rights in relation to the processing of personal data and how to exercise their rights in relation to such processing. In particular, the specific purposes for which personal data are processed should be explicit and legitimate and determined at the time of the collection of the personal data. The personal data should be adequate, relevant and limited to what is necessary for the purposes for which they are processed. This requires, in particular, ensuring that the period for which the personal data are stored is limited to a strict minimum. Personal data should be processed only if the purpose of the processing could not reasonably be fulfilled by other means. In order to ensure that the personal data are not kept longer than necessary, time limits should be established by the controller for erasure or for a periodic review. Every reasonable step should be taken to ensure that personal data which are inaccurate are rectified or deleted. Personal data should be processed in a manner that ensures appropriate security and confidentiality of the personal data, including for preventing unauthorised access to or use of personal data and the equipment used for the processing.

(40) In order for processing to be lawful, personal data should be processed on the basis of the consent of the data subject concerned or some other legitimate basis, laid down by law, either in this Regulation or in other Union or Member State law as referred to in this Regulation, including the necessity for compliance with the legal obligation to which the controller is subject or the necessity for the performance of a contract to which the data subject is party or in order to take steps at the request of the data subject prior to entering into a contract.

(41) Where this Regulation refers to a legal basis or a legislative measure, this does not necessarily require a legislative act adopted by a parliament, without prejudice to requirements pursuant to the constitutional order of the Member State concerned. However, such a legal basis or legislative measure should be clear and precise and its application should be foreseeable to persons subject to it, in accordance with the case-law of the Court of Justice of the European Union (the 'Court of Justice') and the European Court of Human Rights.

(42) Where processing is based on the data subject's consent, the controller should be able to demonstrate that the data subject has given consent to the processing operation. In particular in the context of a written declaration on another matter, safeguards should ensure that the data subject is aware of the fact that and the extent to which consent

is given. In accordance with Council Directive 93/13/EEC [10] a declaration of consent pre-formulated by the controller should be provided in an intelligible and easily accessible form, using clear and plain language and it should not contain unfair terms. For consent to be informed, the data subject should be aware at least of the identity of the controller and the purposes of the processing for which the personal data are intended. Consent should not be regarded as freely given if the data subject has no genuine or free choice or is unable to refuse or withdraw consent without detriment.

(43) In order to ensure that consent is freely given, consent should not provide a valid legal ground for the processing of personal data in a specific case where there is a clear imbalance between the data subject and the controller, in particular where the controller is a public authority and it is therefore unlikely that consent was freely given in all the circumstances of that specific situation. Consent is presumed not to be freely given if it does not allow separate consent to be given to different personal data processing operations despite it being appropriate in the individual case, or if the performance of a contract, including the provision of a service, is dependent on the consent despite such consent not being necessary for such performance.

(44) Processing should be lawful where it is necessary in the context of a contract or the intention to enter into a contract.

(45) Where processing is carried out in accordance with a legal obligation to which the controller is subject or where processing is necessary for the performance of a task carried out in the public interest or in the exercise of official authority, the processing should have a basis in Union or Member State law. This Regulation does not require a specific law for each individual processing. A law as a basis for several processing operations based on a legal obligation to which the controller is subject or where processing is necessary for the performance of a task carried out in the public interest or in the exercise of an official authority may be sufficient. It should also be for Union or Member State law to determine the purpose of processing. Furthermore, that law could specify the general conditions of this Regulation governing the lawfulness of personal data processing, establish specifications for determining the controller, the type of personal data which are subject to the processing, the data subjects concerned, the entities to which the personal data may be disclosed, the purpose limitations, the storage period and other measures to ensure lawful and fair processing. It should also be for Union or Member State law to determine whether the controller performing a task carried out in the public interest or in the exercise of official authority should be a public authority or another natural or legal person governed by public law, or, where it is in the public interest to do so, including for health purposes such as public health and social protection and the management of health care services, by private law, such as a professional association.

(46) The processing of personal data should also be regarded to be lawful where it is necessary to protect an interest which is essential for the life of the data subject or that of another natural person. Processing of personal data based on the vital interest of another natural person should in principle take place only where the processing cannot be manifestly based on another legal basis. Some types of processing may serve both important grounds of public interest and the vital interests of the data subject as for instance when processing is necessary for humanitarian purposes, including for monitoring epidemics

---

[10] Council Directive 93/13/EEC of 5 April 1993 on unfair terms in consumer contracts (OJ L 95, 21.4.1993, p. 29).

and their spread or in situations of humanitarian emergencies, in particular in situations of natural and man-made disasters.

(47) The legitimate interests of a controller, including those of a controller to which the personal data may be disclosed, or of a third party, may provide a legal basis for processing, provided that the interests or the fundamental rights and freedoms of the data subject are not overriding, taking into consideration the reasonable expectations of data subjects based on their relationship with the controller. Such legitimate interest could exist for example where there is a relevant and appropriate relationship between the data subject and the controller in situations such as where the data subject is a client or in the service of the controller. At any rate the existence of a legitimate interest would need careful assessment including whether a data subject can reasonably expect at the time and in the context of the collection of the personal data that processing for that purpose may take place. The interests and fundamental rights of the data subject could in particular override the interest of the data controller where personal data are processed in circumstances where data subjects do not reasonably expect further processing. Given that it is for the legislator to provide by law for the legal basis for public authorities to process personal data, that legal basis should not apply to the processing by public authorities in the performance of their tasks. The processing of personal data strictly necessary for the purposes of preventing fraud also constitutes a legitimate interest of the data controller concerned. The processing of personal data for direct marketing purposes may be regarded as carried out for a legitimate interest.

(48) Controllers that are part of a group of undertakings or institutions affiliated to a central body may have a legitimate interest in transmitting personal data within the group of undertakings for internal administrative purposes, including the processing of clients' or employees' personal data. The general principles for the transfer of personal data, within a group of undertakings, to an undertaking located in a third country remain unaffected.

(49) The processing of personal data to the extent strictly necessary and proportionate for the purposes of ensuring network and information security, i.e. the ability of a network or an information system to resist, at a given level of confidence, accidental events or unlawful or malicious actions that compromise the availability, authenticity, integrity and confidentiality of stored or transmitted personal data, and the security of the related services offered by, or accessible via, those networks and systems, by public authorities, by computer emergency response teams (CERTs), computer security incident response teams (CSIRTs), by providers of electronic communications networks and services and by providers of security technologies and services, constitutes a legitimate interest of the data controller concerned. This could, for example, include preventing unauthorised access to electronic communications networks and malicious code distribution and stopping 'denial of service' attacks and damage to computer and electronic communication systems.

(50) The processing of personal data for purposes other than those for which the personal data were initially collected should be allowed only where the processing is compatible with the purposes for which the personal data were initially collected. In such a case, no legal basis separate from that which allowed the collection of the personal data is required. If the processing is necessary for the performance of a task carried out in the public interest or in the exercise of official authority vested in the controller, Union or Member State law may determine and specify the tasks and purposes for which the further processing should be regarded as compatible and lawful. Further processing for archiving purposes in the public interest, scientific or historical research purposes

or statistical purposes should be considered to be compatible lawful processing operations. The legal basis provided by Union or Member State law for the processing of personal data may also provide a legal basis for further processing. In order to ascertain whether a purpose of further processing is compatible with the purpose for which the personal data are initially collected, the controller, after having met all the requirements for the lawfulness of the original processing, should take into account, inter alia: any link between those purposes and the purposes of the intended further processing; the context in which the personal data have been collected, in particular the reasonable expectations of data subjects based on their relationship with the controller as to their further use; the nature of the personal data; the consequences of the intended further processing for data subjects; and the existence of appropriate safeguards in both the original and intended further processing operations.

Where the data subject has given consent or the processing is based on Union or Member State law which constitutes a necessary and proportionate measure in a democratic society to safeguard, in particular, important objectives of general public interest, the controller should be allowed to further process the personal data irrespective of the compatibility of the purposes. In any case, the application of the principles set out in this Regulation and in particular the information of the data subject on those other purposes and on his or her rights including the right to object, should be ensured. Indicating possible criminal acts or threats to public security by the controller and transmitting the relevant personal data in individual cases or in several cases relating to the same criminal act or threats to public security to a competent authority should be regarded as being in the legitimate interest pursued by the controller. However, such transmission in the legitimate interest of the controller or further processing of personal data should be prohibited if the processing is not compatible with a legal, professional or other binding obligation of secrecy.

(51) Personal data which are, by their nature, particularly sensitive in relation to fundamental rights and freedoms merit specific protection as the context of their processing could create significant risks to the fundamental rights and freedoms. Those personal data should include personal data revealing racial or ethnic origin, whereby the use of the term 'racial origin' in this Regulation does not imply an acceptance by the Union of theories which attempt to determine the existence of separate human races. The processing of photographs should not systematically be considered to be processing of special categories of personal data as they are covered by the definition of biometric data only when processed through a specific technical means allowing the unique identification or authentication of a natural person. Such personal data should not be processed, unless processing is allowed in specific cases set out in this Regulation, taking into account that Member States law may lay down specific provisions on data protection in order to adapt the application of the rules of this Regulation for compliance with a legal obligation or for the performance of a task carried out in the public interest or in the exercise of official authority vested in the controller. In addition to the specific requirements for such processing, the general principles and other rules of this Regulation should apply, in particular as regards the conditions for lawful processing. Derogations from the general prohibition for processing such special categories of personal data should be explicitly provided, inter alia, where the data subject gives his or her explicit consent or in respect of specific needs in particular where the processing is carried out in the course of legitimate activities by certain associations or foundations the purpose of which is to permit the exercise of fundamental freedoms.

(52) Derogating from the prohibition on processing special categories of personal data should also be allowed when provided for in Union or Member State law and subject to suitable safeguards, so as to protect personal data and other fundamental rights, where it is in the public interest to do so, in particular processing personal data in the field of employment law, social protection law including pensions and for health security, monitoring and alert purposes, the prevention or control of communicable diseases and other serious threats to health. Such a derogation may be made for health purposes, including public health and the management of health-care services, especially in order to ensure the quality and cost-effectiveness of the procedures used for settling claims for benefits and services in the health insurance system, or for archiving purposes in the public interest, scientific or historical research purposes or statistical purposes. A derogation should also allow the processing of such personal data where necessary for the establishment, exercise or defence of legal claims, whether in court proceedings or in an administrative or out-of-court procedure.

(53) Special categories of personal data which merit higher protection should be processed for health-related purposes only where necessary to achieve those purposes for the benefit of natural persons and society as a whole, in particular in the context of the management of health or social care services and systems, including processing by the management and central national health authorities of such data for the purpose of quality control, management information and the general national and local supervision of the health or social care system, and ensuring continuity of health or social care and cross-border healthcare or health security, monitoring and alert purposes, or for archiving purposes in the public interest, scientific or historical research purposes or statistical purposes, based on Union or Member State law which has to meet an objective of public interest, as well as for studies conducted in the public interest in the area of public health. Therefore, this Regulation should provide for harmonised conditions for the processing of special categories of personal data concerning health, in respect of specific needs, in particular where the processing of such data is carried out for certain health-related purposes by persons subject to a legal obligation of professional secrecy. Union or Member State law should provide for specific and suitable measures so as to protect the fundamental rights and the personal data of natural persons. Member States should be allowed to maintain or introduce further conditions, including limitations, with regard to the processing of genetic data, biometric data or data concerning health. However, this should not hamper the free flow of personal data within the Union when those conditions apply to cross-border processing of such data.

(54) The processing of special categories of personal data may be necessary for reasons of public interest in the areas of public health without consent of the data subject. Such processing should be subject to suitable and specific measures so as to protect the rights and freedoms of natural persons. In that context, 'public health' should be interpreted as defined in Regulation (EC) No 1338/2008 of the European Parliament and of the Council [11], namely all elements related to health, namely health status, including morbidity and disability, the determinants having an effect on that health status, health care needs, resources allocated to health care, the provision of, and universal access to, health

---

[11] Regulation (EC) No 1338/2008 of the European Parliament and of the Council of 16 December 2008 on Community statistics on public health and health and safety at work (OJ L 354, 31.12.2008, p. 70).

care as well as health care expenditure and financing, and the causes of mortality. Such processing of data concerning health for reasons of public interest should not result in personal data being processed for other purposes by third parties such as employers or insurance and banking companies.

(55) Moreover, the processing of personal data by official authorities for the purpose of achieving the aims, laid down by constitutional law or by international public law, of officially recognised religious associations, is carried out on grounds of public interest.

(56) Where in the course of electoral activities, the operation of the democratic system in a Member State requires that political parties compile personal data on people's political opinions, the processing of such data may be permitted for reasons of public interest, provided that appropriate safeguards are established.

(57) If the personal data processed by a controller do not permit the controller to identify a natural person, the data controller should not be obliged to acquire additional information in order to identify the data subject for the sole purpose of complying with any provision of this Regulation. However, the controller should not refuse to take additional information provided by the data subject in order to support the exercise of his or her rights. Identification should include the digital identification of a data subject, for example through authentication mechanism such as the same credentials, used by the data subject to log-in to the on-line service offered by the data controller.

(58) The principle of transparency requires that any information addressed to the public or to the data subject be concise, easily accessible and easy to understand, and that clear and plain language and, additionally, where appropriate, visualisation be used. Such information could be provided in electronic form, for example, when addressed to the public, through a website. This is of particular relevance in situations where the proliferation of actors and the technological complexity of practice make it difficult for the data subject to know and understand whether, by whom and for what purpose personal data relating to him or her are being collected, such as in the case of online advertising. Given that children merit specific protection, any information and communication, where processing is addressed to a child, should be in such a clear and plain language that the child can easily understand.

(59) Modalities should be provided for facilitating the exercise of the data subject's rights under this Regulation, including mechanisms to request and, if applicable, obtain, free of charge, in particular, access to and rectification or erasure of personal data and the exercise of the right to object. The controller should also provide means for requests to be made electronically, especially where personal data are processed by electronic means. The controller should be obliged to respond to requests from the data subject without undue delay and at the latest within one month and to give reasons where the controller does not intend to comply with any such requests.

(60) The principles of fair and transparent processing require that the data subject be informed of the existence of the processing operation and its purposes. The controller should provide the data subject with any further information necessary to ensure fair and transparent processing taking into account the specific circumstances and context in which the personal data are processed. Furthermore, the data subject should be informed of the existence of profiling and the consequences of such profiling. Where the personal data are collected from the data subject, the data subject should also be informed whether he or she is obliged to provide the personal data and of the consequences, where he or she does not provide such data. That information may be provided in combination with standardised icons in order to give in an easily visible, intelligible

and clearly legible manner, a meaningful overview of the intended processing. Where the icons are presented electronically, they should be machine-readable.

(61) The information in relation to the processing of personal data relating to the data subject should be given to him or her at the time of collection from the data subject, or, where the personal data are obtained from another source, within a reasonable period, depending on the circumstances of the case. Where personal data can be legitimately disclosed to another recipient, the data subject should be informed when the personal data are first disclosed to the recipient. Where the controller intends to process the personal data for a purpose other than that for which they were collected, the controller should provide the data subject prior to that further processing with information on that other purpose and other necessary information. Where the origin of the personal data cannot be provided to the data subject because various sources have been used, general information should be provided.

(62) However, it is not necessary to impose the obligation to provide information where the data subject already possesses the information, where the recording or disclosure of the personal data is expressly laid down by law or where the provision of information to the data subject proves to be impossible or would involve a disproportionate effort. The latter could in particular be the case where processing is carried out for archiving purposes in the public interest, scientific or historical research purposes or statistical purposes. In that regard, the number of data subjects, the age of the data and any appropriate safeguards adopted should be taken into consideration.

(63) A data subject should have the right of access to personal data which have been collected concerning him or her, and to exercise that right easily and at reasonable intervals, in order to be aware of, and verify, the lawfulness of the processing. This includes the right for data subjects to have access to data concerning their health, for example the data in their medical records containing information such as diagnoses, examination results, assessments by treating physicians and any treatment or interventions provided. Every data subject should therefore have the right to know and obtain communication in particular with regard to the purposes for which the personal data are processed, where possible the period for which the personal data are processed, the recipients of the personal data, the logic involved in any automatic personal data processing and, at least when based on profiling, the consequences of such processing. Where possible, the controller should be able to provide remote access to a secure system which would provide the data subject with direct access to his or her personal data. That right should not adversely affect the rights or freedoms of others, including trade secrets or intellectual property and in particular the copyright protecting the software. However, the result of those considerations should not be a refusal to provide all information to the data subject. Where the controller processes a large quantity of information concerning the data subject, the controller should be able to request that, before the information is delivered, the data subject specify the information or processing activities to which the request relates.

(64) The controller should use all reasonable measures to verify the identity of a data subject who requests access, in particular in the context of online services and online identifiers. A controller should not retain personal data for the sole purpose of being able to react to potential requests.

(65) A data subject should have the right to have personal data concerning him or her rectified and a 'right to be forgotten' where the retention of such data infringes this Regulation or Union or Member State law to which the controller is subject. In particular, a data subject should have the right to have his or her personal data erased and

no longer processed where the personal data are no longer necessary in relation to the purposes for which they are collected or otherwise processed, where a data subject has withdrawn his or her consent or objects to the processing of personal data concerning him or her, or where the processing of his or her personal data does not otherwise comply with this Regulation. That right is relevant in particular where the data subject has given his or her consent as a child and is not fully aware of the risks involved by the processing, and later wants to remove such personal data, especially on the internet. The data subject should be able to exercise that right notwithstanding the fact that he or she is no longer a child. However, the further retention of the personal data should be lawful where it is necessary, for exercising the right of freedom of expression and information, for compliance with a legal obligation, for the performance of a task carried out in the public interest or in the exercise of official authority vested in the controller, on the grounds of public interest in the area of public health, for archiving purposes in the public interest, scientific or historical research purposes or statistical purposes, or for the establishment, exercise or defence of legal claims.

(66) To strengthen the right to be forgotten in the online environment, the right to erasure should also be extended in such a way that a controller who has made the personal data public should be obliged to inform the controllers which are processing such personal data to erase any links to, or copies or replications of those personal data. In doing so, that controller should take reasonable steps, taking into account available technology and the means available to the controller, including technical measures, to inform the controllers which are processing the personal data of the data subject's request.

(67) Methods by which to restrict the processing of personal data could include, inter alia, temporarily moving the selected data to another processing system, making the selected personal data unavailable to users, or temporarily removing published data from a website. In automated filing systems, the restriction of processing should in principle be ensured by technical means in such a manner that the personal data are not subject to further processing operations and cannot be changed. The fact that the processing of personal data is restricted should be clearly indicated in the system.

(68) To further strengthen the control over his or her own data, where the processing of personal data is carried out by automated means, the data subject should also be allowed to receive personal data concerning him or her which he or she has provided to a controller in a structured, commonly used, machine-readable and interoperable format, and to transmit it to another controller. Data controllers should be encouraged to develop interoperable formats that enable data portability. That right should apply where the data subject provided the personal data on the basis of his or her consent or the processing is necessary for the performance of a contract. It should not apply where processing is based on a legal ground other than consent or contract. By its very nature, that right should not be exercised against controllers processing personal data in the exercise of their public duties. It should therefore not apply where the processing of the personal data is necessary for compliance with a legal obligation to which the controller is subject or for the performance of a task carried out in the public interest or in the exercise of an official authority vested in the controller. The data subject's right to transmit or receive personal data concerning him or her should not create an obligation for the controllers to adopt or maintain processing systems which are technically compatible. Where, in a certain set of personal data, more than one data subject is concerned, the right to receive the personal data should be without prejudice to the rights and freedoms of other data subjects in accordance with this Regulation. Furthermore, that right should not prejudice the right of the data subject to obtain the erasure of personal data

and the limitations of that right as set out in this Regulation and should, in particular, not imply the erasure of personal data concerning the data subject which have been provided by him or her for the performance of a contract to the extent that and for as long as the personal data are necessary for the performance of that contract. Where technically feasible, the data subject should have the right to have the personal data transmitted directly from one controller to another.

(69) Where personal data might lawfully be processed because processing is necessary for the performance of a task carried out in the public interest or in the exercise of official authority vested in the controller, or on grounds of the legitimate interests of a controller or a third party, a data subject should, nevertheless, be entitled to object to the processing of any personal data relating to his or her particular situation. It should be for the controller to demonstrate that its compelling legitimate interest overrides the interests or the fundamental rights and freedoms of the data subject.

(70) Where personal data are processed for the purposes of direct marketing, the data subject should have the right to object to such processing, including profiling to the extent that it is related to such direct marketing, whether with regard to initial or further processing, at any time and free of charge. That right should be explicitly brought to the attention of the data subject and presented clearly and separately from any other information.

(71) The data subject should have the right not to be subject to a decision, which may include a measure, evaluating personal aspects relating to him or her which is based solely on automated processing and which produces legal effects concerning him or her or similarly significantly affects him or her, such as automatic refusal of an online credit application or e-recruiting practices without any human intervention. Such processing includes 'profiling' that consists of any form of automated processing of personal data evaluating the personal aspects relating to a natural person, in particular to analyse or predict aspects concerning the data subject's performance at work, economic situation, health, personal preferences or interests, reliability or behaviour, location or movements, where it produces legal effects concerning him or her or similarly significantly affects him or her. However, decision-making based on such processing, including profiling, should be allowed where expressly authorised by Union or Member State law to which the controller is subject, including for fraud and tax-evasion monitoring and prevention purposes conducted in accordance with the regulations, standards and recommendations of Union institutions or national oversight bodies and to ensure the security and reliability of a service provided by the controller, or necessary for the entering or performance of a contract between the data subject and a controller, or when the data subject has given his or her explicit consent. In any case, such processing should be subject to suitable safeguards, which should include specific information to the data subject and the right to obtain human intervention, to express his or her point of view, to obtain an explanation of the decision reached after such assessment and to challenge the decision. Such measure should not concern a child.

In order to ensure fair and transparent processing in respect of the data subject, taking into account the specific circumstances and context in which the personal data are processed, the controller should use appropriate mathematical or statistical procedures for the profiling, implement technical and organisational measures appropriate to ensure, in particular, that factors which result in inaccuracies in personal data are corrected and the risk of errors is minimised, secure personal data in a manner that takes account of the potential risks involved for the interests and rights of the data subject and that prevents, inter alia, discriminatory effects on natural persons on the basis of racial or ethnic origin, political opinion, religion or beliefs, trade union membership, genetic or health status or sexual orientation, or that result in measures having such an effect. Automated decision-making and profiling based on special categories of personal data should be allowed only under specific conditions.

(72) Profiling is subject to the rules of this Regulation governing the processing of personal data, such as the legal grounds for processing or data protection principles. The European Data Protection Board established by this Regulation (the 'Board') should be able to issue guidance in that context.

(73) Restrictions concerning specific principles and the rights of information, access to and rectification or erasure of personal data, the right to data portability, the right to object, decisions based on profiling, as well as the communication of a personal data breach to a data subject and certain related obligations of the controllers may be imposed by Union or Member State law, as far as necessary and proportionate in a democratic society to safeguard public security, including the protection of human life especially in response to natural or manmade disasters, the prevention, investigation and prosecution of criminal offences or the execution of criminal penalties, including the safeguarding against and the prevention of threats to public security, or of breaches of ethics for regulated professions, other important objectives of general public interest of the Union or of a Member State, in particular an important economic or financial interest of the Union or of a Member State, the keeping of public registers kept for reasons of general public interest, further processing of archived personal data to provide specific information related to the political behaviour under former totalitarian state regimes or the protection of the data subject or the rights and freedoms of others, including social protection, public health and humanitarian purposes. Those restrictions should be in accordance with the requirements set out in the Charter and in the European Convention for the Protection of Human Rights and Fundamental Freedoms.

(74) The responsibility and liability of the controller for any processing of personal data carried out by the controller or on the controller's behalf should be established. In particular, the controller should be obliged to implement appropriate and effective measures and be able to demonstrate the compliance of processing activities with this Regulation, including the effectiveness of the measures. Those measures should take into account the nature, scope, context and purposes of the processing and the risk to the rights and freedoms of natural persons.

(75) The risk to the rights and freedoms of natural persons, of varying likelihood and severity, may result from personal data processing which could lead to physical, material or non-material damage, in particular: where the processing may give rise to discrimination, identity theft or fraud, financial loss, damage to the reputation, loss of confidentiality of personal data protected by professional secrecy, unauthorised reversal of pseudonymisation, or any other significant economic or social disadvantage; where data subjects might be deprived of their rights and freedoms or prevented from exercising control over their personal data; where personal data are processed which reveal racial or ethnic origin, political opinions, religion or philosophical beliefs, trade union membership, and the processing of genetic data, data concerning health or data concerning sex life or criminal convictions and offences or related security measures; where personal aspects are evaluated, in particular analysing or predicting aspects concerning performance at work, economic situation, health, personal preferences or interests, reliability or behaviour, location or movements, in order to create or use personal profiles; where personal data of vulnerable natural persons, in particular of children, are

processed; or where processing involves a large amount of personal data and affects a large number of data subjects.

(76) The likelihood and severity of the risk to the rights and freedoms of the data subject should be determined by reference to the nature, scope, context and purposes of the processing. Risk should be evaluated on the basis of an objective assessment, by which it is established whether data processing operations involve a risk or a high risk.

(77) Guidance on the implementation of appropriate measures and on the demonstration of compliance by the controller or the processor, especially as regards the identification of the risk related to the processing, their assessment in terms of origin, nature, likelihood and severity, and the identification of best practices to mitigate the risk, could be provided in particular by means of approved codes of conduct, approved certifications, guidelines provided by the Board or indications provided by a data protection officer. The Board may also issue guidelines on processing operations that are considered to be unlikely to result in a high risk to the rights and freedoms of natural persons and indicate what measures may be sufficient in such cases to address such risk.

(78) The protection of the rights and freedoms of natural persons with regard to the processing of personal data require that appropriate technical and organisational measures be taken to ensure that the requirements of this Regulation are met. In order to be able to demonstrate compliance with this Regulation, the controller should adopt internal policies and implement measures which meet in particular the principles of data protection by design and data protection by default. Such measures could consist, inter alia, of minimising the processing of personal data, pseudonymising personal data as soon as possible, transparency with regard to the functions and processing of personal data, enabling the data subject to monitor the data processing, enabling the controller to create and improve security features. When developing, designing, selecting and using applications, services and products that are based on the processing of personal data or process personal data to fulfil their task, producers of the products, services and applications should be encouraged to take into account the right to data protection when developing and designing such products, services and applications and, with due regard to the state of the art, to make sure that controllers and processors are able to fulfil their data protection obligations. The principles of data protection by design and by default should also be taken into consideration in the context of public tenders.

(79) The protection of the rights and freedoms of data subjects as well as the responsibility and liability of controllers and processors, also in relation to the monitoring by and measures of supervisory authorities, requires a clear allocation of the responsibilities under this Regulation, including where a controller determines the purposes and means of the processing jointly with other controllers or where a processing operation is carried out on behalf of a controller.

(80) Where a controller or a processor not established in the Union is processing personal data of data subjects who are in the Union whose processing activities are related to the offering of goods or services, irrespective of whether a payment of the data subject is required, to such data subjects in the Union, or to the monitoring of their behaviour as far as their behaviour takes place within the Union, the controller or the processor should designate a representative, unless the processing is occasional, does not include processing, on a large scale, of special categories of personal data or the processing of personal data relating to criminal convictions and offences, and is unlikely to result in a risk to the rights and freedoms of natural persons, taking into account the nature, context, scope and purposes of the processing or if the controller is a public authority or body. The representative should act on behalf of the controller or the processor and

may be addressed by any supervisory authority. The representative should be explicitly designated by a written mandate of the controller or of the processor to act on its behalf with regard to its obligations under this Regulation. The designation of such a representative does not affect the responsibility or liability of the controller or of the processor under this Regulation. Such a representative should perform its tasks according to the mandate received from the controller or processor, including cooperating with the competent supervisory authorities with regard to any action taken to ensure compliance with this Regulation. The designated representative should be subject to enforcement proceedings in the event of non-compliance by the controller or processor.

(81) To ensure compliance with the requirements of this Regulation in respect of the processing to be carried out by the processor on behalf of the controller, when entrusting a processor with processing activities, the controller should use only processors providing sufficient guarantees, in particular in terms of expert knowledge, reliability and resources, to implement technical and organisational measures which will meet the requirements of this Regulation, including for the security of processing. The adherence of the processor to an approved code of conduct or an approved certification mechanism may be used as an element to demonstrate compliance with the obligations of the controller. The carrying-out of processing by a processor should be governed by a contract or other legal act under Union or Member State law, binding the processor to the controller, setting out the subject-matter and duration of the processing, the nature and purposes of the processing, the type of personal data and categories of data subjects, taking into account the specific tasks and responsibilities of the processor in the context of the processing to be carried out and the risk to the rights and freedoms of the data subject. The controller and processor may choose to use an individual contract or standard contractual clauses which are adopted either directly by the Commission or by a supervisory authority in accordance with the consistency mechanism and then adopted by the Commission. After the completion of the processing on behalf of the controller, the processor should, at the choice of the controller, return or delete the personal data, unless there is a requirement to store the personal data under Union or Member State law to which the processor is subject.

(82) In order to demonstrate compliance with this Regulation, the controller or processor should maintain records of processing activities under its responsibility. Each controller and processor should be obliged to cooperate with the supervisory authority and make those records, on request, available to it, so that it might serve for monitoring those processing operations.

(83) In order to maintain security and to prevent processing in infringement of this Regulation, the controller or processor should evaluate the risks inherent in the processing and implement measures to mitigate those risks, such as encryption. Those measures should ensure an appropriate level of security, including confidentiality, taking into account the state of the art and the costs of implementation in relation to the risks and the nature of the personal data to be protected. In assessing data security risk, consideration should be given to the risks that are presented by personal data processing, such as accidental or unlawful destruction, loss, alteration, unauthorised disclosure of, or access to, personal data transmitted, stored or otherwise processed which may in particular lead to physical, material or non-material damage.

(84) In order to enhance compliance with this Regulation where processing operations are likely to result in a high risk to the rights and freedoms of natural persons, the controller should be responsible for the carrying-out of a data protection impact assessment to evaluate, in particular, the origin, nature, particularity and severity of that risk.

The outcome of the assessment should be taken into account when determining the appropriate measures to be taken in order to demonstrate that the processing of personal data complies with this Regulation. Where a data-protection impact assessment indicates that processing operations involve a high risk which the controller cannot mitigate by appropriate measures in terms of available technology and costs of implementation, a consultation of the supervisory authority should take place prior to the processing.

(85) A personal data breach may, if not addressed in an appropriate and timely manner, result in physical, material or non-material damage to natural persons such as loss of control over their personal data or limitation of their rights, discrimination, identity theft or fraud, financial loss, unauthorised reversal of pseudonymisation, damage to reputation, loss of confidentiality of personal data protected by professional secrecy or any other significant economic or social disadvantage to the natural person concerned. Therefore, as soon as the controller becomes aware that a personal data breach has occurred, the controller should notify the personal data breach to the supervisory authority without undue delay and, where feasible, not later than 72 hours after having become aware of it, unless the controller is able to demonstrate, in accordance with the accountability principle, that the personal data breach is unlikely to result in a risk to the rights and freedoms of natural persons. Where such notification cannot be achieved within 72 hours, the reasons for the delay should accompany the notification and information may be provided in phases without undue further delay.

(86) The controller should communicate to the data subject a personal data breach, without undue delay, where that personal data breach is likely to result in a high risk to the rights and freedoms of the natural person in order to allow him or her to take the necessary precautions. The communication should describe the nature of the personal data breach as well as recommendations for the natural person concerned to mitigate potential adverse effects. Such communications to data subjects should be made as soon as reasonably feasible and in close cooperation with the supervisory authority, respecting guidance provided by it or by other relevant authorities such as law-enforcement authorities. For example, the need to mitigate an immediate risk of damage would call for prompt communication with data subjects whereas the need to implement appropriate measures against continuing or similar personal data breaches may justify more time for communication.

(87) It should be ascertained whether all appropriate technological protection and organisational measures have been implemented to establish immediately whether a personal data breach has taken place and to inform promptly the supervisory authority and the data subject. The fact that the notification was made without undue delay should be established taking into account in particular the nature and gravity of the personal data breach and its consequences and adverse effects for the data subject. Such notification may result in an intervention of the supervisory authority in accordance with its tasks and powers laid down in this Regulation.

(88) In setting detailed rules concerning the format and procedures applicable to the notification of personal data breaches, due consideration should be given to the circumstances of that breach, including whether or not personal data had been protected by appropriate technical protection measures, effectively limiting the likelihood of identity fraud or other forms of misuse. Moreover, such rules and procedures should take into account the legitimate interests of law-enforcement authorities where early disclosure could unnecessarily hamper the investigation of the circumstances of a personal data breach.

(89) Directive 95/46/EC provided for a general obligation to notify the processing of personal data to the supervisory authorities. While that obligation produces administrative and financial burdens, it did not in all cases contribute to improving the protection of personal data. Such indiscriminate general notification obligations should therefore be abolished, and replaced by effective procedures and mechanisms which focus instead on those types of processing operations which are likely to result in a high risk to the rights and freedoms of natural persons by virtue of their nature, scope, context and purposes. Such types of processing operations may be those which in, particular, involve using new technologies, or are of a new kind and where no data protection impact assessment has been carried out before by the controller, or where they become necessary in the light of the time that has elapsed since the initial processing.

(90) In such cases, a data protection impact assessment should be carried out by the controller prior to the processing in order to assess the particular likelihood and severity of the high risk, taking into account the nature, scope, context and purposes of the processing and the sources of the risk. That impact assessment should include, in particular, the measures, safeguards and mechanisms envisaged for mitigating that risk, ensuring the protection of personal data and demonstrating compliance with this Regulation.

(91) This should in particular apply to large-scale processing operations which aim to process a considerable amount of personal data at regional, national or supranational level and which could affect a large number of data subjects and which are likely to result in a high risk, for example, on account of their sensitivity, where in accordance with the achieved state of technological knowledge a new technology is used on a large scale as well as to other processing operations which result in a high risk to the rights and freedoms of data subjects, in particular where those operations render it more difficult for data subjects to exercise their rights. A data protection impact assessment should also be made where personal data are processed for taking decisions regarding specific natural persons following any systematic and extensive evaluation of personal aspects relating to natural persons based on profiling those data or following the processing of special categories of personal data, biometric data, or data on criminal convictions and offences or related security measures. A data protection impact assessment is equally required for monitoring publicly accessible areas on a large scale, especially when using optic-electronic devices or for any other operations where the competent supervisory authority considers that the processing is likely to result in a high risk to the rights and freedoms of data subjects, in particular because they prevent data subjects from exercising a right or using a service or a contract, or because they are carried out systematically on a large scale. The processing of personal data should not be considered to be on a large scale if the processing concerns personal data from patients or clients by an individual physician, other health care professional or lawyer. In such cases, a data protection impact assessment should not be mandatory.

(92) There are circumstances under which it may be reasonable and economical for the subject of a data protection impact assessment to be broader than a single project, for example where public authorities or bodies intend to establish a common application or processing platform or where several controllers plan to introduce a common application or processing environment across an industry sector or segment or for a widely used horizontal activity.

(93) In the context of the adoption of the Member State law on which the performance of the tasks of the public authority or public body is based and which regulates the specific processing operation or set of operations in question, Member States may deem it necessary to carry out such assessment prior to the processing activities.

(94) Where a data protection impact assessment indicates that the processing would, in the absence of safeguards, security measures and mechanisms to mitigate the risk, result in a high risk to the rights and freedoms of natural persons and the controller is of the opinion that the risk cannot be mitigated by reasonable means in terms of available technologies and costs of implementation, the supervisory authority should be consulted prior to the start of processing activities. Such high risk is likely to result from certain types of processing and the extent and frequency of processing, which may result also in a realisation of damage or interference with the rights and freedoms of the natural person. The supervisory authority should respond to the request for consultation within a specified period. However, the absence of a reaction of the supervisory authority within that period should be without prejudice to any intervention of the supervisory authority in accordance with its tasks and powers laid down in this Regulation, including the power to prohibit processing operations. As part of that consultation process, the outcome of a data protection impact assessment carried out with regard to the processing at issue may be submitted to the supervisory authority, in particular the measures envisaged to mitigate the risk to the rights and freedoms of natural persons.

(95) The processor should assist the controller, where necessary and upon request, in ensuring compliance with the obligations deriving from the carrying out of data protection impact assessments and from prior consultation of the supervisory authority.

(96) A consultation of the supervisory authority should also take place in the course of the preparation of a legislative or regulatory measure which provides for the processing of personal data, in order to ensure compliance of the intended processing with this Regulation and in particular to mitigate the risk involved for the data subject.

(97) Where the processing is carried out by a public authority, except for courts or independent judicial authorities when acting in their judicial capacity, where, in the private sector, processing is carried out by a controller whose core activities consist of processing operations that require regular and systematic monitoring of the data subjects on a large scale, or where the core activities of the controller or the processor consist of processing on a large scale of special categories of personal data and data relating to criminal convictions and offences, a person with expert knowledge of data protection law and practices should assist the controller or processor to monitor internal compliance with this Regulation. In the private sector, the core activities of a controller relate to its primary activities and do not relate to the processing of personal data as ancillary activities. The necessary level of expert knowledge should be determined in particular according to the data processing operations carried out and the protection required for the personal data processed by the controller or the processor. Such data protection officers, whether or not they are an employee of the controller, should be in a position to perform their duties and tasks in an independent manner.

(98) Associations or other bodies representing categories of controllers or processors should be encouraged to draw up codes of conduct, within the limits of this Regulation, so as to facilitate the effective application of this Regulation, taking account of the specific characteristics of the processing carried out in certain sectors and the specific needs of micro, small and medium enterprises. In particular, such codes of conduct could calibrate the obligations of controllers and processors, taking into account the risk likely to result from the processing for the rights and freedoms of natural persons.

(99) When drawing up a code of conduct, or when amending or extending such a code, associations and other bodies representing categories of controllers or processors should consult relevant stakeholders, including data subjects where feasible, and have regard to submissions received and views expressed in response to such consultations.

(100) In order to enhance transparency and compliance with this Regulation, the establishment of certification mechanisms and data protection seals and marks should be encouraged, allowing data subjects to quickly assess the level of data protection of relevant products and services.

(101) Flows of personal data to and from countries outside the Union and international organisations are necessary for the expansion of international trade and international cooperation. The increase in such flows has raised new challenges and concerns with regard to the protection of personal data. However, when personal data are transferred from the Union to controllers, processors or other recipients in third countries or to international organisations, the level of protection of natural persons ensured in the Union by this Regulation should not be undermined, including in cases of onward transfers of personal data from the third country or international organisation to controllers, processors in the same or another third country or international organisation. In any event, transfers to third countries and international organisations may only be carried out in full compliance with this Regulation. A transfer could take place only if, subject to the other provisions of this Regulation, the conditions laid down in the provisions of this Regulation relating to the transfer of personal data to third countries or international organisations are complied with by the controller or processor.

(102) This Regulation is without prejudice to international agreements concluded between the Union and third countries regulating the transfer of personal data including appropriate safeguards for the data subjects. Member States may conclude international agreements which involve the transfer of personal data to third countries or international organisations, as far as such agreements do not affect this Regulation or any other provisions of Union law and include an appropriate level of protection for the fundamental rights of the data subjects.

(103) The Commission may decide with effect for the entire Union that a third country, a territory or specified sector within a third country, or an international organisation, offers an adequate level of data protection, thus providing legal certainty and uniformity throughout the Union as regards the third country or international organisation which is considered to provide such level of protection. In such cases, transfers of personal data to that third country or international organisation may take place without the need to obtain any further authorisation. The Commission may also decide, having given notice and a full statement setting out the reasons to the third country or international organisation, to revoke such a decision.

(104) In line with the fundamental values on which the Union is founded, in particular the protection of human rights, the Commission should, in its assessment of the third country, or of a territory or specified sector within a third country, take into account how a particular third country respects the rule of law, access to justice as well as international human rights norms and standards and its general and sectoral law, including legislation concerning public security, defence and national security as well as public order and criminal law. The adoption of an adequacy decision with regard to a territory or a specified sector in a third country should take into account clear and objective criteria, such as specific processing activities and the scope of applicable legal standards and legislation in force in the third country. The third country should offer guarantees ensuring an adequate level of protection essentially equivalent to that ensured within the Union, in particular where personal data are processed in one or several specific sectors. In particular, the third country should ensure effective independent data protection supervision and should provide for cooperation mechanisms with the Member States' data protection authorities, and the data subjects should be

provided with effective and enforceable rights and effective administrative and judicial redress.

(105) Apart from the international commitments the third country or international organisation has entered into, the Commission should take account of obligations arising from the third country's or international organisation's participation in multilateral or regional systems in particular in relation to the protection of personal data, as well as the implementation of such obligations. In particular, the third country's accession to the Council of Europe Convention of 28 January 1981 for the Protection of Individuals with regard to the Automatic Processing of Personal Data and its Additional Protocol should be taken into account. The Commission should consult the Board when assessing the level of protection in third countries or international organisations.

(106) The Commission should monitor the functioning of decisions on the level of protection in a third country, a territory or specified sector within a third country, or an international organisation, and monitor the functioning of decisions adopted on the basis of Article 25(6) or Article 26(4) of Directive 95/46/EC. In its adequacy decisions, the Commission should provide for a periodic review mechanism of their functioning. That periodic review should be conducted in consultation with the third country or international organisation in question and take into account all relevant developments in the third country or international organisation. For the purposes of monitoring and of carrying out the periodic reviews, the Commission should take into consideration the views and findings of the European Parliament and of the Council as well as of other relevant bodies and sources. The Commission should evaluate, within a reasonable time, the functioning of the latter decisions and report any relevant findings to the Committee within the meaning of Regulation (EU) No 182/2011 of the European Parliament and of the Council [12] as established under this Regulation, to the European Parliament and to the Council.

(107) The Commission may recognise that a third country, a territory or a specified sector within a third country, or an international organisation no longer ensures an adequate level of data protection. Consequently the transfer of personal data to that third country or international organisation should be prohibited, unless the requirements in this Regulation relating to transfers subject to appropriate safeguards, including binding corporate rules, and derogations for specific situations are fulfilled. In that case, provision should be made for consultations between the Commission and such third countries or international organisations. The Commission should, in a timely manner, inform the third country or international organisation of the reasons and enter into consultations with it in order to remedy the situation.

(108) In the absence of an adequacy decision, the controller or processor should take measures to compensate for the lack of data protection in a third country by way of appropriate safeguards for the data subject. Such appropriate safeguards may consist of making use of binding corporate rules, standard data protection clauses adopted by the Commission, standard data protection clauses adopted by a supervisory authority or contractual clauses authorised by a supervisory authority. Those safeguards should ensure compliance with data protection requirements and the rights of the

---

[12] Regulation (EU) No 182/2011 of the European Parliament and of the Council of 16 February 2011 laying down the rules and general principles concerning mechanisms for control by Member States of the Commission's exercise of implementing powers (OJ L 55, 28.2.2011, p. 13).

data subjects appropriate to processing within the Union, including the availability of enforceable data subject rights and of effective legal remedies, including to obtain effective administrative or judicial redress and to claim compensation, in the Union or in a third country. They should relate in particular to compliance with the general principles relating to personal data processing, the principles of data protection by design and by default. Transfers may also be carried out by public authorities or bodies with public authorities or bodies in third countries or with international organisations with corresponding duties or functions, including on the basis of provisions to be inserted into administrative arrangements, such as a memorandum of understanding, providing for enforceable and effective rights for data subjects. Authorisation by the competent supervisory authority should be obtained when the safeguards are provided for in administrative arrangements that are not legally binding.

(109) The possibility for the controller or processor to use standard data-protection clauses adopted by the Commission or by a supervisory authority should prevent controllers or processors neither from including the standard data-protection clauses in a wider contract, such as a contract between the processor and another processor, nor from adding other clauses or additional safeguards provided that they do not contradict, directly or indirectly, the standard contractual clauses adopted by the Commission or by a supervisory authority or prejudice the fundamental rights or freedoms of the data subjects. Controllers and processors should be encouraged to provide additional safeguards via contractual commitments that supplement standard protection clauses.

(110) A group of undertakings, or a group of enterprises engaged in a joint economic activity, should be able to make use of approved binding corporate rules for its international transfers from the Union to organisations within the same group of undertakings, or group of enterprises engaged in a joint economic activity, provided that such corporate rules include all essential principles and enforceable rights to ensure appropriate safeguards for transfers or categories of transfers of personal data.

(111) Provisions should be made for the possibility for transfers in certain circumstances where the data subject has given his or her explicit consent, where the transfer is occasional and necessary in relation to a contract or a legal claim, regardless of whether in a judicial procedure or whether in an administrative or any out-of-court procedure, including procedures before regulatory bodies. Provision should also be made for the possibility for transfers where important grounds of public interest laid down by Union or Member State law so require or where the transfer is made from a register established by law and intended for consultation by the public or persons having a legitimate interest. In the latter case, such a transfer should not involve the entirety of the personal data or entire categories of the data contained in the register and, when the register is intended for consultation by persons having a legitimate interest, the transfer should be made only at the request of those persons or, if they are to be the recipients, taking into full account the interests and fundamental rights of the data subject.

(112) Those derogations should in particular apply to data transfers required and necessary for important reasons of public interest, for example in cases of international data exchange between competition authorities, tax or customs administrations, between financial supervisory authorities, between services competent for social security matters, or for public health, for example in the case of contact tracing for contagious diseases or in order to reduce and/or eliminate doping in sport. A transfer of personal data should also be regarded as lawful where it is necessary to protect an interest which is essential for the data subject's or another person's vital interests, including physical integrity or life, if the data subject is incapable of giving consent. In the absence of an

adequacy decision, Union or Member State law may, for important reasons of public interest, expressly set limits to the transfer of specific categories of data to a third country or an international organisation. Member States should notify such provisions to the Commission. Any transfer to an international humanitarian organisation of personal data of a data subject who is physically or legally incapable of giving consent, with a view to accomplishing a task incumbent under the Geneva Conventions or to complying with international humanitarian law applicable in armed conflicts, could be considered to be necessary for an important reason of public interest or because it is in the vital interest of the data subject.

(113) Transfers which can be qualified as not repetitive and that only concern a limited number of data subjects, could also be possible for the purposes of the compelling legitimate interests pursued by the controller, when those interests are not overridden by the interests or rights and freedoms of the data subject and when the controller has assessed all the circumstances surrounding the data transfer. The controller should give particular consideration to the nature of the personal data, the purpose and duration of the proposed processing operation or operations, as well as the situation in the country of origin, the third country and the country of final destination, and should provide suitable safeguards to protect fundamental rights and freedoms of natural persons with regard to the processing of their personal data. Such transfers should be possible only in residual cases where none of the other grounds for transfer are applicable. For scientific or historical research purposes or statistical purposes, the legitimate expectations of society for an increase of knowledge should be taken into consideration. The controller should inform the supervisory authority and the data subject about the transfer.

(114) In any case, where the Commission has taken no decision on the adequate level of data protection in a third country, the controller or processor should make use of solutions that provide data subjects with enforceable and effective rights as regards the processing of their data in the Union once those data have been transferred so that that they will continue to benefit from fundamental rights and safeguards.

(115) Some third countries adopt laws, regulations and other legal acts which purport to directly regulate the processing activities of natural and legal persons under the jurisdiction of the Member States. This may include judgments of courts or tribunals or decisions of administrative authorities in third countries requiring a controller or processor to transfer or disclose personal data, and which are not based on an international agreement, such as a mutual legal assistance treaty, in force between the requesting third country and the Union or a Member State. The extraterritorial application of those laws, regulations and other legal acts may be in breach of international law and may impede the attainment of the protection of natural persons ensured in the Union by this Regulation. Transfers should only be allowed where the conditions of this Regulation for a transfer to third countries are met. This may be the case, inter alia, where disclosure is necessary for an important ground of public interest recognised in Union or Member State law to which the controller is subject.

(116) When personal data moves across borders outside the Union it may put at increased risk the ability of natural persons to exercise data protection rights in particular to protect themselves from the unlawful use or disclosure of that information. At the same time, supervisory authorities may find that they are unable to pursue complaints or conduct investigations relating to the activities outside their borders. Their efforts to work together in the cross-border context may also be hampered by insufficient preventative or remedial powers, inconsistent legal regimes, and practical obstacles

like resource constraints. Therefore, there is a need to promote closer cooperation among data protection supervisory authorities to help them exchange information and carry out investigations with their international counterparts. For the purposes of developing international cooperation mechanisms to facilitate and provide international mutual assistance for the enforcement of legislation for the protection of personal data, the Commission and the supervisory authorities should exchange information and cooperate in activities related to the exercise of their powers with competent authorities in third countries, based on reciprocity and in accordance with this Regulation.

(117) The establishment of supervisory authorities in Member States, empowered to perform their tasks and exercise their powers with complete independence, is an essential component of the protection of natural persons with regard to the processing of their personal data. Member States should be able to establish more than one supervisory authority, to reflect their constitutional, organisational and administrative structure.

(118) The independence of supervisory authorities should not mean that the supervisory authorities cannot be subject to control or monitoring mechanisms regarding their financial expenditure or to judicial review.

(119) Where a Member State establishes several supervisory authorities, it should establish by law mechanisms for ensuring the effective participation of those supervisory authorities in the consistency mechanism. That Member State should in particular designate the supervisory authority which functions as a single contact point for the effective participation of those authorities in the mechanism, to ensure swift and smooth cooperation with other supervisory authorities, the Board and the Commission.

(120) Each supervisory authority should be provided with the financial and human resources, premises and infrastructure necessary for the effective performance of their tasks, including those related to mutual assistance and cooperation with other supervisory authorities throughout the Union. Each supervisory authority should have a separate, public annual budget, which may be part of the overall state or national budget.

(121) The general conditions for the member or members of the supervisory authority should be laid down by law in each Member State and should in particular provide that those members are to be appointed, by means of a transparent procedure, either by the parliament, government or the head of State of the Member State on the basis of a proposal from the government, a member of the government, the parliament or a chamber of the parliament, or by an independent body entrusted under Member State law. In order to ensure the independence of the supervisory authority, the member or members should act with integrity, refrain from any action that is incompatible with their duties and should not, during their term of office, engage in any incompatible occupation, whether gainful or not. The supervisory authority should have its own staff, chosen by the supervisory authority or an independent body established by Member State law, which should be subject to the exclusive direction of the member or members of the supervisory authority.

(122) Each supervisory authority should be competent on the territory of its own Member State to exercise the powers and to perform the tasks conferred on it in accordance with this Regulation. This should cover in particular the processing in the context of the activities of an establishment of the controller or processor on the territory of its own Member State, the processing of personal data carried out by public authorities or private bodies acting in the public interest, processing affecting data subjects on its territory or processing carried out by a controller or processor not established in the

Union when targeting data subjects residing on its territory. This should include handling complaints lodged by a data subject, conducting investigations on the application of this Regulation and promoting public awareness of the risks, rules, safeguards and rights in relation to the processing of personal data.

(123) The supervisory authorities should monitor the application of the provisions pursuant to this Regulation and contribute to its consistent application throughout the Union, in order to protect natural persons in relation to the processing of their personal data and to facilitate the free flow of personal data within the internal market. For that purpose, the supervisory authorities should cooperate with each other and with the Commission, without the need for any agreement between Member States on the provision of mutual assistance or on such cooperation.

(124) Where the processing of personal data takes place in the context of the activities of an establishment of a controller or a processor in the Union and the controller or processor is established in more than one Member State, or where processing taking place in the context of the activities of a single establishment of a controller or processor in the Union substantially affects or is likely to substantially affect data subjects in more than one Member State, the supervisory authority for the main establishment of the controller or processor or for the single establishment of the controller or processor should act as lead authority. It should cooperate with the other authorities concerned, because the controller or processor has an establishment on the territory of their Member State, because data subjects residing on their territory are substantially affected, or because a complaint has been lodged with them. Also where a data subject not residing in that Member State has lodged a complaint, the supervisory authority with which such complaint has been lodged should also be a supervisory authority concerned. Within its tasks to issue guidelines on any question covering the application of this Regulation, the Board should be able to issue guidelines in particular on the criteria to be taken into account in order to ascertain whether the processing in question substantially affects data subjects in more than one Member State and on what constitutes a relevant and reasoned objection.

(125) The lead authority should be competent to adopt binding decisions regarding measures applying the powers conferred on it in accordance with this Regulation. In its capacity as lead authority, the supervisory authority should closely involve and coordinate the supervisory authorities concerned in the decision-making process. Where the decision is to reject the complaint by the data subject in whole or in part, that decision should be adopted by the supervisory authority with which the complaint has been lodged.

(126) The decision should be agreed jointly by the lead supervisory authority and the supervisory authorities concerned and should be directed towards the main or single establishment of the controller or processor and be binding on the controller and processor. The controller or processor should take the necessary measures to ensure compliance with this Regulation and the implementation of the decision notified by the lead supervisory authority to the main establishment of the controller or processor as regards the processing activities in the Union.

(127) Each supervisory authority not acting as the lead supervisory authority should be competent to handle local cases where the controller or processor is established in more than one Member State, but the subject matter of the specific processing concerns only processing carried out in a single Member State and involves only data subjects in that single Member State, for example, where the subject matter concerns the processing of employees' personal data in the specific employment context of a Member

State. In such cases, the supervisory authority should inform the lead supervisory authority without delay about the matter. After being informed, the lead supervisory authority should decide, whether it will handle the case pursuant to the provision on cooperation between the lead supervisory authority and other supervisory authorities concerned ('one-stop-shop mechanism'), or whether the supervisory authority which informed it should handle the case at local level. When deciding whether it will handle the case, the lead supervisory authority should take into account whether there is an establishment of the controller or processor in the Member State of the supervisory authority which informed it in order to ensure effective enforcement of a decision vis-à-vis the controller or processor. Where the lead supervisory authority decides to handle the case, the supervisory authority which informed it should have the possibility to submit a draft for a decision, of which the lead supervisory authority should take utmost account when preparing its draft decision in that one-stop-shop mechanism.

(128) The rules on the lead supervisory authority and the one-stop-shop mechanism should not apply where the processing is carried out by public authorities or private bodies in the public interest. In such cases the only supervisory authority competent to exercise the powers conferred to it in accordance with this Regulation should be the supervisory authority of the Member State where the public authority or private body is established.

(129) In order to ensure consistent monitoring and enforcement of this Regulation throughout the Union, the supervisory authorities should have in each Member State the same tasks and effective powers, including powers of investigation, corrective powers and sanctions, and authorisation and advisory powers, in particular in cases of complaints from natural persons, and without prejudice to the powers of prosecutorial authorities under Member State law, to bring infringements of this Regulation to the attention of the judicial authorities and engage in legal proceedings. Such powers should also include the power to impose a temporary or definitive limitation, including a ban, on processing. Member States may specify other tasks related to the protection of personal data under this Regulation. The powers of supervisory authorities should be exercised in accordance with appropriate procedural safeguards set out in Union and Member State law, impartially, fairly and within a reasonable time. In particular each measure should be appropriate, necessary and proportionate in view of ensuring compliance with this Regulation, taking into account the circumstances of each individual case, respect the right of every person to be heard before any individual measure which would affect him or her adversely is taken and avoid superfluous costs and excessive inconveniences for the persons concerned. Investigatory powers as regards access to premises should be exercised in accordance with specific requirements in Member State procedural law, such as the requirement to obtain a prior judicial authorisation. Each legally binding measure of the supervisory authority should be in writing, be clear and unambiguous, indicate the supervisory authority which has issued the measure, the date of issue of the measure, bear the signature of the head, or a member of the supervisory authority authorised by him or her, give the reasons for the measure, and refer to the right of an effective remedy. This should not preclude additional requirements pursuant to Member State procedural law. The adoption of a legally binding decision implies that it may give rise to judicial review in the Member State of the supervisory authority that adopted the decision.

(130) Where the supervisory authority with which the complaint has been lodged is not the lead supervisory authority, the lead supervisory authority should closely cooperate with the supervisory authority with which the complaint has been lodged in

accordance with the provisions on cooperation and consistency laid down in this Regulation. In such cases, the lead supervisory authority should, when taking measures intended to produce legal effects, including the imposition of administrative fines, take utmost account of the view of the supervisory authority with which the complaint has been lodged and which should remain competent to carry out any investigation on the territory of its own Member State in liaison with the competent supervisory authority.

(131) Where another supervisory authority should act as a lead supervisory authority for the processing activities of the controller or processor but the concrete subject matter of a complaint or the possible infringement concerns only processing activities of the controller or processor in the Member State where the complaint has been lodged or the possible infringement detected and the matter does not substantially affect or is not likely to substantially affect data subjects in other Member States, the supervisory authority receiving a complaint or detecting or being informed otherwise of situations that entail possible infringements of this Regulation should seek an amicable settlement with the controller and, if this proves unsuccessful, exercise its full range of powers. This should include: specific processing carried out in the territory of the Member State of the supervisory authority or with regard to data subjects on the territory of that Member State; processing that is carried out in the context of an offer of goods or services specifically aimed at data subjects in the territory of the Member State of the supervisory authority; or processing that has to be assessed taking into account relevant legal obligations under Member State law.

(132) Awareness-raising activities by supervisory authorities addressed to the public should include specific measures directed at controllers and processors, including micro, small and medium-sized enterprises, as well as natural persons in particular in the educational context.

(133) The supervisory authorities should assist each other in performing their tasks and provide mutual assistance, so as to ensure the consistent application and enforcement of this Regulation in the internal market. A supervisory authority requesting mutual assistance may adopt a provisional measure if it receives no response to a request for mutual assistance within one month of the receipt of that request by the other supervisory authority.

(134) Each supervisory authority should, where appropriate, participate in joint operations with other supervisory authorities. The requested supervisory authority should be obliged to respond to the request within a specified time period.

(135) In order to ensure the consistent application of this Regulation throughout the Union, a consistency mechanism for cooperation between the supervisory authorities should be established. That mechanism should in particular apply where a supervisory authority intends to adopt a measure intended to produce legal effects as regards processing operations which substantially affect a significant number of data subjects in several Member States. It should also apply where any supervisory authority concerned or the Commission requests that such matter should be handled in the consistency mechanism. That mechanism should be without prejudice to any measures that the Commission may take in the exercise of its powers under the Treaties.

(136) In applying the consistency mechanism, the Board should, within a determined period of time, issue an opinion, if a majority of its members so decides or if so requested by any supervisory authority concerned or the Commission. The Board should also be empowered to adopt legally binding decisions where there are disputes between supervisory authorities. For that purpose, it should issue, in principle by

a two-thirds majority of its members, legally binding decisions in clearly specified cases where there are conflicting views among supervisory authorities, in particular in the cooperation mechanism between the lead supervisory authority and supervisory authorities concerned on the merits of the case, in particular whether there is an infringement of this Regulation.

(137) There may be an urgent need to act in order to protect the rights and freedoms of data subjects, in particular when the danger exists that the enforcement of a right of a data subject could be considerably impeded. A supervisory authority should therefore be able to adopt duly justified provisional measures on its territory with a specified period of validity which should not exceed three months.

(138) The application of such mechanism should be a condition for the lawfulness of a measure intended to produce legal effects by a supervisory authority in those cases where its application is mandatory. In other cases of cross-border relevance, the cooperation mechanism between the lead supervisory authority and supervisory authorities concerned should be applied and mutual assistance and joint operations might be carried out between the supervisory authorities concerned on a bilateral or multilateral basis without triggering the consistency mechanism.

(139) In order to promote the consistent application of this Regulation, the Board should be set up as an independent body of the Union. To fulfil its objectives, the Board should have legal personality. The Board should be represented by its Chair. It should replace the Working Party on the Protection of Individuals with Regard to the Processing of Personal Data established by Directive 95/46/EC. It should consist of the head of a supervisory authority of each Member State and the European Data Protection Supervisor or their respective representatives. The Commission should participate in the Board's activities without voting rights and the European Data Protection Supervisor should have specific voting rights. The Board should contribute to the consistent application of this Regulation throughout the Union, including by advising the Commission, in particular on the level of protection in third countries or international organisations, and promoting cooperation of the supervisory authorities throughout the Union. The Board should act independently when performing its tasks.

(140) The Board should be assisted by a secretariat provided by the European Data Protection Supervisor. The staff of the European Data Protection Supervisor involved in carrying out the tasks conferred on the Board by this Regulation should perform its tasks exclusively under the instructions of, and report to, the Chair of the Board.

(141) Every data subject should have the right to lodge a complaint with a single supervisory authority, in particular in the Member State of his or her habitual residence, and the right to an effective judicial remedy in accordance with Article 47 of the Charter if the data subject considers that his or her rights under this Regulation are infringed or where the supervisory authority does not act on a complaint, partially or wholly rejects or dismisses a complaint or does not act where such action is necessary to protect the rights of the data subject. The investigation following a complaint should be carried out, subject to judicial review, to the extent that is appropriate in the specific case. The supervisory authority should inform the data subject of the progress and the outcome of the complaint within a reasonable period. If the case requires further investigation or coordination with another supervisory authority, intermediate information should be given to the data subject. In order to facilitate the submission of complaints, each supervisory authority should take measures such as providing a complaint submission form which can also be completed electronically, without excluding other means of communication.

(142) Where a data subject considers that his or her rights under this Regulation are infringed, he or she should have the right to mandate a not-for-profit body, organisation or association which is constituted in accordance with the law of a Member State, has statutory objectives which are in the public interest and is active in the field of the protection of personal data to lodge a complaint on his or her behalf with a supervisory authority, exercise the right to a judicial remedy on behalf of data subjects or, if provided for in Member State law, exercise the right to receive compensation on behalf of data subjects. A Member State may provide for such a body, organisation or association to have the right to lodge a complaint in that Member State, independently of a data subject's mandate, and the right to an effective judicial remedy where it has reasons to consider that the rights of a data subject have been infringed as a result of the processing of personal data which infringes this Regulation. That body, organisation or association may not be allowed to claim compensation on a data subject's behalf independently of the data subject's mandate.

(143) Any natural or legal person has the right to bring an action for annulment of decisions of the Board before the Court of Justice under the conditions provided for in Article 263 TFEU. As addressees of such decisions, the supervisory authorities concerned which wish to challenge them have to bring action within two months of being notified of them, in accordance with Article 263 TFEU. Where decisions of the Board are of direct and individual concern to a controller, processor or complainant, the latter may bring an action for annulment against those decisions within two months of their publication on the website of the Board, in accordance with Article 263 TFEU. Without prejudice to this right under Article 263 TFEU, each natural or legal person should have an effective judicial remedy before the competent national court against a decision of a supervisory authority which produces legal effects concerning that person. Such a decision concerns in particular the exercise of investigative, corrective and authorisation powers by the supervisory authority or the dismissal or rejection of complaints. However, the right to an effective judicial remedy does not encompass measures taken by supervisory authorities which are not legally binding, such as opinions issued by or advice provided by the supervisory authority. Proceedings against a supervisory authority should be brought before the courts of the Member State where the supervisory authority is established and should be conducted in accordance with that Member State's procedural law. Those courts should exercise full jurisdiction, which should include jurisdiction to examine all questions of fact and law relevant to the dispute before them.

Where a complaint has been rejected or dismissed by a supervisory authority, the complainant may bring proceedings before the courts in the same Member State. In the context of judicial remedies relating to the application of this Regulation, national courts which consider a decision on the question necessary to enable them to give judgment, may, or in the case provided for in Article 267 TFEU, must, request the Court of Justice to give a preliminary ruling on the interpretation of Union law, including this Regulation. Furthermore, where a decision of a supervisory authority implementing a decision of the Board is challenged before a national court and the validity of the decision of the Board is at issue, that national court does not have the power to declare the Board's decision invalid but must refer the question of validity to the Court of Justice in accordance with Article 267 TFEU as interpreted by the Court of Justice, where it considers the decision invalid. However, a national court may not refer a question on the validity of the decision of the Board at the request of a natural or legal person which had the opportunity to bring an action for annulment of that decision, in particular if it was directly and individually concerned by that decision, but had not done so within the period laid down in Article 263 TFEU.

(144) Where a court seized of proceedings against a decision by a supervisory authority has reason to believe that proceedings concerning the same processing, such as the same subject matter as regards processing by the same controller or processor, or the same cause of action, are brought before a competent court in another Member State, it should contact that court in order to confirm the existence of such related proceedings. If related proceedings are pending before a court in another Member State, any court other than the court first seized may stay its proceedings or may, on request of one of the parties, decline jurisdiction in favour of the court first seized if that court has jurisdiction over the proceedings in question and its law permits the consolidation of such related proceedings. Proceedings are deemed to be related where they are so closely connected that it is expedient to hear and determine them together in order to avoid the risk of irreconcilable judgments resulting from separate proceedings.

(145) For proceedings against a controller or processor, the plaintiff should have the choice to bring the action before the courts of the Member States where the controller or processor has an establishment or where the data subject resides, unless the controller is a public authority of a Member State acting in the exercise of its public powers.

(146) The controller or processor should compensate any damage which a person may suffer as a result of processing that infringes this Regulation. The controller or processor should be exempt from liability if it proves that it is not in any way responsible for the damage. The concept of damage should be broadly interpreted in the light of the case-law of the Court of Justice in a manner which fully reflects the objectives of this Regulation. This is without prejudice to any claims for damage deriving from the violation of other rules in Union or Member State law. Processing that infringes this Regulation also includes processing that infringes delegated and implementing acts adopted in accordance with this Regulation and Member State law specifying rules of this Regulation. Data subjects should receive full and effective compensation for the damage they have suffered. Where controllers or processors are involved in the same processing, each controller or processor should be held liable for the entire damage. However, where they are joined to the same judicial proceedings, in accordance with Member State law, compensation may be apportioned according to the responsibility of each controller or processor for the damage caused by the processing, provided that full and effective compensation of the data subject who suffered the damage is ensured. Any controller or processor which has paid full compensation may subsequently institute recourse proceedings against other controllers or processors involved in the same processing.

(147) Where specific rules on jurisdiction are contained in this Regulation, in particular as regards proceedings seeking a judicial remedy including compensation, against a controller or processor, general jurisdiction rules such as those of Regulation (EU) No 1215/2012 of the European Parliament and of the Council [13] should not prejudice the application of such specific rules.

(148) In order to strengthen the enforcement of the rules of this Regulation, penalties including administrative fines should be imposed for any infringement of this Regulation, in addition to, or instead of appropriate measures imposed by the supervisory authority

[13] Regulation (EU) No 1215/2012 of the European Parliament and of the Council of 12 December 2012 on jurisdiction and the recognition and enforcement of judgments in civil and commercial matters (OJ L 351, 20.12.2012, p. 1).

pursuant to this Regulation. In a case of a minor infringement or if the fine likely to be imposed would constitute a disproportionate burden to a natural person, a reprimand may be issued instead of a fine. Due regard should however be given to the nature, gravity and duration of the infringement, the intentional character of the infringement, actions taken to mitigate the damage suffered, degree of responsibility or any relevant previous infringements, the manner in which the infringement became known to the supervisory authority, compliance with measures ordered against the controller or processor, adherence to a code of conduct and any other aggravating or mitigating factor. The imposition of penalties including administrative fines should be subject to appropriate procedural safeguards in accordance with the general principles of Union law and the Charter, including effective judicial protection and due process.

(149) Member States should be able to lay down the rules on criminal penalties for infringements of this Regulation, including for infringements of national rules adopted pursuant to and within the limits of this Regulation. Those criminal penalties may also allow for the deprivation of the profits obtained through infringements of this Regulation. However, the imposition of criminal penalties for infringements of such national rules and of administrative penalties should not lead to a breach of the principle of ne bis in idem, as interpreted by the Court of Justice.

(150) In order to strengthen and harmonise administrative penalties for infringements of this Regulation, each supervisory authority should have the power to impose administrative fines. This Regulation should indicate infringements and the upper limit and criteria for setting the related administrative fines, which should be determined by the competent supervisory authority in each individual case, taking into account all relevant circumstances of the specific situation, with due regard in particular to the nature, gravity and duration of the infringement and of its consequences and the measures taken to ensure compliance with the obligations under this Regulation and to prevent or mitigate the consequences of the infringement. Where administrative fines are imposed on an undertaking, an undertaking should be understood to be an undertaking in accordance with Articles 101 and 102 TFEU for those purposes. Where administrative fines are imposed on persons that are not an undertaking, the supervisory authority should take account of the general level of income in the Member State as well as the economic situation of the person in considering the appropriate amount of the fine. The consistency mechanism may also be used to promote a consistent application of administrative fines. It should be for the Member States to determine whether and to which extent public authorities should be subject to administrative fines. Imposing an administrative fine or giving a warning does not affect the application of other powers of the supervisory authorities or of other penalties under this Regulation.

(151) The legal systems of Denmark and Estonia do not allow for administrative fines as set out in this Regulation. The rules on administrative fines may be applied in such a manner that in Denmark the fine is imposed by competent national courts as a criminal penalty and in Estonia the fine is imposed by the supervisory authority in the framework of a misdemeanour procedure, provided that such an application of the rules in those Member States has an equivalent effect to administrative fines imposed by supervisory authorities. Therefore the competent national courts should take into account the recommendation by the supervisory authority initiating the fine. In any event, the fines imposed should be effective, proportionate and dissuasive.

(152) Where this Regulation does not harmonise administrative penalties or where necessary in other cases, for example in cases of serious infringements of this Regulation,

Member States should implement a system which provides for effective, proportionate and dissuasive penalties. The nature of such penalties, criminal or administrative, should be determined by Member State law.

(153) Member States law should reconcile the rules governing freedom of expression and information, including journalistic, academic, artistic and or literary expression with the right to the protection of personal data pursuant to this Regulation. The processing of personal data solely for journalistic purposes, or for the purposes of academic, artistic or literary expression should be subject to derogations or exemptions from certain provisions of this Regulation if necessary to reconcile the right to the protection of personal data with the right to freedom of expression and information, as enshrined in Article 11 of the Charter. This should apply in particular to the processing of personal data in the audiovisual field and in news archives and press libraries. Therefore, Member States should adopt legislative measures which lay down the exemptions and derogations necessary for the purpose of balancing those fundamental rights. Member States should adopt such exemptions and derogations on general principles, the rights of the data subject, the controller and the processor, the transfer of personal data to third countries or international organisations, the independent supervisory authorities, cooperation and consistency, and specific data-processing situations. Where such exemptions or derogations differ from one Member State to another, the law of the Member State to which the controller is subject should apply. In order to take account of the importance of the right to freedom of expression in every democratic society, it is necessary to interpret notions relating to that freedom, such as journalism, broadly.

(154) This Regulation allows the principle of public access to official documents to be taken into account when applying this Regulation. Public access to official documents may be considered to be in the public interest. Personal data in documents held by a public authority or a public body should be able to be publicly disclosed by that authority or body if the disclosure is provided for by Union or Member State law to which the public authority or public body is subject. Such laws should reconcile public access to official documents and the reuse of public sector information with the right to the protection of personal data and may therefore provide for the necessary reconciliation with the right to the protection of personal data pursuant to this Regulation. The reference to public authorities and bodies should in that context include all authorities or other bodies covered by Member State law on public access to documents. Directive 2003/98/EC of the European Parliament and of the Council [14] leaves intact and in no way affects the level of protection of natural persons with regard to the processing of personal data under the provisions of Union and Member State law, and in particular does not alter the obligations and rights set out in this Regulation. In particular, that Directive should not apply to documents to which access is excluded or restricted by virtue of the access regimes on the grounds of protection of personal data, and parts of documents accessible by virtue of those regimes which contain personal data the re-use of which has been provided for by law as being incompatible with the law concerning the protection of natural persons with regard to the processing of personal data.

(155) Member State law or collective agreements, including 'works agreements', may provide for specific rules on the processing of employees' personal data in the employment context, in particular for the conditions under which personal data in the employment context may be processed on the basis of the consent of the employee,

---

[14] Directive 2003/98/EC of the European Parliament and of the Council of 17 November 2003 on the re-use of public sector information (OJ L 345, 31.12.2003, p. 90).

the purposes of the recruitment, the performance of the contract of employment, including discharge of obligations laid down by law or by collective agreements, management, planning and organisation of work, equality and diversity in the workplace, health and safety at work, and for the purposes of the exercise and enjoyment, on an individual or collective basis, of rights and benefits related to employment, and for the purpose of the termination of the employment relationship.

(156) The processing of personal data for archiving purposes in the public interest, scientific or historical research purposes or statistical purposes should be subject to appropriate safeguards for the rights and freedoms of the data subject pursuant to this Regulation. Those safeguards should ensure that technical and organisational measures are in place in order to ensure, in particular, the principle of data minimisation. The further processing of personal data for archiving purposes in the public interest, scientific or historical research purposes or statistical purposes is to be carried out when the controller has assessed the feasibility to fulfil those purposes by processing data which do not permit or no longer permit the identification of data subjects, provided that appropriate safeguards exist (such as, for instance, pseudonymisation of the data). Member States should provide for appropriate safeguards for the processing of personal data for archiving purposes in the public interest, scientific or historical research purposes or statistical purposes. Member States should be authorised to provide, under specific conditions and subject to appropriate safeguards for data subjects, specifications and derogations with regard to the information requirements and rights to rectification, to erasure, to be forgotten, to restriction of processing, to data portability, and to object when processing personal data for archiving purposes in the public interest, scientific or historical research purposes or statistical purposes. The conditions and safeguards in question may entail specific procedures for data subjects to exercise those rights if this is appropriate in the light of the purposes sought by the specific processing along with technical and organisational measures aimed at minimising the processing of personal data in pursuance of the proportionality and necessity principles. The processing of personal data for scientific purposes should also comply with other relevant legislation such as on clinical trials.

(157) By coupling information from registries, researchers can obtain new knowledge of great value with regard to widespread medical conditions such as cardiovascular disease, cancer and depression. On the basis of registries, research results can be enhanced, as they draw on a larger population. Within social science, research on the basis of registries enables researchers to obtain essential knowledge about the long-term correlation of a number of social conditions such as unemployment and education with other life conditions. Research results obtained through registries provide solid, high-quality knowledge which can provide the basis for the formulation and implementation of knowledge-based policy, improve the quality of life for a number of people and improve the efficiency of social services. In order to facilitate scientific research, personal data can be processed for scientific research purposes, subject to appropriate conditions and safeguards set out in Union or Member State law.

(158) Where personal data are processed for archiving purposes, this Regulation should also apply to that processing, bearing in mind that this Regulation should not apply to deceased persons. Public authorities or public or private bodies that hold records of public interest should be services which, pursuant to Union or Member State law, have a legal obligation to acquire, preserve, appraise, arrange, describe, communicate, promote, disseminate and provide access to records of enduring value for general public interest. Member States should also be authorised to provide for the further processing of personal data for archiving purposes, for example with a view to providing specific

information related to the political behaviour under former totalitarian state regimes, genocide, crimes against humanity, in particular the Holocaust, or war crimes.

(159) Where personal data are processed for scientific research purposes, this Regulation should also apply to that processing. For the purposes of this Regulation, the processing of personal data for scientific research purposes should be interpreted in a broad manner including for example technological development and demonstration, fundamental research, applied research and privately funded research. In addition, it should take into account the Union's objective under Article 179(1) TFEU of achieving a European Research Area. Scientific research purposes should also include studies conducted in the public interest in the area of public health. To meet the specificities of processing personal data for scientific research purposes, specific conditions should apply in particular as regards the publication or otherwise disclosure of personal data in the context of scientific research purposes. If the result of scientific research in particular in the health context gives reason for further measures in the interest of the data subject, the general rules of this Regulation should apply in view of those measures.

(160) Where personal data are processed for historical research purposes, this Regulation should also apply to that processing. This should also include historical research and research for genealogical purposes, bearing in mind that this Regulation should not apply to deceased persons.

(161) For the purpose of consenting to the participation in scientific research activities in clinical trials, the relevant provisions of Regulation (EU) No 536/2014 of the European Parliament and of the Council [15] should apply.

(162) Where personal data are processed for statistical purposes, this Regulation should apply to that processing. Union or Member State law should, within the limits of this Regulation, determine statistical content, control of access, specifications for the processing of personal data for statistical purposes and appropriate measures to safeguard the rights and freedoms of the data subject and for ensuring statistical confidentiality. Statistical purposes mean any operation of collection and the processing of personal data necessary for statistical surveys or for the production of statistical results. Those statistical results may further be used for different purposes, including a scientific research purpose. The statistical purpose implies that the result of processing for statistical purposes is not personal data, but aggregate data, and that this result or the personal data are not used in support of measures or decisions regarding any particular natural person.

(163) The confidential information which the Union and national statistical authorities collect for the production of official European and official national statistics should be protected. European statistics should be developed, produced and disseminated in accordance with the statistical principles as set out in Article 338(2) TFEU, while national statistics should also comply with Member State law. Regulation (EC) No 223/2009 of the European Parliament and of the Council [16] provides further specifications on statistical confidentiality for European statistics.

---

[15] Regulation (EU) No 536/2014 of the European Parliament and of the Council of 16 April 2014 on clinical trials on medicinal products for human use, and repealing Directive 2001/20/EC (OJ L 158, 27.5.2014, p. 1).

[16] Regulation (EC) No 223/2009 of the European Parliament and of the Council of 11 March 2009 on European statistics and repealing Regulation (EC, Euratom) No 1101/2008 of the European Parliament and of the Council on the transmission of data subject to statistical confidentiality to the Statistical Office of the European Communities, Council Regulation (EC) No 322/97 on Community Statistics, and Council Decision 89/382/EEC, Euratom establishing a Committee on the Statistical Programmes of the European Communities (OJ L 87, 31.3.2009, p. 164).

(164) As regards the powers of the supervisory authorities to obtain from the controller or processor access to personal data and access to their premises, Member States may adopt by law, within the limits of this Regulation, specific rules in order to safeguard the professional or other equivalent secrecy obligations, in so far as necessary to reconcile the right to the protection of personal data with an obligation of professional secrecy. This is without prejudice to existing Member State obligations to adopt rules on professional secrecy where required by Union law.

(165) This Regulation respects and does not prejudice the status under existing constitutional law of churches and religious associations or communities in the Member States, as recognised in Article 17 TFEU.

(166) In order to fulfil the objectives of this Regulation, namely to protect the fundamental rights and freedoms of natural persons and in particular their right to the protection of personal data and to ensure the free movement of personal data within the Union, the power to adopt acts in accordance with Article 290 TFEU should be delegated to the Commission. In particular, delegated acts should be adopted in respect of criteria and requirements for certification mechanisms, information to be presented by standardised icons and procedures for providing such icons. It is of particular importance that the Commission carry out appropriate consultations during its preparatory work, including at expert level. The Commission, when preparing and drawing-up delegated acts, should ensure a simultaneous, timely and appropriate transmission of relevant documents to the European Parliament and to the Council.

(167) In order to ensure uniform conditions for the implementation of this Regulation, implementing powers should be conferred on the Commission when provided for by this Regulation. Those powers should be exercised in accordance with Regulation (EU) No 182/2011. In that context, the Commission should consider specific measures for micro, small and medium-sized enterprises.

(168) The examination procedure should be used for the adoption of implementing acts on standard contractual clauses between controllers and processors and between processors; codes of conduct; technical standards and mechanisms for certification; the adequate level of protection afforded by a third country, a territory or a specified sector within that third country, or an international organisation; standard protection clauses; formats and procedures for the exchange of information by electronic means between controllers, processors and supervisory authorities for binding corporate rules; mutual assistance; and arrangements for the exchange of information by electronic means between supervisory authorities, and between supervisory authorities and the Board.

(169) The Commission should adopt immediately applicable implementing acts where available evidence reveals that a third country, a territory or a specified sector within that third country, or an international organisation does not ensure an adequate level of protection, and imperative grounds of urgency so require.

(170) Since the objective of this Regulation, namely to ensure an equivalent level of protection of natural persons and the free flow of personal data throughout the Union, cannot be sufficiently achieved by the Member States and can rather, by reason of the scale or effects of the action, be better achieved at Union level, the Union may adopt measures, in accordance with the principle of subsidiarity as set out in Article 5 of the Treaty on European Union (TEU). In accordance with the principle of proportionality as set out in that Article, this Regulation does not go beyond what is necessary in order to achieve that objective.

(171) Directive 95/46/EC should be repealed by this Regulation. Processing already under way on the date of application of this Regulation should be brought into conformity with this Regulation within the period of two years after which this Regulation enters into force. Where processing is based on consent pursuant to Directive 95/46/EC, it is not necessary for the data subject to give his or her consent again if the manner in which the consent has been given is in line with the conditions of this Regulation, so as to allow the controller to continue such processing after the date of application of this Regulation. Commission decisions adopted and authorisations by supervisory authorities based on Directive 95/46/EC remain in force until amended, replaced or repealed.

(172) The European Data Protection Supervisor was consulted in accordance with Article 28(2) of Regulation (EC) No 45/2001 and delivered an opinion on 7 March 2012 [17].

(173) This Regulation should apply to all matters concerning the protection of fundamental rights and freedoms vis-à-vis the processing of personal data which are not subject to specific obligations with the same objective set out in Directive 2002/58/EC of the European Parliament and of the Council [18], including the obligations on the controller and the rights of natural persons. In order to clarify the relationship between this Regulation and Directive 2002/58/EC, that Directive should be amended accordingly. Once this Regulation is adopted, Directive 2002/58/EC should be reviewed in particular in order to ensure consistency with this Regulation,

HAVE ADOPTED THIS REGULATION:

CHAPTER I GENERAL PROVISIONS

Article 1
Subject-matter and objectives

1. This Regulation lays down rules relating to the protection of natural persons with regard to the processing of personal data and rules relating to the free movement of personal data.
2. This Regulation protects fundamental rights and freedoms of natural persons and in particular their right to the protection of personal data.
3. The free movement of personal data within the Union shall be neither restricted nor prohibited for reasons connected with the protection of natural persons with regard to the processing of personal data.

Article 2
Material scope

1. This Regulation applies to the processing of personal data wholly or partly by automated means and to the processing other than by automated means of personal data which form part of a filing system or are intended to form part of a filing system.

---

[17] OJ C 192, 30.6.2012, p. 7.
[18] Directive 2002/58/EC of the European Parliament and of the Council of 12 July 2002 concerning the processing of personal data and the protection of privacy in the electronic communications sector (Directive on privacy and electronic communications) (OJ L 201, 31.7.2002, p. 37).

2. This Regulation does not apply to the processing of personal data:
   (a) in the course of an activity which falls outside the scope of Union law;
   (b) by the Member States when carrying out activities which fall within the scope of Chapter 2 of Title V of the TEU;
   (c) by a natural person in the course of a purely personal or household activity;
   (d) by competent authorities for the purposes of the prevention, investigation, detection or prosecution of criminal offences or the execution of criminal penalties, including the safeguarding against and the prevention of threats to public security.
3. For the processing of personal data by the Union institutions, bodies, offices and agencies, Regulation (EC) No 45/2001 applies. Regulation (EC) No 45/2001 and other Union legal acts applicable to such processing of personal data shall be adapted to the principles and rules of this Regulation in accordance with Article 98.
4. This Regulation shall be without prejudice to the application of Directive 2000/31/EC, in particular of the liability rules of intermediary service providers in Articles 12 to 15 of that Directive.

Article 3
Territorial scope

1. This Regulation applies to the processing of personal data in the context of the activities of an establishment of a controller or a processor in the Union, regardless of whether the processing takes place in the Union or not.
2. This Regulation applies to the processing of personal data of data subjects who are in the Union by a controller or processor not established in the Union, where the processing activities are related to:
   (a) the offering of goods or services, irrespective of whether a payment of the data subject is required, to such data subjects in the Union; or
   (b) the monitoring of their behaviour as far as their behaviour takes place within the Union.
3. This Regulation applies to the processing of personal data by a controller not established in the Union, but in a place where Member State law applies by virtue of public international law.

Article 4
Definitions

For the purposes of this Regulation:
   (1) 'personal data' means any information relating to an identified or identifiable natural person ('data subject'); an identifiable natural person is one who can be identified, directly or indirectly, in particular by reference to an identifier such as a name, an identification number, location data, an online identifier or to one or more factors specific to the physical, physiological, genetic, mental, economic, cultural or social identity of that natural person;
   (2) 'processing' means any operation or set of operations which is performed on personal data or on sets of personal data, whether or not by automated means, such as collection, recording, organisation, structuring, storage, adaptation or alteration, retrieval, consultation, use, disclosure by transmission, dissemination or otherwise making available, alignment or combination, restriction, erasure or destruction;
   (3) 'restriction of processing' means the marking of stored personal data with the aim of limiting their processing in the future;

(4) 'profiling' means any form of automated processing of personal data consisting of the use of personal data to evaluate certain personal aspects relating to a natural person, in particular to analyse or predict aspects concerning that natural person's performance at work, economic situation, health, personal preferences, interests, reliability, behaviour, location or movements;

(5) 'pseudonymisation' means the processing of personal data in such a manner that the personal data can no longer be attributed to a specific data subject without the use of additional information, provided that such additional information is kept separately and is subject to technical and organisational measures to ensure that the personal data are not attributed to an identified or identifiable natural person;

(6) 'filing system' means any structured set of personal data which are accessible according to specific criteria, whether centralised, decentralised or dispersed on a functional or geographical basis;

(7) 'controller' means the natural or legal person, public authority, agency or other body which, alone or jointly with others, determines the purposes and means of the processing of personal data; where the purposes and means of such processing are determined by Union or Member State law, the controller or the specific criteria for its nomination may be provided for by Union or Member State law;

(8) 'processor' means a natural or legal person, public authority, agency or other body which processes personal data on behalf of the controller;

(9) 'recipient' means a natural or legal person, public authority, agency or another body, to which the personal data are disclosed, whether a third party or not. However, public authorities which may receive personal data in the framework of a particular inquiry in accordance with Union or Member State law shall not be regarded as recipients; the processing of those data by those public authorities shall be in compliance with the applicable data protection rules according to the purposes of the processing;

(10) 'third party' means a natural or legal person, public authority, agency or body other than the data subject, controller, processor and persons who, under the direct authority of the controller or processor, are authorised to process personal data;

(11) 'consent' of the data subject means any freely given, specific, informed and unambiguous indication of the data subject's wishes by which he or she, by a statement or by a clear affirmative action, signifies agreement to the processing of personal data relating to him or her;

(12) 'personal data breach' means a breach of security leading to the accidental or unlawful destruction, loss, alteration, unauthorised disclosure of, or access to, personal data transmitted, stored or otherwise processed;

(13) 'genetic data' means personal data relating to the inherited or acquired genetic characteristics of a natural person which give unique information about the physiology or the health of that natural person and which result, in particular, from an analysis of a biological sample from the natural person in question;

(14) 'biometric data' means personal data resulting from specific technical processing relating to the physical, physiological or behavioural characteristics of a natural person, which allow or confirm the unique identification of that natural person, such as facial images or dactyloscopic data;

(15) 'data concerning health' means personal data related to the physical or mental health of a natural person, including the provision of health care services, which reveal information about his or her health status;

(16) 'main establishment' means:
  (a) as regards a controller with establishments in more than one Member State, the place of its central administration in the Union, unless the decisions on the purposes and means of the processing of personal data are taken in another establishment of the controller in the Union and the latter establishment has the power to have such decisions implemented, in which case the establishment having taken such decisions is to be considered to be the main establishment;
  (b) as regards a processor with establishments in more than one Member State, the place of its central administration in the Union, or, if the processor has no central administration in the Union, the establishment of the processor in the Union where the main processing activities in the context of the activities of an establishment of the processor take place to the extent that the processor is subject to specific obligations under this Regulation;

(17) 'representative' means a natural or legal person established in the Union who, designated by the controller or processor in writing pursuant to Article 27, represents the controller or processor with regard to their respective obligations under this Regulation;

(18) 'enterprise' means a natural or legal person engaged in an economic activity, irrespective of its legal form, including partnerships or associations regularly engaged in an economic activity;

(19) 'group of undertakings' means a controlling undertaking and its controlled undertakings;

(20) 'binding corporate rules' means personal data protection policies which are adhered to by a controller or processor established on the territory of a Member State for transfers or a set of transfers of personal data to a controller or processor in one or more third countries within a group of undertakings, or group of enterprises engaged in a joint economic activity;

(21) 'supervisory authority' means an independent public authority which is established by a Member State pursuant to Article 51;

(22) 'supervisory authority concerned' means a supervisory authority which is concerned by the processing of personal data because:
  (a) the controller or processor is established on the territory of the Member State of that supervisory authority;
  (b) data subjects residing in the Member State of that supervisory authority are substantially affected or likely to be substantially affected by the processing; or
  (c) a complaint has been lodged with that supervisory authority;

(23) 'cross-border processing' means either:
  (a) processing of personal data which takes place in the context of the activities of establishments in more than one Member State of a controller or processor in the Union where the controller or processor is established in more than one Member State; or
  (b) processing of personal data which takes place in the context of the activities of a single establishment of a controller or processor in the Union but which substantially affects or is likely to substantially affect data subjects in more than one Member State.

(24) 'relevant and reasoned objection' means an objection to a draft decision as to whether there is an infringement of this Regulation, or whether envisaged action in relation to the controller or processor complies with this Regulation, which clearly demonstrates the significance of the risks posed by the draft decision as regards the fundamental rights and freedoms of data subjects and, where applicable, the free flow of personal data within the Union;

(25) 'information society service' means a service as defined in point (b) of Article 1(1) of Directive (EU) 2015/1535 of the European Parliament and of the Council [19];

(26) 'international organisation' means an organisation and its subordinate bodies governed by public international law, or any other body which is set up by, or on the basis of, an agreement between two or more countries.

CHAPTER II PRINCIPLES

Article 5
Principles relating to processing of personal data

1. Personal data shall be:
   (a) processed lawfully, fairly and in a transparent manner in relation to the data subject ('lawfulness, fairness and transparency');
   (b) collected for specified, explicit and legitimate purposes and not further processed in a manner that is incompatible with those purposes; further processing for archiving purposes in the public interest, scientific or historical research purposes or statistical purposes shall, in accordance with Article 89(1), not be considered to be incompatible with the initial purposes ('purpose limitation');
   (c) adequate, relevant and limited to what is necessary in relation to the purposes for which they are processed ('data minimisation');
   (d) accurate and, where necessary, kept up to date; every reasonable step must be taken to ensure that personal data that are inaccurate, having regard to the purposes for which they are processed, are erased or rectified without delay ('accuracy');
   (e) kept in a form which permits identification of data subjects for no longer than is necessary for the purposes for which the personal data are processed; personal data may be stored for longer periods insofar as the personal data will be processed solely for archiving purposes in the public interest, scientific or historical research purposes or statistical purposes in accordance with Article 89(1) subject to implementation of the appropriate technical and organisational measures required by this Regulation in order to safeguard the rights and freedoms of the data subject ('storage limitation');
   (f) processed in a manner that ensures appropriate security of the personal data, including protection against unauthorised or unlawful processing and against accidental loss, destruction or damage, using appropriate technical or organisational measures ('integrity and confidentiality').

2. The controller shall be responsible for, and be able to demonstrate compliance with, paragraph 1 ('accountability').

Article 6
Lawfulness of processing

1. Processing shall be lawful only if and to the extent that at least one of the following applies:
   (a) the data subject has given consent to the processing of his or her personal data for one or more specific purposes;

---

[19] Directive (EU) 2015/1535 of the European Parliament and of the Council of 9 September 2015 laying down a procedure for the provision of information in the field of technical regulations and of rules on Information Society services (OJ L 241, 17.9.2015, p. 1).

(b) processing is necessary for the performance of a contract to which the data subject is party or in order to take steps at the request of the data subject prior to entering into a contract;

(c) processing is necessary for compliance with a legal obligation to which the controller is subject;

(d) processing is necessary in order to protect the vital interests of the data subject or of another natural person;

(e) processing is necessary for the performance of a task carried out in the public interest or in the exercise of official authority vested in the controller;

(f) processing is necessary for the purposes of the legitimate interests pursued by the controller or by a third party, except where such interests are overridden by the interests or fundamental rights and freedoms of the data subject which require protection of personal data, in particular where the data subject is a child.

Point (f) of the first subparagraph shall not apply to processing carried out by public authorities in the performance of their tasks.

2. Member States may maintain or introduce more specific provisions to adapt the application of the rules of this Regulation with regard to processing for compliance with points (c) and (e) of paragraph 1 by determining more precisely specific requirements for the processing and other measures to ensure lawful and fair processing including for other specific processing situations as provided for in Chapter IX.

3. The basis for the processing referred to in point (c) and (e) of paragraph 1 shall be laid down by:
   (a) Union law; or
   (b) Member State law to which the controller is subject.

The purpose of the processing shall be determined in that legal basis or, as regards the processing referred to in point (e) of paragraph 1, shall be necessary for the performance of a task carried out in the public interest or in the exercise of official authority vested in the controller. That legal basis may contain specific provisions to adapt the application of rules of this Regulation, inter alia: the general conditions governing the lawfulness of processing by the controller; the types of data which are subject to the processing; the data subjects concerned; the entities to, and the purposes for which, the personal data may be disclosed; the purpose limitation; storage periods; and processing operations and processing procedures, including measures to ensure lawful and fair processing such as those for other specific processing situations as provided for in Chapter IX. The Union or the Member State law shall meet an objective of public interest and be proportionate to the legitimate aim pursued.

4. Where the processing for a purpose other than that for which the personal data have been collected is not based on the data subject's consent or on a Union or Member State law which constitutes a necessary and proportionate measure in a democratic society to safeguard the objectives referred to in Article 23(1), the controller shall, in order to ascertain whether processing for another purpose is compatible with the purpose for which the personal data are initially collected, take into account, inter alia:

   (a) any link between the purposes for which the personal data have been collected and the purposes of the intended further processing;

   (b) the context in which the personal data have been collected, in particular regarding the relationship between data subjects and the controller;

(c) the nature of the personal data, in particular whether special categories of personal data are processed, pursuant to Article 9, or whether personal data related to criminal convictions and offences are processed, pursuant to Article 10;

(d) the possible consequences of the intended further processing for data subjects;

(e) the existence of appropriate safeguards, which may include encryption or pseudonymisation.

Article 7
Conditions for consent

1. Where processing is based on consent, the controller shall be able to demonstrate that the data subject has consented to processing of his or her personal data.

2. If the data subject's consent is given in the context of a written declaration which also concerns other matters, the request for consent shall be presented in a manner which is clearly distinguishable from the other matters, in an intelligible and easily accessible form, using clear and plain language. Any part of such a declaration which constitutes an infringement of this Regulation shall not be binding.

3. The data subject shall have the right to withdraw his or her consent at any time. The withdrawal of consent shall not affect the lawfulness of processing based on consent before its withdrawal. Prior to giving consent, the data subject shall be informed thereof. It shall be as easy to withdraw as to give consent.

4. When assessing whether consent is freely given, utmost account shall be taken of whether, inter alia, the performance of a contract, including the provision of a service, is conditional on consent to the processing of personal data that is not necessary for the performance of that contract.

Article 8

Conditions applicable to child's consent in relation to information society services

1. Where point (a) of Article 6(1) applies, in relation to the offer of information society services directly to a child, the processing of the personal data of a child shall be lawful where the child is at least 16 years old. Where the child is below the age of 16 years, such processing shall be lawful only if and to the extent that consent is given or authorised by the holder of parental responsibility over the child.

Member States may provide by law for a lower age for those purposes provided that such lower age is not below 13 years.

2. The controller shall make reasonable efforts to verify in such cases that consent is given or authorised by the holder of parental responsibility over the child, taking into consideration available technology.

3. Paragraph 1 shall not affect the general contract law of Member States such as the rules on the validity, formation or effect of a contract in relation to a child.

Article 9

Processing of special categories of personal data

1. Processing of personal data revealing racial or ethnic origin, political opinions, religious or philosophical beliefs, or trade union membership, and the processing of genetic data, biometric data for the purpose of uniquely identifying a natural person, data

concerning health or data concerning a natural person's sex life or sexual orientation shall be prohibited.

2. Paragraph 1 shall not apply if one of the following applies:

    (a) the data subject has given explicit consent to the processing of those personal data for one or more specified purposes, except where Union or Member State law provide that the prohibition referred to in paragraph 1 may not be lifted by the data subject;

    (b) processing is necessary for the purposes of carrying out the obligations and exercising specific rights of the controller or of the data subject in the field of employment and social security and social protection law in so far as it is authorised by Union or Member State law or a collective agreement pursuant to Member State law providing for appropriate safeguards for the fundamental rights and the interests of the data subject;

    (c) processing is necessary to protect the vital interests of the data subject or of another natural person where the data subject is physically or legally incapable of giving consent;

    (d) processing is carried out in the course of its legitimate activities with appropriate safeguards by a foundation, association or any other not-for-profit body with a political, philosophical, religious or trade union aim and on condition that the processing relates solely to the members or to former members of the body or to persons who have regular contact with it in connection with its purposes and that the personal data are not disclosed outside that body without the consent of the data subjects;

    (e) processing relates to personal data which are manifestly made public by the data subject;

    (f) processing is necessary for the establishment, exercise or defence of legal claims or whenever courts are acting in their judicial capacity;

    (g) processing is necessary for reasons of substantial public interest, on the basis of Union or Member State law which shall be proportionate to the aim pursued, respect the essence of the right to data protection and provide for suitable and specific measures to safeguard the fundamental rights and the interests of the data subject;

    (h) processing is necessary for the purposes of preventive or occupational medicine, for the assessment of the working capacity of the employee, medical diagnosis, the provision of health or social care or treatment or the management of health or social care systems and services on the basis of Union or Member State law or pursuant to contract with a health professional and subject to the conditions and safeguards referred to in paragraph 3;

    (i) processing is necessary for reasons of public interest in the area of public health, such as protecting against serious cross-border threats to health or ensuring high standards of quality and safety of health care and of medicinal products or medical devices, on the basis of Union or Member State law which provides for suitable and specific measures to safeguard the rights and freedoms of the data subject, in particular professional secrecy;

    (j) processing is necessary for archiving purposes in the public interest, scientific or historical research purposes or statistical purposes in accordance with Article 89(1) based on Union or Member State law which shall be proportionate to the aim pursued, respect the essence of the right to data protection and provide for suitable and specific measures to safeguard the fundamental rights and the interests of the data subject.

3. Personal data referred to in paragraph 1 may be processed for the purposes referred to in point (h) of paragraph 2 when those data are processed by or under the responsibility of a professional subject to the obligation of professional secrecy under Union or Member State law or rules established by national competent bodies or by another person also subject to an obligation of secrecy under Union or Member State law or rules established by national competent bodies.

4. Member States may maintain or introduce further conditions, including limitations, with regard to the processing of genetic data, biometric data or data concerning health.

Article 10
Processing of personal data relating to criminal convictions and offences

Processing of personal data relating to criminal convictions and offences or related security measures based on Article 6(1) shall be carried out only under the control of official authority or when the processing is authorised by Union or Member State law providing for appropriate safeguards for the rights and freedoms of data subjects. Any comprehensive register of criminal convictions shall be kept only under the control of official authority.

Article 11
Processing which does not require identification

1. If the purposes for which a controller processes personal data do not or do no longer require the identification of a data subject by the controller, the controller shall not be obliged to maintain, acquire or process additional information in order to identify the data subject for the sole purpose of complying with this Regulation.

2. Where, in cases referred to in paragraph 1 of this Article, the controller is able to demonstrate that it is not in a position to identify the data subject, the controller shall inform the data subject accordingly, if possible. In such cases, Articles 15 to 20 shall not apply except where the data subject, for the purpose of exercising his or her rights under those articles, provides additional information enabling his or her identification.

CHAPTER III RIGHTS OF THE DATA SUBJECT

Section 1
Transparency and modalities

Article 12
Transparent information, communication and modalities
for the exercise of the rights of the data subject

1. The controller shall take appropriate measures to provide any information referred to in Articles 13 and 14 and any communication under Articles 15 to 22 and 34 relating to processing to the data subject in a concise, transparent, intelligible and easily accessible form, using clear and plain language, in particular for any information addressed specifically to a child. The information shall be provided in writing, or by other means, including, where appropriate, by electronic means. When requested by the data subject, the information may be provided orally, provided that the identity of the data subject is proven by other means.

2. The controller shall facilitate the exercise of data subject rights under Articles 15 to 22. In the cases referred to in Article 11(2), the controller shall not refuse to act

on the request of the data subject for exercising his or her rights under Articles 15 to 22, unless the controller demonstrates that it is not in a position to identify the data subject.

3. The controller shall provide information on action taken on a request under Articles 15 to 22 to the data subject without undue delay and in any event within one month of receipt of the request. That period may be extended by two further months where necessary, taking into account the complexity and number of the requests. The controller shall inform the data subject of any such extension within one month of receipt of the request, together with the reasons for the delay. Where the data subject makes the request by electronic form means, the information shall be provided by electronic means where possible, unless otherwise requested by the data subject.

4. If the controller does not take action on the request of the data subject, the controller shall inform the data subject without delay and at the latest within one month of receipt of the request of the reasons for not taking action and on the possibility of lodging a complaint with a supervisory authority and seeking a judicial remedy.

5. Information provided under Articles 13 and 14 and any communication and any actions taken under Articles 15 to 22 and 34 shall be provided free of charge. Where requests from a data subject are manifestly unfounded or excessive, in particular because of their repetitive character, the controller may either:
   (a) charge a reasonable fee taking into account the administrative costs of providing the information or communication or taking the action requested; or
   (b) refuse to act on the request.

The controller shall bear the burden of demonstrating the manifestly unfounded or excessive character of the request.

6. Without prejudice to Article 11, where the controller has reasonable doubts concerning the identity of the natural person making the request referred to in Articles 15 to 21, the controller may request the provision of additional information necessary to confirm the identity of the data subject.

7. The information to be provided to data subjects pursuant to Articles 13 and 14 may be provided in combination with standardised icons in order to give in an easily visible, intelligible and clearly legible manner a meaningful overview of the intended processing. Where the icons are presented electronically they shall be machine-readable.

8. The Commission shall be empowered to adopt delegated acts in accordance with Article 92 for the purpose of determining the information to be presented by the icons and the procedures for providing standardised icons.

Section 2
Information and access to personal data

Article 13
Information to be provided where personal data are collected from the data subject

1. Where personal data relating to a data subject are collected from the data subject, the controller shall, at the time when personal data are obtained, provide the data subject with all of the following information:
   (a) the identity and the contact details of the controller and, where applicable, of the controller's representative;
   (b) the contact details of the data protection officer, where applicable;
   (c) the purposes of the processing for which the personal data are intended as well as the legal basis for the processing;

(d) where the processing is based on point (f) of Article 6(1), the legitimate interests pursued by the controller or by a third party;

(e) the recipients or categories of recipients of the personal data, if any;

(f) where applicable, the fact that the controller intends to transfer personal data to a third country or international organisation and the existence or absence of an adequacy decision by the Commission, or in the case of transfers referred to in Article 46 or 47, or the second subparagraph of Article 49(1), reference to the appropriate or suitable safeguards and the means by which to obtain a copy of them or where they have been made available.

2. In addition to the information referred to in paragraph 1, the controller shall, at the time when personal data are obtained, provide the data subject with the following further information necessary to ensure fair and transparent processing:

(a) the period for which the personal data will be stored, or if that is not possible, the criteria used to determine that period;

(b) the existence of the right to request from the controller access to and rectification or erasure of personal data or restriction of processing concerning the data subject or to object to processing as well as the right to data portability;

(c) where the processing is based on point (a) of Article 6(1) or point (a) of Article 9(2), the existence of the right to withdraw consent at any time, without affecting the lawfulness of processing based on consent before its withdrawal;

(d) the right to lodge a complaint with a supervisory authority;

(e) whether the provision of personal data is a statutory or contractual requirement, or a requirement necessary to enter into a contract, as well as whether the data subject is obliged to provide the personal data and of the possible consequences of failure to provide such data;

(f) the existence of automated decision-making, including profiling, referred to in Article 22(1) and (4) and, at least in those cases, meaningful information about the logic involved, as well as the significance and the envisaged consequences of such processing for the data subject.

3. Where the controller intends to further process the personal data for a purpose other than that for which the personal data were collected, the controller shall provide the data subject prior to that further processing with information on that other purpose and with any relevant further information as referred to in paragraph 2.

4. Paragraphs 1, 2 and 3 shall not apply where and insofar as the data subject already has the information.

Article 14
Information to be provided where personal data have not been obtained
from the data subject

1. Where personal data have not been obtained from the data subject, the controller shall provide the data subject with the following information:

(a) the identity and the contact details of the controller and, where applicable, of the controller's representative;

(b) the contact details of the data protection officer, where applicable;

(c) the purposes of the processing for which the personal data are intended as well as the legal basis for the processing;

(d) the categories of personal data concerned;

(e) the recipients or categories of recipients of the personal data, if any;

(f) where applicable, that the controller intends to transfer personal data to a recipient in a third country or international organisation and the existence or absence of an adequacy decision by the Commission, or in the case of transfers referred to in Article 46 or 47, or the second subparagraph of Article 49(1), reference to the appropriate or suitable safeguards and the means to obtain a copy of them or where they have been made available.

2. In addition to the information referred to in paragraph 1, the controller shall provide the data subject with the following information necessary to ensure fair and transparent processing in respect of the data subject:

(a) the period for which the personal data will be stored, or if that is not possible, the criteria used to determine that period;

(b) where the processing is based on point (f) of Article 6(1), the legitimate interests pursued by the controller or by a third party;

(c) the existence of the right to request from the controller access to and rectification or erasure of personal data or restriction of processing concerning the data subject and to object to processing as well as the right to data portability;

(d) where processing is based on point (a) of Article 6(1) or point (a) of Article 9(2), the existence of the right to withdraw consent at any time, without affecting the lawfulness of processing based on consent before its withdrawal;

(e) the right to lodge a complaint with a supervisory authority;

(f) from which source the personal data originate, and if applicable, whether it came from publicly accessible sources;

(g) the existence of automated decision-making, including profiling, referred to in Article 22(1) and (4) and, at least in those cases, meaningful information about the logic involved, as well as the significance and the envisaged consequences of such processing for the data subject.

3. The controller shall provide the information referred to in paragraphs 1 and 2:

(a) within a reasonable period after obtaining the personal data, but at the latest within one month, having regard to the specific circumstances in which the personal data are processed;

(b) if the personal data are to be used for communication with the data subject, at the latest at the time of the first communication to that data subject; or

(c) if a disclosure to another recipient is envisaged, at the latest when the personal data are first disclosed.

4. Where the controller intends to further process the personal data for a purpose other than that for which the personal data were obtained, the controller shall provide the data subject prior to that further processing with information on that other purpose and with any relevant further information as referred to in paragraph 2.

5. Paragraphs 1 to 4 shall not apply where and insofar as:

(a) the data subject already has the information;

(b) the provision of such information proves impossible or would involve a disproportionate effort, in particular for processing for archiving purposes in the public interest, scientific or historical research purposes or statistical purposes, subject to the conditions and safeguards referred to in Article 89(1) or in so far as the obligation referred to in paragraph 1 of this Article is likely to render impossible or seriously impair the achievement of the objectives of that processing. In such cases the controller shall take appropriate measures to protect the data subject's rights and freedoms and legitimate interests, including making the information publicly available;

(c) obtaining or disclosure is expressly laid down by Union or Member State law to which the controller is subject and which provides appropriate measures to protect the data subject's legitimate interests; or

(d) where the personal data must remain confidential subject to an obligation of professional secrecy regulated by Union or Member State law, including a statutory obligation of secrecy.

Article 15
Right of access by the data subject

1. The data subject shall have the right to obtain from the controller confirmation as to whether or not personal data concerning him or her are being processed, and, where that is the case, access to the personal data and the following information:

    (a) the purposes of the processing;

    (b) the categories of personal data concerned;

    (c) the recipients or categories of recipient to whom the personal data have been or will be disclosed, in particular recipients in third countries or international organisations;

    (d) where possible, the envisaged period for which the personal data will be stored, or, if not possible, the criteria used to determine that period;

    (e) the existence of the right to request from the controller rectification or erasure of personal data or restriction of processing of personal data concerning the data subject or to object to such processing;

    (f) the right to lodge a complaint with a supervisory authority;

    (g) where the personal data are not collected from the data subject, any available information as to their source;

    (h) the existence of automated decision-making, including profiling, referred to in Article 22(1) and (4) and, at least in those cases, meaningful information about the logic involved, as well as the significance and the envisaged consequences of such processing for the data subject.

2. Where personal data are transferred to a third country or to an international organisation, the data subject shall have the right to be informed of the appropriate safeguards pursuant to Article 46 relating to the transfer.

3. The controller shall provide a copy of the personal data undergoing processing. For any further copies requested by the data subject, the controller may charge a reasonable fee based on administrative costs. Where the data subject makes the request by electronic means, and unless otherwise requested by the data subject, the information shall be provided in a commonly used electronic form.

4. The right to obtain a copy referred to in paragraph 3 shall not adversely affect the rights and freedoms of others.

Section 3
Rectification and erasure

Article 16
Right to rectification

The data subject shall have the right to obtain from the controller without undue delay the rectification of inaccurate personal data concerning him or her. Taking into account the purposes of the processing, the data subject shall have the right to have incomplete personal data completed, including by means of providing a supplementary statement.

Article 17
Right to erasure ('right to be forgotten')

1. The data subject shall have the right to obtain from the controller the erasure of personal data concerning him or her without undue delay and the controller shall have the obligation to erase personal data without undue delay where one of the following grounds applies:
    (a) the personal data are no longer necessary in relation to the purposes for which they were collected or otherwise processed;
    (b) the data subject withdraws consent on which the processing is based according to point (a) of Article 6(1), or point (a) of Article 9(2), and where there is no other legal ground for the processing;
    (c) the data subject objects to the processing pursuant to Article 21(1) and there are no overriding legitimate grounds for the processing, or the data subject objects to the processing pursuant to Article 21(2);
    (d) the personal data have been unlawfully processed;
    (e) the personal data have to be erased for compliance with a legal obligation in Union or Member State law to which the controller is subject;
    (f) the personal data have been collected in relation to the offer of information society services referred to in Article 8(1).
2. Where the controller has made the personal data public and is obliged pursuant to paragraph 1 to erase the personal data, the controller, taking account of available technology and the cost of implementation, shall take reasonable steps, including technical measures, to inform controllers which are processing the personal data that the data subject has requested the erasure by such controllers of any links to, or copy or replication of, those personal data.
3. Paragraphs 1 and 2 shall not apply to the extent that processing is necessary:
    (a) for exercising the right of freedom of expression and information;
    (b) for compliance with a legal obligation which requires processing by Union or Member State law to which the controller is subject or for the performance of a task carried out in the public interest or in the exercise of official authority vested in the controller;
    (c) for reasons of public interest in the area of public health in accordance with points (h) and (i) of Article 9(2) as well as Article 9(3);
    (d) for archiving purposes in the public interest, scientific or historical research purposes or statistical purposes in accordance with Article 89(1) in so far as the right referred to in paragraph 1 is likely to render impossible or seriously impair the achievement of the objectives of that processing; or
    (e) for the establishment, exercise or defence of legal claims.

Article 18
Right to restriction of processing

1. The data subject shall have the right to obtain from the controller restriction of processing where one of the following applies:
    (a) the accuracy of the personal data is contested by the data subject, for a period enabling the controller to verify the accuracy of the personal data;
    (b) the processing is unlawful and the data subject opposes the erasure of the personal data and requests the restriction of their use instead;
    (c) the controller no longer needs the personal data for the purposes of the processing, but they are required by the data subject for the establishment, exercise or defence of legal claims;

(d) the data subject has objected to processing pursuant to Article 21(1) pending the verification whether the legitimate grounds of the controller override those of the data subject.

2. Where processing has been restricted under paragraph 1, such personal data shall, with the exception of storage, only be processed with the data subject's consent or for the establishment, exercise or defence of legal claims or for the protection of the rights of another natural or legal person or for reasons of important public interest of the Union or of a Member State.

3. A data subject who has obtained restriction of processing pursuant to paragraph 1 shall be informed by the controller before the restriction of processing is lifted.

Article 19
Notification obligation regarding rectification or erasure
of personal data or restriction of processing

The controller shall communicate any rectification or erasure of personal data or restriction of processing carried out in accordance with Article 16, Article 17(1) and Article 18 to each recipient to whom the personal data have been disclosed, unless this proves impossible or involves disproportionate effort. The controller shall inform the data subject about those recipients if the data subject requests it.

Article 20
Right to data portability

1. The data subject shall have the right to receive the personal data concerning him or her, which he or she has provided to a controller, in a structured, commonly used and machine-readable format and have the right to transmit those data to another controller without hindrance from the controller to which the personal data have been provided, where:
    (a) the processing is based on consent pursuant to point (a) of Article 6(1) or point (a) of Article 9(2) or on a contract pursuant to point (b) of Article 6(1); and
    (b) the processing is carried out by automated means.

2. In exercising his or her right to data portability pursuant to paragraph 1, the data subject shall have the right to have the personal data transmitted directly from one controller to another, where technically feasible.

3. The exercise of the right referred to in paragraph 1 of this Article shall be without prejudice to Article 17. That right shall not apply to processing necessary for the performance of a task carried out in the public interest or in the exercise of official authority vested in the controller.

4. The right referred to in paragraph 1 shall not adversely affect the rights and freedoms of others.

Section 4
Right to object and automated individual decision-making

Article 21
Right to object

1. The data subject shall have the right to object, on grounds relating to his or her particular situation, at any time to processing of personal data concerning him or her which is based on point (e) or (f) of Article 6(1), including profiling based on those provisions. The controller shall no longer process the personal data unless the controller

demonstrates compelling legitimate grounds for the processing which override the interests, rights and freedoms of the data subject or for the establishment, exercise or defence of legal claims.

2. Where personal data are processed for direct marketing purposes, the data subject shall have the right to object at any time to processing of personal data concerning him or her for such marketing, which includes profiling to the extent that it is related to such direct marketing.

3. Where the data subject objects to processing for direct marketing purposes, the personal data shall no longer be processed for such purposes.

4. At the latest at the time of the first communication with the data subject, the right referred to in paragraphs 1 and 2 shall be explicitly brought to the attention of the data subject and shall be presented clearly and separately from any other information.

5. In the context of the use of information society services, and notwithstanding Directive 2002/58/EC, the data subject may exercise his or her right to object by automated means using technical specifications.

6. Where personal data are processed for scientific or historical research purposes or statistical purposes pursuant to Article 89(1), the data subject, on grounds relating to his or her particular situation, shall have the right to object to processing of personal data concerning him or her, unless the processing is necessary for the performance of a task carried out for reasons of public interest.

Article 22
Automated individual decision-making, including profiling

1. The data subject shall have the right not to be subject to a decision based solely on automated processing, including profiling, which produces legal effects concerning him or her or similarly significantly affects him or her.

2. Paragraph 1 shall not apply if the decision:
   (a) is necessary for entering into, or performance of, a contract between the data subject and a data controller;
   (b) is authorised by Union or Member State law to which the controller is subject and which also lays down suitable measures to safeguard the data subject's rights and freedoms and legitimate interests; or
   (c) is based on the data subject's explicit consent.

3. In the cases referred to in points (a) and (c) of paragraph 2, the data controller shall implement suitable measures to safeguard the data subject's rights and freedoms and legitimate interests, at least the right to obtain human intervention on the part of the controller, to express his or her point of view and to contest the decision.

4. Decisions referred to in paragraph 2 shall not be based on special categories of personal data referred to in Article 9(1), unless point (a) or (g) of Article 9(2) applies and suitable measures to safeguard the data subject's rights and freedoms and legitimate interests are in place.

Section 5
Restrictions

Article 23
Restrictions

1. Union or Member State law to which the data controller or processor is subject may restrict by way of a legislative measure the scope of the obligations and rights provided

for in Articles 12 to 22 and Article 34, as well as Article 5 in so far as its provisions correspond to the rights and obligations provided for in Articles 12 to 22, when such a restriction respects the essence of the fundamental rights and freedoms and is a necessary and proportionate measure in a democratic society to safeguard:

(a) national security;
(b) defence;
(c) public security;
(d) the prevention, investigation, detection or prosecution of criminal offences or the execution of criminal penalties, including the safeguarding against and the prevention of threats to public security;
(e) other important objectives of general public interest of the Union or of a Member State, in particular an important economic or financial interest of the Union or of a Member State, including monetary, budgetary and taxation a matters, public health and social security;
(f) the protection of judicial independence and judicial proceedings;
(g) the prevention, investigation, detection and prosecution of breaches of ethics for regulated professions;
(h) a monitoring, inspection or regulatory function connected, even occasionally, to the exercise of official authority in the cases referred to in points (a) to (e) and (g);
(i) the protection of the data subject or the rights and freedoms of others;
(j) the enforcement of civil law claims.

2. In particular, any legislative measure referred to in paragraph 1 shall contain specific provisions at least, where relevant, as to:

(a) the purposes of the processing or categories of processing;
(b) the categories of personal data;
(c) the scope of the restrictions introduced;
(d) the safeguards to prevent abuse or unlawful access or transfer;
(e) the specification of the controller or categories of controllers;
(f) the storage periods and the applicable safeguards taking into account the nature, scope and purposes of the processing or categories of processing;
(g) the risks to the rights and freedoms of data subjects; and
(h) the right of data subjects to be informed about the restriction, unless that may be prejudicial to the purpose of the restriction.

CHAPTER IV CONTROLLER AND PROCESSOR

Section 1
General obligations

Article 24
Responsibility of the controller

1. Taking into account the nature, scope, context and purposes of processing as well as the risks of varying likelihood and severity for the rights and freedoms of natural persons, the controller shall implement appropriate technical and organisational measures to ensure and to be able to demonstrate that processing is performed in accordance with this Regulation. Those measures shall be reviewed and updated where necessary.

2. Where proportionate in relation to processing activities, the measures referred to in paragraph 1 shall include the implementation of appropriate data protection policies by the controller.

3. Adherence to approved codes of conduct as referred to in Article 40 or approved certification mechanisms as referred to in Article 42 may be used as an element by which to demonstrate compliance with the obligations of the controller.

Article 25
Data protection by design and by default

1. Taking into account the state of the art, the cost of implementation and the nature, scope, context and purposes of processing as well as the risks of varying likelihood and severity for rights and freedoms of natural persons posed by the processing, the controller shall, both at the time of the determination of the means for processing and at the time of the processing itself, implement appropriate technical and organisational measures, such as pseudonymisation, which are designed to implement data-protection principles, such as data minimisation, in an effective manner and to integrate the necessary safeguards into the processing in order to meet the requirements of this Regulation and protect the rights of data subjects.
2. The controller shall implement appropriate technical and organisational measures for ensuring that, by default, only personal data which are necessary for each specific purpose of the processing are processed. That obligation applies to the amount of personal data collected, the extent of their processing, the period of their storage and their accessibility. In particular, such measures shall ensure that by default personal data are not made accessible without the individual's intervention to an indefinite number of natural persons.
3. An approved certification mechanism pursuant to Article 42 may be used as an element to demonstrate compliance with the requirements set out in paragraphs 1 and 2 of this Article.

Article 26
Joint controllers

1. Where two or more controllers jointly determine the purposes and means of processing, they shall be joint controllers. They shall in a transparent manner determine their respective responsibilities for compliance with the obligations under this Regulation, in particular as regards the exercising of the rights of the data subject and their respective duties to provide the information referred to in Articles 13 and 14, by means of an arrangement between them unless, and in so far as, the respective responsibilities of the controllers are determined by Union or Member State law to which the controllers are subject. The arrangement may designate a contact point for data subjects.
2. The arrangement referred to in paragraph 1 shall duly reflect the respective roles and relationships of the joint controllers vis-à-vis the data subjects. The essence of the arrangement shall be made available to the data subject.
3. Irrespective of the terms of the arrangement referred to in paragraph 1, the data subject may exercise his or her rights under this Regulation in respect of and against each of the controllers.

Article 27
Representatives of controllers or processors not established in the Union

1. Where Article 3(2) applies, the controller or the processor shall designate in writing a representative in the Union.

2. The obligation laid down in paragraph 1 of this Article shall not apply to:
   (a) processing which is occasional, does not include, on a large scale, processing of special categories of data as referred to in Article 9(1) or processing of personal data relating to criminal convictions and offences referred to in Article 10, and is unlikely to result in a risk to the rights and freedoms of natural persons, taking into account the nature, context, scope and purposes of the processing; or
   (b) a public authority or body.
3. The representative shall be established in one of the Member States where the data subjects, whose personal data are processed in relation to the offering of goods or services to them, or whose behaviour is monitored, are.
4. The representative shall be mandated by the controller or processor to be addressed in addition to or instead of the controller or the processor by, in particular, supervisory authorities and data subjects, on all issues related to processing, for the purposes of ensuring compliance with this Regulation.
5. The designation of a representative by the controller or processor shall be without prejudice to legal actions which could be initiated against the controller or the processor themselves.

Article 28
Processor

1. Where processing is to be carried out on behalf of a controller, the controller shall use only processors providing sufficient guarantees to implement appropriate technical and organisational measures in such a manner that processing will meet the requirements of this Regulation and ensure the protection of the rights of the data subject.
2. The processor shall not engage another processor without prior specific or general written authorisation of the controller. In the case of general written authorisation, the processor shall inform the controller of any intended changes concerning the addition or replacement of other processors, thereby giving the controller the opportunity to object to such changes.
3. Processing by a processor shall be governed by a contract or other legal act under Union or Member State law, that is binding on the processor with regard to the controller and that sets out the subject-matter and duration of the processing, the nature and purpose of the processing, the type of personal data and categories of data subjects and the obligations and rights of the controller. That contract or other legal act shall stipulate, in particular, that the processor:
   (a) processes the personal data only on documented instructions from the controller, including with regard to transfers of personal data to a third country or an international organisation, unless required to do so by Union or Member State law to which the processor is subject; in such a case, the processor shall inform the controller of that legal requirement before processing, unless that law prohibits such information on important grounds of public interest;
   (b) ensures that persons authorised to process the personal data have committed themselves to confidentiality or are under an appropriate statutory obligation of confidentiality;
   (c) takes all measures required pursuant to Article 32;
   (d) respects the conditions referred to in paragraphs 2 and 4 for engaging another processor;

    (e) taking into account the nature of the processing, assists the controller by appropriate technical and organisational measures, insofar as this is possible, for the fulfilment of the controller's obligation to respond to requests for exercising the data subject's rights laid down in Chapter III;

    (f) assists the controller in ensuring compliance with the obligations pursuant to Articles 32 to 36 taking into account the nature of processing and the information available to the processor;

    (g) at the choice of the controller, deletes or returns all the personal data to the controller after the end of the provision of services relating to processing, and deletes existing copies unless Union or Member State law requires storage of the personal data;

    (h) makes available to the controller all information necessary to demonstrate compliance with the obligations laid down in this Article and allow for and contribute to audits, including inspections, conducted by the controller or another auditor mandated by the controller.

With regard to point (h) of the first subparagraph, the processor shall immediately inform the controller if, in its opinion, an instruction infringes this Regulation or other Union or Member State data protection provisions.

4. Where a processor engages another processor for carrying out specific processing activities on behalf of the controller, the same data protection obligations as set out in the contract or other legal act between the controller and the processor as referred to in paragraph 3 shall be imposed on that other processor by way of a contract or other legal act under Union or Member State law, in particular providing sufficient guarantees to implement appropriate technical and organisational measures in such a manner that the processing will meet the requirements of this Regulation. Where that other processor fails to fulfil its data protection obligations, the initial processor shall remain fully liable to the controller for the performance of that other processor's obligations.

5. Adherence of a processor to an approved code of conduct as referred to in Article 40 or an approved certification mechanism as referred to in Article 42 may be used as an element by which to demonstrate sufficient guarantees as referred to in paragraphs 1 and 4 of this Article.

6. Without prejudice to an individual contract between the controller and the processor, the contract or the other legal act referred to in paragraphs 3 and 4 of this Article may be based, in whole or in part, on standard contractual clauses referred to in paragraphs 7 and 8 of this Article, including when they are part of a certification granted to the controller or processor pursuant to Articles 42 and 43.

7. The Commission may lay down standard contractual clauses for the matters referred to in paragraph 3 and 4 of this Article and in accordance with the examination procedure referred to in Article 93(2).

8. A supervisory authority may adopt standard contractual clauses for the matters referred to in paragraph 3 and 4 of this Article and in accordance with the consistency mechanism referred to in Article 63.

9. The contract or the other legal act referred to in paragraphs 3 and 4 shall be in writing, including in electronic form.

10. Without prejudice to Articles 82, 83 and 84, if a processor infringes this Regulation by determining the purposes and means of processing, the processor shall be considered to be a controller in respect of that processing.

Article 29
Processing under the authority of the controller or processor

The processor and any person acting under the authority of the controller or of the processor, who has access to personal data, shall not process those data except on instructions from the controller, unless required to do so by Union or Member State law.

Article 30
Records of processing activities

1. Each controller and, where applicable, the controller's representative, shall maintain a record of processing activities under its responsibility. That record shall contain all of the following information:
    (a) the name and contact details of the controller and, where applicable, the joint controller, the controller's representative and the data protection officer;
    (b) the purposes of the processing;
    (c) a description of the categories of data subjects and of the categories of personal data;
    (d) the categories of recipients to whom the personal data have been or will be disclosed including recipients in third countries or international organisations;
    (e) where applicable, transfers of personal data to a third country or an international organisation, including the identification of that third country or international organisation and, in the case of transfers referred to in the second subparagraph of Article 49(1), the documentation of suitable safeguards;
    (f) where possible, the envisaged time limits for erasure of the different categories of data;
    (g) where possible, a general description of the technical and organisational security measures referred to in Article 32(1).
2. Each processor and, where applicable, the processor's representative shall maintain a record of all categories of processing activities carried out on behalf of a controller, containing:
    (a) the name and contact details of the processor or processors and of each controller on behalf of which the processor is acting, and, where applicable, of the controller's or the processor's representative, and the data protection officer;
    (b) the categories of processing carried out on behalf of each controller;
    (c) where applicable, transfers of personal data to a third country or an international organisation, including the identification of that third country or international organisation and, in the case of transfers referred to in the second subparagraph of Article 49(1), the documentation of suitable safeguards;
    (d) where possible, a general description of the technical and organisational security measures referred to in Article 32(1).
3. The records referred to in paragraphs 1 and 2 shall be in writing, including in electronic form.
4. The controller or the processor and, where applicable, the controller's or the processor's representative, shall make the record available to the supervisory authority on request.
5. The obligations referred to in paragraphs 1 and 2 shall not apply to an enterprise or an organisation employing fewer than 250 persons unless the processing it carries out is likely to result in a risk to the rights and freedoms of data subjects, the processing is not occasional, or the processing includes special categories of data as referred to in Article 9(1) or personal data relating to criminal convictions and offences referred to in Article 10.

Article 31
Cooperation with the supervisory authority

The controller and the processor and, where applicable, their representatives, shall cooperate, on request, with the supervisory authority in the performance of its tasks.

Section 2
Security of personal data

Article 32
Security of processing

1. Taking into account the state of the art, the costs of implementation and the nature, scope, context and purposes of processing as well as the risk of varying likelihood and severity for the rights and freedoms of natural persons, the controller and the processor shall implement appropriate technical and organisational measures to ensure a level of security appropriate to the risk, including inter alia as appropriate:
   (a) the pseudonymisation and encryption of personal data;
   (b) the ability to ensure the ongoing confidentiality, integrity, availability and resilience of processing systems and services;
   (c) the ability to restore the availability and access to personal data in a timely manner in the event of a physical or technical incident;
   (d) a process for regularly testing, assessing and evaluating the effectiveness of technical and organisational measures for ensuring the security of the processing.
2. In assessing the appropriate level of security account shall be taken in particular of the risks that are presented by processing, in particular from accidental or unlawful destruction, loss, alteration, unauthorised disclosure of, or access to personal data transmitted, stored or otherwise processed.
3. Adherence to an approved code of conduct as referred to in Article 40 or an approved certification mechanism as referred to in Article 42 may be used as an element by which to demonstrate compliance with the requirements set out in paragraph 1 of this Article.
4. The controller and processor shall take steps to ensure that any natural person acting under the authority of the controller or the processor who has access to personal data does not process them except on instructions from the controller, unless he or she is required to do so by Union or Member State law.

Article 33
Notification of a personal data breach to the supervisory authority

1. In the case of a personal data breach, the controller shall without undue delay and, where feasible, not later than 72 hours after having become aware of it, notify the personal data breach to the supervisory authority competent in accordance with Article 55, unless the personal data breach is unlikely to result in a risk to the rights and freedoms of natural persons. Where the notification to the supervisory authority is not made within 72 hours, it shall be accompanied by reasons for the delay.
2. The processor shall notify the controller without undue delay after becoming aware of a personal data breach.
3. The notification referred to in paragraph 1 shall at least:
   (a) describe the nature of the personal data breach including where possible, the categories and approximate number of data subjects concerned and the categories and approximate number of personal data records concerned;

    (b) communicate the name and contact details of the data protection officer or other contact point where more information can be obtained;

    (c) describe the likely consequences of the personal data breach;

    (d) describe the measures taken or proposed to be taken by the controller to address the personal data breach, including, where appropriate, measures to mitigate its possible adverse effects.

4. Where, and in so far as, it is not possible to provide the information at the same time, the information may be provided in phases without undue further delay.

5. The controller shall document any personal data breaches, comprising the facts relating to the personal data breach, its effects and the remedial action taken. That documentation shall enable the supervisory authority to verify compliance with this Article.

Article 34
Communication of a personal data breach to the data subject

1. When the personal data breach is likely to result in a high risk to the rights and freedoms of natural persons, the controller shall communicate the personal data breach to the data subject without undue delay.

2. The communication to the data subject referred to in paragraph 1 of this Article shall describe in clear and plain language the nature of the personal data breach and contain at least the information and measures referred to in points (b), (c) and (d) of Article 33(3).

3. The communication to the data subject referred to in paragraph 1 shall not be required if any of the following conditions are met:

    (a) the controller has implemented appropriate technical and organisational protection measures, and those measures were applied to the personal data affected by the personal data breach, in particular those that render the personal data unintelligible to any person who is not authorised to access it, such as encryption;

    (b) the controller has taken subsequent measures which ensure that the high risk to the rights and freedoms of data subjects referred to in paragraph 1 is no longer likely to materialise;

    (c) it would involve disproportionate effort. In such a case, there shall instead be a public communication or similar measure whereby the data subjects are informed in an equally effective manner.

4. If the controller has not already communicated the personal data breach to the data subject, the supervisory authority, having considered the likelihood of the personal data breach resulting in a high risk, may require it to do so or may decide that any of the conditions referred to in paragraph 3 are met.

Section 3
Data protection impact assessment and prior consultation

Article 35
Data protection impact assessment

1. Where a type of processing in particular using new technologies, and taking into account the nature, scope, context and purposes of the processing, is likely to result in a high risk to the rights and freedoms of natural persons, the controller shall, prior to the processing, carry out an assessment of the impact of the envisaged processing operations on the protection of personal data. A single assessment may address a set of similar processing operations that present similar high risks.

2. The controller shall seek the advice of the data protection officer, where designated, when carrying out a data protection impact assessment.

3. A data protection impact assessment referred to in paragraph 1 shall in particular be required in the case of:

   (a) a systematic and extensive evaluation of personal aspects relating to natural persons which is based on automated processing, including profiling, and on which decisions are based that produce legal effects concerning the natural person or similarly significantly affect the natural person;

   (b) processing on a large scale of special categories of data referred to in Article 9(1), or of personal data relating to criminal convictions and offences referred to in Article 10; or

   (c) a systematic monitoring of a publicly accessible area on a large scale.

4. The supervisory authority shall establish and make public a list of the kind of processing operations which are subject to the requirement for a data protection impact assessment pursuant to paragraph 1. The supervisory authority shall communicate those lists to the Board referred to in Article 68.

5. The supervisory authority may also establish and make public a list of the kind of processing operations for which no data protection impact assessment is required. The supervisory authority shall communicate those lists to the Board.

6. Prior to the adoption of the lists referred to in paragraphs 4 and 5, the competent supervisory authority shall apply the consistency mechanism referred to in Article 63 where such lists involve processing activities which are related to the offering of goods or services to data subjects or to the monitoring of their behaviour in several Member States, or may substantially affect the free movement of personal data within the Union.

7. The assessment shall contain at least:

   (a) a systematic description of the envisaged processing operations and the purposes of the processing, including, where applicable, the legitimate interest pursued by the controller;

   (b) an assessment of the necessity and proportionality of the processing operations in relation to the purposes;

   (c) an assessment of the risks to the rights and freedoms of data subjects referred to in paragraph 1; and

   (d) the measures envisaged to address the risks, including safeguards, security measures and mechanisms to ensure the protection of personal data and to demonstrate compliance with this Regulation taking into account the rights and legitimate interests of data subjects and other persons concerned.

8. Compliance with approved codes of conduct referred to in Article 40 by the relevant controllers or processors shall be taken into due account in assessing the impact of the processing operations performed by such controllers or processors, in particular for the purposes of a data protection impact assessment.

9. Where appropriate, the controller shall seek the views of data subjects or their representatives on the intended processing, without prejudice to the protection of commercial or public interests or the security of processing operations.

10. Where processing pursuant to point (c) or (e) of Article 6(1) has a legal basis in Union law or in the law of the Member State to which the controller is subject, that law regulates the specific processing operation or set of operations in question, and a data protection impact assessment has already been carried out as part of a general impact assessment in the context of the adoption of that legal basis, paragraphs 1 to 7 shall not

apply unless Member States deem it to be necessary to carry out such an assessment prior to processing activities.

11. Where necessary, the controller shall carry out a review to assess if processing is performed in accordance with the data protection impact assessment at least when there is a change of the risk represented by processing operations.

Article 36
Prior consultation

1. The controller shall consult the supervisory authority prior to processing where a data protection impact assessment under Article 35 indicates that the processing would result in a high risk in the absence of measures taken by the controller to mitigate the risk.

2. Where the supervisory authority is of the opinion that the intended processing referred to in paragraph 1 would infringe this Regulation, in particular where the controller has insufficiently identified or mitigated the risk, the supervisory authority shall, within period of up to eight weeks of receipt of the request for consultation, provide written advice to the controller and, where applicable to the processor, and may use any of its powers referred to in Article 58. That period may be extended by six weeks, taking into account the complexity of the intended processing. The supervisory authority shall inform the controller and, where applicable, the processor, of any such extension within one month of receipt of the request for consultation together with the reasons for the delay. Those periods may be suspended until the supervisory authority has obtained information it has requested for the purposes of the consultation.

3. When consulting the supervisory authority pursuant to paragraph 1, the controller shall provide the supervisory authority with:
   (a) where applicable, the respective responsibilities of the controller, joint controllers and processors involved in the processing, in particular for processing within a group of undertakings;
   (b) the purposes and means of the intended processing;
   (c) the measures and safeguards provided to protect the rights and freedoms of data subjects pursuant to this Regulation;
   (d) where applicable, the contact details of the data protection officer;
   (e) the data protection impact assessment provided for in Article 35; and
   (f) any other information requested by the supervisory authority.

4. Member States shall consult the supervisory authority during the preparation of a proposal for a legislative measure to be adopted by a national parliament, or of a regulatory measure based on such a legislative measure, which relates to processing.

5. Notwithstanding paragraph 1, Member State law may require controllers to consult with, and obtain prior authorisation from, the supervisory authority in relation to processing by a controller for the performance of a task carried out by the controller in the public interest, including processing in relation to social protection and public health.

Section 4
Data protection officer

Article 37
Designation of the data protection officer

1. The controller and the processor shall designate a data protection officer in any case where:
   (a) the processing is carried out by a public authority or body, except for courts acting in their judicial capacity;

(b) the core activities of the controller or the processor consist of processing operations which, by virtue of their nature, their scope and/or their purposes, require regular and systematic monitoring of data subjects on a large scale; or

(c) the core activities of the controller or the processor consist of processing on a large scale of special categories of data pursuant to Article 9 and personal data relating to criminal convictions and offences referred to in Article 10.

2. A group of undertakings may appoint a single data protection officer provided that a data protection officer is easily accessible from each establishment.

3. Where the controller or the processor is a public authority or body, a single data protection officer may be designated for several such authorities or bodies, taking account of their organisational structure and size.

4. In cases other than those referred to in paragraph 1, the controller or processor or associations and other bodies representing categories of controllers or processors may or, where required by Union or Member State law shall, designate a data protection officer. The data protection officer may act for such associations and other bodies representing controllers or processors.

5. The data protection officer shall be designated on the basis of professional qualities and, in particular, expert knowledge of data protection law and practices and the ability to fulfil the tasks referred to in Article 39.

6. The data protection officer may be a staff member of the controller or processor, or fulfil the tasks on the basis of a service contract.

7. The controller or the processor shall publish the contact details of the data protection officer and communicate them to the supervisory authority.

Article 38
Position of the data protection officer

1. The controller and the processor shall ensure that the data protection officer is involved, properly and in a timely manner, in all issues which relate to the protection of personal data.

2. The controller and processor shall support the data protection officer in performing the tasks referred to in Article 39 by providing resources necessary to carry out those tasks and access to personal data and processing operations, and to maintain his or her expert knowledge.

3. The controller and processor shall ensure that the data protection officer does not receive any instructions regarding the exercise of those tasks. He or she shall not be dismissed or penalised by the controller or the processor for performing his tasks. The data protection officer shall directly report to the highest management level of the controller or the processor.

4. Data subjects may contact the data protection officer with regard to all issues related to processing of their personal data and to the exercise of their rights under this Regulation.

5. The data protection officer shall be bound by secrecy or confidentiality concerning the performance of his or her tasks, in accordance with Union or Member State law.

6. The data protection officer may fulfil other tasks and duties. The controller or processor shall ensure that any such tasks and duties do not result in a conflict of interests.

Article 39
Tasks of the data protection officer

1. The data protection officer shall have at least the following tasks:
   (a) to inform and advise the controller or the processor and the employees who carry out processing of their obligations pursuant to this Regulation and to other Union or Member State data protection provisions;

(b) to monitor compliance with this Regulation, with other Union or Member State data protection provisions and with the policies of the controller or processor in relation to the protection of personal data, including the assignment of responsibilities, awareness-raising and training of staff involved in processing operations, and the related audits;

(c) to provide advice where requested as regards the data protection impact assessment and monitor its performance pursuant to Article 35;

(d) to cooperate with the supervisory authority;

(e) to act as the contact point for the supervisory authority on issues relating to processing, including the prior consultation referred to in Article 36, and to consult, where appropriate, with regard to any other matter.

2. The data protection officer shall in the performance of his or her tasks have due regard to the risk associated with processing operations, taking into account the nature, scope, context and purposes of processing.

Section 5
Codes of conduct and certification

Article 40
Codes of conduct

1. The Member States, the supervisory authorities, the Board and the Commission shall encourage the drawing up of codes of conduct intended to contribute to the proper application of this Regulation, taking account of the specific features of the various processing sectors and the specific needs of micro, small and medium-sized enterprises.

2. Associations and other bodies representing categories of controllers or processors may prepare codes of conduct, or amend or extend such codes, for the purpose of specifying the application of this Regulation, such as with regard to:

(a) fair and transparent processing;

(b) the legitimate interests pursued by controllers in specific contexts;

(c) the collection of personal data;

(d) the pseudonymisation of personal data;

(e) the information provided to the public and to data subjects;

(f) the exercise of the rights of data subjects;

(g) the information provided to, and the protection of, children, and the manner in which the consent of the holders of parental responsibility over children is to be obtained;

(h) the measures and procedures referred to in Articles 24 and 25 and the measures to ensure security of processing referred to in Article 32;

(i) the notification of personal data breaches to supervisory authorities and the communication of such personal data breaches to data subjects;

(j) the transfer of personal data to third countries or international organisations; or

(k) out-of-court proceedings and other dispute resolution procedures for resolving disputes between controllers and data subjects with regard to processing, without prejudice to the rights of data subjects pursuant to Articles 77 and 79.

3. In addition to adherence by controllers or processors subject to this Regulation, codes of conduct approved pursuant to paragraph 5 of this Article and having general validity pursuant to paragraph 9 of this Article may also be adhered to by controllers or processors that are not subject to this Regulation pursuant to Article 3 in order to provide appropriate safeguards within the framework of personal data transfers to third countries or international organisations under the terms referred to in point (e) of Article

46(2). Such controllers or processors shall make binding and enforceable commitments, via contractual or other legally binding instruments, to apply those appropriate safeguards including with regard to the rights of data subjects.

4. A code of conduct referred to in paragraph 2 of this Article shall contain mechanisms which enable the body referred to in Article 41(1) to carry out the mandatory monitoring of compliance with its provisions by the controllers or processors which undertake to apply it, without prejudice to the tasks and powers of supervisory authorities competent pursuant to Article 55 or 56.

5. Associations and other bodies referred to in paragraph 2 of this Article which intend to prepare a code of conduct or to amend or extend an existing code shall submit the draft code, amendment or extension to the supervisory authority which is competent pursuant to Article 55. The supervisory authority shall provide an opinion on whether the draft code, amendment or extension complies with this Regulation and shall approve that draft code, amendment or extension if it finds that it provides sufficient appropriate safeguards.

6. Where the draft code, or amendment or extension is approved in accordance with paragraph 5, and where the code of conduct concerned does not relate to processing activities in several Member States, the supervisory authority shall register and publish the code.

7. Where a draft code of conduct relates to processing activities in several Member States, the supervisory authority which is competent pursuant to Article 55 shall, before approving the draft code, amendment or extension, submit it in the procedure referred to in Article 63 to the Board which shall provide an opinion on whether the draft code, amendment or extension complies with this Regulation or, in the situation referred to in paragraph 3 of this Article, provides appropriate safeguards.

8. Where the opinion referred to in paragraph 7 confirms that the draft code, amendment or extension complies with this Regulation, or, in the situation referred to in paragraph 3, provides appropriate safeguards, the Board shall submit its opinion to the Commission.

9. The Commission may, by way of implementing acts, decide that the approved code of conduct, amendment or extension submitted to it pursuant to paragraph 8 of this Article have general validity within the Union. Those implementing acts shall be adopted in accordance with the examination procedure set out in Article 93(2).

10. The Commission shall ensure appropriate publicity for the approved codes which have been decided as having general validity in accordance with paragraph 9.

11. The Board shall collate all approved codes of conduct, amendments and extensions in a register and shall make them publicly available by way of appropriate means.

Article 41
Monitoring of approved codes of conduct

1. Without prejudice to the tasks and powers of the competent supervisory authority under Articles 57 and 58, the monitoring of compliance with a code of conduct pursuant to Article 40 may be carried out by a body which has an appropriate level of expertise in relation to the subject-matter of the code and is accredited for that purpose by the competent supervisory authority.

2. A body as referred to in paragraph 1 may be accredited to monitor compliance with a code of conduct where that body has:
   (a) demonstrated its independence and expertise in relation to the subject-matter of the code to the satisfaction of the competent supervisory authority;

    (b) established procedures which allow it to assess the eligibility of controllers and processors concerned to apply the code, to monitor their compliance with its provisions and to periodically review its operation;

    (c) established procedures and structures to handle complaints about infringements of the code or the manner in which the code has been, or is being, implemented by a controller or processor, and to make those procedures and structures transparent to data subjects and the public; and

    (d) demonstrated to the satisfaction of the competent supervisory authority that its tasks and duties do not result in a conflict of interests.

3. The competent supervisory authority shall submit the draft criteria for accreditation of a body as referred to in paragraph 1 of this Article to the Board pursuant to the consistency mechanism referred to in Article 63.

4. Without prejudice to the tasks and powers of the competent supervisory authority and the provisions of Chapter VIII, a body as referred to in paragraph 1 of this Article shall, subject to appropriate safeguards, take appropriate action in cases of infringement of the code by a controller or processor, including suspension or exclusion of the controller or processor concerned from the code. It shall inform the competent supervisory authority of such actions and the reasons for taking them.

5. The competent supervisory authority shall revoke the accreditation of a body as referred to in paragraph 1 if the conditions for accreditation are not, or are no longer, met or where actions taken by the body infringe this Regulation.

6. This Article shall not apply to processing carried out by public authorities and bodies.

Article 42
Certification

1. The Member States, the supervisory authorities, the Board and the Commission shall encourage, in particular at Union level, the establishment of data protection certification mechanisms and of data protection seals and marks, for the purpose of demonstrating compliance with this Regulation of processing operations by controllers and processors. The specific needs of micro, small and medium-sized enterprises shall be taken into account.

2. In addition to adherence by controllers or processors subject to this Regulation, data protection certification mechanisms, seals or marks approved pursuant to paragraph 5 of this Article may be established for the purpose of demonstrating the existence of appropriate safeguards provided by controllers or processors that are not subject to this Regulation pursuant to Article 3 within the framework of personal data transfers to third countries or international organisations under the terms referred to in point (f) of Article 46(2). Such controllers or processors shall make binding and enforceable commitments, via contractual or other legally binding instruments, to apply those appropriate safeguards, including with regard to the rights of data subjects.

3. The certification shall be voluntary and available via a process that is transparent.

4. A certification pursuant to this Article does not reduce the responsibility of the controller or the processor for compliance with this Regulation and is without prejudice to the tasks and powers of the supervisory authorities which are competent pursuant to Article 55 or 56.

5. A certification pursuant to this Article shall be issued by the certification bodies referred to in Article 43 or by the competent supervisory authority, on the basis of criteria approved by that competent supervisory authority pursuant to Article 58(3) or

by the Board pursuant to Article 63. Where the criteria are approved by the Board, this may result in a common certification, the European Data Protection Seal.

6. The controller or processor which submits its processing to the certification mechanism shall provide the certification body referred to in Article 43, or where applicable, the competent supervisory authority, with all information and access to its processing activities which are necessary to conduct the certification procedure.

7. Certification shall be issued to a controller or processor for a maximum period of three years and may be renewed, under the same conditions, provided that the relevant requirements continue to be met. Certification shall be withdrawn, as applicable, by the certification bodies referred to in Article 43 or by the competent supervisory authority where the requirements for the certification are not or are no longer met.

8. The Board shall collate all certification mechanisms and data protection seals and marks in a register and shall make them publicly available by any appropriate means.

Article 43
Certification bodies

1. Without prejudice to the tasks and powers of the competent supervisory authority under Articles 57 and 58, certification bodies which have an appropriate level of expertise in relation to data protection shall, after informing the supervisory authority in order to allow it to exercise its powers pursuant to point (h) of Article 58(2) where necessary, issue and renew certification. Member States shall ensure that those certification bodies are accredited by one or both of the following:
   (a) the supervisory authority which is competent pursuant to Article 55 or 56;
   (b) the national accreditation body named in accordance with Regulation (EC) No 765/2008 of the European Parliament and of the Council [20] in accordance with EN-ISO/IEC 17065/2012 and with the additional requirements established by the supervisory authority which is competent pursuant to Article 55 or 56.

2. Certification bodies referred to in paragraph 1 shall be accredited in accordance with that paragraph only where they have:
   (a) demonstrated their independence and expertise in relation to the subject-matter of the certification to the satisfaction of the competent supervisory authority;
   (b) undertaken to respect the criteria referred to in Article 42(5) and approved by the supervisory authority which is competent pursuant to Article 55 or 56 or by the Board pursuant to Article 63;
   (c) established procedures for the issuing, periodic review and withdrawal of data protection certification, seals and marks;
   (d) established procedures and structures to handle complaints about infringements of the certification or the manner in which the certification has been, or is being, implemented by the controller or processor, and to make those procedures and structures transparent to data subjects and the public; and
   (e) demonstrated, to the satisfaction of the competent supervisory authority, that their tasks and duties do not result in a conflict of interests.

[20] Regulation (EC) No 765/2008 of the European Parliament and of the Council of 9 July 2008 setting out the requirements for accreditation and market surveillance relating to the marketing of products and repealing Regulation (EEC) No 339/93 (OJ L 218, 13.8.2008, p. 30).

3. The accreditation of certification bodies as referred to in paragraphs 1 and 2 of this Article shall take place on the basis of criteria approved by the supervisory authority which is competent pursuant to Article 55 or 56 or by the Board pursuant to Article 63. In the case of accreditation pursuant to point (b) of paragraph 1 of this Article, those requirements shall complement those envisaged in Regulation (EC) No 765/2008 and the technical rules that describe the methods and procedures of the certification bodies.

4. The certification bodies referred to in paragraph 1 shall be responsible for the proper assessment leading to the certification or the withdrawal of such certification without prejudice to the responsibility of the controller or processor for compliance with this Regulation. The accreditation shall be issued for a maximum period of five years and may be renewed on the same conditions provided that the certification body meets the requirements set out in this Article.

5. The certification bodies referred to in paragraph 1 shall provide the competent supervisory authorities with the reasons for granting or withdrawing the requested certification.

6. The requirements referred to in paragraph 3 of this Article and the criteria referred to in Article 42(5) shall be made public by the supervisory authority in an easily accessible form. The supervisory authorities shall also transmit those requirements and criteria to the Board. The Board shall collate all certification mechanisms and data protection seals in a register and shall make them publicly available by any appropriate means.

7. Without prejudice to Chapter VIII, the competent supervisory authority or the national accreditation body shall revoke an accreditation of a certification body pursuant to paragraph 1 of this Article where the conditions for the accreditation are not, or are no longer, met or where actions taken by a certification body infringe this Regulation.

8. The Commission shall be empowered to adopt delegated acts in accordance with Article 92 for the purpose of specifying the requirements to be taken into account for the data protection certification mechanisms referred to in Article 42(1).

9. The Commission may adopt implementing acts laying down technical standards for certification mechanisms and data protection seals and marks, and mechanisms to promote and recognise those certification mechanisms, seals and marks. Those implementing acts shall be adopted in accordance with the examination procedure referred to in Article 93(2).

CHAPTER V TRANSFERS OF PERSONAL DATA TO THIRD COUNTRIES OR INTERNATIONAL ORGANISATIONS

Article 44
General principle for transfers

Any transfer of personal data which are undergoing processing or are intended for processing after transfer to a third country or to an international organisation shall take place only if, subject to the other provisions of this Regulation, the conditions laid down in this Chapter are complied with by the controller and processor, including for onward transfers of personal data from the third country or an international organisation to another third country or to another international organisation. All provisions in this Chapter shall be applied in order to ensure that the level of protection of natural persons guaranteed by this Regulation is not undermined.

Article 45
Transfers on the basis of an adequacy decision

1. A transfer of personal data to a third country or an international organisation may take place where the Commission has decided that the third country, a territory or one or more specified sectors within that third country, or the international organisation in question ensures an adequate level of protection. Such a transfer shall not require any specific authorisation.

2. When assessing the adequacy of the level of protection, the Commission shall, in particular, take account of the following elements:

   (a) the rule of law, respect for human rights and fundamental freedoms, relevant legislation, both general and sectoral, including concerning public security, defence, national security and criminal law and the access of public authorities to personal data, as well as the implementation of such legislation, data protection rules, professional rules and security measures, including rules for the onward transfer of personal data to another third country or international organisation which are complied with in that country or international organisation, case-law, as well as effective and enforceable data subject rights and effective administrative and judicial redress for the data subjects whose personal data are being transferred;

   (b) the existence and effective functioning of one or more independent supervisory authorities in the third country or to which an international organisation is subject, with responsibility for ensuring and enforcing compliance with the data protection rules, including adequate enforcement powers, for assisting and advising the data subjects in exercising their rights and for cooperation with the supervisory authorities of the Member States; and

   (c) the international commitments the third country or international organisation concerned has entered into, or other obligations arising from legally binding conventions or instruments as well as from its participation in multilateral or regional systems, in particular in relation to the protection of personal data.

3. The Commission, after assessing the adequacy of the level of protection, may decide, by means of implementing act, that a third country, a territory or one or more specified sectors within a third country, or an international organisation ensures an adequate level of protection within the meaning of paragraph 2 of this Article. The implementing act shall provide for a mechanism for a periodic review, at least every four years, which shall take into account all relevant developments in the third country or international organisation. The implementing act shall specify its territorial and sectoral application and, where applicable, identify the supervisory authority or authorities referred to in point (b) of paragraph 2 of this Article. The implementing act shall be adopted in accordance with the examination procedure referred to in Article 93(2).

4. The Commission shall, on an ongoing basis, monitor developments in third countries and international organisations that could affect the functioning of decisions adopted pursuant to paragraph 3 of this Article and decisions adopted on the basis of Article 25(6) of Directive 95/46/EC.

5. The Commission shall, where available information reveals, in particular following the review referred to in paragraph 3 of this Article, that a third country, a territory or one or more specified sectors within a third country, or an international organisation no longer ensures an adequate level of protection within the meaning of paragraph 2 of this Article, to the extent necessary, repeal, amend or suspend the decision referred to in paragraph 3 of this Article by means of implementing acts without retro-active

effect. Those implementing acts shall be adopted in accordance with the examination procedure referred to in Article 93(2).

On duly justified imperative grounds of urgency, the Commission shall adopt immediately applicable implementing acts in accordance with the procedure referred to in Article 93(3).

6. The Commission shall enter into consultations with the third country or international organisation with a view to remedying the situation giving rise to the decision made pursuant to paragraph 5.

7. A decision pursuant to paragraph 5 of this Article is without prejudice to transfers of personal data to the third country, a territory or one or more specified sectors within that third country, or the international organisation in question pursuant to Articles 46 to 49.

8. The Commission shall publish in the Official Journal of the European Union and on its website a list of the third countries, territories and specified sectors within a third country and international organisations for which it has decided that an adequate level of protection is or is no longer ensured.

9. Decisions adopted by the Commission on the basis of Article 25(6) of Directive 95/46/EC shall remain in force until amended, replaced or repealed by a Commission Decision adopted in accordance with paragraph 3 or 5 of this Article.

Article 46
Transfers subject to appropriate safeguards

1. In the absence of a decision pursuant to Article 45(3), a controller or processor may transfer personal data to a third country or an international organisation only if the controller or processor has provided appropriate safeguards, and on condition that enforceable data subject rights and effective legal remedies for data subjects are available.

2. The appropriate safeguards referred to in paragraph 1 may be provided for, without requiring any specific authorisation from a supervisory authority, by:
    (a) a legally binding and enforceable instrument between public authorities or bodies;
    (b) binding corporate rules in accordance with Article 47;
    (c) standard data protection clauses adopted by the Commission in accordance with the examination procedure referred to in Article 93(2);
    (d) standard data protection clauses adopted by a supervisory authority and approved by the Commission pursuant to the examination procedure referred to in Article 93(2);
    (e) an approved code of conduct pursuant to Article 40 together with binding and enforceable commitments of the controller or processor in the third country to apply the appropriate safeguards, including as regards data subjects' rights; or
    (f) an approved certification mechanism pursuant to Article 42 together with binding and enforceable commitments of the controller or processor in the third country to apply the appropriate safeguards, including as regards data subjects' rights.

3. Subject to the authorisation from the competent supervisory authority, the appropriate safeguards referred to in paragraph 1 may also be provided for, in particular, by:
    (a) contractual clauses between the controller or processor and the controller, processor or the recipient of the personal data in the third country or international organisation; or
    (b) provisions to be inserted into administrative arrangements between public authorities or bodies which include enforceable and effective data subject rights.

4. The supervisory authority shall apply the consistency mechanism referred to in Article 63 in the cases referred to in paragraph 3 of this Article.

5. Authorisations by a Member State or supervisory authority on the basis of Article 26(2) of Directive 95/46/EC shall remain valid until amended, replaced or repealed, if necessary, by that supervisory authority. Decisions adopted by the Commission on the basis of Article 26(4) of Directive 95/46/EC shall remain in force until amended, replaced or repealed, if necessary, by a Commission Decision adopted in accordance with paragraph 2 of this Article.

Article 47
Binding corporate rules

1. The competent supervisory authority shall approve binding corporate rules in accordance with the consistency mechanism set out in Article 63, provided that they:
   (a) are legally binding and apply to and are enforced by every member concerned of the group of undertakings, or group of enterprises engaged in a joint economic activity, including their employees;
   (b) expressly confer enforceable rights on data subjects with regard to the processing of their personal data; and
   (c) fulfil the requirements laid down in paragraph 2.

2. The binding corporate rules referred to in paragraph 1 shall specify at least:
   (a) the structure and contact details of the group of undertakings, or group of enterprises engaged in a joint economic activity and of each of its members;
   (b) the data transfers or set of transfers, including the categories of personal data, the type of processing and its purposes, the type of data subjects affected and the identification of the third country or countries in question;
   (c) their legally binding nature, both internally and externally;
   (d) the application of the general data protection principles, in particular purpose limitation, data minimisation, limited storage periods, data quality, data protection by design and by default, legal basis for processing, processing of special categories of personal data, measures to ensure data security, and the requirements in respect of onward transfers to bodies not bound by the binding corporate rules;
   (e) the rights of data subjects in regard to processing and the means to exercise those rights, including the right not to be subject to decisions based solely on automated processing, including profiling in accordance with Article 22, the right to lodge a complaint with the competent supervisory authority and before the competent courts of the Member States in accordance with Article 79, and to obtain redress and, where appropriate, compensation for a breach of the binding corporate rules;
   (f) the acceptance by the controller or processor established on the territory of a Member State of liability for any breaches of the binding corporate rules by any member concerned not established in the Union; the controller or the processor shall be exempt from that liability, in whole or in part, only if it proves that that member is not responsible for the event giving rise to the damage;
   (g) how the information on the binding corporate rules, in particular on the provisions referred to in points (d), (e) and (f) of this paragraph is provided to the data subjects in addition to Articles 13 and 14;
   (h) the tasks of any data protection officer designated in accordance with Article 37 or any other person or entity in charge of the monitoring compliance with the

binding corporate rules within the group of undertakings, or group of enter-prises engaged in a joint economic activity, as well as monitoring training and complaint-handling;

(i) the complaint procedures;

(j) the mechanisms within the group of undertakings, or group of enterprises engaged in a joint economic activity for ensuring the verification of compliance with the binding corporate rules. Such mechanisms shall include data protection audits and methods for ensuring corrective actions to protect the rights of the data subject. Results of such verification should be communicated to the person or entity referred to in point (h) and to the board of the controlling undertaking of a group of undertakings, or of the group of enterprises engaged in a joint eco-nomic activity, and should be available upon request to the competent supervis-ory authority;

(k) the mechanisms for reporting and recording changes to the rules and reporting those changes to the supervisory authority;

(l) the cooperation mechanism with the supervisory authority to ensure compliance by any member of the group of undertakings, or group of enterprises engaged in a joint economic activity, in particular by making available to the supervisory authority the results of verifications of the measures referred to in point (j);

(m) the mechanisms for reporting to the competent supervisory authority any legal requirements to which a member of the group of undertakings, or group of enter-prises engaged in a joint economic activity is subject in a third country which are likely to have a substantial adverse effect on the guarantees provided by the bind-ing corporate rules; and

(n) the appropriate data protection training to personnel having permanent or regular access to personal data.

3. The Commission may specify the format and procedures for the exchange of informa-tion between controllers, processors and supervisory authorities for binding corporate rules within the meaning of this Article. Those implementing acts shall be adopted in accordance with the examination procedure set out in Article 93(2).

Article 48
Transfers or disclosures not authorised by Union law

Any judgment of a court or tribunal and any decision of an administrative authority of a third country requiring a controller or processor to transfer or disclose personal data may only be recognised or enforceable in any manner if based on an international agreement, such as a mutual legal assistance treaty, in force between the requesting third country and the Union or a Member State, without prejudice to other grounds for transfer pursuant to this Chapter.

Article 49
Derogations for specific situations

1. In the absence of an adequacy decision pursuant to Article 45(3), or of appropriate safeguards pursuant to Article 46, including binding corporate rules, a transfer or a set of transfers of personal data to a third country or an international organisation shall take place only on one of the following conditions:

(a) the data subject has explicitly consented to the proposed transfer, after having been informed of the possible risks of such transfers for the data subject due to the absence of an adequacy decision and appropriate safeguards;

(b) the transfer is necessary for the performance of a contract between the data subject and the controller or the implementation of pre-contractual measures taken at the data subject's request;

(c) the transfer is necessary for the conclusion or performance of a contract concluded in the interest of the data subject between the controller and another natural or legal person;

(d) the transfer is necessary for important reasons of public interest;

(e) the transfer is necessary for the establishment, exercise or defence of legal claims;

(f) the transfer is necessary in order to protect the vital interests of the data subject or of other persons, where the data subject is physically or legally incapable of giving consent;

(g) the transfer is made from a register which according to Union or Member State law is intended to provide information to the public and which is open to consultation either by the public in general or by any person who can demonstrate a legitimate interest, but only to the extent that the conditions laid down by Union or Member State law for consultation are fulfilled in the particular case.

Where a transfer could not be based on a provision in Article 45 or 46, including the provisions on binding corporate rules, and none of the derogations for a specific situation referred to in the first subparagraph of this paragraph is applicable, a transfer to a third country or an international organisation may take place only if the transfer is not repetitive, concerns only a limited number of data subjects, is necessary for the purposes of compelling legitimate interests pursued by the controller which are not overridden by the interests or rights and freedoms of the data subject, and the controller has assessed all the circumstances surrounding the data transfer and has on the basis of that assessment provided suitable safeguards with regard to the protection of personal data. The controller shall inform the supervisory authority of the transfer. The controller shall, in addition to providing the information referred to in Articles 13 and 14, inform the data subject of the transfer and on the compelling legitimate interests pursued.

2. A transfer pursuant to point (g) of the first subparagraph of paragraph 1 shall not involve the entirety of the personal data or entire categories of the personal data contained in the register. Where the register is intended for consultation by persons having a legitimate interest, the transfer shall be made only at the request of those persons or if they are to be the recipients.

3. Points (a), (b) and (c) of the first subparagraph of paragraph 1 and the second subparagraph thereof shall not apply to activities carried out by public authorities in the exercise of their public powers.

4. The public interest referred to in point (d) of the first subparagraph of paragraph 1 shall be recognised in Union law or in the law of the Member State to which the controller is subject.

5. In the absence of an adequacy decision, Union or Member State law may, for important reasons of public interest, expressly set limits to the transfer of specific categories of personal data to a third country or an international organisation. Member States shall notify such provisions to the Commission.

6. The controller or processor shall document the assessment as well as the suitable safeguards referred to in the second subparagraph of paragraph 1 of this Article in the records referred to in Article 30.

Article 50
International cooperation for the protection of personal data

In relation to third countries and international organisations, the Commission and supervisory authorities shall take appropriate steps to:

(a) develop international cooperation mechanisms to facilitate the effective enforcement of legislation for the protection of personal data;

(b) provide international mutual assistance in the enforcement of legislation for the protection of personal data, including through notification, complaint referral, investigative assistance and information exchange, subject to appropriate safeguards for the protection of personal data and other fundamental rights and freedoms;

(c) engage relevant stakeholders in discussion and activities aimed at furthering international cooperation in the enforcement of legislation for the protection of personal data;

(d) promote the exchange and documentation of personal data protection legislation and practice, including on jurisdictional conflicts with third countries.

CHAPTER VI INDEPENDENT SUPERVISORY AUTHORITIES

Section 1
Independent status

Article 51
Supervisory authority

1. Each Member State shall provide for one or more independent public authorities to be responsible for monitoring the application of this Regulation, in order to protect the fundamental rights and freedoms of natural persons in relation to processing and to facilitate the free flow of personal data within the Union ('supervisory authority').

2. Each supervisory authority shall contribute to the consistent application of this Regulation throughout the Union. For that purpose, the supervisory authorities shall cooperate with each other and the Commission in accordance with Chapter VII.

3. Where more than one supervisory authority is established in a Member State, that Member State shall designate the supervisory authority which is to represent those authorities in the Board and shall set out the mechanism to ensure compliance by the other authorities with the rules relating to the consistency mechanism referred to in Article 63.

4. Each Member State shall notify to the Commission the provisions of its law which it adopts pursuant to this Chapter, by 25 May 2018 and, without delay, any subsequent amendment affecting them.

Article 52
Independence

1. Each supervisory authority shall act with complete independence in performing its tasks and exercising its powers in accordance with this Regulation.

2. The member or members of each supervisory authority shall, in the performance of their tasks and exercise of their powers in accordance with this Regulation, remain

free from external influence, whether direct or indirect, and shall neither seek nor take instructions from anybody.

3. Member or members of each supervisory authority shall refrain from any action incompatible with their duties and shall not, during their term of office, engage in any incompatible occupation, whether gainful or not.

4. Each Member State shall ensure that each supervisory authority is provided with the human, technical and financial resources, premises and infrastructure necessary for the effective performance of its tasks and exercise of its powers, including those to be carried out in the context of mutual assistance, cooperation and participation in the Board.

5. Each Member State shall ensure that each supervisory authority chooses and has its own staff which shall be subject to the exclusive direction of the member or members of the supervisory authority concerned.

6. Each Member State shall ensure that each supervisory authority is subject to financial control which does not affect its independence and that it has separate, public annual budgets, which may be part of the overall state or national budget.

Article 53
General conditions for the members of the supervisory authority

1. Member States shall provide for each member of their supervisory authorities to be appointed by means of a transparent procedure by:
   — their parliament;
   — their government;
   — their head of State; or
   — an independent body entrusted with the appointment under Member State law.

2. Each member shall have the qualifications, experience and skills, in particular in the area of the protection of personal data, required to perform its duties and exercise its powers.

3. The duties of a member shall end in the event of the expiry of the term of office, resignation or compulsory retirement, in accordance with the law of the Member State concerned.

4. A member shall be dismissed only in cases of serious misconduct or if the member no longer fulfils the conditions required for the performance of the duties.

Article 54
Rules on the establishment of the supervisory authority

1. Each Member State shall provide by law for all of the following:
   (a) the establishment of each supervisory authority;
   (b) the qualifications and eligibility conditions required to be appointed as member of each supervisory authority;
   (c) the rules and procedures for the appointment of the member or members of each supervisory authority;
   (d) the duration of the term of the member or members of each supervisory authority of no less than four years, except for the first appointment after 24 May 2016, part of which may take place for a shorter period where that is necessary to protect the independence of the supervisory authority by means of a staggered appointment procedure;
   (e) whether and, if so, for how many terms the member or members of each supervisory authority is eligible for reappointment;

(f) the conditions governing the obligations of the member or members and staff of each supervisory authority, prohibitions on actions, occupations and benefits incompatible therewith during and after the term of office and rules governing the cessation of employment.

2. The member or members and the staff of each supervisory authority shall, in accordance with Union or Member State law, be subject to a duty of professional secrecy both during and after their term of office, with regard to any confidential information which has come to their knowledge in the course of the performance of their tasks or exercise of their powers. During their term of office, that duty of professional secrecy shall in particular apply to reporting by natural persons of infringements of this Regulation.

Section 2
Competence, tasks and powers

Article 55
Competence

1. Each supervisory authority shall be competent for the performance of the tasks assigned to and the exercise of the powers conferred on it in accordance with this Regulation on the territory of its own Member State.
2. Where processing is carried out by public authorities or private bodies acting on the basis of point (c) or (e) of Article 6(1), the supervisory authority of the Member State concerned shall be competent. In such cases Article 56 does not apply.
3. Supervisory authorities shall not be competent to supervise processing operations of courts acting in their judicial capacity.

Article 56
Competence of the lead supervisory authority

1. Without prejudice to Article 55, the supervisory authority of the main establishment or of the single establishment of the controller or processor shall be competent to act as lead supervisory authority for the cross-border processing carried out by that controller or processor in accordance with the procedure provided in Article 60.
2. By derogation from paragraph 1, each supervisory authority shall be competent to handle a complaint lodged with it or a possible infringement of this Regulation, if the subject matter relates only to an establishment in its Member State or substantially affects data subjects only in its Member State.
3. In the cases referred to in paragraph 2 of this Article, the supervisory authority shall inform the lead supervisory authority without delay on that matter. Within a period of three weeks after being informed the lead supervisory authority shall decide whether or not it will handle the case in accordance with the procedure provided in Article 60, taking into account whether or not there is an establishment of the controller or processor in the Member State of which the supervisory authority informed it.
4. Where the lead supervisory authority decides to handle the case, the procedure provided in Article 60 shall apply. The supervisory authority which informed the lead supervisory authority may submit to the lead supervisory authority a draft for a decision. The lead supervisory authority shall take utmost account of that draft when preparing the draft decision referred to in Article 60(3).

5. Where the lead supervisory authority decides not to handle the case, the supervisory authority which informed the lead supervisory authority shall handle it according to Articles 61 and 62.

6. The lead supervisory authority shall be the sole interlocutor of the controller or processor for the cross-border processing carried out by that controller or processor.

Article 57
Tasks

1. Without prejudice to other tasks set out under this Regulation, each supervisory authority shall on its territory:

   (a) monitor and enforce the application of this Regulation;

   (b) promote public awareness and understanding of the risks, rules, safeguards and rights in relation to processing. Activities addressed specifically to children shall receive specific attention;

   (c) advise, in accordance with Member State law, the national parliament, the government, and other institutions and bodies on legislative and administrative measures relating to the protection of natural persons' rights and freedoms with regard to processing;

   (d) promote the awareness of controllers and processors of their obligations under this Regulation;

   (e) upon request, provide information to any data subject concerning the exercise of their rights under this Regulation and, if appropriate, cooperate with the supervisory authorities in other Member States to that end;

   (f) handle complaints lodged by a data subject, or by a body, organisation or association in accordance with Article 80, and investigate, to the extent appropriate, the subject matter of the complaint and inform the complainant of the progress and the outcome of the investigation within a reasonable period, in particular if further investigation or coordination with another supervisory authority is necessary;

   (g) cooperate with, including sharing information and provide mutual assistance to, other supervisory authorities with a view to ensuring the consistency of application and enforcement of this Regulation;

   (h) conduct investigations on the application of this Regulation, including on the basis of information received from another supervisory authority or other public authority;

   (i) monitor relevant developments, insofar as they have an impact on the protection of personal data, in particular the development of information and communication technologies and commercial practices;

   (j) adopt standard contractual clauses referred to in Article 28(8) and in point (d) of Article 46(2);

   (k) establish and maintain a list in relation to the requirement for data protection impact assessment pursuant to Article 35(4);

   (l) give advice on the processing operations referred to in Article 36(2);

   (m) encourage the drawing up of codes of conduct pursuant to Article 40(1) and provide an opinion and approve such codes of conduct which provide sufficient safeguards, pursuant to Article 40(5);

   (n) encourage the establishment of data protection certification mechanisms and of data protection seals and marks pursuant to Article 42(1), and approve the criteria of certification pursuant to Article 42(5);

(o) where applicable, carry out a periodic review of certifications issued in accordance with Article 42(7);

(p) draft and publish the criteria for accreditation of a body for monitoring codes of conduct pursuant to Article 41 and of a certification body pursuant to Article 43;

(q) conduct the accreditation of a body for monitoring codes of conduct pursuant to Article 41 and of a certification body pursuant to Article 43;

(r) authorise contractual clauses and provisions referred to in Article 46(3);

(s) approve binding corporate rules pursuant to Article 47;

(t) contribute to the activities of the Board;

(u) keep internal records of infringements of this Regulation and of measures taken in accordance with Article 58(2); and

(v) fulfil any other tasks related to the protection of personal data.

2. Each supervisory authority shall facilitate the submission of complaints referred to in point (f) of paragraph 1 by measures such as a complaint submission form which can also be completed electronically, without excluding other means of communication.

3. The performance of the tasks of each supervisory authority shall be free of charge for the data subject and, where applicable, for the data protection officer.

4. Where requests are manifestly unfounded or excessive, in particular because of their repetitive character, the supervisory authority may charge a reasonable fee based on administrative costs, or refuse to act on the request. The supervisory authority shall bear the burden of demonstrating the manifestly unfounded or excessive character of the request.

Article 58
Powers

1. Each supervisory authority shall have all of the following investigative powers:

    (a) to order the controller and the processor, and, where applicable, the controller's or the processor's representative to provide any information it requires for the performance of its tasks;

    (b) to carry out investigations in the form of data protection audits;

    (c) to carry out a review on certifications issued pursuant to Article 42(7);

    (d) to notify the controller or the processor of an alleged infringement of this Regulation;

    (e) to obtain, from the controller and the processor, access to all personal data and to all information necessary for the performance of its tasks;

    (f) to obtain access to any premises of the controller and the processor, including to any data processing equipment and means, in accordance with Union or Member State procedural law.

2. Each supervisory authority shall have all of the following corrective powers:

    (a) to issue warnings to a controller or processor that intended processing operations are likely to infringe provisions of this Regulation;

    (b) to issue reprimands to a controller or a processor where processing operations have infringed provisions of this Regulation;

    (c) to order the controller or the processor to comply with the data subject's requests to exercise his or her rights pursuant to this Regulation;

    (d) to order the controller or processor to bring processing operations into compliance with the provisions of this Regulation, where appropriate, in a specified manner and within a specified period;

    (e) to order the controller to communicate a personal data breach to the data subject;

(f) to impose a temporary or definitive limitation including a ban on processing;

(g) to order the rectification or erasure of personal data or restriction of processing pursuant to Articles 16, 17 and 18 and the notification of such actions to recipients to whom the personal data have been disclosed pursuant to Article 17(2) and Article 19;

(h) to withdraw a certification or to order the certification body to withdraw a certification issued pursuant to Articles 42 and 43, or to order the certification body not to issue certification if the requirements for the certification are not or are no longer met;

(i) to impose an administrative fine pursuant to Article 83, in addition to, or instead of measures referred to in this paragraph, depending on the circumstances of each individual case;

(j) to order the suspension of data flows to a recipient in a third country or to an international organisation.

3. Each supervisory authority shall have all of the following authorisation and advisory powers:

(a) to advise the controller in accordance with the prior consultation procedure referred to in Article 36;

(b) to issue, on its own initiative or on request, opinions to the national parliament, the Member State government or, in accordance with Member State law, to other institutions and bodies as well as to the public on any issue related to the protection of personal data;

(c) to authorise processing referred to in Article 36(5), if the law of the Member State requires such prior authorisation;

(d) to issue an opinion and approve draft codes of conduct pursuant to Article 40(5);

(e) to accredit certification bodies pursuant to Article 43;

(f) to issue certifications and approve criteria of certification in accordance with Article 42(5);

(g) to adopt standard data protection clauses referred to in Article 28(8) and in point (d) of Article 46(2);

(h) to authorise contractual clauses referred to in point (a) of Article 46(3);

(i) to authorise administrative arrangements referred to in point (b) of Article 46(3);

(j) to approve binding corporate rules pursuant to Article 47.

4. The exercise of the powers conferred on the supervisory authority pursuant to this Article shall be subject to appropriate safeguards, including effective judicial remedy and due process, set out in Union and Member State law in accordance with the Charter.

5. Each Member State shall provide by law that its supervisory authority shall have the power to bring infringements of this Regulation to the attention of the judicial authorities and where appropriate, to commence or engage otherwise in legal proceedings, in order to enforce the provisions of this Regulation.

6. Each Member State may provide by law that its supervisory authority shall have additional powers to those referred to in paragraphs 1, 2 and 3. The exercise of those powers shall not impair the effective operation of Chapter VII.

Article 59
Activity reports

Each supervisory authority shall draw up an annual report on its activities, which may include a list of types of infringement notified and types of measures taken in accordance with Article 58(2). Those reports shall be transmitted to the national parliament, the government and other authorities as designated by Member State law. They shall be made available to the public, to the Commission and to the Board.

CHAPTER VII COOPERATION AND CONSISTENCY

Section 1
Cooperation

Article 60
Cooperation between the lead supervisory authority and
the other supervisory authorities concerned

1. The lead supervisory authority shall cooperate with the other supervisory authorities concerned in accordance with this Article in an endeavour to reach consensus. The lead supervisory authority and the supervisory authorities concerned shall exchange all relevant information with each other.
2. The lead supervisory authority may request at any time other supervisory authorities concerned to provide mutual assistance pursuant to Article 61 and may conduct joint operations pursuant to Article 62, in particular for carrying out investigations or for monitoring the implementation of a measure concerning a controller or processor established in another Member State.
3. The lead supervisory authority shall, without delay, communicate the relevant information on the matter to the other supervisory authorities concerned. It shall without delay submit a draft decision to the other supervisory authorities concerned for their opinion and take due account of their views.
4. Where any of the other supervisory authorities concerned within a period of four weeks after having been consulted in accordance with paragraph 3 of this Article, expresses a relevant and reasoned objection to the draft decision, the lead supervisory authority shall, if it does not follow the relevant and reasoned objection or is of the opinion that the objection is not relevant or reasoned, submit the matter to the consistency mechanism referred to in Article 63.
5. Where the lead supervisory authority intends to follow the relevant and reasoned objection made, it shall submit to the other supervisory authorities concerned a revised draft decision for their opinion. That revised draft decision shall be subject to the procedure referred to in paragraph 4 within a period of two weeks.
6. Where none of the other supervisory authorities concerned has objected to the draft decision submitted by the lead supervisory authority within the period referred to in paragraphs 4 and 5, the lead supervisory authority and the supervisory authorities concerned shall be deemed to be in agreement with that draft decision and shall be bound by it.
7. The lead supervisory authority shall adopt and notify the decision to the main establishment or single establishment of the controller or processor, as the case may be and inform the other supervisory authorities concerned and the Board of the decision in question, including a summary of the relevant facts and grounds. The supervisory authority with which a complaint has been lodged shall inform the complainant on the decision.
8. By derogation from paragraph 7, where a complaint is dismissed or rejected, the supervisory authority with which the complaint was lodged shall adopt the decision and notify it to the complainant and shall inform the controller thereof.

9. Where the lead supervisory authority and the supervisory authorities concerned agree to dismiss or reject parts of a complaint and to act on other parts of that complaint, a separate decision shall be adopted for each of those parts of the matter. The lead supervisory authority shall adopt the decision for the part concerning actions in relation to the controller, shall notify it to the main establishment or single establishment of the controller or processor on the territory of its Member State and shall inform the complainant thereof, while the supervisory authority of the complainant shall adopt the decision for the part concerning dismissal or rejection of that complaint, and shall notify it to that complainant and shall inform the controller or processor thereof.

10. After being notified of the decision of the lead supervisory authority pursuant to paragraphs 7 and 9, the controller or processor shall take the necessary measures to ensure compliance with the decision as regards processing activities in the context of all its establishments in the Union. The controller or processor shall notify the measures taken for complying with the decision to the lead supervisory authority, which shall inform the other supervisory authorities concerned.

11. Where, in exceptional circumstances, a supervisory authority concerned has reasons to consider that there is an urgent need to act in order to protect the interests of data subjects, the urgency procedure referred to in Article 66 shall apply.

12. The lead supervisory authority and the other supervisory authorities concerned shall supply the information required under this Article to each other by electronic means, using a standardised format.

Article 61
Mutual assistance

1. Supervisory authorities shall provide each other with relevant information and mutual assistance in order to implement and apply this Regulation in a consistent manner, and shall put in place measures for effective cooperation with one another. Mutual assistance shall cover, in particular, information requests and supervisory measures, such as requests to carry out prior authorisations and consultations, inspections and investigations.

2. Each supervisory authority shall take all appropriate measures required to reply to a request of another supervisory authority without undue delay and no later than one month after receiving the request. Such measures may include, in particular, the transmission of relevant information on the conduct of an investigation.

3. Requests for assistance shall contain all the necessary information, including the purpose of and reasons for the request. Information exchanged shall be used only for the purpose for which it was requested.

4. The requested supervisory authority shall not refuse to comply with the request unless:
   (a) it is not competent for the subject-matter of the request or for the measures it is requested to execute; or
   (b) compliance with the request would infringe this Regulation or Union or Member State law to which the supervisory authority receiving the request is subject.

5. The requested supervisory authority shall inform the requesting supervisory authority of the results or, as the case may be, of the progress of the measures taken in order to respond to the request. The requested supervisory authority shall provide reasons for any refusal to comply with a request pursuant to paragraph 4.

6. Requested supervisory authorities shall, as a rule, supply the information requested by other supervisory authorities by electronic means, using a standardised format.

7. Requested supervisory authorities shall not charge a fee for any action taken by them pursuant to a request for mutual assistance. Supervisory authorities may agree on rules to indemnify each other for specific expenditure arising from the provision of mutual assistance in exceptional circumstances.

8. Where a supervisory authority does not provide the information referred to in paragraph 5 of this Article within one month of receiving the request of another supervisory authority, the requesting supervisory authority may adopt a provisional measure on the territory of its Member State in accordance with Article 55(1). In that case, the urgent need to act under Article 66(1) shall be presumed to be met and require an urgent binding decision from the Board pursuant to Article 66(2).

9. The Commission may, by means of implementing acts, specify the format and procedures for mutual assistance referred to in this Article and the arrangements for the exchange of information by electronic means between supervisory authorities, and between supervisory authorities and the Board, in particular the standardised format referred to in paragraph 6 of this Article. Those implementing acts shall be adopted in accordance with the examination procedure referred to in Article 93(2).

Article 62
Joint operations of supervisory authorities

1. The supervisory authorities shall, where appropriate, conduct joint operations including joint investigations and joint enforcement measures in which members or staff of the supervisory authorities of other Member States are involved.

2. Where the controller or processor has establishments in several Member States or where a significant number of data subjects in more than one Member State are likely to be substantially affected by processing operations, a supervisory authority of each of those Member States shall have the right to participate in joint operations. The supervisory authority which is competent pursuant to Article 56(1) or (4) shall invite the supervisory authority of each of those Member States to take part in the joint operations and shall respond without delay to the request of a supervisory authority to participate.

3. A supervisory authority may, in accordance with Member State law, and with the seconding supervisory authority's authorisation, confer powers, including investigative powers on the seconding supervisory authority's members or staff involved in joint operations or, in so far as the law of the Member State of the host supervisory authority permits, allow the seconding supervisory authority's members or staff to exercise their investigative powers in accordance with the law of the Member State of the seconding supervisory authority. Such investigative powers may be exercised only under the guidance and in the presence of members or staff of the host supervisory authority. The seconding supervisory authority's members or staff shall be subject to the Member State law of the host supervisory authority.

4. Where, in accordance with paragraph 1, staff of a seconding supervisory authority operate in another Member State, the Member State of the host supervisory authority shall assume responsibility for their actions, including liability, for any damage caused by them during their operations, in accordance with the law of the Member State in whose territory they are operating.

5. The Member State in whose territory the damage was caused shall make good such damage under the conditions applicable to damage caused by its own staff. The Member State of the seconding supervisory authority whose staff has caused damage

to any person in the territory of another Member State shall reimburse that other Member State in full any sums it has paid to the persons entitled on their behalf.

6. Without prejudice to the exercise of its rights vis-à-vis third parties and with the exception of paragraph 5, each Member State shall refrain, in the case provided for in paragraph 1, from requesting reimbursement from another Member State in relation to damage referred to in paragraph 4.

7. Where a joint operation is intended and a supervisory authority does not, within one month, comply with the obligation laid down in the second sentence of paragraph 2 of this Article, the other supervisory authorities may adopt a provisional measure on the territory of its Member State in accordance with Article 55. In that case, the urgent need to act under Article 66(1) shall be presumed to be met and require an opinion or an urgent binding decision from the Board pursuant to Article 66(2).

Section 2
Consistency

Article 63
Consistency mechanism

In order to contribute to the consistent application of this Regulation throughout the Union, the supervisory authorities shall cooperate with each other and, where relevant, with the Commission, through the consistency mechanism as set out in this Section.

Article 64
Opinion of the Board

1. The Board shall issue an opinion where a competent supervisory authority intends to adopt any of the measures below. To that end, the competent supervisory authority shall communicate the draft decision to the Board, when it:
   (a) aims to adopt a list of the processing operations subject to the requirement for a data protection impact assessment pursuant to Article 35(4);
   (b) concerns a matter pursuant to Article 40(7) whether a draft code of conduct or an amendment or extension to a code of conduct complies with this Regulation;
   (c) aims to approve the criteria for accreditation of a body pursuant to Article 41(3) or a certification body pursuant to Article 43(3);
   (d) aims to determine standard data protection clauses referred to in point (d) of Article 46(2) and in Article 28(8);
   (e) aims to authorise contractual clauses referred to in point (a) of Article 46(3); or
   (f) aims to approve binding corporate rules within the meaning of Article 47.

2. Any supervisory authority, the Chair of the Board or the Commission may request that any matter of general application or producing effects in more than one Member State be examined by the Board with a view to obtaining an opinion, in particular where a competent supervisory authority does not comply with the obligations for mutual assistance in accordance with Article 61 or for joint operations in accordance with Article 62.

3. In the cases referred to in paragraphs 1 and 2, the Board shall issue an opinion on the matter submitted to it provided that it has not already issued an opinion on the same matter. That opinion shall be adopted within eight weeks by simple majority of the members of the Board. That period may be extended by a further six weeks, taking into

account the complexity of the subject matter. Regarding the draft decision referred to in paragraph 1 circulated to the members of the Board in accordance with paragraph 5, a member which has not objected within a reasonable period indicated by the Chair, shall be deemed to be in agreement with the draft decision.

4. Supervisory authorities and the Commission shall, without undue delay, communicate by electronic means to the Board, using a standardised format any relevant information, including as the case may be a summary of the facts, the draft decision, the grounds which make the enactment of such measure necessary, and the views of other supervisory authorities concerned.

5. The Chair of the Board shall, without undue, delay inform by electronic means:
   (a) the members of the Board and the Commission of any relevant information which has been communicated to it using a standardised format. The secretariat of the Board shall, where necessary, provide translations of relevant information; and
   (b) the supervisory authority referred to, as the case may be, in paragraphs 1 and 2, and the Commission of the opinion and make it public.

6. The competent supervisory authority shall not adopt its draft decision referred to in paragraph 1 within the period referred to in paragraph 3.

7. The supervisory authority referred to in paragraph 1 shall take utmost account of the opinion of the Board and shall, within two weeks after receiving the opinion, communicate to the Chair of the Board by electronic means whether it will maintain or amend its draft decision and, if any, the amended draft decision, using a standardised format.

8. Where the supervisory authority concerned informs the Chair of the Board within the period referred to in paragraph 7 of this Article that it does not intend to follow the opinion of the Board, in whole or in part, providing the relevant grounds, Article 65(1) shall apply.

Article 65
Dispute resolution by the Board

1. In order to ensure the correct and consistent application of this Regulation in individual cases, the Board shall adopt a binding decision in the following cases:
   (a) where, in a case referred to in Article 60(4), a supervisory authority concerned has raised a relevant and reasoned objection to a draft decision of the lead authority or the lead authority has rejected such an objection as being not relevant or reasoned. The binding decision shall concern all the matters which are the subject of the relevant and reasoned objection, in particular whether there is an infringement of this Regulation;
   (b) where there are conflicting views on which of the supervisory authorities concerned is competent for the main establishment;
   (c) where a competent supervisory authority does not request the opinion of the Board in the cases referred to in Article 64(1), or does not follow the opinion of the Board issued under Article 64. In that case, any supervisory authority concerned or the Commission may communicate the matter to the Board.

2. The decision referred to in paragraph 1 shall be adopted within one month from the referral of the subject-matter by a two-thirds majority of the members of the Board. That period may be extended by a further month on account of the complexity of the subject-matter. The decision referred to in paragraph 1 shall be reasoned and addressed to the lead supervisory authority and all the supervisory authorities concerned and binding on them.

3. Where the Board has been unable to adopt a decision within the periods referred to in paragraph 2, it shall adopt its decision within two weeks following the expiration of the second month referred to in paragraph 2 by a simple majority of the members of the Board. Where the members of the Board are split, the decision shall by adopted by the vote of its Chair.

4. The supervisory authorities concerned shall not adopt a decision on the subject matter submitted to the Board under paragraph 1 during the periods referred to in paragraphs 2 and 3.

5. The Chair of the Board shall notify, without undue delay, the decision referred to in paragraph 1 to the supervisory authorities concerned. It shall inform the Commission thereof. The decision shall be published on the website of the Board without delay after the supervisory authority has notified the final decision referred to in paragraph 6.

6. The lead supervisory authority or, as the case may be, the supervisory authority with which the complaint has been lodged shall adopt its final decision on the basis of the decision referred to in paragraph 1 of this Article, without undue delay and at the latest by one month after the Board has notified its decision. The lead supervisory authority or, as the case may be, the supervisory authority with which the complaint has been lodged, shall inform the Board of the date when its final decision is notified respectively to the controller or the processor and to the data subject. The final decision of the supervisory authorities concerned shall be adopted under the terms of Article 60(7), (8) and (9). The final decision shall refer to the decision referred to in paragraph 1 of this Article and shall specify that the decision referred to in that paragraph will be published on the website of the Board in accordance with paragraph 5 of this Article. The final decision shall attach the decision referred to in paragraph 1 of this Article.

Article 66
Urgency procedure

1. In exceptional circumstances, where a supervisory authority concerned considers that there is an urgent need to act in order to protect the rights and freedoms of data subjects, it may, by way of derogation from the consistency mechanism referred to in Articles 63, 64 and 65 or the procedure referred to in Article 60, immediately adopt provisional measures intended to produce legal effects on its own territory with a specified period of validity which shall not exceed three months. The supervisory authority shall, without delay, communicate those measures and the reasons for adopting them to the other supervisory authorities concerned, to the Board and to the Commission.

2. Where a supervisory authority has taken a measure pursuant to paragraph 1 and considers that final measures need urgently be adopted, it may request an urgent opinion or an urgent binding decision from the Board, giving reasons for requesting such opinion or decision.

3. Any supervisory authority may request an urgent opinion or an urgent binding decision, as the case may be, from the Board where a competent supervisory authority has not taken an appropriate measure in a situation where there is an urgent need to act, in order to protect the rights and freedoms of data subjects, giving reasons for requesting such opinion or decision, including for the urgent need to act.

4. By derogation from Article 64(3) and Article 65(2), an urgent opinion or an urgent binding decision referred to in paragraphs 2 and 3 of this Article shall be adopted within two weeks by simple majority of the members of the Board.

Article 67
Exchange of information

The Commission may adopt implementing acts of general scope in order to specify the arrangements for the exchange of information by electronic means between supervisory authorities, and between supervisory authorities and the Board, in particular the standardised format referred to in Article 64.

Those implementing acts shall be adopted in accordance with the examination procedure referred to in Article 93(2).

Section 3
European data protection board

Article 68
European Data Protection Board

1. The European Data Protection Board (the 'Board') is hereby established as a body of the Union and shall have legal personality.
2. The Board shall be represented by its Chair.
3. The Board shall be composed of the head of one supervisory authority of each Member State and of the European Data Protection Supervisor, or their respective representatives.
4. Where in a Member State more than one supervisory authority is responsible for monitoring the application of the provisions pursuant to this Regulation, a joint representative shall be appointed in accordance with that Member State's law.
5. The Commission shall have the right to participate in the activities and meetings of the Board without voting right. The Commission shall designate a representative. The Chair of the Board shall communicate to the Commission the activities of the Board.
6. In the cases referred to in Article 65, the European Data Protection Supervisor shall have voting rights only on decisions which concern principles and rules applicable to the Union institutions, bodies, offices and agencies which correspond in substance to those of this Regulation.

Article 69
Independence

1. The Board shall act independently when performing its tasks or exercising its powers pursuant to Articles 70 and 71.
2. Without prejudice to requests by the Commission referred to in point (b) of Article 70(1) and in Article 70(2), the Board shall, in the performance of its tasks or the exercise of its powers, neither seek nor take instructions from anybody.

Article 70
Tasks of the Board

1. The Board shall ensure the consistent application of this Regulation. To that end, the Board shall, on its own initiative or, where relevant, at the request of the Commission, in particular:
   (a) monitor and ensure the correct application of this Regulation in the cases provided for in Articles 64 and 65 without prejudice to the tasks of national supervisory authorities;
   (b) advise the Commission on any issue related to the protection of personal data in the Union, including on any proposed amendment of this Regulation;

(c) advise the Commission on the format and procedures for the exchange of information between controllers, processors and supervisory authorities for binding corporate rules;

(d) issue guidelines, recommendations, and best practices on procedures for erasing links, copies or replications of personal data from publicly available communication services as referred to in Article 17(2);

(e) examine, on its own initiative, on request of one of its members or on request of the Commission, any question covering the application of this Regulation and issue guidelines, recommendations and best practices in order to encourage consistent application of this Regulation;

(f) issue guidelines, recommendations and best practices in accordance with point (e) of this paragraph for further specifying the criteria and conditions for decisions based on profiling pursuant to Article 22(2);

(g) issue guidelines, recommendations and best practices in accordance with point (e) of this paragraph for establishing the personal data breaches and determining the undue delay referred to in Article 33(1) and (2) and for the particular circumstances in which a controller or a processor is required to notify the personal data breach;

(h) issue guidelines, recommendations and best practices in accordance with point (e) of this paragraph as to the circumstances in which a personal data breach is likely to result in a high risk to the rights and freedoms of the natural persons referred to in Article 34(1).

(i) issue guidelines, recommendations and best practices in accordance with point (e) of this paragraph for the purpose of further specifying the criteria and requirements for personal data transfers based on binding corporate rules adhered to by controllers and binding corporate rules adhered to by processors and on further necessary requirements to ensure the protection of personal data of the data subjects concerned referred to in Article 47;

(j) issue guidelines, recommendations and best practices in accordance with point (e) of this paragraph for the purpose of further specifying the criteria and requirements for the personal data transfers on the basis of Article 49(1);

(k) draw up guidelines for supervisory authorities concerning the application of measures referred to in Article 58(1), (2) and (3) and the setting of administrative fines pursuant to Article 83;

(l) review the practical application of the guidelines, recommendations and best practices referred to in points (e) and (f);

(m) issue guidelines, recommendations and best practices in accordance with point (e) of this paragraph for establishing common procedures for reporting by natural persons of infringements of this Regulation pursuant to Article 54(2);

(n) encourage the drawing-up of codes of conduct and the establishment of data protection certification mechanisms and data protection seals and marks pursuant to Articles 40 and 42;

(o) carry out the accreditation of certification bodies and its periodic review pursuant to Article 43 and maintain a public register of accredited bodies pursuant to Article 43(6) and of the accredited controllers or processors established in third countries pursuant to Article 42(7);

(p) specify the requirements referred to in Article 43(3) with a view to the accreditation of certification bodies under Article 42;

(q) provide the Commission with an opinion on the certification requirements referred to in Article 43(8);

(r)   provide the Commission with an opinion on the icons referred to in Article 12(7);

(s)   provide the Commission with an opinion for the assessment of the adequacy of the level of protection in a third country or international organisation, including for the assessment whether a third country, a territory or one or more specified sectors within that third country, or an international organisation no longer ensures an adequate level of protection. To that end, the Commission shall provide the Board with all necessary documentation, including correspondence with the government of the third country, with regard to that third country, territory or specified sector, or with the international organisation.

(t)   issue opinions on draft decisions of supervisory authorities pursuant to the consistency mechanism referred to in Article 64(1), on matters submitted pursuant to Article 64(2) and to issue binding decisions pursuant to Article 65, including in cases referred to in Article 66;

(u)   promote the cooperation and the effective bilateral and multilateral exchange of information and best practices between the supervisory authorities;

(v)   promote common training programmes and facilitate personnel exchanges between the supervisory authorities and, where appropriate, with the supervisory authorities of third countries or with international organisations;

(w)   promote the exchange of knowledge and documentation on data protection legislation and practice with data protection supervisory authorities worldwide.

(x)   issue opinions on codes of conduct drawn up at Union level pursuant to Article 40(9); and

(y)   maintain a publicly accessible electronic register of decisions taken by supervisory authorities and courts on issues handled in the consistency mechanism.

2. Where the Commission requests advice from the Board, it may indicate a time limit, taking into account the urgency of the matter.

3. The Board shall forward its opinions, guidelines, recommendations, and best practices to the Commission and to the committee referred to in Article 93 and make them public.

4. The Board shall, where appropriate, consult interested parties and give them the opportunity to comment within a reasonable period. The Board shall, without prejudice to Article 76, make the results of the consultation procedure publicly available.

Article 71
Reports

1. The Board shall draw up an annual report regarding the protection of natural persons with regard to processing in the Union and, where relevant, in third countries and international organisations. The report shall be made public and be transmitted to the European Parliament, to the Council and to the Commission.

2. The annual report shall include a review of the practical application of the guidelines, recommendations and best practices referred to in point (l) of Article 70(1) as well as of the binding decisions referred to in Article 65.

Article 72
Procedure

1. The Board shall take decisions by a simple majority of its members, unless otherwise provided for in this Regulation.

2. The Board shall adopt its own rules of procedure by a two-thirds majority of its members and organise its own operational arrangements.

Article 73
Chair

1. The Board shall elect a chair and two deputy chairs from amongst its members by simple majority.
2. The term of office of the Chair and of the deputy chairs shall be five years and be renewable once.

Article 74
Tasks of the Chair

1. The Chair shall have the following tasks:
   (a) to convene the meetings of the Board and prepare its agenda;
   (b) to notify decisions adopted by the Board pursuant to Article 65 to the lead supervisory authority and the supervisory authorities concerned;
   (c) to ensure the timely performance of the tasks of the Board, in particular in relation to the consistency mechanism referred to in Article 63.
2. The Board shall lay down the allocation of tasks between the Chair and the deputy chairs in its rules of procedure.

Article 75
Secretariat

1. The Board shall have a secretariat, which shall be provided by the European Data Protection Supervisor.
2. The secretariat shall perform its tasks exclusively under the instructions of the Chair of the Board.
3. The staff of the European Data Protection Supervisor involved in carrying out the tasks conferred on the Board by this Regulation shall be subject to separate reporting lines from the staff involved in carrying out tasks conferred on the European Data Protection Supervisor.
4. Where appropriate, the Board and the European Data Protection Supervisor shall establish and publish a Memorandum of Understanding implementing this Article, determining the terms of their cooperation, and applicable to the staff of the European Data Protection Supervisor involved in carrying out the tasks conferred on the Board by this Regulation.
5. The secretariat shall provide analytical, administrative and logistical support to the Board.
6. The secretariat shall be responsible in particular for:
   (a) the day-to-day business of the Board;
   (b) communication between the members of the Board, its Chair and the Commission;
   (c) communication with other institutions and the public;
   (d) the use of electronic means for the internal and external communication;
   (e) the translation of relevant information;
   (f) the preparation and follow-up of the meetings of the Board;
   (g) the preparation, drafting and publication of opinions, decisions on the settlement of disputes between supervisory authorities and other texts adopted by the Board.

Article 76
Confidentiality

1. The discussions of the Board shall be confidential where the Board deems it necessary, as provided for in its rules of procedure.

2. Access to documents submitted to members of the Board, experts and representatives of third parties shall be governed by Regulation (EC) No 1049/2001 of the European Parliament and of the Council [21].

CHAPTER VIII REMEDIES, LIABILITY AND PENALTIES

Article 77
Right to lodge a complaint with a supervisory authority

1. Without prejudice to any other administrative or judicial remedy, every data subject shall have the right to lodge a complaint with a supervisory authority, in particular in the Member State of his or her habitual residence, place of work or place of the alleged infringement if the data subject considers that the processing of personal data relating to him or her infringes this Regulation.
2. The supervisory authority with which the complaint has been lodged shall inform the complainant on the progress and the outcome of the complaint including the possibility of a judicial remedy pursuant to Article 78.

Article 78
Right to an effective judicial remedy against a supervisory authority

1. Without prejudice to any other administrative or non-judicial remedy, each natural or legal person shall have the right to an effective judicial remedy against a legally binding decision of a supervisory authority concerning them.
2. Without prejudice to any other administrative or non-judicial remedy, each data subject shall have the right to a an effective judicial remedy where the supervisory authority which is competent pursuant to Articles 55 and 56 does not handle a complaint or does not inform the data subject within three months on the progress or outcome of the complaint lodged pursuant to Article 77.
3. Proceedings against a supervisory authority shall be brought before the courts of the Member State where the supervisory authority is established.
4. Where proceedings are brought against a decision of a supervisory authority which was preceded by an opinion or a decision of the Board in the consistency mechanism, the supervisory authority shall forward that opinion or decision to the court.

Article 79
Right to an effective judicial remedy against a controller or processor

1. Without prejudice to any available administrative or non-judicial remedy, including the right to lodge a complaint with a supervisory authority pursuant to Article 77, each data subject shall have the right to an effective judicial remedy where he or she considers that his or her rights under this Regulation have been infringed as a result of the processing of his or her personal data in non-compliance with this Regulation.
2. Proceedings against a controller or a processor shall be brought before the courts of the Member State where the controller or processor has an establishment. Alternatively,

[21] Regulation (EC) No 1049/2001 of the European Parliament and of the Council of 30 May 2001 regarding public access to European Parliament, Council and Commission documents (OJ L 145, 31.5.2001, p. 43).

such proceedings may be brought before the courts of the Member State where the data subject has his or her habitual residence, unless the controller or processor is a public authority of a Member State acting in the exercise of its public powers.

Article 80
Representation of data subjects

1. The data subject shall have the right to mandate a not-for-profit body, organisation or association which has been properly constituted in accordance with the law of a Member State, has statutory objectives which are in the public interest, and is active in the field of the protection of data subjects' rights and freedoms with regard to the protection of their personal data to lodge the complaint on his or her behalf, to exercise the rights referred to in Articles 77, 78 and 79 on his or her behalf, and to exercise the right to receive compensation referred to in Article 82 on his or her behalf where provided for by Member State law.

2. Member States may provide that any body, organisation or association referred to in paragraph 1 of this Article, independently of a data subject's mandate, has the right to lodge, in that Member State, a complaint with the supervisory authority which is competent pursuant to Article 77 and to exercise the rights referred to in Articles 78 and 79 if it considers that the rights of a data subject under this Regulation have been infringed as a result of the processing.

Article 81
Suspension of proceedings

1. Where a competent court of a Member State has information on proceedings, concerning the same subject matter as regards processing by the same controller or processor, that are pending in a court in another Member State, it shall contact that court in the other Member State to confirm the existence of such proceedings.

2. Where proceedings concerning the same subject matter as regards processing of the same controller or processor are pending in a court in another Member State, any competent court other than the court first seized may suspend its proceedings.

3. Where those proceedings are pending at first instance, any court other than the court first seized may also, on the application of one of the parties, decline jurisdiction if the court first seized has jurisdiction over the actions in question and its law permits the consolidation thereof.

Article 82
Right to compensation and liability

1. Any person who has suffered material or non-material damage as a result of an infringement of this Regulation shall have the right to receive compensation from the controller or processor for the damage suffered.

2. Any controller involved in processing shall be liable for the damage caused by processing which infringes this Regulation. A processor shall be liable for the damage caused by processing only where it has not complied with obligations of this Regulation specifically directed to processors or where it has acted outside or contrary to lawful instructions of the controller.

3. A controller or processor shall be exempt from liability under paragraph 2 if it proves that it is not in any way responsible for the event giving rise to the damage.

4. Where more than one controller or processor, or both a controller and a processor, are involved in the same processing and where they are, under paragraphs 2 and 3,

responsible for any damage caused by processing, each controller or processor shall be held liable for the entire damage in order to ensure effective compensation of the data subject.

5. Where a controller or processor has, in accordance with paragraph 4, paid full compensation for the damage suffered, that controller or processor shall be entitled to claim back from the other controllers or processors involved in the same processing that part of the compensation corresponding to their part of responsibility for the damage, in accordance with the conditions set out in paragraph 2.

6. Court proceedings for exercising the right to receive compensation shall be brought before the courts competent under the law of the Member State referred to in Article 79(2).

Article 83
General conditions for imposing administrative fines

1. Each supervisory authority shall ensure that the imposition of administrative fines pursuant to this Article in respect of infringements of this Regulation referred to in paragraphs 4, 5 and 6 shall in each individual case be effective, proportionate and dissuasive.

2. Administrative fines shall, depending on the circumstances of each individual case, be imposed in addition to, or instead of, measures referred to in points (a) to (h) and (j) of Article 58(2). When deciding whether to impose an administrative fine and deciding on the amount of the administrative fine in each individual case due regard shall be given to the following:

   (a) the nature, gravity and duration of the infringement taking into account the nature scope or purpose of the processing concerned as well as the number of data subjects affected and the level of damage suffered by them;

   (b) the intentional or negligent character of the infringement;

   (c) any action taken by the controller or processor to mitigate the damage suffered by data subjects;

   (d) the degree of responsibility of the controller or processor taking into account technical and organisational measures implemented by them pursuant to Articles 25 and 32;

   (e) any relevant previous infringements by the controller or processor;

   (f) the degree of cooperation with the supervisory authority, in order to remedy the infringement and mitigate the possible adverse effects of the infringement;

   (g) the categories of personal data affected by the infringement;

   (h) the manner in which the infringement became known to the supervisory authority, in particular whether, and if so to what extent, the controller or processor notified the infringement;

   (i) where measures referred to in Article 58(2) have previously been ordered against the controller or processor concerned with regard to the same subject-matter, compliance with those measures;

   (j) adherence to approved codes of conduct pursuant to Article 40 or approved certification mechanisms pursuant to Article 42; and

   (k) any other aggravating or mitigating factor applicable to the circumstances of the case, such as financial benefits gained, or losses avoided, directly or indirectly, from the infringement.

3. If a controller or processor intentionally or negligently, for the same or linked processing operations, infringes several provisions of this Regulation, the total amount of the administrative fine shall not exceed the amount specified for the gravest infringement.

4. Infringements of the following provisions shall, in accordance with paragraph 2, be subject to administrative fines up to 10 000 000 EUR, or in the case of an undertaking, up to 2 % of the total worldwide annual turnover of the preceding financial year, whichever is higher:

   (a) the obligations of the controller and the processor pursuant to Articles 8, 11, 25 to 39 and 42 and 43;

   (b) the obligations of the certification body pursuant to Articles 42 and 43;

   (c) the obligations of the monitoring body pursuant to Article 41(4).

5. Infringements of the following provisions shall, in accordance with paragraph 2, be subject to administrative fines up to 20 000 000 EUR, or in the case of an undertaking, up to 4 % of the total worldwide annual turnover of the preceding financial year, whichever is higher:

   (a) the basic principles for processing, including conditions for consent, pursuant to Articles 5, 6, 7 and 9;

   (b) the data subjects' rights pursuant to Articles 12 to 22;

   (c) the transfers of personal data to a recipient in a third country or an international organisation pursuant to Articles 44 to 49;

   (d) any obligations pursuant to Member State law adopted under Chapter IX;

   (e) non-compliance with an order or a temporary or definitive limitation on processing or the suspension of data flows by the supervisory authority pursuant to Article 58(2) or failure to provide access in violation of Article 58(1).

6. Non-compliance with an order by the supervisory authority as referred to in Article 58(2) shall, in accordance with paragraph 2 of this Article, be subject to administrative fines up to 20 000 000 EUR, or in the case of an undertaking, up to 4 % of the total worldwide annual turnover of the preceding financial year, whichever is higher.

7. Without prejudice to the corrective powers of supervisory authorities pursuant to Article 58(2), each Member State may lay down the rules on whether and to what extent administrative fines may be imposed on public authorities and bodies established in that Member State.

8. The exercise by the supervisory authority of its powers under this Article shall be subject to appropriate procedural safeguards in accordance with Union and Member State law, including effective judicial remedy and due process.

9. Where the legal system of the Member State does not provide for administrative fines, this Article may be applied in such a manner that the fine is initiated by the competent supervisory authority and imposed by competent national courts, while ensuring that those legal remedies are effective and have an equivalent effect to the administrative fines imposed by supervisory authorities. In any event, the fines imposed shall be effective, proportionate and dissuasive. Those Member States shall notify to the Commission the provisions of their laws which they adopt pursuant to this paragraph by 25 May 2018 and, without delay, any subsequent amendment law or amendment affecting them.

Article 84
Penalties

1. Member States shall lay down the rules on other penalties applicable to infringements of this Regulation in particular for infringements which are not subject to administrative fines pursuant to Article 83, and shall take all measures necessary to ensure that they are implemented. Such penalties shall be effective, proportionate and dissuasive.

2. Each Member State shall notify to the Commission the provisions of its law which it adopts pursuant to paragraph 1, by 25 May 2018 and, without delay, any subsequent amendment affecting them.

CHAPTER IX PROVISIONS RELATING TO SPECIFIC PROCESSING SITUATIONS

Article 85
Processing and freedom of expression and information

1. Member States shall by law reconcile the right to the protection of personal data pursuant to this Regulation with the right to freedom of expression and information, including processing for journalistic purposes and the purposes of academic, artistic or literary expression.
2. For processing carried out for journalistic purposes or the purpose of academic artistic or literary expression, Member States shall provide for exemptions or derogations from Chapter II (principles), Chapter III (rights of the data subject), Chapter IV (controller and processor), Chapter V (transfer of personal data to third countries or international organisations), Chapter VI (independent supervisory authorities), Chapter VII (cooperation and consistency) and Chapter IX (specific data processing situations) if they are necessary to reconcile the right to the protection of personal data with the freedom of expression and information.
3. Each Member State shall notify to the Commission the provisions of its law which it has adopted pursuant to paragraph 2 and, without delay, any subsequent amendment law or amendment affecting them.

Article 86
Processing and public access to official documents

Personal data in official documents held by a public authority or a public body or a private body for the performance of a task carried out in the public interest may be disclosed by the authority or body in accordance with Union or Member State law to which the public authority or body is subject in order to reconcile public access to official documents with the right to the protection of personal data pursuant to this Regulation.

Article 87
Processing of the national identification number

Member States may further determine the specific conditions for the processing of a national identification number or any other identifier of general application. In that case the national identification number or any other identifier of general application shall be used only under appropriate safeguards for the rights and freedoms of the data subject pursuant to this Regulation.

Article 88
Processing in the context of employment

1. Member States may, by law or by collective agreements, provide for more specific rules to ensure the protection of the rights and freedoms in respect of the processing of employees' personal data in the employment context, in particular for the purposes of

the recruitment, the performance of the contract of employment, including discharge of obligations laid down by law or by collective agreements, management, planning and organisation of work, equality and diversity in the workplace, health and safety at work, protection of employer's or customer's property and for the purposes of the exercise and enjoyment, on an individual or collective basis, of rights and benefits related to employment, and for the purpose of the termination of the employment relationship.

2. Those rules shall include suitable and specific measures to safeguard the data subject's human dignity, legitimate interests and fundamental rights, with particular regard to the transparency of processing, the transfer of personal data within a group of undertakings, or a group of enterprises engaged in a joint economic activity and monitoring systems at the work place.

3. Each Member State shall notify to the Commission those provisions of its law which it adopts pursuant to paragraph 1, by 25 May 2018 and, without delay, any subsequent amendment affecting them.

Article 89
Safeguards and derogations relating to processing for archiving purposes in the public interest, scientific or historical research purposes or statistical purposes

1. Processing for archiving purposes in the public interest, scientific or historical research purposes or statistical purposes, shall be subject to appropriate safeguards, in accordance with this Regulation, for the rights and freedoms of the data subject. Those safeguards shall ensure that technical and organisational measures are in place in particular in order to ensure respect for the principle of data minimisation. Those measures may include pseudonymisation provided that those purposes can be fulfilled in that manner. Where those purposes can be fulfilled by further processing which does not permit or no longer permits the identification of data subjects, those purposes shall be fulfilled in that manner.

2. Where personal data are processed for scientific or historical research purposes or statistical purposes, Union or Member State law may provide for derogations from the rights referred to in Articles 15, 16, 18 and 21 subject to the conditions and safeguards referred to in paragraph 1 of this Article in so far as such rights are likely to render impossible or seriously impair the achievement of the specific purposes, and such derogations are necessary for the fulfilment of those purposes.

3. Where personal data are processed for archiving purposes in the public interest, Union or Member State law may provide for derogations from the rights referred to in Articles 15, 16, 18, 19, 20 and 21 subject to the conditions and safeguards referred to in paragraph 1 of this Article in so far as such rights are likely to render impossible or seriously impair the achievement of the specific purposes, and such derogations are necessary for the fulfilment of those purposes.

4. Where processing referred to in paragraphs 2 and 3 serves at the same time another purpose, the derogations shall apply only to processing for the purposes referred to in those paragraphs.

Article 90
Obligations of secrecy

1. Member States may adopt specific rules to set out the powers of the supervisory authorities laid down in points (e) and (f) of Article 58(1) in relation to controllers or processors that are subject, under Union or Member State law or rules established by national

competent bodies, to an obligation of professional secrecy or other equivalent obligations of secrecy where this is necessary and proportionate to reconcile the right of the protection of personal data with the obligation of secrecy. Those rules shall apply only with regard to personal data which the controller or processor has received as a result of or has obtained in an activity covered by that obligation of secrecy.

2. Each Member State shall notify to the Commission the rules adopted pursuant to paragraph 1, by 25 May 2018 and, without delay, any subsequent amendment affecting them.

Article 91
Existing data protection rules of churches and religious associations

1. Where in a Member State, churches and religious associations or communities apply, at the time of entry into force of this Regulation, comprehensive rules relating to the protection of natural persons with regard to processing, such rules may continue to apply, provided that they are brought into line with this Regulation.

2. Churches and religious associations which apply comprehensive rules in accordance with paragraph 1 of this Article shall be subject to the supervision of an independent supervisory authority, which may be specific, provided that it fulfils the conditions laid down in Chapter VI of this Regulation.

CHAPTER X DELEGATED ACTS AND IMPLEMENTING ACTS

Article 92
Exercise of the delegation

1. The power to adopt delegated acts is conferred on the Commission subject to the conditions laid down in this Article.

2. The delegation of power referred to in Article 12(8) and Article 43(8) shall be conferred on the Commission for an indeterminate period of time from 24 May 2016.

3. The delegation of power referred to in Article 12(8) and Article 43(8) may be revoked at any time by the European Parliament or by the Council. A decision of revocation shall put an end to the delegation of power specified in that decision. It shall take effect the day following that of its publication in the Official Journal of the European Union or at a later date specified therein. It shall not affect the validity of any delegated acts already in force.

4. As soon as it adopts a delegated act, the Commission shall notify it simultaneously to the European Parliament and to the Council.

5. A delegated act adopted pursuant to Article 12(8) and Article 43(8) shall enter into force only if no objection has been expressed by either the European Parliament or the Council within a period of three months of notification of that act to the European Parliament and the Council or if, before the expiry of that period, the European Parliament and the Council have both informed the Commission that they will not object. That period shall be extended by three months at the initiative of the European Parliament or of the Council.

Article 93
Committee procedure

1. The Commission shall be assisted by a committee. That committee shall be a committee within the meaning of Regulation (EU) No 182/2011.

2. Where reference is made to this paragraph, Article 5 of Regulation (EU) No 182/2011 shall apply.
3. Where reference is made to this paragraph, Article 8 of Regulation (EU) No 182/2011, in conjunction with Article 5 thereof, shall apply.

CHAPTER XI FINAL PROVISIONS

Article 94
Repeal of Directive 95/46/EC

1. Directive 95/46/EC is repealed with effect from 25 May 2018.
2. References to the repealed Directive shall be construed as references to this Regulation. References to the Working Party on the Protection of Individuals with regard to the Processing of Personal Data established by Article 29 of Directive 95/46/EC shall be construed as references to the European Data Protection Board established by this Regulation.

Article 95
Relationship with Directive 2002/58/EC

This Regulation shall not impose additional obligations on natural or legal persons in relation to processing in connection with the provision of publicly available electronic communications services in public communication networks in the Union in relation to matters for which they are subject to specific obligations with the same objective set out in Directive 2002/58/EC.

Article 96

Relationship with previously concluded Agreements
International agreements involving the transfer of personal data to third countries or international organisations which were concluded by Member States prior to 24 May 2016, and which comply with Union law as applicable prior to that date, shall remain in force until amended, replaced or revoked.

Article 97
Commission reports

1. By 25 May 2020 and every four years thereafter, the Commission shall submit a report on the evaluation and review of this Regulation to the European Parliament and to the Council. The reports shall be made public.
2. In the context of the evaluations and reviews referred to in paragraph 1, the Commission shall examine, in particular, the application and functioning of:
   (a) Chapter V on the transfer of personal data to third countries or international organisations with particular regard to decisions adopted pursuant to Article 45(3) of this Regulation and decisions adopted on the basis of Article 25(6) of Directive 95/46/EC;
   (b) Chapter VII on cooperation and consistency.
3. For the purpose of paragraph 1, the Commission may request information from Member States and supervisory authorities.
4. In carrying out the evaluations and reviews referred to in paragraphs 1 and 2, the Commission shall take into account the positions and findings of the European Parliament, of the Council, and of other relevant bodies or sources.

5. The Commission shall, if necessary, submit appropriate proposals to amend this Regulation, in particular taking into account of developments in information technology and in the light of the state of progress in the information society.

Article 98
Review of other Union legal acts on data protection

The Commission shall, if appropriate, submit legislative proposals with a view to amending other Union legal acts on the protection of personal data, in order to ensure uniform and consistent protection of natural persons with regard to processing. This shall in particular concern the rules relating to the protection of natural persons with regard to processing by Union institutions, bodies, offices and agencies and on the free movement of such data.

Article 99
Entry into force and application

1. This Regulation shall enter into force on the twentieth day following that of its publication in the Official Journal of the European Union.
2. It shall apply from 25 May 2018.

This Regulation shall be binding in its entirety and directly applicable in all Member States. Done at Brussels, 27 April 2016.

For the European Parliament
The President
M. SCHULZ

For the Council
The President
J.A. HENNIS-PLASSCHAERT

Addresses and Websites

For enquiries relating to British, European, and International Standards:

British Standards Institution
389 Chiswick High Road
London
W4 4AL

Tel: +44 (0) 845 086 9001
Email: cservices@bsigroup.com
<http://www.bsigroup.com>

For enquiries on government initiatives in Information Security Management:

Department for Business, Energy & Industrial Strategy
1 Victoria Street
London
SW1H 0ET

Tel: +44 (0) 20 7215 5000
Fax: +44 (0) 20 7215 0105
Email: enquiries@beis.gov.uk
<http://www.bis.gov.uk>

To join the Direct Marketing Association and to obtain a copy of the DMA's code of practice on direct marketing:

Direct Marketing Association
DMA House
70 Margaret Street
London
W1W 8SS

Tel: 020 7291 3300
Fax: 020 7921 3301
<http://www.dma.org.uk>

To obtain a copy of the register of fax numbers registered by subscribers indicating that they do not wish to receive marketing faxes:

Fax Preference Service
DMA House
70 Margaret Street
London
W1W 8SS

Tel: +44 (0) 20 7291 3330
Email: fps@dma.org.uk
<http://www.fpsonline.org.uk>

For Data Protection Guidelines and Codes of Practice, and to make contact regarding data breaches or other compliance issues:

Information Commissioner's Office
Wycliffe House
Water Lane
Wilmslow
Cheshire
SK9 5AF

Tel: +44 (0) 1625 545 745
Fax: +44 (0) 1625 524 510
<http://www.ico.org.uk>

To obtain a copy of the register of addresses registered by residents indicating that they do not wish to receive marketing materials by post:

Mailing Preference Service
DMA House
70 Margaret Street
London
W1W 8SS

Tel: +44 (0) 20 7291 3310
Email: mps@dma.org.uk
<http://www.mpsonline.org.uk>

To subscribe to Privacy & Data Protection *journal*:

PDP Journals
Canterbury Court
Kennington Park
London
SW9 6DE

Tel: +44 (0) 20 7014 3399
Fax: +44 (0) 870 137 7871
Email: subs@pdpjournals.com
<http://www.pdpjournals.com>

For professional training courses on data protection law and practice including the Practitioner Certificate in Data Protection:

PDP Training
Canterbury Court
Kennington Park
London
SW9 6DE

Tel: +44 (0) 20 7014 3399
Fax: +44 (0) 870 137 7871
Email: bookings@pdptraining.com
<http://www.pdptraining.com>
<http://www.dataprotectionqualification.com>

To obtain a list of the US Privacy Shield companies:

Safe Harbor Website
<http://www.privacyshield.gov/list>

To obtain official copies of relevant legislation:

The Stationery Office Publications Centre
PO Box 276
London
SW8 5DT

Tel: +44 (0) 870 600 5522
<http://www.tso.co.uk>

To obtain a copy of the register of telephone numbers registered by subscribers indicating that they do not wish to receive marketing calls:

Telephone Preference Service
DMA House
70 Margaret Street
London
W1W 8SS

Tel: +44 (0) 20 7291 3320
Email: tps@dma.org.uk
<http://www.tpsonline.org.uk>

Index

access rights
  automated decision-making 132–3
  data protection impact assessments
      (DPIAs) 222
  data transfers 133
  excessive requests 129
  fees and time limits 136
  GDPR, under the 126–7
  nature and extent of 127–8
  'purpose' of subject access requests 128–9
  requests and legal proceedings 135–6
  required information 130–1
  searches 129–30
  simple, example of 136
  subject access and emails 131–2
  third party information 133–5
  travellers 108
  UK public authorities 133
accessibility, of DPOs 231–2
accountability
  concept 223
  Data Protection Bill 2017 225
  Data Protection Principles 40
  GDPR Articles 225
  requirement 224–6
accounts and records
  DPO, duties of 238–9
  filing system 16–18
  paper-based records, see paper-based
      records
accurate and up-to-date data
  Data Protection Principles 37–8
  inaccurate data 37
  special categories of personal data 83
adequate, relevant and not excessive data
  level of protection 108–10
  safeguards, providing 114–15
  transfers of international
      data 108–10, 114–15
advertising, marketing and public relations
  behavioural advertising 6, 140, 208, 228, 229
  direct marketing, see direct marketing
  email marketing 189–94
    compliance with existing law 193–4
    exceptions for existing customer
        relationship 192–3
    identity of sender and return address 194
    similar products/services 193
  fax marketing 196
  sales negotiations 190, 191, 193
  telephone marketing
    automated calling systems, use of 196

  Telephone Preference Service
      (TPS) 196
  unsolicited calls for direct
      marketing 195–6
  text message marketing 194
advice
  for data controllers 138–9, 142,
      143, 146–7, 150
  data portability 138–9
  data protection impact assessments
      (DPIAs) 218–19
  of DPO 218–19
  individual rights 138–9, 142, 143
  notification of security breaches 104
  for organizations 121
  security breaches, notification of 104
  special categories of personal
      data, processing 83–7
  transfers of international data 121
amendments to data 135
anonymized data 23, 39
appeals 173
apps
  consent of children 54
  location tracking 208
  privacy 45
  smartphones 67
archiving 79–81
armed forces 55
Article 29 Working Party 237
  Binding Corporate Rules (BCR) 117
  cloud services 183
  cookies 199–200
  data protection impact assessments
      (DPIAs) 206, 208, 219, 221
  Data Protection Officer (DPO)
      226–32, 235
  DPIA Guidelines 214
  and EDPB 28
  email marketing 192, 194
  erasure of data 147
  legitimate interests 58, 59
  Opinion document on definition
      of personal data 12
  portability of data 138, 139
  Privacy Shield 112–13
  purpose limitation Principle 34
  special categories of personal data 86
  transfers of data 110
  see also European Data Protection
      Board (EDPB)
Assessment Notices 156, 169–70

audits
  breach notification 203
  compliance programme, creating 241,
    244, 245, 246, 247, 249
  data protection impact assessments
    (DPIAs) 218, 221
  enforcement 157, 159
  outsourcing 181
  special categories of personal data 67, 85
automated calling systems,
    telephone marketing 196
automated decision-making
  access rights 132–3
  data protection impact assessments
    (DPIAs) 209
  example 151
  individual rights 132–3, 149–51
awareness, raising of 244–6

banks
  case law 11–12
  and data controllers 18
  data protection impact assessments
    (DPIAs) 209
  and Data Protection Officer (DPO) 228
  and Directive on Security of Network
    and Information Systems 30
  and enforcement 171, 172
  files, held by FSA 17
  lawfulness conditions 54, 55
  monetary penalties 91
  personal data, determining 11
  security considerations 91
  transfers of data 113
BCR *see* Binding Corporate Rules (BCR)
behavioural advertising 6, 140, 208
  and role of the DPO 228, 229
'big data' 22
Binding Corporate Rules (BCR)
  concept 117
  consistency mechanism 117
  foreign processors 183
  practical advantages 118–19
  requirements 117–19
biological samples 25
biometric data 25, 66
blocking *see* rectification, blocking,
    erasure and destruction
breaches
  advice on breach notification 104
  confidentiality 59–60
  Data Protection Principles 32, 36
  defining 24
  and enforcement 158
  financial gain as result of 161
  by health care system 67
  notification of security breaches 100,
    101–2, 104
  penalties for, *see* fines; monetary penalties

  personal data 24, 98
  of security 98, 100, 101–2, 104, 161, 245
  sensitive personal data 84
Brexit (UK's withdrawal from the EU)
  codes of conduct following 27
  controller/processor based outside the
    UK 22
  and the GDPR 4
  and personal data inside and outside the EU 5
  UK data protection law following 7
  see also United Kingdom

call forwarding 202
Calling Line Identification (CLI) 200, 201
categorization of personal data *see* special
    categories of personal data
CCTV 15, 81, 207
certification
  certificating bodies 28, 29, 161
  defining 28–9
  transfers of international data 116
Charter of Fundamental Rights 4
children
  autonomy 55
  communication with 125
  consent of 54–5
  definition of 'child' 24–5
  individual rights 123, 125
  and information society services 24, 54–5
cloud services 183
codes of conduct
  defining 26–7
  transfers of international data 116
  see also under Information
    Commissioner's Office (ICO)
collection of data *see* obtaining data
collective agreements 71–2
commercial transactions, consent
    'freely given' in 52
companies
  access rights 134
  advice for 121
  breach of data protection law by 32
  Company Secretariat papers 17
  information used by, as personal data 11
  limited, database on 14
  non-profit-making organizations 73–4
  raising awareness of data protection 246
  security measures 94
  small or medium-sized enterprises (SMEs) 92
  technical and organizational measures 93, 94
compensation
  details of claims 152–3
  liability for claims 151–2
  persons bringing claims 152
complaints
  files held by FSA 17
  to Financial Services Authority 11
  investigation of 166–7

to Irish Data Protection Commissioner 112
to UK Information Commissioner 154
compliance
annual review process 249–50
assessment of data processing activities 241–2
audits 241, 244, 245, 246, 247, 249
compliance programme, creating 240–50
data protection policies, creating 242–4
Data Protection Principles 32
data protection training/awareness
raising 244–6
email marketing 193–4
fair, lawful and legitimate processing 65
with the GDPR 213
implementing controls to reduce/
monitor risk 246–8
monitoring 248–9
with notices 167–8, 171
outsourcing arrangements 176
reporting 249
stages in programme creation 241
time limits 167–8
transfers of data 244
**Computer Security Incident Response
Teams (CSIRTs)** 30
confidentiality
Data Protection Principles 39–40
fair, lawful and legitimate processing 49–50
unlawful processing 59–60
conflicts of interest 237–8
consent
active opt-in requirement 53
of children 54–5
clear affirmative action requirement 53, 74
commercial transactions 52
data subjects 24
explicit 70
'freely given' 52
where not applicable 70
granular requirement 53
naming of those relying on 53
parental 25, 159
public authorities 52
special personal data 70
transfers of data 119–20
unbundled requirement 53
withdrawal 53
consistency mechanism 117, 162–3
**Consolidated Fund, Monetary
Penalty Notices** 171
consultation
with data protection authorities 181
with the EDPB 162, 163
with stakeholders 211
with supervisory authorities 206, 220–1
contractual obligations
data processors, pre-contractual
checks on 178
necessity 55

performance 120
transfers of international data 115–16, 120
written contract, outsourcing 180–1
cookies 198–9
**cooperation between supervisory
authorities** 165
Council of Ministers 28
counselling 24, 76
credit scoring 132–3
criminal convictions 81–3
criminal offences
Data Protection Act 1984 2
electoral registration 61–2
enforcement 169, 174
Information Commissioner,
obstruction of 174
Information Notices 169
special categories of personal data 67, 81–3
cross-border processing
cooperation between supervisory
authorities 165
defining 163
identifying the lead authority 164–5
lead authority not appointed 163–4
transfers of data 106
see also processing; transfers of data
Crown Prosecution Service, fining of 84

dactyloscopic data 25
damaging or distressful processing 4, 170
individual rights 143, 152–3
special categories of personal data 80, 83
data
anonymized 23, 39
'big data' 22
biometric 25, 66
collecting, *see* obtaining data
dactyloscopic 25
encryption of 92, 93
genetic 10, 25
inaccurate 37
inferred 138
location data 22, 196
observed 138
pseudonymization 23
suppression 39
vulnerable data subjects 209
see also personal data; sensitive personal data;
special categories of personal data
data audit questionnaires 241
data controllers
advice for, regarding individual rights 150
erasure of data, informing about 146–7
objection rights 142, 143
portability of data 138–9
appropriate measures, transparency 44
based outside the EU 21–2
data mapping by 85
versus data processors 182–3

data controllers (*cont.*)
defining role of 18–19
distinguished from data processors 19
distinguished from DPOs 18–19
DPIAs, obligation to carry out 211
individual rights 123, 124
joint 27
main establishment 21
outsourcing arrangements 176
security obligations 88, 91–4, 99
specific rights, processing conditions 71–2
storage limitation Principle 38
see also Data Protection Principles; notification
data exports *see* export of data
data mapping 85, 241
'data minimization' Principle 35–6, 79, 89–90
data processors
based outside the EU 21–2
choice of 179
versus data controllers 182–3
defining of role 19–20, 177
distinguished from data controllers 19
foreign 183
and the GDPR 177, 178
nature of 177–8
obligations on 178
pre-contractual checks on 178
processor DPOs 230
responsibilities 41
security obligations 88, 91–4
sub-processors 181
see also outsourcing of data
processing operations
Data Protection Act 1984
compared to 1998 regime 3–4
criminal offences 2
introduction 2
principles 2–3
Data Protection Act 1998
access rights 129
compared to 1984 regime 3–4
and Data Protection Directive 3, 7
definitions/provisions
data subject 23
filing system 16, 17
personal data 8
special categories of personal data 20
Fair Processing Notices 27
inaccurate data 37
Information Commissioner,
extension of powers 186
outsourcing arrangements 175, 180, 181
Privacy Notices 27
purpose 7
sensitive personal data 77–8
special categories of personal data 87
Data Protection Bill 2017
access rights 125, 131
accountability 224, 225

and competence of the EU 5
competent authorities 227
compliance programme, creating 240
Data Protection Officer (DPO) 226, 239
definitions/provisions
certification 29
children 24
data controller 18
filing system 16
processing 15
enforcement powers 156
individual rights 125, 131, 143, 150
introduction 5
objection rights 143
special categories of personal data 68, 69
advice on processing 83, 85
processing conditions 79, 80
structure (Parts and Schedules) 5
Data Protection Directive
adoption 3
aims 3
data minimization 35
and Data Protection Act 1984 3
and Data Protection Act 1998 7
Data Protection Principles 40
definitions/provisions
data controller 18
data processor 19
personal data 7, 10
special categories of personal data 20
electronic communications 187
failure to adequately implement,
allegations of 12
fair, lawful and legitimate processing 62
GDPR replacing 4
outsourcing arrangements 175, 180, 181
Safe Harbor framework 111
scope of application 3
transfers of data 109–10
**data protection impact assessments
(DPIAs)** 205–22
accountability 40
activities and purposes of the processing 212
advice of DPO 218–19
Article 29 Working Party 206, 208, 219, 222
assessing necessity and proportionality in
relation to the purposes 212–13
audits 218, 221
conducting 212–21
consultation with supervisory
authority 220–1
data subjects, seeking views of 220
defining 206–7
determining measures to address
the risks 215–18
determining when to carry out 207–10
and DPO 238
identifying whether required 210–11
obligation to carry out by controller 211

publication 221–2
reporting 221–2
requirements for 209
reviewing for compliance 221
risk assessment 213–15
    determining measures to address
        the risks 215–18
    risk register 216–17
Data Protection Officer (DPO)
accessibility 231–2
accountability 40
advice of, regarding DPIAs 218–19
Article 29 Working Party 226–32, 235
compliance monitoring by 248, 249
compulsory to appoint, where 19
conflict of interest 237–8
core activities 227–8
distinguished from data controllers 18–19
and DPIAs 238
and enforcement powers 157
expertise and skill 233–4
independence 236
involvement 234–5
key requirements and characteristics 233–4
and local data processing laws 243
necessary resources 235–6
policies and procedures 239
processor DPOs 230
and processors 41
record keeping 238–9
reporting responsibilities 249
risk minimization duties 247
role 226
security considerations 90
security of tenure 236–7
tasks/functions 230
and training 246
when mandatory 226–30
Data Protection Principles 32–41
accountability 40
compliance with all 32
data accuracy 37–8
'data minimization' 35–6
design and default, data protection by 41
exemptions 40
integrity, confidentiality and security 39–40
lawfulness, fairness and
        transparency 33–4, 42
processors, responsibilities 41
purpose limitation 34–5
storage limitation 38–9
data protection supervisors 162
Data Protection Tribunal 43
data security *see* security considerations
data subject access right *see* access rights
data subjects
consent 24, 70
contractual necessity 55
data obtained from 46–7

defining 22–3
exercise of rights free of charge 124
explicit consent to processing of
        special personal data 70
expressions of opinion about 11
identifiability 10, 22
information provided to 44–50
method of providing information to 45
personal data, defining 9
personal data manifestly made public by 74
processing restrictions, informing about 148
pseudonymization 23
seeking views of, regarding DPIAs 220
specific rights, processing conditions 71–2
systematic monitoring on a large scale 228–9
vital interests, protecting 72–3
vulnerable 209
data transfers *see* transfers of data
deceased persons, and personal data 13–14
default
data protection by 26, 41
privacy by 95
delegated acts
and certification 29
defining 28
design
data protection by 26, 41
privacy by 95
destruction *see* rectification, blocking,
        erasure and destruction
direct marketing
charitable fundraising 144
fair, lawful and legitimate processing 61, 62
objections unrelated to 142–3
political canvassing 144
right to object to 140–3
unsolicited calls for 195–6
unsolicited emails 191
dispute resolution, 'safe harbor'
        exports 111–12
distress *see* damaging or distressful processing
DNA (deoxyribonucleic acid) 25
domestic activities 3, 135
DPIAs *see* data protection impact
        assessments (DPIAs)
DPO *see* Data Protection Officer (DPO)

EDPB *see* European Data Protection
        Board (EDPB)
EEA *see* European Economic Area (EEA)
elected representatives 76
electronic communications *see* emails;
        Internet; telecommunications
emails
access rights 131–2
marketing 189–94
    Article 29 Working Party 192, 194
    compliance with existing law 193–4
    consent 54

emails (*cont.*)
    exceptions for existing customer
        relationship 192–3
    'host mailing' services 191
    identity of sender and return address 194
    similar products/services 193
    'soft opt-in' provisions 191
    unsolicited emails 191
  searches 132
  web-based services 186
emergency calls 198, 201
employees
  access to personal data 93
  junior 246
  racial or sexual discrimination
    against 71–2
  special categories of personal data,
    processing conditions 71–2
  training and awareness regarding
    data protection 244–6
encrypted biometric access systems 97
encryption 92, 93
enforcement 155–74
  appeals 173
  Assessment Notices 169–70
  consistency mechanism 162–3
  criminal offences 174
  cross-border processing 163–5
  Directive on Personal Data Processed for
    Criminal Law Enforcement 31
  Enforcement Notices 170–1
  Information Notice 167–9
  investigation of complaints 166–7
  Monetary Penalty Notices 171–3
  powers of entry and inspection 173–4
  procedures 166–7
  special categories of personal data 82, 83
  special purposes 168, 171
  supervisory authorities, *see*
    supervisory authorities
  telecommunications issues 203–4
  in United Kingdom 166
Enforcement Notices 156, 170–1
entry and inspection powers 173–4
E-Privacy Directive
  breach notification 203
  compliance with existing law 193–4
  cookies 199
  email marketing 189–90, 191
  'existing customer relationship,'
    exception for 192
  historical background 184–5
  implementation in the UK 185
  location data 196, 198
  REFIT evaluation 185
  review 185
  short message service (SMS) 194
  similar products/services 192
  telephone marketing 195

E-Privacy Regulation, proposed
  breach notification 203
  consent 54
  cookies 199
  direct marketing 191–2
  enforcement 204
  extra-territorial effect 186
  and the GDPR 185
  historical background 185–6
  similar products/services 192
  telephone directories 202
  telephone marketing 195–6
equality of opportunity tracing 75
erasure *see* rectification, blocking,
  erasure and destruction
'establishment'
  concept 7
  main establishments
    defining 21–2
    lead authorities 164, 165
  multiple establishments across Europe 165
EU law
  competence of the EU 5
  Data Protection Directive, *see* Data
    Protection Directive
  Directive on Personal Data Processed for
    Criminal Law Enforcement 31
  Directive on Security of Network and
    Information Systems 30
  E-Privacy Directive, *see* E-Privacy Directive
  EU–US Privacy Shield framework,
    adequacy 112
  and law of Member States 6
  lawfulness conditions 50
  main establishment of controller in 21
  personal data inside and outside 5
  territorial scope 5–7
  see also Brexit (UK's withdrawal from the EU)
European Commission
  and Data Protection Act 1998 4
  legal proceedings against the UK 12
  and transfers of data 108–9,
    111–12, 115, 116
European Data Protection Board (EDPB)
  and accountability 226
  certificates issued by 28
  codes of conduct 26–7
  collation of certificates by 29
  composition 28
  consultation with 162, 163
  establishment 27
  members 28
  see also Article 29 Working Party
European Economic Area (EEA)
  and Data Protection Directive 3
  defining 21
  members 21
  outsourcing outside 177
  transfers of data to countries outside 105

European Parliament 4, 28
European Research Area, objectives 80
excessive data *see* adequate, relevant
    and not excessive data
exemptions
    Data Protection Principles 40
    disproportionate effort 49
    erasure of data 145
    General Data Protection Regulation
        (GDPR) 4–5
    individual rights 125
    Information Notice, compliance with 168
    insurance 77
    journalism 76–7
    legal or confidentiality obligation 49–50
    location of main establishment 22
    see also under General Data Protection
        Regulation (GDPR)
export of data
    and Data Protection Act 1998 3
    restrictions on 106
    security considerations 98
    see also transfers of data

facial images 25
fair, lawful and legitimate processing 42–65
    cases of significance 61–5
        electoral registration 61–2
        naming of professionals by website 65
        public figures 63
        sensitive personal data, disclosure
            of 63–4, 68
    compliance with requirements 65
    Data Protection Principles 33–4, 42
    data subjects, data obtained from 46–7
    disproportionate effort exemption 49
    duty not to mislead 43
    information supplied to data subject 44–50
    lawfulness conditions 50–9
    legal or confidentiality obligation
        exemption 49–50
    notices 44–6
    obtaining data 43–50
    third parties, data obtained from 47–9
    see also unfair processing
Fair Processing Notices 27
fax marketing 196
fees
    access rights 136
    electoral registration 61
filing system, defining 16–18
Financial Conduct Authority (FCA) 11, 172
financial penalties 159–61
financial services 113, 172, 233
Financial Services Authority (FSA)
    complaints to 11
    manual files held by 17
fines
    breaches of security 161

cap on 90
conditions for imposing 186
failure to notify of security breaches 104
imposed by supervisory authorities 159–61
special categories of personal data 84–5
see also monetary penalties
First Tier Tribunal, appeals from 173
fraud prevention 77, 208
FSA *see* Financial Services Authority (FSA)

General Data Protection Regulation (GDPR)
    accountability 224, 225
    amendments to data 135
    applied regime 5
    breaches 24, 159
    children, protection of 54
    cloud services 183
    compliance with 213, 249
    on creation of compliance
        programmes 240, 242
    data processors
        defining 177
        obligations on 178
    and Data Protection Act 1984 2
    data protection impact assessments
        (DPIAs) 205
        carrying out 207–10
        defining 206–7
        identifying whether required 210, 211
    Data Protection Officer (DPO)
        advice of 206
        dismissal or replacement 237
        expertise and skill 233
        involvement 234
        record keeping 238–9
        risk assessment/management 213–14, 215
        role 226
        when mandatory 226, 227, 228, 229
        where customary to appoint 19
    Data Protection Principles
        accountability 40
        data accuracy 37
        data minimization 35
        design and default, data protection by 41
        integrity, confidentiality and
            security 39–40
        lawfulness, fairness and transparency 33–4
        storage 38
    definitions/provisions
        biometric data 25
        codes of conduct 26
        data controller 18
        data processor 19, 177
        data protection by design or default 26
        data subject 22
        delegated acts 28
        filing system 16
        genetic data 25
        personal data 8, 9

General Data Protection
  Regulation (GDPR) (*cont.*)
    processing 15
    profiling 23
    recipient 25
    special categories of personal
      data 20
  derogations under (data transfers)
    consent 119–20
    contract performance 120
    legal claims 120
    public registers 121
    substantial public interest 120
    vital interests 120
  direct effect, date of 4
  direct marketing 140
  on enforcement powers 155, 158, 162
  and E-Privacy Regulation 185
  exemptions 4–5
  extra-territorial effect 186
  fines, cap on 90
  foreign processors 183
  ICO GDPR Consent Guidance 53
  incorporation into UK law 4
  individual rights 122, 123
    access rights 126–30, 132–5
    advice for controllers 138–9, 142, 143
    automated decision-making 149
    compensation 151, 152
    complaints 154
    erasure of data 143–7
    informing data subject and
      third parties 148
    judicial remedy, right to 153
    objection 140, 142
    portability of data 137
    rectification 139–40
    responding to individuals 123, 124
    restriction of processing 147–8
  infringements 154, 159–60
  joint data controllers 182–3
  lawfulness conditions 50
    consent 51–2, 53, 54–5
    contractual necessity 55
    legal obligations 55–6
    legitimate interests 57
    public functions 56–7
    vital interests 56
  non-compliance with 221
  outsourcing 177, 178, 179, 180
    pre-GDPR arrangements 181
  public authorities 59
  replacing Data Protection Directive 4
  scope of application 4, 6, 7
  security considerations 88, 89
    breaches 98
    data exports 98
    notification of security breaches 101–3

    obligations of data controllers
      and processors 92
    outsourcing 98, 99
    privacy by design and by default 95–6
    pseudonymization 96
    technical and organizational measures 93
  special categories of personal data 68–9
    advice on processing 83, 85, 86, 87
    processing, conditions for 69–81
  supervisory authorities, cooperation
    between 165
  text 251–330
  third parties, information from 47–8, 49
  on training 245
  transfers of data 105–6
    adequacy safeguards, providing 114
    concept of transfer 108
    data export restrictions 106
    derogations 119–21
    examples of international transfers 107
    levels of protection 109–10
    wording, breadth of 13
General Medical Council (GMC) 78
genetic data 10, 25
Global Witness, investigation of 77
government departments
  competent authorities 82
  fining of 91
  and legitimate interests 59

health and medical matters
  genetic data 25
  HIV patients, revealing identities of 84
  medical research 80
  special categories of personal data,
    processing conditions 78–9
  staff members, inadvertently
    publishing details of 84, 90
  vital interests 56, 73
historical research, special categories of personal
  data, processing conditions 79–81
history of data protection 2–5
human rights
  Convention on 4
  legitimate interests 58
  medical records 77–8
  privacy 61, 62

ICO *see* Information Commissioner's
  Office (ICO)
identification of individuals 9
identifiers
  examples 9
  hidden 86
  online 8, 9, 22
  personal identifier, removal 79
  unique 11
indecent photographs 82

independence, of DPO 236
individual rights 122–54
 access, *see* access rights
 advice for controllers 138–9
 automated decision-making 132–3, 149–51
 children 123
 compensation 151–3
 and Data Protection Act 1998 4
 erasure of data
  advice for controllers 146–7
  exemptions 145
  informing recipients 145–6
  scope of right 143–5
 exemptions 125
 Information Commissioner, complaints to 154
 judicial remedy, right to 153
 objection, right of 140–3
 paper-based records 129, 130
 portability of data 137–9
 processing, right to restriction of 147–8
 responding to individuals 123–5
 right to know 'logic' 150
inferred data 138
Information Commissioner
 on access rights 132
 Assessment Notices served by 169–70
 complaints to 154
 Enforcement Notices 170–1
 entry and inspection powers 173, 174
 extension of powers under the DPA 186
 guidance
  breach notification 104
  filing systems 17–18
  identification of individuals 9, 10
  storage limitation Principle 39
 obstruction of 174
 offences in relation to 174
 outsourcing arrangements 179
 on privacy enhancing technologies 97
 special purposes for Information
   Notices determined by 168–9
 and UK enforcement procedures 167, 168–9
 see also Information Commissioner's
   Office (ICO)
Information Commissioner's Office (ICO)
 and accountability 223
 Codes of Practice 45–6, 206, 220
 data protection, defining 12, 13
 data protection impact assessments
   (DPIAs) 205, 206
 guidance
  email marketing 192
  GDPR Consent Guidance 53, 70
  Guide to Data Protection 72–3
  lawfulness conditions 51
  records management in health care sector 67
  special categories of personal
    data 67, 68, 70, 86

investigations by 77
monetary penalty issued by 37, 84
and outsourcing 247
PECR, enforcement 203–4
on training 245
and UK enforcement procedures 167
undertakings by 79
see also Information Commissioner
Information Notices 156, 167–9
 criminal offences 169
 exemptions from compliance 168
 special purposes 168–9
 time limit for compliance 167–8
information provision
 access rights 130–1
 companies 134
 confidential information 59–60
 data collection from data subject 46–7
 to data subjects 44–50
 limited companies 14
 method 45
 multiple requests for information 124, 136
 notices 44, 45–6
 notification of security breaches 99
 prisoner information 91, 131
 public information 74
 third parties 47–9, 133–5
 use by organizations, as personal data 11
 see also Information Commissioner;
   Information Notices
Information Rights Tribunal 43
information society services, and
   children 24, 54–5
instant messaging 186
insurance
 data protection impact assessments
   (DPIAs) 208
 and Data Protection Officer (DPO) 228, 229
 monetary penalties 90, 172
 Prudential, monetary penalty
   issued against 37
 security considerations 90
 special categories of personal data 76, 77, 78, 82
 terminology 18
 third party contracts 76
integrity, Data Protection Principles 39–40
International Chamber of
   Commerce (ICC) 115
Internet
 and E-Privacy Regulation 185–6
 failure to keep online information secure 91
 internet service providers (ISPs) 18
 recently developed or expanded
   services, concerns 185–6
 search engines 15–16
 see also emails; E-Privacy Directive; E-
   Privacy Regulation, proposed;
   telecommunications

investigation
　of complaints 166–7
　supervisory authorities, powers of 157–8
ISO 27001 97

joint controllers, defining 27
judicial authorities 112, 157, 224, 227
judicial remedy, right to 153

keeping of data *see* storage

lawfulness conditions 50–9
　consent, *see* consent
　contractual necessity 55
　legitimate interests 57–9
　necessity 50, 51, 55
　public functions 56–7
　vital interests 56
lead authorities
　appointment 164
　and cooperation between supervisory
　　authorities 165
　designation of 29
　identifying 164–5
　not appointed 163–4
　see also public authorities;
　　supervisory authorities
legal claims
　compensation 151–3
　liability for 151–2
　persons bringing 152
　special categories of personal data,
　　processing conditions 74–5
　transfers of international data 120
legal obligations
　fair, lawful and legitimate processing 49–50
　lawfulness conditions 55–6
　see also lawfulness conditions
legal proceedings
　access rights 135–6
　and claims 75
　by European Commission 12
legal professional privilege 129, 136, 222
legislation
　data protection legislation,
　　arising of need for 2
　see also Data Protection Act 1984;
　　Data Protection Act 1998; Data
　　Protection Bill 2017; Data Protection
　　Directive; EU law; General Data
　　Protection Regulation (GDPR)
legitimate interests
　Article 29 Working Party 58, 59
　human rights 58
　lawfulness conditions 57–9
　not-for-profit body 73–4
legitimizing conditions
　see also fair, lawful and legitimate processing
line identification 184, 187, 200–2

'list rental' business 191
living persons
　genetic data 25
　and personal data 9, 13–14
　see also natural persons
location data 22, 197–8

main establishments
　defining 21–2
　lead authorities 164, 165
malicious calls 201–2
manual filing systems *see* paper-based records
market research 81
marketing *see* advertising, marketing
　and public relations
medical matters *see* health and medical
　matters
medical research 80
mislead, duty not to 43
monetary penalties
　issued by ICO 37, 84, 90
　in public sector 173
　security considerations 90, 91
　service of 172
　see also fines; Monetary Penalty Notices
Monetary Penalty Notices 171–3
　examples 172–3
　formalities 172
multimedia messaging service (MMS) 54, 186
multiple requests for information 124, 136

names
　of legal professionals 65
　obtaining data 43
　personal data 14, 68
　security considerations 91
　transfers of data 107
National Health Service (NHS) 78, 173
national security
　electronic communications 200
　entry and inspection powers 174
　individual rights 125
　personal data 4, 5
　special categories of personal data 69
　transfers of data 108, 111, 112, 120
natural persons
　biometric data 66
　data protection impact assessments
　　(DPIAs) 207
　electronic communications 194
　historical perspective 4
　identifiable 9–10, 22
　lawfulness conditions 51, 56
　personal data relating to 13–14
　as recipients 25
　security considerations 89, 92,
　　95, 96, 100, 101, 102
　terminology 8–9, 10, 22–6
　transfers of data 106, 192

necessity
  contractual 55
  defining 55
  DPIAs, conducting 212–13
  lawfulness conditions 50, 51, 55
  special categories of personal data,
    processing conditions 72
negotiations, sales 190, 191, 193
non-itemised billing 202
non-profit-making organizations,
  legitimate interests 73–4
notices
  compliance with 167–8, 171
  fair, lawful and legitimate processing 44–6
  layered 45–6
  see also Assessment Notices; Enforcement
    Notices; Fair Processing Notices;
    Information Notices; Monetary
    Penalty Notices; Privacy Notices
notification
  of security breaches 104
  telecommunications breaches 203
nuisance calls 201–2

objection rights
  advice for controllers 142, 143
  direct marketing 140–3
  scope of right 141
  unrelated to direct marketing 142–3
observed data 138
obtaining data
  from data subject 46–7
  duty not to mislead 43
  information requirements 46
  from third party 47–9
  transparency 44–50
  see also information provision
OFCOM (Office of Communications) 195,
  196, 203
Office of the Data Protection Registrar 2
One Stop Shop 29
organizational measures *see* technical
  and organizational measures
organizations *see* companies
outsourcing of data processing operations
  cloud services 183
  data processors
    choice of 179
    versus data controllers 182–3
    defining role of 177
    foreign 183
    nature of 177–8
    obligations on 178
    pre-contractual checks on 178
    terminology 19
  ongoing assurance 179–80
  personal data processing 175–83
  pre-GDPR arrangements 181
  security considerations 98, 99

sub-processors 181
  written contract 180–1
'Over-the-Top' (OTT) services 186

packet-switch technology, technical
  routing of 108
paper-based records
  and 1998 regime 3
  individual rights 129, 130
  obtaining data 43
  security considerations 94
  terminology 11, 16
parental authority/responsibility 55
parental consent 25, 159
PECR (Privacy and Electronic
  Communications (EC Directive)
  Regulations) 2003
  automated calling systems, use of 196
  breach notification 203
  Calling Line Identification (CLI) 201
  compliance with existing law 193–4
  cookies 198, 199
  definitions in relation to 187–9
  email marketing 189, 190, 191
  emergency calls 201
  enforcement 203–4
  'existing customer relationship,'
    exception for 192
  fax marketing 196
  identity of sender and return address 194
  implementation of E-Privacy
    Directive in the UK 185
  key provisions 187
  malicious or nuisance calls 201
  short message service (SMS) 194
  similar products/services 192
  telephone directories 202
  Telephone Preference Service (TPS) 196
  traffic data, limitations on processing of 200
penalties 159–61
pensions 76
personal data
  access rights 130, 131
  automated 16
  breaches 24, 98
  collecting, *see* obtaining data
  deceased persons 13–14
  defining 8–15, 22
  electronic access by travellers 108
  examples amounting to 14
  living persons 9, 13–14
  multiple persons 14
  natural persons, *see* natural persons
  outsourcing, *see* outsourcing of data
    processing operations
  past interpretations by the courts 11–15
  portability of 137–8
  rectification 139–40
  retention periods 39

personal data (*cont.*)
  special categories, *see* special
      categories of personal data
  unstructured, access rights to 133
  see also access rights; data;
      sensitive personal data
police
  covert surveillance powers 69
  fining of 84, 90–1
  information provision 56
  obtaining data 46
  penalising 84, 90
  public authorities 59
  terminology 18
policies
  compliance programme, creating 242–4
  Data Protection Officer (DPO) 239
political opinions 20, 34
  special categories of personal data 66, 76
portability of data
  advice for controllers 138–9
  Article 29 Working Party 138, 139
  scope of right 137–8
Practitioner Certificate in Data Protection 94
Principles *see* Data Protection Principles
prisoner information 91, 131
privacy
  apps 45
  design and default, by 95
  Safe Harbor Privacy Principles 111
  see also E-Privacy Directive; E-Privacy
      Regulation, proposed; privacy enhancing
      technologies (PETs); Privacy Impact
      Assessments (PIAs); Privacy Shield
privacy enhancing technologies (PETs) 97
Privacy Impact Assessments (PIAs)
Privacy Notices 27
Privacy Shield
  Article 29 Working Party 112–13
  and EU law 6, 112
  operation 113–14
  origins 112–13
  Principles 113
  see also Safe Harbor framework; United States
privilege *see* legal professional privilege
processing
  advice on processing special category
      personal data 83–7
  assessment of activities 241–2
  breadth of term 15
  by competent authorities 81, 82, 83
  in compliance with DPIA, assessment 221
  conditions for, *see* processing conditions,
      special category personal data
  cross-border 163–5
  and Data Protection Act 1998 3
  data protection impact assessments
      (DPIAs) 212
  defining 15–16

  on large scale 209
  legitimacy 3
  manual 3
  restriction of, right to 147–8
  of traffic data, limitations on 200
  unfair 50
  unlawful 59–61
  see also Data Protection Principles; fair,
      lawful and legitimate processing
**processing conditions, special category
    personal data** 69–81
  archiving 79–81
  explicit consent by data subject 70
  fraud prevention 77
  journalism exemption 76–7
  legal claims 74–5
  legitimate interests of not-for-
      profit body 73–4
  obligations exercising specific rights of
      controller/data subject 71–2
  outline of 69
  personal data manifestly made
      public by data subject 74
  protection of vital interests of data
      subject/another person 72–3
  provision of medical or social
      care or treatment 78
  public health 78–9
  substantial public interest 75–8
profiling
  data protection impact assessments
      (DPIAs) 209
  defining 23
proportionality principle
  access rights 129
  DPIAs, conducting 212–13
pseudonymization
  defining 23, 96
  security considerations 92, 96
  and storage 38, 39
public authorities
  consent 'freely given' to 52
  and DPO 227
  examples 59
  lack of definition in the GDPR 59
  public functions 57
  recipients, not classed as 25
  see also lead authorities; supervisory authorities
public functions, lawfulness conditions 56–7
public information 74
public interest
  access rights 133
  archiving in 79–81
  and health 78–9
  public functions 57
  special categories of personal data,
      processing conditions 75–9
  substantial 75–8, 120
  transfers of data 120

public relations *see* advertising,
   marketing and public relations
publication, of DPIAs 221–2
'purpose'
   of Data Protection Act 1998 7
   DPIAs, conducting 212–13
   purpose limitation Principle 34–5
   of subject access requests 128–9

recipient 25, 145–6
records *see* accounts and records
rectification, blocking, erasure and destruction
   Article 29 Working Party 147
   exemptions 145
   individual rights 139–40, 143–7
   informing recipients 145–6
   scope of right 143–5
   storage limitation Principle 38
references 94, 179, 224
registers 121, 216–17
regulatory activity 156
relevance *see* adequate, relevant
   and not excessive data
religion 214
reporting 221–2, 249
research, special categories of
   personal data 79–81
retention of data *see* storage
reverse search directories 202
risk assessment/management
   controls, implementing 246–8
   data protection impact assessments
     (DPIAs) 213–15
     compliance with GDPR 213
     determining measures to address
       the risks 215–18
     risk register 216–17
RNA (ribonucleic acid) 25

Safe Harbor framework
   amendments to data 135
   and EU law 6
   Privacy Principles 111
   'Safe Harbor II' 111–12
   and transfers to the US 110–11
   validity, questioning 112
   see also Privacy Shield; United States
scientific research 79–81
search engines 15–16
searches, access rights 129–30
secondary legislation
   Directives
     Data Protection, *see* Data
       Protection Directive
     Directive on Personal Data Processed for
       Criminal Law Enforcement 31
     Directive on Security of Network and
       Information Systems 30
     E-Privacy Directive, *see* E-Privacy Directive

E-Privacy Directive implemented
     by way of 185
General Data Protection Regulation
     (GDPR), *see* General Data
     Protection Regulation (GDPR)
   see also Data Protection Bill 2017; E-Privacy
     Regulation, proposed; General Data
     Protection Regulation (GDPR)
security considerations
   appropriate measures 92–3
   Binding Corporate Rules (BCR) 117–19
   breaches of security 98, 100, 101–2,
     161, 245
   'data minimization' 89–90
   and Data Protection Act 1998 3
   Data Protection Principles 39–40
   Directive on Security of Network and
     Information Systems 30
   encryption of data 92, 93
   exports 98
   ISO 27001 97
   laptops 93
   monetary penalties 90, 91
   natural persons 92, 95, 96, 100, 101, 102
   obligations of data controllers and
     processors 88, 91–4, 99
   organizational measures 94
   and outsourcing 98, 99
   privacy by design and by default 95
   privacy enhancing technologies (PETs) 97
   pseudonymization 96
   security of tenure of the DPO 236–7
   technical measures 93
   telecommunications 202–3
   see also national security
sensitive personal data
   advice on processing 84, 85
   breaches involving 84
   and Data Protection Act 1998 3
   data protection impact assessments
     (DPIAs) 209
   Data Protection Officer (DPO) 231, 244
   fair, lawful and legitimate processing 63
   processing conditions 76, 77, 79
   public interest exception 77–8
   replacement by special categories
     of personal data 20, 66
   special categories of personal data 66,
     67, 68, 76, 77, 79, 84, 85
   training and awareness 244
   see also personal data; processing
     conditions, special category personal
     data; special categories of personal data
short message service (SMS) 194
small or medium-sized enterprises
   (SMEs) 92
social security, specific rights,
   processing conditions 71–2
social work, processing conditions 78

special categories of personal data
  advice on processing 83–7
  audits 67, 85
  contextual importance 68
  criminal convictions and offences 67, 81–3
  defining 20
  ethnic origin 68
  examples 67–8
  fair, lawful and legitimate processing 66–8
  on a large scale 229
  law enforcement 82, 83
  listing of types of personal data forming 66
  money laundering prevention 76
  processing, conditions for, *see* processing
      conditions, special category personal data
  replacement of sensitive personal
      data by 20, 66
  terrorism prevention 76
  see also personal data
statistics *see* research
storage, Data Protection Principles 38–9
structuring 15, 16
subject access requests
  and emails 131–2
  example of a simple request 136
  'purpose' 128–9
  third parties 135
  see also access rights
sub-processors 181
substantial public interest
  special categories of personal data,
      processing conditions 75–8
  transfers of international data 120
  see also public interest
supervisory authorities
  certificates issued by 28
  codes of conduct 26, 27
  consultation with, regarding DPIAs 220–1
  cooperation between 165
  enforcement role 156–62
  fines imposed by 159–61
  harmonization duties 156
  identifying the lead authority 164–5
  lead authority not appointed 163–4
  main establishments 21
  non-regulatory enforcement action 162
  notification of security breaches to 99
  powers
      authorization and advisory 162
      bans 155
      corrective 158
      investigative 157–8
      and processors 41
  sanctions imposed by 177
  see also enforcement; Information
      Commissioner; lead authorities;
      public authorities
suppression data 39

Talk Talk Telecom Group plc, monetary
      penalty affecting 172
taxation matters 56, 125
technical and organizational measures
  data transfer agreements 116
  packet-switch technology, technical
      routing of 108
  privacy enhancing technologies (PETs) 97
  security considerations 93
  special categories of personal data,
      processing conditions 79
telecommunications 184–204
  Calling Line Identification (CLI) 200
  cookies 198–9
  data controllers 18
  definitions 186–9
  Directive provisions 187
  email marketing 189–94
      compliance with existing law 193–4
      exceptions for existing customer
          relationship 192–3
      identity of sender and return address 194
      similar products/services 193
  enforcement 203–4
  fax marketing 196
  historical background 184–6
  incoming calls 201
  location data 22, 197–8
  malicious calls 201–2
  monetary penalties, security failings 90
  999 or 112 calls 201
  non-itemised billing 202
  nuisance calls 201–2
  outgoing calls 201
  reverse search directories 202
  security considerations 202–3
  telephone directories 202
  telephone marketing
      automated calling systems, use of 196
      Telephone Preference Service (TPS) 196
      unsolicited calls for direct
          marketing 195–6
  text message marketing 194
  traffic data, limitations on processing of 200
  unwanted call forwarding, termination of 202
  see also advertising, marketing and public
      relations; emails; Internet
telephone directories 202
Telephone Preference Service (TPS) 195, 196
terminology
  biometric data 25
  certification 28–9
  children 24–5
  codes of conduct 26–7
  data controllers 18–19
  data processors 19–20
  data subjects 22–3
  default, data protection by 26

delegated acts 28
design, data protection by 26
European Data Protection Board
    (EDPB) 27–8
European Economic Area (EEA) 21
filing system 16–18
genetic data 25
joint controllers 27
main establishments 21–2
personal data 8–15, 22
processing 15–16
profiling 23
pseudonymization 23
recipient 25
territorial scope of law 5–7
text message marketing 54, 194
third parties
    access rights 133–5
    data obtained from 47–9
    insurance contracts 76
    processing restrictions, informing about 148
time limits
    access rights 136
    compliance with notices 167–8, 171
traffic data, limitations on processing of 200
training, data protection 244–6
transfers of data
    access rights 133
    adequacy safeguards, providing 114–15
    adequate level of protection 108–10
    advice for organizations 121
    codes of conduct and certification
        mechanisms 116
    compliance 244
    contractual route 115–16
    data transfer agreements 116
    and European Commission 108–
        9, 111–12, 115, 116
    examples 107
    GDPR, derogations under
        consent 119–20
        contract performance 120
        legal claims 120
        public registers 121
        substantial public interest 120
        vital interests 120
    international data 105–21
    model clauses 115–16
    national security 108, 111, 112, 120
    non-repetitive 121
    outsourcing arrangements 176–7
    Privacy Shield 110–11
    restrictions on data exports 106

'Safe Habor II' 111–12
scope 108
Snowden effect 111
standard contractual clauses 115–16
to the United States 110–11
see also export of data
transparency
    appropriate measures 44
    Data Protection Principles 33–4
    obtaining data 44–50

ultra vires activities 60, 145
unfair processing 50
United Kingdom
    enforcement in 166
    E-Privacy Directive, implementing 185
    legal proceedings against 12
    limitation periods 38
    main establishment in 165
    personal data, defining 7–10
    public authorities, access requests to 133
    withdrawal from the EU, *see* Brexit
        (UK's withdrawal from the EU)
    see also Data Protection Act 1984;
        Data Protection Act 1998;
        Data Protection Bill 2017
United Kingdom Accreditation
    Service (UKAS) 29
United States
    data transfers to, *see* Privacy Shield
    Department of Commerce 114
    Department of Transportation 113
    Federal Trade Commission 113
    National Security Agency 111
    surveillance activities 111
    see also Safe Harbor framework
unlawful processing 59–61
    confidential information 59–60
    legal provisions 60–1
up-to-date data *see* accurate and up-to-date data

value-added services 194
vital interests
    examples 56
    lawfulness conditions 56
    and public health 73
    special categories of personal data,
        processing conditions 72–3
    transfers of international data 120
Voice over IP (VoIP) 186
voice-activated telephone
    systems 156, 195, 196
voluntary certification 28